STORY OF A DEATH FORETOLD

STORY OF
A DEATH FORETOLD

The Coup against Salvador Allende,
September 11, 1973

Oscar Guardiola-Rivera

BLOOMSBURY PRESS

NEW YORK · LONDON · NEW DELHI · SYDNEY

Published by Bloomsbury Press, New York

All papers used by Bloomsbury Press are natural, recyclable products made from wood grown in well-managed forests. The manufacturing processes conform to the environmental regulations of the country of origin.

LIBRARY OF CONGRESS CATALOGING-IN-PUBLICATION DATA HAS BEEN APPLIED FOR

ISBN: 978-1-60819-896-2

First U.S. Edition 2013

1 3 5 7 9 10 8 6 4 2

Typeset by Hewer Text UK Ltd, Edinburgh
Printed and bound in the U.S.A. by Thomson-Shore Inc., Dexter, Michigan

To the memory of my mother

A constitutional solution, for instance, could result from massive internal disorders, strikes, urban and rural warfare. This would morally justify an armed forces intervention for an indefinite period.

Letter from H. Hendrix and R. Berrelez to E. J. Gerrity,
vice-president of ITT, 1970

An action prepared to the last detail. Brilliantly executed . . . Allende's government has encountered the end it deserved . . . In the future, Chile will be an ever more interesting market for our products.

Cable sent from Hoechst Chemical Chile to its Frankfurt
headquarters, 1973, cited by Julio Cortázar in Fantomas
contra los vampires multinationals (*1975*)

Contents

Acknowledgements

Books are living creatures and collective creations. They respond to the presence or absence of others. This one is no exception. In the process of writing it some people departed and others have arrived. Those who I am proud to call true friends remained constant. I could not have written this book without them. I cannot name them all here, but I hope they know how grateful and fortunate I am to enjoy their friendship, wisdom and love.

My mother lost her final battle while I was working on this book. I wish to acknowledge her enduring example of courage.

My daughter Zoe has been, and will always be, light, love and life.

Bill Swainson, my editor at Bloomsbury, never stopped believing in this project. He and Caroline stood by my side all along. I am grateful to them.

Thanks, also, to Steve Cox and Catherine Best.

I'd like to acknowledge the poet Alejandro Zambra, and through him, the youth of Chile. They have defied the tide, and in doing so made history. This story belongs to them.

Alejandro once said to me that if the story of Salvador Allende and the Chilean Way were to be told today, it should be a story of heroism and love, but most of all, it should be told honestly. I have endeavoured to do this.

As the book's title informs the reader, I acknowledge the example of Gabriel García Márquez. I first heard about the story of 11 September 1973 from him.

Eric Hobsbawm pointed me towards his work on popular intellectuals during a conversation in Wales. His chapter on political cobblers became my entry point to the story told in this book.

Jon Lee Anderson shared many of his personal stories and firsthand knowledge of the period with me, during conversations over beer and *huevos rancheros* in Xalapa, Beirut and London.

Thanks to Cristina Fuentes de la Roche and Peter Florence for making possible the encounters and conversations with many of the people I mention here, as well as others, in the course of the brilliant Hay Festivals.

I've learned from the example, commitment and rigour that characterise Birkbeck scholars, as well as those who often visit and teach at the college. Among them Costas Douzinas, Slavoj Zizek, Etienne Balibar, Joanna Bourke, Drucilla Cornell, John Kraniauskas, and, especially, my friends and colleagues at Birkbeck School of Law and the Institute for the Humanities.

I am grateful to many other friends and colleagues whose work and commitment to justice illuminate these pages: Lewis R. Gordon, Jane Anna Gordon, Linda Martín Alcoff, Eduardo Mendieta, Enrique Dussel, Nelson Maldonado-Torres, Michael Hardt, Gayatri Spivak, Bruno Bosteels, Ramón Grosfoguel, Santiago Castro-Gómez, John Beverley, Gerald Martin and Marcus Rediker. Mireille Fanon-Mendès France, Michael Mansfield QC, Santiago Gamboa, Mario Mendoza, Juan Gabriel Vásquez, Javier Cercas, Jane Teller, David Whittaker, Peter Griffin and Alberto Manguel.

I am grateful to Natalie Hanman and Claire Armitstead.

The support of the Leverhulme Trust helped me to test some of these ideas with my students in the company of the sociologist Boaventura de Sousa Santos.

I also acknowledge, with gratitude, the support of the Colombian embassy in London, especially Ambassador Mauricio Rodríguez Múnera.

I wish to thank my agents, Kevin Conroy-Scott and Sophie Lambert.

My gratitude to Alexandra Pringle, for her unwavering enthusiasm about the work that writers at Bloomsbury do.

My infinite debt is to Nayra Bello O'Shanahan, whose passion for books and life I treasure.

Introduction

The story told and the arguments developed in this book show that what became known as Allende's Chilean Way – *la vía chilena* – was tuned to the desire of the most disadvantaged people in the country, and the globe, to wipe out their ongoing disadvantage. It aimed to turn that desire into law. Such a law could be called a law of life, and light, in the sense that it sought the creative affirmation and illumination of humanity as such. The narrative that sustained it was one of courage and love.

Allende's notion of resistance and revolution entailed divorcing democracy and law from coercion, force and privilege in the national as well as the international arena. The commitment to divorce force from law may in fact summarise the ends as well as the means of the Chilean Way.

Privilege and coercion had been factors in the uneven development of capitalism, politics and social regulation in Chile from the outset. They can be traced back to the arrival of the British naval hero Lord Cochrane in the summer of 1818. Having abandoned his initial scheme of placing Napoleon on the throne of South America, Cochrane persuaded himself he had 'every prospect of making a fortune' in Chile.[1] To that end he bought a coastal estate north of Valparaíso, planning to make it the centre of an economic empire. Cochrane imported agricultural equipment from Britain, machinery to roll copper for a new national coinage, and set up Chile's first lithographic printing press, thereby making sure that his polemics

and opinions would be distributed and discussed all over the southern cone. In the meantime he lived up to his legendary status as
Master and Commander, leading the Chilean navy that wrested the
country's seas from the Spaniards, whom he then helped, alongside
General José de San Martín, to expel from Peru altogether.

When news of their victory in July 1821 reached London, *The
Times* told the English public about Lord Cochrane being driven
into the city of Lima in a magnificent coach pulled by four white
horses. Cochrane received all the credit. Lord Byron reacted to the
news by saying: 'There is no man I envy so much as Lord Cochrane.'[2]

Cochrane's fame became as well entrenched as his fortune.[3] The
records show that after the capture of the schooner *Sacramento* in
September 1821 he sent home $13,507 in HMS *Superb*, and upon his
return to Valparaíso in June 1822 some $16,997 in the British
warships *Alacrity* and *Doris*. When he finally left for Brazil in the
Colonel Allen on 18 January 1823, Cochrane took with him several
boxes of gold bullion worth £10,400.[4]

His legacy in Chile would endure. By the time of his departure,
a colony of British smugglers and merchants was better established
than ever in Valparaíso, making profits and shipping the gains back
to England. They and their Anglo-Chilean inheritors, who sported
such English-sounding names as Edwards or Brown, owned and
administered small lending companies in the mining areas and the
seafront warehouses of the port of Valparaíso, and settled in the
smartest residential areas in the hills, not far from where both
General Augusto Pinochet and Salvador Allende would be born
many years later. They plundered, they became bankers, they
funded Cochrane's fleet, traded in agricultural exports during the
European winter and imported European manufactures into Chile
all the year around, skimming the difference.

Their economic gains quickly converted into social status and
political influence. As early as 1819 the British traders' association, a
guild or *gremio* in local parlance, was consulted on economic matters
by the Chilean government, which followed its advice closely.[5]

Cochrane relied on these British merchants and financiers, people like George Edwards Brown, founder of the powerful Edwards clan, 'to obtain considerable quantities of naval and military stores', and persuaded them to pay a subscription towards his army in exchange for 'protection and the creation of further commercial opportunities'.[6] Not only did this establish an important connection for the first time in Chile – between the financial health and survival of the Chilean government, on the one hand, and British and other foreign business interests on the other – but also it throws into relief another connection between the use of military force and the creation 'of further commercial opportunities' along with the opening of new markets.

Many things would change in Chile after Cochrane's departure. The more prosperous urban sectors of the country would transform from old colonial backwaters into modern cities with electricity, sanitation, broad avenues, courts of law, a presidential palace, national poets and European pretensions. But such sectors and the late inheritors of the banking, transport and trading families would continue to relate to the southern regions inhabited by the Mapuche, or the northern regions full of natural resources, in a manner not too far removed from the way in which London would relate to Santiago and Valparaíso.

Force would be used time and again to grab land from the southern Mapuches or secure the exploitation of minerals in the north, thereby creating further opportunities for commerce and prosperity in the much-envied cities. Finally, the financial health and survival of the admired republican institutions of Chile would continue to depend on the prosperity of British (and thereafter other foreign) business interests.

The breakdown of this combined system of unequal relations would only begin when local politicians and the sectors of the population displaced in the south, migrants in the north and the main cities, and the youth of Chile, finally found such influences over their country and their personal lives intolerable.

This is the point where our story of death foretold begins in earnest. It will be told in three parts. Part I, 'Precedents and Causes', introduces the main characters – political cobblers, those they inspired, and the owners of Chile – taking the narrative up to the time of the Cold War (here termed, after W. H. Auden, 'The Age of Anxiety') and the 1960s and 1970s. Part II, 'The Coup', sets the leadership of the Chilean Way and the people who were its engine in the context of the interests of foreign and local powers. An image taken from a little-known novella by Argentinian writer Julio Cortázar serves to stage the drama that follows. The circumstances leading to and including the events of 11 September 1973 are described as a tragedy in three parts, loosely modelled on Sartre's retelling of the drama of Orestes for the twentieth century. Part III deals with the aftermath of 11 September 1973 and its consequences, up to the political action of the youth of Chile between 2011 and 2013, striving to recover once again the ability to make history and tell the story in their own voice. This book is theirs.

I

PRECEDENTS
AND CAUSES

I

Outlaws and Political Cobblers

When he was a teenager, Salvador Allende used to visit the work-
shop of a cobbler named Juan Demarchi after classes at the Liceo
Eduardo de la Barra in his native Valparaíso had finished for the day.
Demarchi lived across the street from Allende. There they would
play chess and talk about life. Allende would listen for hours to the
sixty-three-year-old European immigrant whose stories amounted
to a memoir of an entire class of people who lived on this planet but
did not seem to share any part of it.

Telling their own stories was important, as it challenged the
commonly held view that such people lacked in some fundamental
way the equipment to acquire knowledge, govern themselves, and
in short become fully human. Allegedly, others did possess such
equipment, and that was supposed to justify their social advantage.
At a time when for an 'uneducated' person to speak in the first
person was first of all to claim that one was a person, such stories
had profound significance. This was the case between the late nineteenth and the early twentieth centuries for peasants and artisans in
Europe, as much as it was for indigenous peoples, descendants of
Africans displaced during the years of slavery, and poor migrants in
the Americas. They were not merely illegal. They were, in fact,
outlaws living outside the walls of the lettered city, the polis, in
short, the fully human. It was this significance that stunned the
young Salvador Allende.[1]

Demarchi opened his library to Allende, who was soon an avid reader of books on politics and society, most of them of egalitarian inspiration. It was through Demarchi that Salvador Allende became acquainted with the works of such thinkers as Mikhail Bakunin, a Russian anarchist who had read the French Enlightenment philosophers, embraced wholeheartedly the philosophy of the most influential among German intellectuals in the nineteenth century, G. W. F. Hegel, and met George Sand, Pierre-Joseph Proudhon and Karl Marx in the tumultuous Paris of the 1840s.

According to Allende's own testimony, Bakunin captured his imagination not so much because of his theories but rather because of his adventurous life and the way it resonated with the lives of Allende's own ancestors: after being deported from France for speaking against Russia's oppression of Poland, Bakunin took part in the Czech rebellion of 1848, was imprisoned in St Petersburg and exiled to a work camp in Siberia, which he escaped, eventually reaching Japan, the USA and London before settling in Italy en route to join the Polish insurrection.[2]

Perhaps it was there, in Italy before migrating to Chile, that Demarchi learned about Bakunin. Since, by his own admission, Allende had little inclination for 'engaging in readings of a certain depth' during his teenage years, the cobbler Demarchi would simplify and explain things to him 'with the clarity and directness that is characteristic of the workers who have come to comprehend the nature of things'.[3]

It is a common error to assume that the lack of a formal education means that shoemakers, weavers, peasants or indigenous peoples cannot be intellectuals. We may even find it difficult to believe that they could acquire a significant book collection, let alone be interested in or able to engage in philosophy or pass on proper knowledge, not just 'culture' or 'traditions', to others. Such a misunderstanding excludes many people from history because it assumes that they can have no impact on history, or even be affected by it. This is the basis of the idea that, for instance, history does not really happen in the global South, or that, at the very least, history and significant advancement have only taken place in privileged locations on the planet in which 'civilisation' reached a certain zenith.

The idea that history does not take place in the South originated in a tradition that conceived of place as the basis for explaining and predicting the nature and behaviour of peoples and creatures around the globe. It drew a fundamental distinction between the lands and peoples in the higher latitudes of the 'temperate' North (Europe) and a 'hot' South (the Caribbean basin and the lands beyond the Equator). This geographical distinction enabled explorers, conquistadors and jurists from the sixteenth century onwards to believe not only that they were venturing into vast and wealthier lands, but also that the peoples they would encounter necessarily possessed a nature – ranging from 'childish' to inhuman – that justified rendering them Europe's subjects. The political lessons drawn from that distinction greatly impacted modern economics, law and geopolitics. This explains their endurance, as well as the fact that such ideas have been held by people as diverse as the founding fathers of international law, classical economists and political liberals such as Adam Smith or John Locke, and contemporary masters of geopolitics like Henry Kissinger.[4]

People like Demarchi gave a voice to those too often excluded from history under the pretext that they are immature or backward. Allende heard that voice, and on the basis of it developed a different view of history and society as well as a more inclusive political practice. His views and practice can be seen as part and parcel of an ongoing effort towards undoing a conception of politics and subjectivity constructed over five centuries of Latin American history. During that period, different regimes of selection and exclusion – colonial, slave-holding, capitalist – were overlaid to form a powerful sense of social hierarchy, deeply entrenched in people's minds. Beginning in the late nineteenth and early twentieth centuries, popular intellectuals like the cobbler Demarchi and his disciple Salvador Allende challenged such established boundaries.

It is no accident that from beginning to end, from Allende's first speeches during the turbulent years of student university politics to his very last words, the constant theme is that of equality, self-determination and independence. His lifelong aim was to show that the oppression which had closed off the lives of many in Chile and elsewhere – the enclosure of history's commons for the benefit of the few – not only produced negative effects, but also insights, and perhaps even a culture of engagement with the question of what and who has value and valid knowledge.[5]

To historians, the reputation of shoemakers and cobblers as worker-philosophers and militant egalitarians is as well known as it is old. In an essay included in his collection *Uncommon People*, Eric Hobsbawm described the historical role played by political shoemakers together with weavers and musicians such as the pioneers of jazz and other forms of popular music and culture, as thinkers and artisans of rebellion.[6]

This is remarkable because it sets in its proper context, both existential and political, the encounter between Salvador Allende and the cobbler Juan Demarchi. But also because it helps us to grasp the extent to which weavers and popular musicians such as the Yarur workers – who went from operating Chile's largest cotton mill in the 1930s, to seizing control of the factory and gaining the political initiative in the 1960s – or the folk singer Víctor Jara forged the Chilean Revolution of the 1960s and 1970s from below.

As Peter Winn, responsible for the most exhaustive account of what he calls the Chilean 'revolution from below', observes, that movement extended from the shoemakers, weavers, poets and musicians to other areas of social creativity and production, such as factory labour, mural painting and literature.[7] As the life and work of the poet and Nobel Prize winner Pablo Neruda attests, the creativity of this movement from below also made possible legal as well as political change. This is so not because of some underlying necessity or historical rule, but because what is at stake in particularly urgent historical situations such as this one is existence itself, and there is no stake higher.

Only that kind of particular urgency, accompanied by a more generic sense that what is at issue is existence itself, awakens in us the spirit that can take us beyond the sinful entrapment of apathy and melancholia that Dante Alighieri called *accidia*.[8] That powerful combination becomes embodied in the kind of political organisation that activists often call a front or a popular block, to be distinguished from the more vertical relation between leader and people that usually goes by the name of representation or populism. These were some of the lifelong lessons that Allende learned early on, from Demarchi and others, and that he consistently applied throughout his political praxis and his life as both dreamer and militant.

Political shoemakers such as Juan Demarchi were quite a visible presence at the end of the nineteenth century. The first anarchist ever recorded in a provincial town (Rio Grande do Sul, Brazil, 1891) was, precisely, an Italian shoemaker. The only craft union reported as participating in the first Workers' Congress in Curitiba was the Shoemakers' Association, as Hobsbawm observes. Certainly, militancy and left-wing activism alone did not distinguish cobblers and shoemakers from some other craftsmen who were, as a group, as prominent in the events of the 1848 German Revolution or in France during the revolts against the July monarchy. In 1850 Joseph Weydemeyer wrote to Karl Marx to inform him that 'the Workers Club [also known as the Communist league] is small and consists only of shoemakers and tailors', but the latter were more prominent.[9] The same would happen during the Chilean Revolution of the 1960s–70s, in which weavers would become more prominent than most other groups active in the revolution from below.[10]

What gave shoemakers their radical reputation was not their prominence in collective action; it was the fact that they were well established as worker intellectuals. Their role as spokespersons and organisers of common folk is well documented, from the 1830 'Swing' Riots in England and the French 'worker-poets' of 1850 to

the organisation of the Federation of Workers of the Argentine
Region in 1890.

Hobsbawm attributes their reputation as popular philosophers to
their independence – the solitude of their work, its physically unde-
manding character requiring little or no division of labour – and the
material conditions of their trade, which in turn explain their ability
to become the village's politician. In addition, according to the
English historian, the humble status of their trade and their relative
poverty help make sense of their proverbial radicalism.

Agreeing with such a depiction of political shoemakers, E. P.
Thompson quotes a Yorkshire satirist's portrayal of the village politician as:

> typically, a cobbler, an old man and the sage of his industrial
> village: He has a library that he rather prides himself upon. It is a
> strange collection . . . There is the 'Pearl of Great Price' and
> Cobbett's 'Twopenny Trash' . . . 'The Wrongs of Labour' and
> 'The Rights of Man', 'The History of the French Revolution'
> and Bunyan's 'Holy War' . . . It warms his old heart like a quart
> of old ale when he hears of a successful revolution – a throne
> tumbled, kings flying and princes scattered abroad.[11]

Thompson's would have been a very good description of the
anarchist cobbler of Valparaíso and his strange collection of books.
Demarchi comes across as an almost fictive character in 1900s Chile,
but he was nevertheless very real and decisive in the life of Salvador
Allende, according to his own account. He taught Allende the most
important lesson of his life.

The lesson was this: in Latin America, as pretty much everywhere else, there thrives the notion that cobblers, tailors, weavers
and the like, as well as indigenous peoples and the sons and daughters of former slaves, do not possess a culture of their own; they are
not civilised or literate enough to make full use in the future of the
fruits of their own labour, let alone to govern themselves. So they

must labour for others and be governed. Literacy implied civilisation, which entailed the right to govern others and benefit from
their efforts as 'brutes of labour'.[12] Put otherwise, with the added
moral rectitude of Victorian or Catholic righteousness, it was
assumed that the more advanced in the world, or among a certain
population, had an obligation to assist the backward and civilise the
savage. Such an ethical duty, wedded to cosmopolitan sentiments of
sympathy and benevolence, suited the needs of empire.

The whole of the Americas had been represented in terms of
such a mould during the 1550 debates that took place in Valladolid,
Spain: as a vast space lacking the basic traits of civilisation, chief
among them the ability to accumulate and plan for the uncertain
future, and thus in need of the ways and values of Renaissance
Europe.[13] This narrative that identifies two sorts of people in the
world – the diligent, intelligent and above all frugal elite who shall
inherit the earth, and the improvident who squander what they
have on mere enjoyment – created the framework of all modern
imperialisms and justified them. By the time of Allende's birth in
1908, people like Diego Portales, a merchant from Valparaíso who
became the country's most prominent nineteenth-century politician, had decisively contributed to the foundation of the Chilean
republic on the basis of that geopolitical and cultural representation:
as a vast blank space in need of conquest and civilisation. That idea,
and the motivations of foreign capital, help explain the expansion of
Chile at the expense of Peru and Bolivia in the north and the
Mapuche Indians in the south, as well as the internecine wars that
in the late nineteenth century cleared the way for the political
designs of Portales and others, which would endure well into the
twentieth century, and with changes, into the twenty-first.

This is the political context in which Allende grew up, at a time
in which the workers' movement that emerged among the miners
and industry of the north and the Mapuche resistance that continued in the south began to challenge the state of affairs established by
people like Portales. That situation was clearly defined by Portales

himself in a letter written at the time, in which he defended the following idea:

> This thing called democracy, which is claimed by dreamers of all kind, is an absurd notion in the countries of the Americas. Our nations are full of vices, and their citizens lack the necessary virtues to establish a true republic . . . As a system, republicanism is what we must adopt. However, do you wish to know how I conceive of it in countries such as this? A strong government, centralised, made of men who can be true models of virtue and patriotism, able to straighten our citizens so that they would follow the righteous path of order and virtue, and thus become part of the city. This is what I think, and every man of sense should think the same.[14]

The ideology expressed in Portales's letter is but a variation on the theme of the two sorts of people, now internalised in the settlers' self-image and transformed into the foundational narrative of Chile's republican constitution. Thus, the Chile in which Allende was born had been built upon two pillars: the imposition of a strong authority backed by force, on the one hand, and on the other the configuration of a group of white men – and they *were* only men (although behind them, as the stereotype goes, there were women ready to defend the stability of home, tradition and family) – virtuous, literate and capable of ruling over national politics for ever in exclusivity. These men, and the interests they served, configured the fate of Chile. That destiny, however, was entangled with the fate of a few resources: nitrates, copper and foreign capital.[15]

These men completed Portales's work after his death in 1837. Men like the Venezuelan grammarian and legal codifier Andrés Bello (perhaps the most influential jurist in nineteenth-century Latin America), Manuel Renjifo, Manuel Montt, Antonio Varas and the Argentinian Domingo Faustino Sarmiento, who contrasted the civilised world of enlightened Europe, where in their eyes democracy, law and order and intelligent thought were valued, with the barbarism of the native, the gaucho and the caudillo in Latin America.

This narrative of 'civilisation versus barbarism' framed the legal and political regime of Chile, which was parliamentarian until 1925 and presidentialist thereafter, featuring a strictly limited male suffrage (limited until 1888 by the possession of property, and thereafter by literacy, age and gender) and without religious freedom until the late nineteenth century. This political edifice was complemented and in fact secured by the use of force aimed at opening markets and new economic opportunities – concretely speaking, the military machine waging war on Chile's neighbours in the north for control of nitrates and copper, and in the south engaging in the genocide of the Mapuche indigenous people for farmland and other natural resources. Force was central: it guaranteed the repression of social unrest and the ever stronger link between the defence of domestic and foreign economic interests, and the financial health and survival of government.

In the late nineteenth century, President José Manuel Balmaceda attempted to loosen the ties between the interests of big miners in the north – chief among them the legendary 'Nitrate King', a British businessman called John T. North – British-controlled finance, the few Chilean importers and exporters who benefited from the status quo, and the security forces. His attempt was quelled by a violent coup, funded in part by North, Agustín Edwards of the powerful banking and media Edwards family, and the financier Eduardo Matte. After Balmaceda's overthrow and suicide in 1891 the tale of civilisation versus barbarism and the political edifice built upon it became further entrenched, as 'it was proven categorically . . . that the economic and social interests of these men were incompatible, to a lesser or higher degree, with transformations of significance and magnitude. That is why they raised their arms against a government acting in a truly revolutionary manner and against a president – Balmaceda – who was the heart of that government.'[16]

One should perhaps correct Ramírez Necochea, the historian quoted above, and specify that the heart and soul of Balmaceda's revolution and of its successors in the late twentieth century was not up there in the presidential palace but down below: among the lesser breeds dismissed as barbarous and unthinking by Portales and his like. Peter Winn's term 'revolution from below' stresses that the most significant political, social and legal changes that have taken place in Chile's more recent history have been forged by ordinary men and women trying to revive and reinvent long-standing struggles against dispossession and tyranny, in the name of securing liberties and commons for all. These are repeatedly discarded when the greed of privatisation, the lust for power and the ambition of empire capture the means of government. Hence the need to transform the state and change the way it and the law relate to the people at its base, making sure that they no longer work merely as tools for repression.[17]

This was clearly the case in the eyes of Salvador Allende, who, as we shall see, held it as an incontrovertible truth throughout his life and even at the moment of his death. Born in 1908, the fifth son in a family of exalted ancestry but economically far from the powerful bourgeoisie, Allende would recall himself late in life as the pupil of a worker philosopher, a true representative of the people.

By the time Allende entered university in 1926, the impact of the Great Depression upon peripheral countries like Chile or Argentina was turning an already difficult situation into a nightmare: in Argentina, urban unemployment had tripled from 6.7 to 19.4 per cent between 1914 and 1917; inflation cut workers' real wages by one-third. The immediate consequence was an upsurge in strikes, legal conflict and social unrest. Those who inaugurated the era of mass politics in Chile at the end of the nineteenth century, during the decline of the mining industry in the north and in the wake of indigenous genocide and resistance in the south, became organised in the early twentieth century, and this gave rise to social and political movements that grew bolder in step with their strength.

Employers in Chile and elsewhere in the Americas retaliated, pushing their governments towards ever more violent means of repression, or using their own, such as private security detachments or paramilitary groups like the Argentine Patriotic League. The Russian Revolution of 1917 further radicalised working-class and peasant grievances, provided new legal, economic and political tools for creating new knowledge, and multiplied tenfold the fears and anxieties of the propertied classes.

In Chile, post-war depression had been exacerbated by the fall in demand for nitrates and the development of a synthetic variety in Germany. Finding themselves out of work, the majority of Chile's labour force migrated south, away from the mines, in search of new opportunities, or clashed with the security forces of the state. Fifteen people were killed when security forces broke a strike in the town of Puerto Natales in February 1919. The recently established Chilean Workers' Federation (FOCH) gathered 100,000 people in Santiago that same year. Anarchist militancy increased, and the communist movement in Chile would become one of the most active in all Latin America, building on an older tradition of trade union activism in Chile's copper and nitrate industries. The situation was similar elsewhere: by 1910, three out of four adults in Argentina's capital Buenos Aires were migrants who had arrived in South America bringing with them new political ideas and militant narratives – among them communism, Marxism and anarcho-syndicalism. A different but no less important militancy had grown up among the Mapuche indigenous peoples of the south of Chile whose struggle had been going on for more than 300 years; the resistant *indianismo* of the Bolivians Juan Lero and Zárate Willka; the anti-slavery narratives from the coasts of Colombia and the north of Brazil; and the pioneering socialism of the Peruvian feminist and worker organiser Flora Tristán.

In 1896, the physician Juan B. Justo founded the Argentine Socialist Party; earlier on he had translated into Spanish Karl Marx's *Capital*. As had happened in Argentina and Chile, anarchism became particularly influential in Bolivia between the 1920s and 1940s, though it had been present there since at least the end of the nineteenth century. Around the time of the Chaco War fought between Bolivia and Paraguay over assumed oil-rich territories in the 1930s, it shared the space of radical politics with canonical Marxism and, as was the case also in Peru, Venezuela and Chile, with a form of revolutionary nationalism that attracted members of the armed forces.[18]

The radical politics of this period in Latin America were also gendered: in 1914, the middle-class Alicia Moreau founded the Socialist Women's Centre while her upper-class counterpart Victoria Ocampo led the Argentinian suffragette movement. Less than ten years later, in Colombia, María Cano would lead the struggle for workers' and women's rights in the country and helped found the Socialist Revolutionary Party between 1925 and 1926. These women were walking in the footsteps of Flora Tristán over half a century earlier.

The elite in these countries responded to growing militancy and activism. On 21 July 1920, Chile's outgoing president Juan Luis Sanfuentes did what was expected of him when he ordered the security forces of the country to put a stop to a series of student uprisings in support of workers' activism, social and university reform taking place in the city of Santiago. The Students' Federation headquarters were destroyed and a young student poet named José Domingo Gómez was beaten and tortured. In 1922 the Communist Party of Chile was formed. Among its long-standing members was the poet and future Nobel Prize winner Neftalí Reyes, who became politicised after news of the brutal repression of the student uprisings in 1920 reached him in the southern town of Temuco, where he was the seventeen-year-old president of the local school's writers' society, known as Ateneo Literario, and secretary of the Students' Association. In the first article he signed as Pablo Neruda, a pen name inspired by the Czech author of a book of stories about the humble people of the Malá Strana neighbourhood in Prague, the poet expressed his anger at the unholy trinity of 'exploitation,

capital, and abuse'.[19] Provincial Temuco was the last heart of the
Mapuche Indian resistance. One of Neruda's mentors there had
been the village poet and popular intellectual Orlando Mason,
editor of the town's daily newspaper *La Mañana*. Mason read his
poetry in public recitals, where he also became well known as an
outspoken critic of the Indian wars. 'Under the pretext of extermi-
nating bandits,' he argued, 'the colonisers have dispossessed the
native inhabitants of their land, and Indians were killed like rabbits.'
After independence in 1810, Chileans of European descent 'devoted
themselves to killing Indians with the same enthusiasm as the
Spanish invaders'.[20] What Demarchi meant for Allende, Mason did
for Neruda. The life and teachings of these popular intellectuals
helped link the emerging struggle of the workers of the Chilean
north with that of the Indians in the south, and the cyclical upheavals in the long duration of five hundred years of capitalism and
conquest with the decisive bifurcation between popular power and
rule by the powerful and the wealthy that began to take shape in the
early twentieth century and would finally explode as a crisis at its
latter end.[21]

Neruda's next stop was the university in Santiago, where the
future Nobel Prize winner reflected in his poetry on what he called
his 'feelings of repulsion towards the bourgeoisie', while identify-
ing himself further with the restless, outraged people.[22] These
people were the persecuted Indians, domestic servants, men in the
mines and women in the mills, plantations and textile factories, the
unemployed, prostitutes, artists and criminals, the same people
identified later on, in the 1950s, by the Latin American thinker
Frantz Fanon as all those 'who turned in circles between suicide
and madness'.[23] These were the same people brought to the screen
by Luis Buñuel in his celebrated 1950 Mexican film *Los Olvidados*,
written about in the 1960s by the Mexican novelist and essayist José
Revueltas, and turned into protagonists of history and political
economy in the Chile of the 1970s by the German-American
Andre Gunder Frank.[24]

Neruda's political awakening took a decisive turn during his years as a university student in the 1920s. He connected his motivations to the fate of the forgotten, as the latter suffered under the uneven impact of global capitalism, which allowed for the faster integration of some regions and sectors of society into global circuits of trade (said to be more 'central') to the detriment of others (said to be more 'peripheral') and confronted the state's forces. Allende made his debut in university politics in a similar context. As a member of the student movement Avance, he would speak of liberty, high-lighting the plight of the leaderless proletariat as specific to Latin American reality and a crucial point of contrast with the dogmas repeated by the ideologues and cadres of orthodox Marxism and communist parties, which tended to exclude them using denigrat-ing terms such as 'lumpenproletariat'.[25] After refusing to sign a manifesto proposed by the leaders of Avance, calling for the forma-tion of Chilean soviets like those emerging in Russia after the 1917 revolution, Allende was expelled from the student group in 1931.

Allende argued that such rhetorical antics ignored the situation in Chile. He was referring to a blind spot in orthodox Marxist politics – the contradiction of exclusive inclusion, which it shares with forms of racism and sexism – and a relation to political practice that tends to view the future in the light of mechanical and deterministic perspectives. The canonical Marxism that troubled the young Allende corresponded to a dogmatic version of 'scientific socialism' according to which one class, the proletariat, embodies with full consciousness the necessary orientation of future history to the exclusion of other, less conscious sectors of society, especially the 'lumpenproletariat'.

In this respect at least, the version of Marxism that advocated the need for a historical vanguard at the helm of other, supposedly less conscious, sectors of the population was not so different from the conservative and liberal position that put the exclusive right to political agency, government and constitution-making into the hands of the literate or civilised classes. This was particularly problematic in the countries of Latin America, given the history of political militancy originating from the plight of indigenous peoples and other sectors often seen as in need of leadership from without.

There is no need to read this issue anachronistically, as a question of multiculturalism or lack of it. But more importantly, it was not how the younger generation of the early twentieth century saw it. For them, it was a matter of realism as well as an existential judgement. Latin American reality could not be reduced to the simple dualities of a Manichean vision portrayed as the 'objective' history of class struggle, in accordance with the formulas regurgitated at the time by fat manuals published by the Soviet Academy. The past and current history of Latin America did not fit such clear-cut schemes; it could not be read as the product of clockwork mechanisms, but rather as the result of a series of encounters and misunderstandings between people, structures and institutions persisting over long periods – at once legal, geopolitical, cultural and economic. In such an uneven history, different turning points, clashes and confrontations were lived and enacted differently by diverse groups and individuals.

At first, people like Allende, Neruda, Fanon and others would speak of 'eliminating feudalism', or 'secularisation', or 'awakening the nation', evoking previous projects of liberation and independence, in the sense of clashes and readjustments within an enduring system. But in the two decades between the 1930s and 1950s, major crises ensued which threatened the enduring structures and relatively stable institutions of the post-colonial Americas. At that point in their lives, Allende, Neruda and others found themselves facing choices that were not only political but also existential.

Allende articulated the new situation in just such terms. He spoke of making a pledge or a promise, and of the 'arduous consistency' of maintaining such a promise.[26] Referring to his early experiences as a student activist in the Avance group, and the contrast he found there between following a ready-made theory or political dogma and devising a plan and sticking to it, he spoke of the 'arduous consistency of being a revolutionary and staying a revolutionary in a bourgeois society'.[27] For Allende, as well as for other activists of his time, Marxism was less a ready-made answer to the question 'What is to be done?' and more like an existential challenge: to ask oneself 'What am I?' and dare to seek an answer to that and other questions in concrete situations not of one's own making, and with no guarantee that there will be a definitive answer.

The virtue involved in such a quest is neither that of the classical warrior nor of the republican soldier, the founding fathers, or the writers of Latin America's constitutions. Rather it belongs to the migrants, the original Indians, the errant slaves and their descendants, and the political cobblers and popular intellectuals of Allende and Neruda's youth. They would be the subjects of the former's politics and the latter's poetry. The political virtue called for by the arduous consistency of action over time would become the key trait of Allende's life.[28]

Having been expelled from the Avance group and then, for a while, from the university because of his opposition to the dictatorship of Colonel Carlos Ibáñez, who led the repression of the emerging mass movement and the Left between 1927 and 1931, Allende committed himself to the cause of socialism during the short life of the so-called Chilean Socialist Republic of 1932. That year, Air Force Colonel Marmaduque Grove and a group of socialist leaders declared the advent of 'something new, serious, and real'.[29] The spirit of change lasted only twelve days after their colleagues in the military and the big landowners accused Grove and the others of leading the country towards communism. They were arrested and exiled to Easter Island (Isla de Pascua) and hundreds of engaged activists and young students were arrested, Salvador Allende among them.

During Allende's captivity, his father fell ill and died. The experience of captivity and the repression of the 1932 Chilean Socialist Republic, coinciding with the death of his father, whose funeral he attended after receiving a special concession to leave jail, would have an enduring impact on the mind of the young Allende. More generally, these events were deeply affecting for an entire generation of Chileans. Arguably, the fall of the 1932 Socialist Republic became the traumatic wound of Chile's twentieth-century history. At his father's funeral, Allende promised to dedicate his life to the struggle for social justice. That was his pledge.[30] He linked his political choice as a legal reformer and a fighter for the cause of social justice and remedial equality to an existential judgement, a promise made at his father's graveside in a situation of captivity and the repression of the 1932 movement, and not to the ecstatic illumination of Marxist doctrine.

As Tomás Moulian has observed, Allende draws a portrait of the entire socialist political generation of the 1930s in his memoir of this early traumatic episode.[31] Coming from the tradition of radical Enlightenment and secular humanism (and in Allende's case also the prophetic Jewish tradition on his mother's side), raised on the legacy and customs of lower-middle-class provincial families and professional parents (Allende's father had said that he left no other inheritance than a good honest education), they became politicised mainly through their actual experiences of misery and existential struggle: as teenagers in contact with popular intellectuals, as students from the provinces living in modest parts of urban centres, mixing with the popular classes as well as with other liberal professions – in Allende's case, as a practitioner of medicine in the Santiago Hospice. These were young men and women immersed in the social struggles of the time and in the uneven and unequal existence of those involved in such conflicts.

Central to their reflections and their theories was the notion that the 'Indian problem', the legal, political and existentially problematic status of forgotten peoples, was related to the extension of the capitalist appropriation of wealth produced collectively 'out to the farthest reaches of society'.[32] As capitalism colonised the globe and society colonised itself, rifts that were at once temporal, economic, legal, political and even subjective became more evident.

No mechanistic historical narrative, based on the vulgar notion of inevitable progress common to some Marxists and most centrist Liberals, could account for such rifts. It is no coincidence that people like Neruda and Allende almost instinctively rejected such narratives in favour of more nuanced theories.

Crucially, those theories reflected upon the reality in which people like Neruda, Salvador Allende, Laura Allende, Carmen Lazo and others immersed themselves. Their experience in Chile would not be dissimilar to that of their contemporaries in Colombia. There, lower- and upper-middle-class young university students inspired by the Mexican and Russian revolutions would gather in the coffee houses and literary associations of the 1920s to form rebel groups such as Los Nuevos, which brought together the likes of Gabriel Turbay, María Cano, a Russian dyer recently arrived in Bogotá named Savinsky, and Jorge Eliécer Gaitán. The latter, although belonging to the lower castes, had distinguished himself through his speeches after the massacre of 16 March 1919. In 1924 some of them would go on to form a communist cell that met periodically in a church located in the Las Nieves quarter of Colombia's capital.

Let us thus observe the variety of rebellious rationalities that began to coalesce in Latin America between the 1920s and 1940s. Some of them, like anarchism, anarcho-syndicalism and Marxism, were more or less recent arrivals, dating back to the late nineteenth or early twentieth century. In Bolivia and Chile anarchism had been present since the late 1800s, managing to voice the experiences of European immigrants and the living memory and demands coming from the emerging working sectors of society in urban areas, associated with low-scale artisan and industrial labour and small businesses. The sociologist Álvaro García Linera observes that anarchism's influence became notable during the 1920s, 30s and 40s as it helped to organise horizontal federations of apprenticeships and labour associations, as well as contributing decisively to the autonomous formation of an egalitarian culture among its affiliates. As we

know, the young Allende would be exposed to this egalitarian tradi-
tion through his early contact with the working-class world of
Valparaíso, embodied in the figure of the anarchist cobbler
Demarchi.[33]

Though this kind of contact between members of the upper and
working classes might seem unlikely, in fact there were several
examples of it throughout Latin America. Many of these cases
involved upper- and lower-middle-class women becoming aware
of the plight of other women working in sectors where female
labour was intensive and conditions inhumane, such as mining
enclaves and the textile industry. This was the case of María Cano
in the Colombian province of Antioquia, or Alicia Moreau in
Buenos Aires.

Cano had been born to a well-off middle-class family imbued
with the tradition of the radical enlightenment and liberalism during
the years of intolerance, counter-reformation, 'regeneration',
constitutionalism, and persecution of radicals and dissidents in late
nineteenth-century Colombia. Internationally, the Mexican
Revolution, anti-dictatorship and anti-imperialist struggles against
the new expansionist policy and free-market adventurism of the
post-1898 United States fired the imagination of these younger
activists. They were also inspired by the literary work of other
women like Gabriela Mistral, Alfonsina Storni, Juana de Ibarborou
and Delmira Agostini, and deeply affected by the consequences of
the First World War, the 1917 Russian Revolution and later on the
Great Depression. Through her continual visits to the public library,
María Cano went on to become a reader for groups of workers
from whom she would learn about the lived experience of work as
the class composition of Colombian society changed, and the
autonomy and creativity of artisans was lost to the experience of
rigorous control over the behaviour of workers in factories and
workshops.

Some eighty-three years after the experience of workerist and
gendered socialism pioneered by Flora Tristán in her 1843 essay

'The Worker's Union', written between Peru and Britain, Cano, Carmen Lazo and Moreau would help to found socialist political organisations in Colombia, Chile and Argentina. In this more auto-chthonous tradition, socialism and radical liberalism were under-stood as implying the further development of civil liberties into economic and social liberties. Similarly, it was argued that political democracy and legal formal equality were necessary but insufficient, and needed to evolve into economic democracy and social equality.

The Socialist Party of Chile, for instance, was founded on this basis in the wake of the electoral result of 30 October 1932 and the fall of the short-lived Socialist Republic. In that election, the right-wing candidate Arturo Alessandri, who did not hide his sympathies for fascism, won 54.6 per cent of the vote while Grove, the leader of the Chilean Socialist Republic, obtained 17.7 per cent without the support of a proper party. That level of support convinced many on the left about the need for a political organisation more respon-sive to Chilean popular sentiment than to canonical dogmas and international directives. The worsening of the situation in Spain and the rest of Europe, the quarrel between Trotsky and Stalin, and later on the signature of the non-aggression pact between the Soviet Union and Nazi Germany, further strained existing differences between socialists and communists.

Among the founders of the Socialist Party were Colonel Marmaduque Grove, Oscar Schnake and his Acción Revolucionaria Socialista, the anarcho-syndicalist Eugenio González, Trotskyites expelled from the Communist Party, Carlos Martínez, Blanca Luz Brum and Salvador Allende.

Allende observed that when the Socialist Party of Chile was founded, the Communist Party appeared to them 'more hermetic, closed-off, dogmatic' and internationally dependent. However, the founders of the Socialist Party saw no essential incompatibility between their organisation and the Communist Party in terms of their shared philosophy and method of historical and social analysis.[34] Allende's Socialist Party of Chile embraced Marxism while at the same time distancing itself from what Allende called at the time the 'sectarian and revolutionary immature stance that called for a dictatorship of the proletariat in our country',[35] and strongly rejected the cult of personality or *caudillismo* that had become fashionable on the left and the right of Europe between the 1920s and 1940s.

As we will see in the next chapter, European events were extremely influential in determining the different but intricately related destinies of socialists and communists in Chile. Chief among them was the Spanish Civil War, widely interpreted in Latin America as the starting point of the Second World War, and thereafter of the Cold War.

2

The Owners of Chile

Political activism in times of repression is no easy task, but difficult circumstances have a way of inspiring people. During the 1940s and 1950s, as socialists and communists were forced underground by unjust laws and persecution, Carmen Lazo, better known as La Negra Lazo, came up with an inventive way of getting people together. She would bring a harmonica to political meetings. When people failed to show up, Carmen would get the harmonica out of her pocket and start playing as if she were a blues musician from the southern United States. At first, some kids would come, attracted by the music, and behind them the kids' mothers. Then the fathers would come. Soon enough a crowd of a few dozen people would form, dancing to the rhythms of *cueca* and *cumbia* coming out of Carmen's harmonica. Finally, the whole town would fill the square, ready to listen.

Now it was Salvador Allende's turn to keep the mood going. These were the early 1950s, and this was his first bid for the presidency of Chile as the popular coalition's candidate, the current incarnation of the anti-fascist Popular Front of the 1930s and 1940s, now known as the People's Front.

Given the prevailing climate of fear and persecution, for the Chilean Left to have made it this far was already an achievement. For leaders, activists and the people, to show up was itself an act of courage. In the post-war years, after the administration of President Gabriel González Videla turned against 'communism' in general and the parties of the left and the unions in particular, to be seen in a political demonstration organised by the People's Front was to risk arrest and internment in the Pisagua concentration camp, far north in Chile's desert.

Strangely enough, González Videla had been elected with the votes of the Communist Party and the Chilean Left, still riding the wave of respect and popularity provoked by their decisive stance against fascism during the 1930s, especially at the time of the Spanish Civil War in Europe and the Second World War.

The importance of these two events cannot be exaggerated. For it was the battle against fascism that helped shape militancy in twentieth-century Latin America, consolidating positions and reshaping the entire landscape of politics, law and economics. Although the region saw little action within its borders, Latin Americans never conceived of the events in Europe as something foreign, a dark undercurrent to the European Enlightenment happening across the ocean, unfortunate perhaps, but in any case too distant to be of real concern. On the contrary, many understood that the plight of the Jews of Central Europe and the fate of the Second Spanish Republic resonated with a story that was as familiar elsewhere in South America as it was in Chile.

After all, racism and the genocide of entire populations had been the rule in the Americas since the arrival of colonialism, and continued apace after the foundation and consolidation of republicanism in the nineteenth century. In fact, republicanism in the Americas had been founded upon the notion that 'the people' – a term with mostly pejorative connotations at the time – did not matter. From the perspective of those who ran the decisive institutions of Chilean society, 'the people' were for the most part an obstacle on the path towards civilisation, legality and progress. Unlike Europeans, they were illiterate and stuck in a permanent past. As such, they needed to be taught the value of austerity and parsimony, of law and order, and so to become civilised or else be removed.

The worldview bequeathed by the founding fathers and the

writers of legal codes and constitutions – Portales, Bello, North and others – was still being made explicit by people like Eduardo Matte, a member of one of Chile's most powerful banking families at the end of the nineteenth century. As Matte proudly pointed out in 1892, 'the sole owners of Chile are ourselves, the owners of capital and of the soil: the rest are the masses who can be influenced and sold.' And if they could not be manipulated or bought, they could always be forcibly displaced or killed off. In any case, he said, 'they do not matter either as opinion or as prestige.'[1] Two years before, in 1890, Matte, together with Agustín Edwards of the Bank of A. Edwards & Co. and some British business interests associated with the Nitrate King, John T. North, had financed the coup against President Balmaceda's 'revolution'. Those names – Agustín Edwards, the Matte family, those of many other foreign tycoons and investors – will keep cropping up in this story. It is not that they are a constant: what is constant and repetitive is the narrative that frames their vision. We know that according to that narrative there are two sorts of peoples in the world: those who run the risks, own the land and thus deserve to reap the benefits, and all the rest, who get left behind. The corollary of this fiction is that the former have a duty to show the latter the way ahead. It is assumed that beneficiaries of past progress constitute the very form and sole possible shape of things to come. The latter, the wretched of the earth, as they would be called in the 1960s, allegedly unwilling or unable to take risks and face the future, have only to follow the former's example in order to catch up and get their share of promised progress and happiness tomorrow.

The likes of Matte and Edwards saw the people as essentially lacking some element that was basic for the progress of society. In consequence, they tended to perceive them as a problem; as in the phrase 'the Indian problem' or 'the Negro problem'. And problems, of course, need to be ironed out.

Likewise, they held a view of time as transcendence: history itself progressed through stages (from the Ancient East to the modern West), which made the South simultaneously invisible from the perspective of universal history, and an opportunity for the self-affirmation of (mostly Western) civilisation. Thus, southern republics internalised the tenets of progress – free trade, competition, positivist science and law, a work ethic, parsimonious austerity, consumerism and 'hygiene', a term that at the time referred to a particularly nineteenth-century mixture of biology, philosophies of regeneration and *élan vital*, eugenics and medicine. This new vitalism infused a particular understanding of the institutions of the state, law and society, chief among them the market, seen from that viewpoint both as the tool for peoples to transcend in time and as the space in which to do it. In the new paradigm, transcendence would be identified with the remaking or regeneration of entire populations. The term most often associated with that idea is 'progress', but there are others that share similar connotations, some more politically correct than others: advancement, regeneration, civilising mission or development.

The generation of Pablo Neruda, Salvador Allende and Carmen Lazo had witnessed the genocide of the Mapuche in Chile's south and knew first-hand of the plight of displaced Indians, peasants and workers in the mining north. Often referred to by pejorative names such as *indios*, *rotos*, *plebe*, *morenos*, *cholos*, *mestizos* and other terms denoting backwardness, these people would usually be marked by skin colour or, more generally, simply referred to by a single label. Their very existence would be the cause of anxiety among the literate, the 'civilised' and the ruling classes. This is the part of society whose labour is needed in order to satisfy the normal desires of that society – to consume, to vote, to maintain order, respect property and follow the law, to keep the show running – but whose desire to affirm its own existence is constantly denied or disavowed: like foreign migrants in the global North, or peasants, indigenous peoples and the lower castes in the global South. In the 1950s, Buñuel turned his camera lens towards the innermost aspects of the legal, social and political relation between the ruling classes of Latin America and those perceived as the rabble down below. In a series of films, mostly set in the slums and mansions of urban Mexico, Buñuel helped make visible the deep and affective relation of dependency between the people of the slums and those enjoying the benefits of progress, which the latter would not be ready to recognise, let alone to remedy.

The need to express the plight of those scraping a living on the border between city and slum, legality and illegality, humanity and the inhuman, inspired the writing and politics of people like Neruda or Allende. They learned from popular intellectuals that this was not simply a matter of progress or transcendence. Occasionally, they experienced that truth themselves. For people like Carmen Lazo, it had always been a matter of existence.

Lazo was born to poverty in the mining town of Chuquicamata, the biggest copper mine in the world, a hole in the desert so big that it has often been compared to a monster, swallowing countless men and women to produce 'the wages of Chile'. She belonged to a humble family with strong roots in the mining community of Potrerillos, Atacama, where her father had migrated in search of work. In Potrerillos she was a colleague of Manuel Ovalle, who would go on to become one of the founders of the Copper Workers' Confederation in the 1950s, and a leader of one of the most influential unions in Chile's history. After the family moved once more, to Valparaíso, displaced by economic and social circumstances, Carmen continued her studies. While in primary school, she heard the word 'socialism' from the lips of a teacher, also a woman and most probably a militant and a community organiser.

At thirteen years of age, Carmen joined the recently founded Socialist Party of Chile. She began her work around the gold and iron mines of the mountainous region of El Tofo, in the town of Coquimbo. Carmen would ride a mule into the areas where gold and iron miners worked under extremely harsh conditions with an issue of the party's newspaper Consigna under her arm. Once there, she would read and discuss with them extracts from the news broad-sheet, or debate the reasons why Ramsay MacDonald – the author of the only book she could find on the subject of socialism, and a critic of it – had got it all wrong.

On one occasion she was asked by the party director of the Tofo region to write a speech that would be read before a congregation of some 2,000 workers. Present at that meeting were also the found-ers of the party, Marmaduque Grove, Oscar Schnake, the young Salvador Allende and the Uruguayan poet Blanca Luz Brum. 'She was extraordinarily beautiful,' Lazo says, '. . . tall, blonde, green eyes. She crossed her legs up on stage and the men were going crazy, she had them eating from the palm of her hand; she was defi-nitely in charge of the whole affair.' When the moment came for Carmen to read the speech she froze. 'I couldn't see the words on the page,' she recalls. 'Then Blanca Luz turned to me and said: "Girl, lose the papers and improvise." That's what I've been doing ever since.'[2]

Blanca Luz Brum had been born to escape. No wall was tall enough, no boundary could stop her; no gender or sexual conven-tion would have the power to tame her desire. Defying laws and social conventions, the seventeen-year-old Blanca Luz escaped on a motorbike from a nuns' convent in Montevideo with a Peruvian poet. They married, had a child and lived together until his death three years later. Widowed, and wishing for her son to see the land of his father, the poet Juan Parra del Riego, she and her son moved to Lima, where she befriended José Carlos Mariátegui. A Peruvian pioneer of the cause of the indigenous peoples of the Andes who, 'nauseated by creole politics', had turned to socialism, Mariátegui went on to become one of the most original interpreters of Marxism, often compared with Antonio Gramsci and M. N. Roy.[3] Blanca Luz began writing for Mariátegui's journal *Amauta*, and edited a journal of her own titled *Guerrilla: Atalaya de la Revolución*, which published 'rupturist poetry' – which aimed to make a break with traditional literatures centred on the figure of the epic warrior or the soldier, and focused instead on disrupting the narrative chain of mainstream language – essays and social commentary.

In the course of a meeting of union organisers in Montevideo in 1929 Blanca Luz met David Alfaro Siqueiros, the famous Mexican muralist and staunch communist. They fell madly in love and during the time of their passionate relationship they got involved in political militancy, the avant-garde and according to some even plotting and political assassination. They spent time in jail, and became part of a circle in Mexico that included, among others, Frida Kahlo, Diego Rivera, Augusto Sandino, Tina Modotti, Pablo Neruda and his beloved friend Federico García Lorca.

The reach of that circle was global in more than one sense. Not only did it include writers, muralists and painters, but also filmmakers like Sergei Eisenstein and Luis Buñuel, a close friend of Lorca, whom he had met while studying philosophy at the University of Madrid. It also reached as far as Egypt, where members of the Art and Liberty group would develop their own work in dialogue with the Mexican group. In the early 1920s, Buñuel, Lorca and Salvador Dalí were at the heart of a new cultural movement centred on the image, searching for new spaces of freedom and other scenes of interiority and expression. 'Images', Buñuel concluded at the time, 'did become for me the true means of expression.'[4]

By the 1930s, Buñuel's films had enraged both the fascists and the Catholic Church, which denounced his imagery as both communist and heretical. His 1932 film *Las Hurdes: Tierra Sin Pan* focused on the grim circumstances of poverty and peasant life in Extremadura. It used a combination of the languages of ethnography and the written press, travelogues and new pedagogic methods as well as a subversive use of sound, photography and documentary, which laid the basis for a contemporary and creative view of the masses directly opposed to their dismissive portrayal in the past.[5] The image, both in painting and film, was central to the aim of portraying and enhancing the existence and importance of 'the people', the rabble, the forgotten peasantry and the lumpen as the other scene and underside of society, not only as a stage in which the dramas of childhood or the traditional past are constantly played and replayed but also, crucially, as society's productive unconscious.

It was among the people, no matter how dismissed and invisible from the top of the social pyramid, that desire could be encountered, explored and manifested in all its radical nature, and therefore also in terms of its political actuality. For Buñuel and others of his mind, desire took the concrete shape of a multi-layered voice, a montage, or a stereoscopic image. They imagined memory and creative desire in the shape of the strata of the mine at Chuquicamata, or like an inverted Mexican pyramid, a juxtaposition of narratives and oral traditions of remembrance and storytelling, and a creative hub of experimentation on the basis of a multiplicity of stored practices.

It is no accident that in circles like the one frequented by Buñuel, Eisenstein, Lorca, Carmen Lazo, Nicanor Parra, Pablo Neruda, García Lorca and others in Mexico and Chile, and elsewhere in Latin America during the effervescent decades spanning the 1930s to the 1960s, the question of existence and the desire of the people, so often dismissed as a mark of backwardness and an obstacle to progress, would be explored and celebrated instead as the untapped source of energies barely understood. Surrealist, rupturist, Marxist and cannibalistic perspectives – in the sense given to that term by the Brazilian poet Oswald de Andrade and the Colombian writer Gabriel García Márquez – were brought to bear on the issue and provided a whole new landscape of meaning, aesthetic as well as legal and political. Such new perspectives were deeply wedded to a love of life lived to the fullest, freedom, and an engaged practice of ethics inseparable from politics.[6]

Such was the case for Blanca Luz Brum, David Alfaro Siqueiros, Luis Buñuel and Lorca in Mexico and Spain, the painter Roberto Matta or Pablo Neruda and Carmen Lazo in Chile, or Oswald de Andrade in Brazil, among others. Love and life lived to the fullest. It is perhaps in this sense that we may recall, with Pablo

Neruda, his memoir of a night of passionate lovemaking with a tall, blonde, green-eyed woman at a dinner in the house of the Argentinian millionaire and newspaper owner Natalio Botana in the 1930s:

> That night Federico [García Lorca] and I sat on each side of our host at the dinner table. A tall, strikingly beautiful blonde woman was sitting in front of us. She kept her green eyes on me, more than on Federico. At some point we stood up and went to the highest tower in the mansion. I kissed her, and soon we were lying on the ground. As I undressed her, I noticed Federico looking at us and shouted at him: go, and make sure no one comes upstairs. He did so, with such bad luck that he stumbled down the stairs in the darkness.[7]

The woman in question, whom Neruda leaves unnamed, was Blanca Luz Brum. She and her husband, the muralist David Alfaro Siqueiros, were the main guests at the Don Torcuato estate of Natalio Botana, a Citizen Kane-like character well known in Buenos Aires society for his stake in the media business as well as the anarchist tendencies of his long-standing partner, Salvadora Medina Onrubia. While David Alfaro Siqueiros decorated the basement of Botana's mansion with images of his naked wife Blanca Luz, she was busy pursuing her desire to its furthest conclusions, all the while inventing and experimenting with a whole new ethics: holding up the mirror of her rupturist poetry to a broken and incomplete reality, passionately falling in and out of love and demanding everything from men as well as women while giving up nothing, challenging the illusion that people must have a single coherent subjectivity well tuned to its place in society. By refusing to fit into 'accepted categories of gender and sexuality, Blanca Luz proposed new modes of identification . . . based on recognition of desire more than on social rules and conventions', the critic Erin Hilda Redmond pointed out. 'She is a poseur in the sense that she represents an officially impossible, unnameable identity that refuses categorization as male or female, straight or gay.'[8]

Refusing to cede their desire to the rules and conventions of their time led women like Brum and Lazo to come into contact with the void at the centre of their societies. While the self-proclaimed 'owners' of those societies anxiously declared them to be built on the firmest of grounds – capital and soil, or blood and fatherland, in that order – Brum and Lazo found the patriarchal order implied by such declarations to be sustained by feet of clay. Like the characters of a Henry James novel, not only did they refuse any simple resolutions, but perhaps also the very idea of a resolution. To them, the ground was moving, and the pillars were shaking. Soon the whole order would come crashing down. The rise of fascism in Spain, Germany and elsewhere turned that perception into a nightmare reality.

Through their lived dilemmas of suffering and paradoxical triumph, women like Brum or Lazo and men like Buñuel, Lorca, Neruda and Allende punched holes through the fabric of a society already bursting at the seams. On the one hand, the recognition that the promise of personal fulfilment and the organic coherence of personal self and society, entailed in the use of such terms as 'we', 'ownership' and 'capital and soil' by people like Matte or Edwards, was an empty pledge. On the other, the turn towards popular politics and aesthetics, new ideas about what humanity could become, militancy, image, experimentation and desire.

In a sense, rather than closing their eyes to the signs of impending apocalypse, the generation that Brum, Lazo and the others represented embraced the violence around them and sought to confront it in their own terms, turning their lived experiences into practical forms of knowledge and truthfulness, aesthetic as well as political, and came through to the other side. The symbols of cultural collapse would become all too real throughout the 1930s and 1940s in the shape of total war, and the fabrication of figures of hatred justifying the state's recourse to ordeals by fire, states of emergency and the systematic rituals of regenerative violence, first in Spain and Germany and then everywhere else. Far from proposing a bullet-proof recipe that would lead into another promised land, they pursued the beast in their respective jungles and held fast to specific truths, imaginations, promises and political declarations. Chief among them was the idea that 'the people' did matter in so far as they were creatively affirming their own existence, and in doing so also created new spaces for a different relation between law, life and desire. Rather than describing society as the result of a conventional pact or the social contract of liberal republican imagination, which should not be broken and must restrict existing desires, they revolted against what they saw as the dictatorship of normal desires. And they did so in the name of a new law, for instance a personal pledge on behalf of creation and the law of life versus the fascist law of death, or even beyond the law in search of a new humanity. This conception of the relation between law, life and desire entailed the notion that one would stay true to one's pledge and desire, come what may.

This is how they confronted their own lives, as a project of salvage and construction amidst the wreckage left by a furious age, with no guarantees as to the outcome. So it is wrong to attribute to these people a fanatical commitment to dogmatic ideologies, or to shrug off their existential dilemmas as the errors of an adolescent age; it is not only disingenuous but also constitutes a serious misunderstanding that refuses to see the facts for what they are. Some of them, for instance Blanca Luz Brum, would be anything but ideologically consistent. However, they were ready to engage in acts of extreme courage: to volunteer in the fight against fascism in Spain or to combat its replications in the streets of Valparaíso and Santiago, as was the case for García Lorca, Alfaro Siqueiros, Buñuel, Neruda, Allende, Brum and Lazo; to defend the workers and their political organisations when these became the new figure of hatred after the Second World War, in the wake of a shift to paranoid politics in much of the Western world; and to raise the voice of the poor against the mighty, defying the odds on the global stage, as Allende would do later on.

In 1935 Blanca Luz Brum divorced from Siqueiros, who would later move to Spain and join the republican side. She went to Chile and helped to organise the anti-fascist Popular Front, together with Allende's Socialist Party and other popular movements of the time. It was while performing such a role that she met the young Carmen Lazo in the union's theatre of Valparaíso, challenging her to forget the script and instead rely on experiment and improvisation.

Carmen Lazo traced her political commitment back to her lived encounter with what Henry James once called 'the great smudge of mortality across the picture'. In her case, this meant her encounters with the precarious existence of the miners in El Tofo, the brief experience of the Socialist Republic, and poverty early on in life. Lazo relates how on one occasion, while walking back home from school, she picked up a leaflet from the ground that read: 'On 4 June the revolution will take place, come what may.' She relates how the sense of courage implicit in such words was engraved in her soul for ever.

Similarly, Allende reflects on his time as a student of medicine, and his opposition to the Ibáñez dictatorship that put an end to the brief experiment begun on 4 June 1932. For twelve days the leaders of the proclaimed Socialist Republic made explicit their 'resolute will to change' the unequal structures of the old republic. Allende linked his vocation as a militant and an activist to the strength of these feelings, to his experience of captivity, and to the symbolic pledge made at his father's graveside.[9] The resonances between this episode and similar lived experiences in the cases of Carmen Lazo and Blanca Brum are not accidental. In emphasising the subjective side of his political commitment over the alleged objectivity of an ideology, Allende provides what one could call a cinematic image, 'a sociological portraiture of the political generation of the 1930s that opted for socialism'. According to Moulian this makes them different from what he sees as the more ideological commitment of the 1960s generation.[10]

Although Moulian is right in his observations about the subjective (rather than objective) reasons behind the militancy of people like Allende in the 1930s, the resonances with the cases of Carmen Lazo and Blanca Luz Brum exhibit the wider appeal of militant politics, as well as the fact that the old class and gender divisions were being challenged across different sections of society, while being replaced with new political ones. In spite of circumstantial differences, they were all responding to existential challenges by proposing new ways of being and new identities, something that the generation of their sons and daughters in the 1960s and 1970s would also do.

There are important lessons to be drawn from these biographical stories as well as from Moulian's observation. One of them is that the decision to engage in political militancy has little to do with the apparent opposition between practice and theory (or ideology) supposedly inherent in the diverse politics of the men and women of the 1930s and the 1960s. Rather, the emergence of new political subjectivities always takes place in response to more complex practical and profoundly existential challenges.

For women like Lazo and Brum, for instance, political militancy also meant questioning deep-seated assumptions about politics, sex and gender. For too long a connection has been made of order or discipline with masculinity on the one side – a masculinity that can only be fully realised through death, as in the literary figures of the warrior and the soldier – and of unruly desire and weakness with femininity, on the other. Both Lazo and Brum struggled to undo such connections, and their responses to the challenges therein were different.

Brum would grow ever more disappointed about the fact that vanguard parties, political leaders and engaged writers commonly demeaned and marginalised women, divorcing the revolution from gender relations. Like many others, then and afterwards, she agonised over the party line that during the Popular Front period and immediately after the Second World War put the revolution on hold, leaving militants waiting for 'objective' conditions to be ripe for revolution. Among other reasons, these led to her disillusion with the revolutionary cause later in life. Lazo did not grow disillusioned, but was no less conscious and critical about a tendency within parts of the Left to idealise a life of sacrifice (an ideal more Christian than leftist) and to disavow feminine self-sacrifice and love of life, as her interviews late in life reveal.[11] Other militant women would have to deal with similar questions in the different circumstances of the 1960s and 1970s, as Beatriz Allende did, from within the debates over armed struggle, the primacy of the guerrilla, and alternative roads to socialism.

The contrasts between men and women, between Brum or Lazo and Allende or Neruda, as well as those between different generations of militants, suggest a more nuanced picture than the one indicated by sharp oppositions between theory and practice or realpolitik and utopia. This is also expressed in the way that members of each generation perceived themselves not as followers or adherents of militant parties and movements, but either as their founders (as with Allende, Lazo and Brum) or their critics and reinventors (as with the militants and engaged writers of the 1960s like Beatriz Allende, Ernesto Che Guevara or the Argentinian author Ricardo Piglia).

Allende and Lazo made their names fighting fascism on the streets of Valparaíso and Santiago, but they struggled at first with the stigma attached to militancy. For instance, upon receiving his licence to practise medicine with a thesis titled 'On Mental Health and Criminality' in 1932, Allende struggled to find a job because of his activist past, was arrested once more for his criticism of the conservative government of Arturo Alessandri – many of whose supporters in Congress watched the rising tide of fascism with a mixture of complacency and approval because of its counter-revolutionary

stance – and then was exiled to the northern port of Caldera. There
he saw the link between declining health conditions among the
population, their class and racial segregation, and poverty.

In his 1932 thesis Allende had questioned the connection between
race and criminality fashionable at the time: 'Among the Jews,
crimes such as fraud, falsity and forgery, but most of all, usury,
appear characteristic, whereas murder and sexual crimes are exceptional,' he wrote, paraphrasing the Italian criminologist Cesare
Lombroso; 'such arguments suggest that race has an effect on criminality. But there are no precise data or evidence to demonstrate
such influence.'[12] And yet, even though Allende's comment on
Lombroso's views shows that he was sceptical – for want of
evidence – of any link between race and criminality, paragraphs
such as this have been read as proof of his allegedly hidden prejudices.[13] On the contrary, Allende was questioning such views and
prejudices, which had become normalised in academic discourse
and political life in 1930s Latin America. Such views associated race,
specifically the fantasised otherness of the Jew, with images of
monetary circulation and the circulation of ideas, as a metaphor for
the alleged sickness of the social body.

In Latin America, these views built upon already existing and
widespread notions that identify certain populations, such as
indigenous peoples, as traditional or archaic, too invested in religious or magical beliefs that make them prone to lawless and
primitive violence to be fit for modernity, or to understand the
need for the protection of law through legitimate violence.
Therefore they become an obstacle to progress and modernity.
These fantasies, derived from early justifications of conquest in
the Americas, have offered the rationale for political and legal
institutions that uphold a national reality based on the segregation
and relegation of the Andean and African masses, and other
displaced peoples, from a modern project 'that drags along a colonial inheritance, as a consequence of which they are considered
less than human'.[14]

Thus, the basis on which to normalise such views in the twentieth century had been laid by the racism of colonial times revived in
the late nineteenth century. Advocating the restoration of order and
the 'regeneration' of an ailing social body, these views fused together
the discourses promoting Europe's 'civilising mission' with the idea
of enforcing rights of conquest through extermination. A disciple of
this linkage, and business partner of the British–Chilean entrepreneur John T. North in the Congo, was King Leopold II of Belgium,
who wrote in 1876: 'to open up to civilisation the only part of our
globe that it has not yet penetrated, to pierce the darkness that
envelops entire populations . . . is a crusade worthy of an age of
progress.'[15] King Leopold's panegyric to colonialism squares with
Eduardo Matte's 1892 proclamation of the owners of capital and soil
as the owners of Chile, for whom the nameless masses simply do not
matter.

People like Neruda, Lazo and Allende had witnessed first-hand
(or learned from popular intellectuals) how mass murder and the
enforcement of the interests of the wealthy and the powerful as
synonymous with the interest of the nation had been combined
to wrest land and resources from neighbouring countries in the
north and Indians in the south. The wars against Peru, Bolivia
and the indigenous Mapuche had provided the *Lebensraum* that
made up the Chilean nation and the institutions of the republic.
To them, the novelty of totalitarian politics in Germany and
Spain could only appear as having extended to civilised European
peoples the methods hitherto reserved for the natives in Chile
and elsewhere.

According to Hannah Arendt's *The Origins of Totalitarianism*, such
convergence cannot be explained without considering European
imperialism, which she identified as essential to the genesis of
Nazism. This in no way denies the uniqueness of Nazi violence, or
relativises the plight of the Jews. On the contrary, it highlights the
universal significance of the fact that such unique violence yoked
the horrors of colonial plunder and extermination to the military

and financial project of bringing about a homogeneous world in the name of naturalised ideas of competition and selection.

Crucial to that synthesis was also the definition of the masses as an impulsive and maniacal beast, played upon by mechanical instincts and habits, easily manipulated by born rebels and criminals whose morphological characteristics included an aquiline nose, flat skull, bloodshot eyes and an uncanny ability to calculate and persuade. It is easy to recognise here, in Lombroso's description of 'criminal man', a number of physical and psychical elements attributed to the Jews that would be inserted in the early twentieth century into the iconography of Bolsheviks, communards, terrorists, anarchists and communists, and which Lombroso included in his classification of the born criminal as a monster and a degenerate whose exorcism he sanctioned and advocated.[16]

The perception of a threat of political revolt by the lowest layers of society was contemporary with the 'swiftly mutating stereotypes of hatred against the Jews', according to the historian Enzo Traverso. These identified neurasthenia and hysteria as one and the same source of the Jewish genius, the leading role played by Jewish figures in revolutionary uprisings, and the idea of socialism and communism as a persuasive lie or a virus foreign to the social body, and in need of extirpation. Jewishness was associated with the power of abstraction and the circulation of dangerous foreign ideas, allegedly at the heart of the masses' revolt. But also with the abstract circulation of money. The resulting paradox was resolved in the fantasy that the calculating mind of the 'Jewish financiers', which the American industrialist Henry Ford contrasted with the entrepreneurial spirit of Anglo-Saxon 'captains of industry' in his 1922 set of four pamphlets *The International Jew*, also accounted for their moral instability and the abstract intellectualism of their radical political conviction.

The stereotype of the abstract theorist of radical conviction, able to manipulate the masses, would be identified in turn-of-the-century Spain with the menacing figure of the Jewish–Bolshevik plotter, the popular intellectual and the Freemason. Those whom the historian Paul Preston calls 'theorists of extermination', hostile to the Spanish Second Republic, insinuated the racial inferiority of their left-wing and liberal enemies 'through the clichés of the theory of the Jewish–Masonic–Bolshevik conspiracy'.[17] The Catalan priest Juan Tusquets Terrats, author of the best-selling *Orígenes de la revolución española*, condemned the Second Republic as the brainchild of Freemasons and Bolsheviks who did their work by means of revolution, constitutional reform, economic mismanagement, unholy propaganda and relaxed moral attitudes towards sexuality. He denounced the republican president Niceto Alcalá Zamora, a Catholic, as both a Jew and a Freemason. 'The message was clear,' says Preston, 'Spain and the Catholic Church could be saved only by the destruction of Jews, Freemasons and Socialists – in other words, of the entire left of the political spectrum.'[18]

The work of Spanish writers like Tusquets, the theologian Aniceto de Castro – rector of the Jesuit University of Comillas in the 1930s – and other influential collaborators of the journal *Acción Española* sold massively in Spain, and circulated widely among Catholic networks in Latin America. Such publications, as well as the Geneva-based *Bulletin de l'Entente Internationale contre la Troisième Internationale* (whose founders were connected with Joseph Goebbels's Anti-Komintern agency), Ángel and Enrique Herrera's *El Debate*, Onésimo Redondo's *La Libertad*, the Fascist monthly *JONS* (*Juntas de Ofensiva Nacional-Sindicalista*), and José Antonio Primo de Rivera's Falangist daily *Arriba*, peddled the notion that the working class and their organisers were unpatriotic foreign enemies.

That identification was based on the twisted logic that viewed Bolshevism as a Masonic or Jewish invention, and Jews and Freemasons as indistinguishable from Muslims or revolutionary African slaves. Hence, leftists had as their aim the subjection of Catholic countries such as Spain or Chile by African or eastern elements. One of the most extreme proponents of this view in Spain was the late nineteenth-century ideologue Juan Vázquez de Mella.

He argued that Jewish funds and ideas lay behind liberal and communist revolutions that aimed, together with Muslim hordes (transformed in Latin America into the spectre of Haitian revolutionaries), to gain control of the state, destroy Christian civilisation and
impose their tyranny.

These ideas were taken seriously in Chile. The priest and theologian Osvaldo Lira popularised the work of Vázquez de Mella among
the students of the School of the Sacred Heart and the Catholic
University of Santiago in the 1930s and 1940s. Together with the
legal theorist Julio Philippi and Jaime Eyzaguirre, editors of
the journal *Estudios*, Lira would become hugely influential among
the new generation of conservatives who would clash violently
with Allende and the Chilean Left in the 1960s and 1970s. Stereotypes
of atheists, Masons, popular intellectuals, foreign importers of
dangerous ideas, and Jewish–Bolsheviks bent on destroying
Christendom, which already infested the conservative Catholic
imagination of self-righteous Spaniards and Latin American promot-
ers of Hispanism, were mobilised as reasons to oppose the Left by all
means. Such images call to mind the anarchist cobbler of Allende's
youth, the popular intellectual of Neruda's early memories, or the
typographer from the town of Iquique, Luis Emilio Recabarren,
who on 4 June 1912 founded the POS (Partido Obrero Socialista)
which in 1922 became the Communist Party of Chile. Collectively,
the ideas of Tusquets, Primo de Rivera, Vázquez de Mella, Osvaldo
Lira, Philippi, Eyzaguirre, the right-wing press, and all those who
alleged the existence of a Masonic or Jewish–Bolshevik conspiracy
against Christian civilisation, natural law and the given order, justified the extermination of the Left.

As the anti-fascist alliance gave way to the anti-communist
crusade following the 1948 shift in Washington's priorities, the
stereotypical image of the engaged intellectual would be extended
to cover all kinds of revolutionary expressions of popular politics,
and justify their extirpation. The political twilight of the New
Deal in the US, after the death of Franklin Delano Roosevelt and

the sidelining of his vice-president Henry A. Wallace by the conservative wing of the Democratic Party, and the ascent to power of Harry S. Truman, signalled a turn in America's political interests from democracy's defence to an orthodox projection of 'American values' and counter-revolutionary reaction both at home and abroad.

In the process, a new figure of hatred was invented: the silver-tongued intellectual turned enchanter of the masses, ready to unleash the destructive force of their resentment against the hard-working, law-abiding middle and propertied classes at home, while sowing chaos abroad in order to disrupt the natural order among nations. He would be a master manipulator of language and imagination, setting the power of his word and charisma before the camera or the microphone in the service of a revolution at best too abstract to correspond to the concrete needs of common people, at worst too beholden to a messianic ideal to be able to curb its own destructive potential. He would be a fraud and a persuasive liar, an atheist and a communist, perhaps even an anti-Semite himself, if not the devil incarnate. Nothing short of an exorcism, the unleashing of regenerative and purifying counter-revolutionary violence, could cast him out. All the while, the cancer he spread throughout the social body with his lies and promises should be rooted out.

By 1937, Salvador Allende was the twenty-nine-year-old president of the Popular Front in Valparaíso, having made his name as the leader of the Socialist Militias confronting the far right Republican Militias and the National Socialist Movement of Chile in the streets, together with Carmen Lazo and others.[19] That year he became a congressman in the first of five victories in parliamentary elections. Between 1934 and 1938, the exemplary struggle of the Second Republic against fascism in the Spanish Civil War helped to create the climate for a new convergence of rebel voices in the formation of the Popular Front. Chile was the only country in the Americas where the various movements of the Left and the progressive centre formed an anti-fascist coalition that, as had happened in France and Spain, took power in presidential elections, this time under the leadership of Pedro Aguirre Cerda in October 1938. The Popular Front initiated a turn in the economic fate of Chile, beginning a policy of agrarian reform and industrialisation through protections and subsidies for local entrepreneurs making products that would replace those currently imported after the creation in 1939 of the Corporación de Fomento de la Producción de Chile (CORFO).

'The Popular Front is a defensive barricade behind which all democratic forces converge,' explained Congressman Allende in response to the attacks of a colleague of the Right in June 1939, 'whose actions are not delimited by an ideological commitment, and whose orientation is directed by the kind of knowledge that recognises the depths and plenitude of Chilean popular character. Its destiny is to serve the people's interest through a people's govern-ment.'[20] On that occasion he also clarified the position of the socialists:

> For as long as there are oligarchic and exploitative classes set in a relationship of dependent servitude in respect to imperialism, antagonistic towards the multitudes of oppressed workers, which can turn the state into an instrument of repression, a true demo-cratic politics and society will continue to be a utopia and it will not be possible to achieve the economic welfare of the labouring sectors.

He was referring to the mining exporters of the north of the country, who were free-traders; the agricultural and livestock exporters of the south, also free-traders; the big import houses of Valparaíso and Santiago, likewise traditionally free-traders; and finally, to the commercial and industrial sectors that in the 1880s had opposed imperialism and pledged their commitment to the idea that 'Chile could and should be industrial', but then, with the advent of light industry, 'lost a large part of its point of view, and many of its members, with some reservation, joined the pro-imperialist band'. Chief among these were people like Agustín Edwards of the Bank of A. Edwards & Co.

In 1883, Edwards had signed, as first president of the Sociedad de Fomento Industrial, that society's Inaugural Prospectus, which called for the industrialisation of the country. In 1890, however, as we have seen, this same Agustín Edwards was financing the coup against Balmaceda in cahoots with British business interests. By the late 1930s, the Edwards family, their bank, their light industries and their newspaper *El Mercurio* were Chile's most influential partner with American interests. Together they campaigned against the popular candidates Aguirre Cerda (1938) and Salvador Allende (1952, 1958, 1964, 1970). Allende 'could well have used the Sociedad's 1883 Inaugural Prospectus as his economic platform'.[21]

The sequence of popular coalitions, initiated in 1938 when the Socialist Party entered the Popular Front, together with the Radical Party, the Communist Party, the liberal Democratic Party, the CTCh trade union, the Mapuche indigenous Frente Único Araucano, and the feminist Movimiento Pro-Emancipación de las Mujeres de Chile, and consolidated in the anti-fascist electoral victory of 1939, was a considered response to the development of a powerful coalition of interests, based on the export of raw materials, light industry and the import and distribution of foreign manufactured goods. This was and would 'continue to be fundamentally concerned that Chilean development be oriented towards the outside', among other reasons, according to the Chilean economist Max Nolff, because of 'the high propensity to luxury consumption of the high-income classes'.[22] This coalition of interests would be at the heart of the counter-revolutionary efforts of the 1960s and 1970s just as it had been against President Balmaceda in the 1890s.

From now on I will refer to them as the 'Import–Export coalition', for two reasons: first, to highlight the fact that domestic power in Chile rested, at least since the end of the colonial era, in the hands of a bourgeoisie that was and continued to be intimately tied to

foreign interests, first British and then American, was and is prima-
rily commercial, and did and does appropriate surplus profit from
most or all of the important sectors of the economy. Second, to
point out that until 1970, law (both international and domestic), the
Chilean state and its institutions, democratic or otherwise, and the
national elite that appointed themselves as exclusive legislators for
most of the country's history, had long been and still are integral
parts of a global market and regulatory system, with which they
have had a relationship of mutual dependence.[23]

In the intervening years, the immediate effect of the 1948 breakdown of relations between Washington and Moscow, and the
reorientation of priorities in the direction of economic and political
orthodoxy, was the outlawing of the Communist Party of Chile,
the persecution of its militants – forced into exile, underground, or
confined to concentration camps such as the one in Pisagua – and
the repression of parties and movements of the Left involved in
popular politics.

In 1891, the London *Times* reported: 'there is in Chile a communist government, a despot or various despots who under the false
name of Executive Power have overturned all the peace, all the
prosperity and all the education of the preceding eighty years.' And
in 1964, Agustín Edwards's *El Mercurio* would point out how 'everywhere . . . they [socialists and communists] have ended systematis-
ing abuse, suppressing the most elementary rights, and imposing
hunger, violence and misery'. This updates for the years of the Cold
War the projection of a figure of universal hatred in the person and
the image of the political militant or engaged intellectual – in this
case, Salvador Allende himself: 'The parties that support the candidate of the Popular Action Front [Allende] have dedicated their
existence to fighting for Marxism and consequently to promoting
the dictatorship of the proletariat, the abolition of property, the
persecution of religion and the suppression of the state and the rule
of law.'[24]

A manipulator and a liar, an atheist and a communist, a Marxist and a democrat, a lover of luxury as well as a critic of the propensity to luxury consumption of the high-income classes, a revolutionary in theory who in practice could not recognise the simple needs of the common man, a defender of constitutionalism who in fact wanted to establish a dictatorship of the rabble and the proletariat, perhaps even an anti-Semite himself, if not the devil incarnate. In the eyes of the Import-Export coalition, their ideologues and their foreign patrons in the global counter-revolutionary crusade, people like Allende, Lazo and Neruda – especially Allende – began to appear as the ultimate contradiction. None of their promises could be believed, and each one of their assertions should be taken for the opposite; for just like the stereotypical Jewish Bolshevik of the interwar years, these were cunning liars and careful calculators, evil geniuses behind an international plot.

Since they were not to be trusted, any promise of revolutionary restraint on their part should be answered with counter-revolutionary violence. As such, in the paranoid view that came to dominate what W. H. Auden called the Age of Anxiety, the only possible resolution to what was perceived as an inherently violent threat would be a readiness to unleash violence on an equal or greater scale: the Furies of counter-revolution, like those of ancient Greece, could only be one-sided. These are the origins of the metaphysics of hatred that dominated the second half of the twentieth century, which would culminate in the matching violence of the Cold War, including MAD (Mutually Assured Destruction), the Bay of Pigs fiasco of 1961, the Cuban Missile Crisis and the Vietnam War, but which would also help seal the destiny of Salvador Allende and his Chilean Way.[25]

3

The Age of Anxiety

As the Cold War became more aggressive, how did America consider the possibility of a leftist government in Chile? For those engaged in the making of such decisions in the US government, the question was not whether America would allow an independent Left to flourish south of the border. It would not. Instead, they grew anxious about whether their eagerness to allow only one type of political vision in the region would be seen as too imperialistic and anti-democratic.

This means that they recognised limits, for instance law and democracy, and yet sought ways to act without restraint in order to impose a single view throughout. If Latin Americans wished to see things their own way, to envisage another law and a different order, such desires must be contained by any and every means. It was a matter of ascribing them to juvenile fads or irresponsible errors and prescribing either a subtle treatment or the harshest medicine. From then on, everything in Latin America would begin with a decision between where to make a subtle cut and where to opt for surgery.[1]

In the subtle language of diplomacy the view was expressed as follows: 'Allende's government is likely to move along lines that will make it very difficult to marshal international or hemisphere censure of him; he (sic) is more likely to appear as an independent socialist country rather than as a Soviet satellite or a "Communist" government.'

But in the language of a country's interests, the formulation is more blunt: 'Yet a Titoist government in Latin America' – here the author refers to the perceived autonomy of the former Yugoslavia vis-à-vis the USSR during the Cold War:

> would be far more dangerous than it is in Europe precisely because it can move against our policies and interests more ambiguously, and because its model effect can be more insidious.
>
> What all of this boils down to is a fundamental dilemma and issue: Do we wait and try to protect our interests in the context of dealing with Allende . . . or do we decide to do something to prevent him from consolidating himself now.[2]

The author of both versions is one and the same: Henry Kissinger. The previous quotes belong to a memo he wrote to US President Richard Nixon immediately after it became clear that Salvador Allende could be the next president of Chile in 1970. The memo, and others like it, helped define US foreign policy in the 1960s and 1970s, and notions of humanity before the language of human rights became common usage. When people hear the phrase 'human rights', the image that comes to mind is of Amnesty International do-gooders, international law experts, and Blue Helmets trying to uphold the highest moral declarations and legal prescriptions alongside the willing democracies of the world. The phrase also connotes a utopian agenda to improve the lot of the least favoured around the world, the dignity and liberty of each individual secured by international standards, and in general, protection against states deciding to use the blunt instrument.

Kissinger's memo reveals a less rosy picture. Willing and powerful democracies like the US do not necessarily think about human rights when designing their policies, particularly not when it comes to southern countries located, like Chile, 'in their backyard'. Even though legally binding human rights declarations existed since the late 1940s (many of them actually drafted by American lawyers acting on behalf of American governments), between the 1950s and early 1970s the phrase 'human rights' meant little, if anything, to US government officials like Henry Kissinger.

It need not have been this way. In the aftermath of the Spanish Civil War and the Second World War, a Universal Declaration of Human Rights was proclaimed. 'It was less the annunciation of a new age, than a funeral wreath laid on the grave of wartime hopes,' says Samuel Moyn.[3] As he puts it, at the end of those fratricidal wars the world did look up for a moment: US President Franklin Delano Roosevelt and Soviet Premier Joseph Stalin got along famously well. Stalin was a brutal dictator, but at the time he was recognised as the leader of a people characterised by their willingness to sacrifice themselves in the fight against Nazism, their strength in defending their freedom, and their 'extraordinary work ethic', according to a *New York Times* 1942 article.[4] Where before there was deep suspicion of the Russians, now the talk was of Soviet people, who had done 'most of the fighting and most of the dying' in the Second World War according to the *Atlanta Constitution*, being a lot like Americans. A March 1945 Gallup poll revealed that 55 per cent of Americans believed the Soviets could be trusted to work with the US after the war.[5]

Moreover, both countries seemed to be on the same page when it came to imperialism. Although Roosevelt was not as passionate a critic of colonialism as his vice-president Henry Wallace, he told Winston Churchill that it was contradictory to wage war against fascist slavery and at the same time 'not work to free people all over the world from a backward colonial policy'.[6] His observation goes to the heart of a dilemma that persisted in most legal and political arrangements after the Enlightenment: the persistence of slavery and subjection amidst declarations of liberty. That contradiction was as evident in the case of the US legal system as in that of worldwide imperialism. Its recognition had inspired the languages of 'higher law', remedial and 'equal' equality, and the 'right to revolution' in the nineteenth-century struggles for independence, as well as calls for a 'second economic independence', decolonisation, self-determination and the 'rights of peoples' as well as civil rights in the twentieth-century Americas.[7]

US vice-president Henry Wallace, an outspoken critic of racial segregation in his own country, paid homage to that important legal and political tradition in the Americas. In 1942 he responded as follows to the publishing tycoon Henry Luce's call to renew the doctrine according to which America had a manifest destiny to become an empire and make this the 'American Century':

> Some have spoken of the 'American Century.' I say . . . the century . . . which will come of this war can and must be the century of the Common Man . . . There must be neither military nor economic imperialism . . . International cartels that serve American greed and the German will to power must go . . . The march of freedom of the past 150 years has been a . . . great revolution of the people, there were the American Revolution of 1775, the French Revolution of 1792, the Latin American revolutions of the Bolivarian era, the German Revolution of 1848, and the Russian Revolution of 1917. Each spoke for the Common Man.[8]

In Wallace's words, and the tradition he appealed to, lay an alternative history and a future for human rights as the rights of the Common Man. Unsurprisingly, when Wallace toured Latin America to unite the continent in the fight against fascism he came back home to Washington with the firm support of most Latin American nations. This support mattered most in terms of the scarce resources needed for the war effort against fascism, not least Chilean copper, which was central to the manufacture of weaponry. It came at no small cost for countries like Chile. During the Second World War, as Washington capped the market price of copper at 11.5 cents per pound, Chile lost $500m. It also compromised its sovereignty. Chile allowed American troops to occupy the main copper mines to prevent an attack by the Axis powers. As it happened, however, it was not the future of human rights and liberty that triumphed. Another future, characterised by a much more feeble support for rights and freedom, would prevail after the second half of the twentieth century.

Its origins may have something to do with the ambiguities of the inter-war period. Roosevelt and Stalin recognised, as did the rest of the world, that the feeble international response to the Spanish Holocaust, German anti-Semitism and racial hygiene policies had been disastrous. That feebleness might be explained by the fact that such policies and attitudes were more widespread than we would like to remember. Today, few will recall that the American icon of free-enterprise capitalism, Henry Ford, did more than supply trucks for the Germans and be decorated by the Nazi government for doing so. He also contributed to the development of the theories of extermination that justified the elimination of the Left in Spain and Nazism's ideology of hatred. As we have seen, in 1922 he published a collection of anti-Semitic pamphlets titled *The International Jew*. In 1927, Ford attempted to impose social engineering and Midwestern Puritanism upon the native peoples of South America by building a town called Fordlandia near the city of Santarém in the Brazilian Amazon, complete with rubber plantation, factories with time clocks, prohibition, a strict diet, and weekly square dances that would cleanse the hearts of Indians of their darkness, giving birth to a new world of individual initiative and belief.[9] Thereafter, Ford sponsored the printing of 500,000 copies of the notorious forgery *The Protocols of the Elders of Zion*, published in Russia in 1903 on the basis of German and French novels of the 1860s.

The first Spanish translations of the *Protocols*, which peddled the fantasy of a secret Jewish conspiracy to destroy Christian civilisation, became available in Leipzig and Barcelona in the early 1930s. Their fantastical plot was popularised in Spain by the writers of *Acción Española*, and especially by Juan Vázquez de Mella – who added the twist that Jews and Blacks were in it together – and the best-selling work of Juan Tusquets, who used the *Protocols* as 'evidence' backing his thesis that Freemasons and socialists were instrumental in the anti-Christian conspiracy.

In late 1933 Tusquets was invited by the Anti-Masonic Association to visit the concentration camp at Dachau established to quarantine Freemasons, communists, socialists and liberal political opponents, as well as homosexuals, Gypsies and other dark-skinned 'deviants'. He declared: 'they did it to show me what we had to do in Spain.'[10] Tusquets and the others had an enormous impact among Spanish military figures active in the African colonies, such as Francisco Franco. Turning from theory to practice, Tusquets got involved in the military plot against the Spanish Republic through his links with Carlist monarchists. In turn, the Carlist ideologue Vázquez de Mella inspired the Chilean theologians and lawyers who not only developed the ideas that justified violence against Allende and the Left, but also took part in the plot against the latter's government in the 1970s, and became the architects of the legal and constitutional institutions of Chile thereafter.

There is a straight line linking intellectual endorsement of the *Protocols*, justifications of violence as the blunt instrument for the extirpation of the Left, Hitler's regard for Henry Ford's free enterprise, the rise and fall of Fordlandia, the triumph of Henry Luce's American Century over Henry Wallace's Century of the Common Man, the Spanish Holocaust and the 1980 Chilean Constitution. It marks the choice between the Common Man and the American Century as set out in Kissinger's memo to Richard Nixon on the Chilean situation in 1970, which embodied, in that single instance, the more general question of the unresolved contradiction between liberty and slavery at the heart of modern law and politics. It is as if, at every point in the story told in this book, we are faced with yet another opportunity to choose between these two alternatives. Crucially, the memo was written before the Chilean Left had a chance to nationalise, reform or mismanage the economy, and before Allende could demonstrate whether he was fool or fraud, or both, or neither. Way before any of the fears expressed about him and his coalition of socialists, slum-dwellers, indigenous peoples, communists, radical Christians, peasants and so on could be confirmed or disproved, his fate had been foretold in the back corridors of the White House and discussed in clandestine meetings between secretive men.

According to these men, the consolidation of a Chilean Way (*la vía chilena*) – as Allende's coalition plan for a peaceful transformation of the state had come to be known at home and abroad – would pose 'very serious threats' to the interests and position of the US government and its clients in the region: 'U.S. investments (totalling some one billion dollars) may be lost, at least in part; Chile might default on debts . . . owed to the government and private banks.'[11] Inherent in the danger represented by Chile to the natural order of finance in the world was its additional potential to become a political threat. In Kissinger's opinion Chile was likely to become a leader of the opposition in the inter-American system, 'and a focal point of subversion in the rest of Latin America'.[12]

One may surmise from this line that Kissinger had heard of Che Guevara's manual *Guerrilla Warfare* – where Guevara explains the *foco* tactics of subversion that advocated the establishment of a guerrilla group that would act as a 'small engine' sparking revolution in larger societies, which led to the success of the 1959 Cuban Revolution. Whether he read it or not, Kissinger seems completely ignorant of the fact that Allende did not believe such tactics and strategy would work in Chile or the rest of Latin America.[13] Furthermore, by 1965, after his disappointing visit to the countries of the Iron Curtain, Guevara himself had moved on. He appeared much more interested in the question of the 'transition' towards socialism and the design of legal and political institutions fit for the task of transformation and the coming of the 'new man', as well as in taking the struggle to his native Argentina, than in the tactics of the past. His ill-fated Bolivian campaign of 1967 would demonstrate to a whole new generation the need to shift tactics: it provoked a debate about Guevarist views of the guerrilla group as 'almost a sect', always at risk of abdication, of being infiltrated, which led to the extreme consequences of notions of the *compañero* as liable to desert and betray. It also deepened current debates about the importance of the institutions of the state and the possibility of transformative uses of law, and prompted serious and self-critical considerations about the persistence of old habits like the idealisation of masculinity, the maintenance of strict sexual boundaries, or looking down on local and native peoples during and even after a revolutionary process.[14]

That generation, which came of age politically in the 1960s and 1970s, included Allende's daughter Beatriz, the Argentinian writers Ricardo Piglia, Julio Cortázar and León Rozitchner, the Mexican author Paco Ignacio Taibo II, the Mapuche activist Rosendo Huenuman, the Chilean film-maker Patricio Guzmán and the Colombian activist Gloria Gaitán, among others. All of them would be touched in one way or another by the events unfolding in Chile. Distancing themselves from the 'old ways' of their parents while at the same time reclaiming those legacies, they set out to develop images and languages of their own. At times, these were critical of the persistence of certain images and values of the past, specifically the tendency to continue to dismiss the will of the people as lacking any substance of its own.

Such tendencies persisted on the left, and were visible, for instance, in the attitude of those who confused the plight of indigenous peoples with peasant grievances in the context of wider class alliances. Others were dismissive of the specific nature of Indians' grievances, the frustration of younger generations over party politics, and feminist criticisms, representing them as particular identity claims with no universal value, or as 'ethnological rather than political' positions.[15] And they were certainly an element in the remnants of 'fascism' present among the owners of Chile, on the right generally, and in the foreign policy of the US after F. D. Roosevelt's death and Henry Wallace's political decline, which nervously swung between assistance and belligerence towards entire populations in Asia and Latin America. The possibility of a 'socialist' contagion – a term that itself reduces the variety and specificity of popular claims to zero, by placing them in the void of absolute enmity and anxiety – spreading among the peoples of Asia, Latin America and southern Europe, frightened the Americans.

What really worried Kissinger was the chance that Chile might set an example: 'The example of a successful elected Marxist government in Chile would surely have an impact in the rest of the world; especially in Italy; the imitative spread of similar phenomena would in turn significantly affect the world balance and our position in it.'[16] Faced with such a threat, Kissinger urged Nixon to make a choice between the subtle dagger and the blunt instrument. In fact he advocated the latter, to loose the Furies upon the peoples of the Andes, but to make sure that US hands could not be seen engineering the plot, or as he put it 'to use [the means of force] quietly and covertly . . . to oppose Allende as strongly as we can and do all we can to keep him from consolidating power, taking care to package those efforts in a style that gives us the appearance of reacting to his moves.'[17] Whatever the choice, the result would ultimately be the same: to induce blindness, to make sure no history was made in the South so that it would keep moving on its God-given and natural course from East (the place of the past) to West (the land of the future) with the light of progress and reason frozen in mid-air directly above America.

The looming power of the US to dazzle and blind had been a salient feature of political debate south of the Rio Grande since at least the period between 1914 and 1930, when the North American nation began expanding its sphere of influence at the expense of the British, Spaniards and others, after the British–American War of 1812, the Mexican–American War of 1848, the seizure of Cuba, Puerto Rico and the islands of the Pacific following the

Spanish–American War of 1898, and the takeover of Panama and the Canal Zone from Colombia in 1903.

Echoes of the 1910 Mexican Revolution and the 1927 Sandinista rebellion against American occupation in Nicaragua resounded throughout the region as writers and activists searched for anti-imperialist alternatives. These, as well as fears of 'pressure and hostility', became more acute during the cycle that began after 1948. The two decades between 1948 and 1968 proved crucial. The period started with a change of direction in Washington after the Potsdam Conference that replaced the anti-German alliance with an anti-Soviet one, resuming in Latin America a sequence of counter-revolutionary violence that in the opinion of Allende's adviser Joan Garcés 'had never been entirely closed'.[18] According to him, the assassination in Bogotá on 9 April 1948 of the left liberal leader Jorge Eliécer Gaitán, a popular lawyer and likely winner of the Colombian presidential elections that year, revived the expedient of preventing those who pledged their faith to the cause of the people, and enjoyed enough support to take over and transform state power in free elections, from ever becoming government leaders. The episode of Gaitán's assassination would become so ingrained in Allende's mind that later on he would try to join his own legacy to Gaitán's in the womb of the murdered Colombian leader's daughter, Gloria Gaitán, his last lover.

Let us consider, in this respect, the Argentinian philosopher León Rozitchner's exploration of his own condition as a politically dissident Jew in Latin America in the late 1960s. Being Jewish, Rozitchner observed at the time, 'is an index of the inhumanity of the human', and the inhuman treatment and persecution of humanity. If fully assumed, he says, that index should make us turn our eyes towards other indices of a different status, such as being black or indigenous, female, homosexual, a worker, a slum-dweller, a Muslim and so on, for these are all indices of non-being and oppression but also of emancipation and revolt, 'that should be able to link up in an international movement of liberation'.[19]

Here Rozitchner proposes a distinction: it is one thing to be robbed of the things of the world, as could be said of owners in general in cases of expropriation or nationalisation. It is a very different thing to be the object of plunder, enslavement, poverty or massacre, for in the latter case one is robbed not only of the things of the world but of 'the very ground of being in the world'.[20] This argument pertains to the motivations and viewpoint of the oppressed as expressed by themselves, for instance in oral history, memoirs, or in the testimonies recorded in Guzmán's film *The Battle of Chile*. It is also the starting point for a cogent critique of some mainstream ideas about property, rights and law, together with the contradiction between slavery and liberty mentioned above.

It throws light on the fact that the nature of oppression in our time is such that it challenges people constantly to question their value, and define who they are. If one is nearly everywhere told that one is not fully human, and yet one struggles every day with responsibilities that are only too human, one ends up critically engaging with the very concept and image of the human as it is applied, or not applied, to oneself. The result is the construction of a new image of the human, more universal than the previous one. From such a perspective our current standpoint and the order it belongs to (which otherwise seems quite natural) now looks partial and profoundly inadequate. In politics, legal philosophy and theology this kind of judgement is often called a chiliastic or last judgement. It entails the need for a rupture in history. This is the kind of judgement people refer to when they have recourse to 'the judgement of history', as Fidel Castro did when he appeared in court on 16 October 1953.[21] In referring to the judgement of history we endeavour in imagination to conceive of a better future that would replace the current order (which appears from that perspective as meagre and inadequate) and attempt to realise it in the present. As in reality there is always scope for incompleteness and failure, the practical lesson we draw is that we struggle and protest because not to do so would be too humiliating, too deadly, too inhuman. We protest by defending ourselves in unjust court proceedings, building a barricade, taking up arms, going on hunger strike, shouting, speaking up, or writing in order to save the present moment, come what may, so that there may be a future.

'To protest is to refuse being reduced to a zero and to an enforced silence', and that moment, although passing like every moment, acquires a certain indelibility. This realisation is of huge importance in any consideration of an ethics of sacrifice, which as we will see, became a central concern for activists in the 1960s and 1970s, and is particularly apposite to our story of a death foretold. It indicates that militancy or protest is not principally a sacrifice made for some alternative future, imagined as more just; 'it is an inconsequential redemption of the present', as the novelist John Berger has said, or does battle for a transformed present and for the very possibility of transformation to take place against the present's logic that insists on calling our efforts pointless.[22]

In the 1960s and 1970s, various artistic and political approaches in Latin America dealt with this practical question. It lay at the heart of the 'revolution from below' in Cuba and in the southern cone of the Americas; taking stock of it may provide us with a privileged entry point to the existential and political dilemmas faced by the protagonists of our story.

Rozitchner's distinction is reminiscent of the critique of absolute property developed in the nineteenth century against the backdrop of colonial plunder and slavery.[23] Furthermore, it is strictly relevant to the anti-imperialist and decolonising politics and the approach to law developed by Allende and the popular movements between the late 1940s and the early 1970s, especially in such crucial areas as agrarian justice and nationalisation. This argument and the politics it fosters involve a shift of perspective: away from the absoluteness of property and the image of history as an evolutionary passage from one stage to another, and towards the centrality of existence, the question of value, and what Rozitchner calls the transit from the old – non-being, social invisibility or slavery – to the new – freedom and the creative exploration of who we are, as subjects of value. Notice, however, that the term 'value' in the second perspective has nothing to do with the value of property and economic prices, but rather with what is priceless, what money can't buy. In short, it has to do with dignity, truthfulness, consistency and humanity, and the conditions that make the latter possible. To create a new humanity means, in practical terms, to stop thinking politics (and economics) like Romans, that is to say, imperially, and instead have the courage to think that empire is not the last word, that something will come after its proclaimed final struggle against all forms of militancy. We do not know what this will be, but we can say that a new sense of urgency is required, for we cannot wait until it is too late. More genuine forms of deliberation are needed now.

This might entail considering seriously the possibility that the current forms of deliberation and social organisation – going from the state presiding over crises and emergencies via the police, to charity and compassion – are not sufficient and can be replaced or complemented. This can be empirically tested: one of the least considered outcomes of financial and security crises is the fact that societies in general do not regress to some state of chaos but actually reinvent networks of solidarity, care and organisation, or create new ones, and carry on. The point is simple: do not treat other people as children, who become people only if and when they enter into contact with your own laws and ways, thereby reflecting some underlying natural code (Romans called this *ius gentium*), unless you want them to act as such. We can pursue, in practice as well as imagination, forms of democracy in which all are treated as adults and equals irrespective of their property or industry.

Such has been the point of prophetic religions like Christianity, Judaism or Islam, which from the outset, in their non-imperial modalities, imposed strict injunctions on the extension of market practices to all aspects of society. The point is practical: transforming political institutions into forms of collective problem-solving, in which the base rather than the hierarchy at the top interprets the unrealised possibilities of tradition into a renewed sense of urgency about the fact that things cannot continue as they are. That has nothing to do with sticking stubbornly to religious dogma, but one important implication is that it is not necessary to stop being Jew or Christian or Muslim to engage in such transformation. For we know that viewing politics and law as common problem-solving entails assuming the fact that the interlocutors will always have mismatching viewpoints and ideas about life, death, and what is yet to come. To rid the world of identity, ethnicity, communal values, identified with the archaic as opposed to modernity, will not solve the problem. A deeper sense of democracy, here and now, can.

It became clear to many between 1948 and 1968 that to change only the economic relations of production would not suffice without also reformulating the conditions of humanity and subjectivity free from their colonial–capitalistic carapace, the political surface if you will. This included US imperialist foreign policy. Guevara, Allende and many others in the world understood this to be the case, and acted together on the basis of such an understanding. They challenged the 'imperialist' bias of international law, and mobilised in the General Assembly of the United Nations and elsewhere so as to change the rules of the international order.[24] This was the kind of global 'demonstration effect' that people like Kissinger feared the most.

In 1948 US Assistant Secretary of State Spruille Braden, who had been a paid lobbyist for the United Fruit Company, threatened the government of Chilean President González Videla with a credit freeze unless it cut its ties to the Communist Party and proscribed it. Until then the party had been the second political force in the country. Not only that, a 'revolution from below' was beginning to gain momentum as southern coalminers went on strike in August and October 1947 and workers in the northern Chuquicamata copper mine followed their example, this time with the presence and support of the communists. In all of these cases the government invoked emergency powers and sent troops to restore order. Seeking to blot out mass politics by the stroke of a pen, in July 1948 the Chilean government introduced the Law for the Permanent Defence of Democracy, banning the Communist Party, striking the names of its activists off the electoral register and creating exceptional rules allowing their persecution. It soon became known among Chileans as 'the Damned Law'.

For people like Neruda, Allende and Carmen Lazo, these events seemed like a repetition of pre-war European history. They had led the Socialist Militias in the struggle against the rightists and Nacistas (as the local version of Nazism was known) in the streets of Valparaíso and Santiago, aided Spanish refugees fleeing Europe into Chile, and signed messages of protest against Hitler in the wake of Kristallnacht.[25] They found support in the emerging Social Christian camp, which appealed to the Chilean middle class and would in time become the Christian Democratic Party. Together they condemned the 'Damned Law' as an 'atom bomb set to destroy Chile's social and political coexistence, built on a long tradition of effective democracy', as Allende put it during an intervention before the Chilean Senate on 8 June 1948.[26]

The law struck from the electoral register more than 20,000 communists, and barred others from participating in the union movement. Party leaders and militants were identified, persecuted and called to surrender themselves for internment and concentration in the prison camp located in the old nitrate port of Pisagua. Many were forced into exile.

Pablo Neruda was one of them. He had joined the Communist Party in July 1945, having concluded during the Spanish Civil War that communism was the only effective way to fight fascism. Fresh in his memory was also the fact that on 5 September 1938 the Chilean Nazi or Nacista Party led by Jorge González von Maráes had attempted a coup d'état with the support of one of the most important figures of Chilean politics at the time, Carlos Ibáñez – the dictator deposed in 1931, who had stood as candidate of the Right in 1942 with an authoritarian programme, and by the late 1940s, in the midst of the persecution of the communists, was successfully courting the support of the socialists.

To understand the appeal of figures like Ibáñez it is necessary to take into account the fact that anti-communist reaction had sent the Left into disarray in Chile and elsewhere in Latin America, pushing many to succumb to the kind of populist temptation embodied by Ibáñez and his ilk. Populism, a pejorative term often applied nowadays to left-of-centre governments in Latin America, referred originally to a form of politics that appeared first in the wake of persecution against the Left and the persistence of fascism and Spanish *falangismo*. As such, it connotes a mishmash of anti-communist sentiment, anti-politics, fears concerning the participation of popular majorities, the persistence of old (Christian) beliefs concerning the natural order of society and the centrality of Church and family, and immediate reactions to demands from below that were seen as threatening the sacrosanct primacy of property. It is a catch-all term, too vague to be useful, and better understood as indexing the confusion of the historical period immediately following the end of the Second World War and the beginning of the Cold War, its Manichean worldview, and its tendency towards reducing politics to essential monolithic differences in place of drawing meaningful distinctions.[27]

People like Neruda, his partner Delia del Carril (a woman as determined to follow her own path as Brum and Lazo, profoundly influential in Neruda's turn to the political left) and Allende read these confused times through the prism of the lessons derived from the Spanish Civil War. Having become a senator for the Communist Party, Neruda denounced in Congress the volte-face of President González Videla. The Damned Law was the result of a secret deal with President Truman's emissary, Admiral William Leahy. According to Neruda, González Videla's actions were comparable to those of the Nazis in Germany:

A president elected by these very same workers – who hoped that at least once someone would hear the voices rising from their hell – has declared in public that the strike is not due to the frightful conditions in the coal regions, but to an international plot, and on the basis of this falsehood, he has treated the workers with a cruelty and savagery found only in Nazi systems of slavery and oppression.[28]

Referring to the American hand at work in these events, Neruda issued a stark warning for the whole of the continent:

The instigators of these crimes threaten not only the freedom of Chile but the order and integrity of our forsaken Latin America. Other governments will repeat these debilitating betrayals. The cruel and bloody dictators in some of our sister countries will today feel more firm and resolute as they tighten the noose around the necks of their people.[29]

On 6 January 1948, Neruda delivered in the Senate one of the bravest speeches in Chilean political history. It is known as 'Yo Acuso' (I accuse), after Zola's rejoinder against the French government for the persecution of the Jewish soldier Alfred Dreyfus fifty years earlier:

The President of the Republic has taken one more step in the unbridled political persecution which will make him notorious in the sad history of these days, by filing an action before the Supreme Court requesting my impeachment . . . They charge me with having spoken against my country because I did not agree with decisions taken by this same Exalted Leader . . . If to disagree with His Excellency is to turn against the nation, what can we say when we recall that Señor González Videla, as president of the Committee for Aid to the Spanish People, supported and defended the rights of expatriate Spaniards to attack from exile the same Franco government with which he is now on such good terms? . . . I am proud that his persecution has fallen on my shoulders. I am proud, because the people who suffer and endure may thus have an opportunity to see which of us have remained loyal to their public obligations and which have betrayed them.[30]

He proceeded to read out the names of 628 men and women in detention in Pisagua concentration camp under the auspices of the Law for the Permanent Defence of Democracy. When Salvador Allende attempted to visit those confined in Pisagua, he was stopped by a young army lieutenant who had been put in charge of rounding up hundreds of workers and leftists in the northern desert. His name was Augusto Pinochet Ugarte. It was thus in January 1948 that Pinochet was given his first role in this story, as jailer and director of the Pisagua concentration camp.[31]

In October that year General Manuel Odría established a dictatorship in Peru. Another was imposed in Venezuela a few months later, opening a long sequence that would lead some twenty years later to the 1964 coup in Brazil and the events of September 1973 in Chile.[32]

The immediate effect of the change of priorities in Washington, the banning of the Communist Party of Chile and the persecution of militants and activists was the liquidation of the Democratic Alliance, a new incarnation of the progressive Popular Front in 1948. The Left and the popular movement were thus thrown into disarray. It would take almost a decade for a new coalition based on the alliance between socialists and communists to be formed, one that could articulate its political programme successfully with the momentum of popular movements leading a 'revolution from below', first as the People's Action Front (FRAP) and then as Popular Unity (UP).

In contrast with what had happened in the previous period, between 1948 and 1968 popular alliances in Latin America were disavowed in the US, when not directly attacked or conspired against. As for the economic element inherent in the new attitude, the US put forward a plan for the hemisphere along traditional lines of international trade, but this time under the aegis of the US as chief market. The plan was announced by General George C. Marshall during the Ninth Pan-American Conference celebrated in April 1948 in Bogotá, on the same day and in the same city where Jorge Eliécer Gaitán was murdered.

The plan was countered a year after in Havana by the Latin American equivalent of John M. Keynes, the Argentinian diplomat and economist Raúl Prebisch. Originally based at the Economic Council for Latin America (ECLA) research centre in Santiago de Chile, an economics and policy think tank funded by the UN, in 1949 Prebisch launched his Havana Manifesto, provoking equal measures of sensation in the Latin American media and consternation among senior UN and US officials in New York and Washington who understood it as a major challenge to the old doctrine of free-tradism and comparative advantage.[33]

Prebisch's Manifesto called for an activist state and indigenous industrialisation, while providing a firm basis for the thesis concerning the uneven nature of the relationship between 'centres' and 'peripheries' in the global economy. This thesis stated that different regions of the world and different sectors of society integrated into the international circuits of trade in diverse ways and at different speeds, and would become its beneficiaries to the detriment of those regions and sectors that did not, and the notion that persistent and increasing inequality would accompany the globalisation of markets and capital. Prebisch denounced as a conspicuous flaw in economic theory as taught in the academies of northern metropolises its bogus sense of universality, its assumption that its descriptions and prescriptions were globally applicable, even though in fact very little effort was put into studying the real economic, social and political conditions of regions of the world beyond the centres, or the ways in which economic views developed in such places might talk back to the centre. His was a riposte to the hold of the tale of the two sorts of people, which distinguished between more advanced and more backward peoples and regions of the world, upon the political and economic imagination of the times.

Prebisch's ECLA, based in Santiago, began to train men who would in time contribute to the economic policy of the Christian Democrat government of Eduardo Frei Montalva of the late 1960s and Allende's UP administration in the 1970s. It received the input and criticism of a new generation of economists and sociologists from Chile and Brazil such as Celso Furtado, Enzo Faletto and Fernando H. Cardoso from the late 1950s onwards. All the while, ECLA members participated in the wider political debates that in the 1960s and 1970s moved the focus from economics and sociology to personal and social psychology, and from the tactics of coalition politics and armed struggle to such strategic and existential questions as global institutional design (the issue of the state in the 'transition' to socialism), democracy and terror.

The newer generation of critics demonstrated that policies for industrialisation, though more desirable than dependency on foreign manufacture and finance, were unable to check the persistent tendency to concentrate income in the upper layers of society, and the tendency of the latter to resort to counter-revolutionary violence and terror. A renewed focus on the global transfer and accumulation of surpluses and profits – including the role of multinationals, the project for a common Latin American market, the need to build an anti-imperialist popular block, the diversity of the roads to transformation, and the crucial question of violence and terror in relation to the anxiety of the times, as seen from the South – would be the themes dominating the economic and political debates of the 1960s and 1970s.

The changing role of the US loomed large in the background, particularly in the wake of the Cuban Revolution. In this respect, the first presidential candidacy of Salvador Allende on behalf of the People's Front, which firmly opposed the 'populist temptation' embodied by Carlos Ibáñez (who in spite of his advanced age and authoritarian past obtained 46.8 per cent of the vote against a meagre 5.4 per cent for Allende) and other US-backed authoritarian rulers in the continent, constituted a breaking point. In February 1953, the launch of the Central Unitaria de Trabajadores (CUT) marked the unification of workers affiliated to communist, socialist, radical, anarchist and Social Christian tendencies. In 1956 the Popular Action front (FRAP) was formed, achieving the reunification of socialism in 1957, and in 1958 Allende's electoral fortunes turned decisively when he ended 30,000 votes short of the presidency, obtaining 28.51 per cent of the vote against 31.18 per cent obtained by the conservative candidate Jorge Alessandri, supported by the beneficiaries of old colonial and neocolonial monopolies of trade and the US, and the 20.46 per cent share of the vote obtained by Eduardo Frei of the newly formed Christian Democratic Party.

The recognition of the influence of *allendismo* among workers, peasants and indigenous peoples, making inroads into the female vote (allowed for the first time in Chile in that election), and of the increasing momentum of the 'revolution from below', fuelled the anxiety of ruling sectors, particularly after rumours emerged that Allende's coalition had been robbed of the election at the last minute. At first, the results indicated a victory for Allende, closely followed by Alessandri. Around six in the evening, as Allende stayed ahead in the vote, an earth tremor occurred near the capital Santiago. The electoral agency argued this had caused some problems with the counting of votes in areas where the Left had few representatives and that were controlled by the Right. Suddenly the results from such voting booths, brought in late, gave Alessandri a slim margin.

Although convinced that the result had been rigged, Allende refused to listen to those within the FRAP coalition who demanded he create 'a social fact of extraordinary magnitude and violence', for instance a general strike that would have paralysed the country, thereby forcing the momentum of the revolution from below in the direction of a forceful rupture. Instead he opted to respect the result, so that 'the people would have a clearer sense of their responsibility'.[34] The programme proposed to the Chilean people by Allende's coalition comprised four pillars of profound legal reform: agrarian reform, nationalisation of copper and nitrates, the creation of a social property sector that would coexist with private and public property, and the strict regulation or nationalisation of the banking sector. In the framework of a gradual transition and transformation of the relationship between the state and the people, these constituted the principles of what in time would be known as 'the Chilean Way to Socialism'.

The political Left now offered a serious alternative in the southern cone of Latin America as well as an alternative revolution within the revolution, a prospect that concerned some in the US as much or even more than the prospect of victorious armed uprising elsewhere. Four months after Allende's electoral challenge in Chile, the bearded guerrilleros of the Sierra Maestra led by Fidel Castro, Ernesto Che Guevara and Camilo Cienfuegos defeated the US-backed authoritarian regime of Fulgencio Batista and entered Havana. The game had changed.

The US fascinated and concerned Latin Americans in equal measure, responses that had been magnified by the near-defeat of Britain and France in the First World War as well as by the events of the Spanish Civil War, the Second World War and the new anti-communist crusade. Until then, the international orthodoxy had been the classical political economy imported from England into the Americas before 1914, and in particular the theories of free trade and comparative advantage developed by David Ricardo, Adam Smith, John Stuart Mill, Alfred Marshall and Jean-Gustave Courcell-Seneuil.

That theory supported Latin American specialisation in raw materials, chiefly mineral and agricultural products for export to industrialised countries in exchange for importing manufactured goods. According to E. J. Dosman, it also reflected the elite structure of pre-war Latin America, the 'aristocratic pact' and the so-called lettered republic that based representativity and law on status, familiarity with Western language and culture, established by people such as Diego Portales in Chile or Miguel A. Caro and Carlos Holguín in Colombia.[35]

So overwhelmingly reliant on a single trading and financial partners were countries like Argentina and Chile that they were seen as virtually another dominion of the British Empire at the end of the nineteenth century. No other country except Cuba was more dependent on a single foreign market, and in that case it was the US. This balance of power was reversed in the post-war era, when the US expanded its dominion from Cuba to the rest of the hemisphere at the expense of Britain. The basic structure of dependency, race and class relations would nevertheless remain much the same, with the important caveat that artisans and peasants began their long transit towards becoming waged and precarious industrial or service labour, while the traditional landowning class faced competition from the rising industrial bourgeoisie.[36]

By the mid-twentieth century two questions remained open: first, to what extent did Latin American states like Chile or Argentina have the wherewithal to perform a similar function to that of states such as Britain or the rising US in the context of an increasingly Darwinian world economy? And second, could the state be made to function in a way that would not reduce its role to that of enforcer of the elite structure of a society inserted in the global economy under uneven rules and terms of dependency?

Allende had given attention early on to the twin questions of the means at the disposal of the state and the functioning of the institutions of law and the state. During an intervention in the lower chamber of the Chilean Congress in 7 June 1939, he put forward as one of his main responses to the question of the state the need to build and rebuild, again and again, a social coalition that would include autonomous base and civic movements, unions and parties. In the context of the rise of fascism in Europe and expansionism in the Americas, this would provide 'a defensive barricade behind which all democratic forces can gather'.[37] As Allende understood it, the socialists would participate in this coalition with middle-class parties as a grouping of 'workers, peasants, employees and the small bourgeoisie . . . who have the will to build and maintain democracy, fight oligarchy, and struggle against fascism and imperialism'.[38]

He also distinguished carefully between a socialist programme and a Popular Front programme, recognising that the latter was created to defend basic democratic guarantees. For Allende, without democracy there could be no revolutionary transformation of the relationship between the state and the people. Moreover, without political parties independent of the elite structure of society established as a consequence of the imbalance of the global economy, which pushed those at the pinnacle of domestic society – the 'Import-Export coalition' – to align themselves with the interests of foreign Big Powers dominating the global economy at the expense of those of their own nations and communities, the independence of the state would be compromised.

Allende was equally sceptical about the plausibility of communist rule in Chile, due to the convergence between the interests of the local 'Import-Export coalition' and the influence of an ever more anxious America. 'If tomorrow Chileans legitimately elected a communist government, I'm absolutely certain that the international pressure would be of such magnitude that it would break the sovereign will of the people of this country,' he said on 4 December 1956. 'The communists know this; they are sufficiently realistic, in the precise sense of the term, to understand the calibre of such limitations. They appreciate the social, economic and geographic reality of a small country such as ours, subjected to considerable and violent pressure from abroad, exercised both politically and economically.'[39] He explained the alliance with the communists along similar lines:

There was no question of a 'cold', 'temperate', or 'hot' war, but rather, the matter of Chile's interests. In those days I concluded that Chile required a clearer political course than that chosen by some within the Socialist Party who supported the Ibáñez candidacy even though, because of his personal characteristics and authoritarian past, he could not have led a revolutionary process.

In addition to his observations about the persistence of conservative elements of the authoritarian past in the revolutionary present, Allende referred to the need for a unitary purpose among the many rebellious tendencies in Chilean society, a theme that would focus his attention until the final moments of his life.[40]

Such was the answer that Allende developed between the 1940s and the 1960s to the persistent questions concerning the nation and the state. According to Joan Garcés, it would stamp his political militancy right up to the 1970s.[41] With the creation of the FRAP and the Popular Unity coalitions, Allende and the communists forged an understanding that became the key for the juncture between the political Left and the revolution from below led by workers, peasants, indigenous peoples and slum-dwellers that kept gaining momentum, a rather exceptional phenomenon given the context of the Cold War. From that time onwards Allende became the champion of the unity of the Left. This was not only a matter of tactics and electoral strategy, but also of the very subjective core of people like Neruda and Carmen Lazo.

To them and to many others in Latin America, a leftist orientation, understood not merely as ideology or as a set of objective beliefs but also as the core of one's political identity and subjectivity, was the answer to persecution and terror. Che Guevara called it 'love'; Allende understood it in terms of courage or consistency. Democratic societies might formally disown the suggestion that they were using terror tactics to exterminate the Left – as the passage of the Damned Law demonstrates in Chile – but the use of lethal force always lurked behind denunciations of the communist or terrorist threat.

The question of political subjectivity – of love in a time of terror –

also provided the link between the purpose of the movements from below and the individual dilemmas of those involved, explored in the cinema of the 1960s and 1970s by filmmakers like Tomás Gutiérrez Alea and Patricio Guzmán.[42]

The background for these practical questions was provided by an eventful time: the implosion and split of the socialist and communist camp after the invasion of Hungary in 1956, which Allende condemned in the strongest terms as he and the socialists distanced themselves from the worst consequences of Stalinism in the USSR,[43] but also the Suez crisis, the entrenchment of French repressive policy in Algeria, war in South Vietnam, and the origins and triumph of the Cuban Revolution. Other features of the time were the emergence of social Catholicism as a response to radical politics and the politicisation of theology from the base of the Church's hierarchy, leading to the formation of the Chilean Christian Democrats in July 1957; the many varieties of armed struggle – from the Guevarist *foco* to combinations of Cuban revolutionary practice with liberation theology, as in the case of the Colombian ELN (National Liberation Army), or Chinese- and indigenous-inspired movements in Argentina and Uruguay; and heightened peasant, anti-racist and student activism, from the formation of the so-called Bolshevik republics in the Colombian town of Líbano to student and civil rights unrest in the US and elsewhere, ending in the massacres of Tlatelolco in Mexico in 1968 and Kent State University in Ohio in 1970.

Such developments were lived and experienced by groups and individuals as slippages, disagreements, conflicts and divisions that were concrete expressions of historical, political and institutional life in a specific situation. According to the Argentinian critic Bruno Bosteels, they could be presented as mere aspects of a great law of imbalance that knows no exceptions.[44]

An instance of that law would be the signature of the US-backed Inter-American Treaty of Reciprocal Assistance in 1948, which inaugurated the expansion of a powerful security network across the

Americas aimed at centralising and speeding up the counter-revolutionary effort. By 1968, the network had made possible an escalation of political violence and state repression that was continent-wide, as well as more capable of reacting to perceived revolutionary dangers with a dynamism of its own that was less dependent on, and not merely a reaction to, revolutionary politics. It is to such dynamics that people like Allende, Neruda and others referred in their observations about the confusion of the post-war years and the threat of a 'populist temptation' that would lead traditionalist conservatives to come out as fully-fledged counter-revolutionaries.[45]

According to such observations, traditional conservatives tend to resist change as a result of a half-baked negative view of human nature and the exaltation of a social order assumed as natural or organic. These conservatives gathered around the views of Diego Portales, Miguel A. Caro and José E. Rodó in Latin America. During periods of relative political stability, this kind of conservative politics finds its roots in a simpler celebration of family, religion, property, status or caste, and distaste for new times and politics of rupture. In contrast, conservative counter-revolutionaries tend to emerge from within an increasingly anxious middle class, complete with an ideology and a programme. The latter can be more openly critical of the moral rot or sickness taking over the heart of society, even going as far as 'to call for its destruction and bring about its purification and regeneration'.[46] These two groups may be opposed during periods of perceived equilibrium, as in the case of Christian Democrats and other sectors of the Chilean Right during the 1950s and early 1960s when persecution and disarray weakened the Left, and specifically during the Frei government at the time of the US-inspired Alliance for Progress and the absorption of the military under the mutual protection alliance. But they cleave together during moments of crisis and perceived threat, as would happen at the end of the Frei government in the mid-1960s. Amidst loss of self-confidence and the need for revisionism in the face of revolutionary threat, conservatives and many self-styled liberals shift their support from freedom to security, from law to exception, and tend to accept a general move from preventive repression to exemplary violence and terror.

As historians Arno Mayer and Greg Grandin observe, for this transformation of conservative politics into counter-revolution to take place, two additional steps are required: the second group has to look outward and attract the attention and support of foreign powers; it also has to look downwards, connecting with and mobilising grassroots discontent.[47] Both orientations were visible in the Chilean case, with the proviso that here the Furies were 'as in Ancient Greece . . . one-sided'.[48] This means that members of the Left, owing largely to its deep humanist tradition, their reading of the Spanish experience and the years of persecution, but also to the debates concerning the persistence of old 'bourgeois' habits in the revolutionary process, such as machismo, the celebration of violence and the tendency to dismiss the masses as ignorant, generally refused to respond in kind and 'enter into the swirl of retribution and reaction' between revolutionary and counter-revolutionary violence.[49]

Yet the expansion of counter-revolutionary efforts throughout the continent, derived from anxiety in America and the over-perception of revolutionary threats – made explicit in Henry Kissinger's advice to the Nixon administration on the eve of Allende's election in 1970 – provide enough evidence to make a case for the notion of an overreaction on the part of the elite, both domestic and foreign. It would push Chile's uneven status quo to the precipice of destruction.

This was in keeping with the Zeitgeist. In 1942 Vice-President Henry Wallace had declared the twentieth century as 'the century of the Common Man'. It became instead, as Auden put it, 'the Age of Anxiety'.

4

Dawn of the New Man

Allende travelled from Venezuela to Cuba in the early days of 1959, after the liberation of Santa Clara and the triumphant entry into Havana of the guerrilleros led by Fidel Castro and Che Guevara. The impact of the triumph of the Cuban Revolution on the geopolitics of the region cannot be sufficiently emphasised. It 'constituted a nationalist, anti-imperialist, popular, anticapitalist and Latin-Americanist experience', according to the Chilean scholar and diplomat Heraldo Muñoz, who was also a protagonist of the 'revolution from below' in the 1970s. Chile and Chilean socialists identified fully with the Cuban cause, he says, 'politically, culturally, geographically, historically and economically', even subjectively. As Muñoz's comment suggests, its geopolitical significance was surpassed only by its psychological impact among many in the US and Latin America.[1]

The victory of a rag-tag group of bearded, young and militarily fairly inexperienced men against the US-friendly dictatorship of Fulgencio Batista, whom Vice-President Richard Nixon had embraced during his 1955 trip to the Caribbean, came as an additional and potentially devastating blow to an American confidence and sense of superiority already in tatters. About a year before, in August 1957, the Soviet Union had successfully tested the world's first intercontinental ballistic missile (ICBM), catching up with and potentially offsetting the enormous military advantage given to the US by the atomic bombers stationed at NATO bases around Europe.

Less than two months later, on 4 October, while the racial desegregation crisis unfolded in the American South – in Little Rock, Arkansas – in the wake of the US Supreme Court *Brown v. Board of Education* decision of 17 May 1954, a Soviet R-7 ICBM launched the first satellite into orbit around the Earth. The Court's decision to end the segregation of white and black children in public schools, which 'denoted the inferiority of the negro group' sanctioned by the law, badly damaged America's image around the world as the land of freedom and equality.[2] In 1957 the extent of the country's division over the *Brown* decision was made evident when the Arkansas governor Orval Faubus called out the National Guard to stop nine courageous black teenagers from entering Little Rock Central High School. The Guard stood by as an angry mob of local white folk viciously attacked the boys and girls, together with the journalists who were covering the story for the Black press. President Dwight D. Eisenhower responded by federalising the Guard and deploying the 101st Airborne Division. Faubus labelled the soldiers an 'army of occupation'. To prevent integration he would privatise the schools next year, a move backed by the white majority of Little Rock's voters. It would take another eighteen years after *Brown* for all schools in Arkansas to end segregation.

If the 1957 crisis in Little Rock shattered the idea of America as one nation undivided under God, democracy and the rule of law, Sputnik punctured the belief that US technological sophistication and its faith in unbridled capitalism, compared with the relative backwardness of the USSR and its lacklustre economic performance, would guarantee a fast and decisive victory for the American Century over its new socialist foe.[3]

It was bad enough that the Russians, who as John Gunther noted at the time, had been for a generation of Americans 'hardly capable of operating a tractor', suddenly overtook them in the space and arms race.[4] It was utterly unthinkable that a group of Latino bandits could tilt the balance so decisively less than ninety miles from the coast of Florida. The Cuban bandits were led by a man who judging by his looks and promises of agrarian reform must surely be a communist. This in spite of the fact that Fidel Castro, such was his name, quoted Jefferson and Paine way before he ever started invoking Lenin.[5]

African Americans and Latin Americans had loomed large in the imagination of mainstream Americans as an obscure and threatening object, far longer than Russians and other 'orientals'. African-Americans and Latin Americans were often represented as lacking some fundamental trait to fully achieve their maturity and potential as human beings, stuck in a state of perennial deficit or vacuum, or as the very embodiment of laziness and disorderly or violent behaviour. The assumed backwardness of Latin Americans reimagined through photography, travel narratives, economic discourse, product advertising, illustrated magazines and thereafter in television and cinema, justified the transformation of the originally anti-imperialist Monroe Doctrine into an imperialist Manifest Destiny that entitled America to intervene elsewhere by its self-appointed and heartfelt duty to aid and civilise. This attitude would determine America's policy towards Latinos and Latin America until at least 1930. Things did change for a while, as demonstrated by the results of Henry Wallace's trip to Latin America in the early 1940s, but by 1948 the old ways had come back with a vengeance.

Some in the US, especially popular movements and grassroots political organisations targeted by the Red Scare campaign of the 1940s and 1950s, made the link between domestic issues of inequality and American foreign policy on the one hand and homegrown racism on the other.[6] They took account of recent history: at the beginning of the century, D. H. Haskell told his American audience that Manifest Destiny was 'a pretty doctrine', thereby perpetuating nineteenth-century themes representing Latin America as a land of atypical racial mixture, cultural simplicity and in a perpetual state of childhood, bar a few exceptions here and there. That view was confirmed when President

Theodore Roosevelt visited Buenos Aires in 1913. Roosevelt told his elite audience at the Teatro Colón that Argentina and other South American countries where European immigration transformed the composition of the population had achieved a certain threshold of socio-economic and political progress he associated with maturity. Between 1890 and 1930, such countries, Chile among them, were now receiving increasing amounts of North American goods in exchange for raw exports while also 'whitening' their populations in bloody Indian wars, the erasure of antislavery conflict from history and miscegenation. As a result, according to historian Ricardo Salvatore some of them could be seen as becoming 'a female consumer fascinated with North American goods and culture', with growing numbers of middle- and upper-class urban women being actively portrayed as defenders of family and consumer values, racial purity and the economy; perhaps even mature enough 'to marry North American capital and culture'.[7]

More powerful countries like Brazil and Argentina, each with respectable armed forces courted by the US military and political establishment, had gone further: 'they had achieved manhood'.[8] And wherever childlike peoples in South American countries showed signs of political consciousness, it was oftentimes concluded that this could only be the consequence of 'foreign' or 'backward' undesirable influences. As in the case of Allende's cobbler, the image evoked in such descriptions is that of the 'popular intellectual' associated with archaic thought and religiosity, Jewishness and, since at least the rise of fascism, leftism.

In contrast with the more 'mature' Latin American countries, others like Puerto Rico and the Dominican Republic were claimed by the US after 1898 as childlike 'protected possessions', or occupied in 1916 and presented as 'a potentially compelling counter-example to the much more uncertain situations facing US capitalists, military personnel and bureaucrats in the Philippines and Cuba'.[9] In the images produced for the consumption of North American audiences at the time, the apparently more docile Puerto Ricans and Dominicans were constantly feminised and infantilised – as needing and desiring US virile or fatherly guidance and rule – while the radical actuality of the early Cuban liberation movement, led by the writer and nationalist intellectual José Martí, and its potential for years to come, were represented in a cartoon published by the *Chicago Inter Ocean* in 1905 as a raucous black child in poor clothing and no shoes, armed with gun and dagger, aptly named Revolt.[10] The Cuban guerrillas of the Sierra Maestra, both Black and Latino, bore out this dangerous potential in the eyes of stunned Americans between 1956 and 1959.

If we take stock of the panic created by the Soviet achievements of October 1957, and the contrast between these and the racial and economic tensions bubbling beneath the surface of American superiority – pointed out by Radio Moscow's announcements every time Sputnik passed over Little Rock[11] – we can get a better sense of the profound impact caused in the US and abroad, especially in Latin America, by the victory of Castro, Guevara and the Afro-Cuban Juan Almeida.

The early Soviet victory in space certainly shook the American establishment. The bearded Latino and black Cuban rebels beating the US and leaving them open to 'communist' (even nuclear) attack ninety miles from the Florida Keys was perceived as an earthquake north and south of the border. For all the deeds that could be attributed to Cuban revolutionaries, and condemned morally or otherwise – repression, the purges and executions of opponents after summary trials at La Cabaña headquarters, overseen by Guevara and executed by the American freebooter Herman Marks, and so on – none had as much historical and political import as the impact of the revolution on a US confidence already shaken by Soviet achievement, Chinese involvement in the Korean War, and the domestic and foreign policy crises of the first half of the 1950s. Up north, anxiety turned into full-blown panic and readiness to unleash the Furies. Down south, the perception of an opening in history was interpreted as a practical lesson: 'a people united, a people conscious of their historical task, goal and responsibility are invincible,' as Salvador Allende put it when reflecting on his encounter with Guevara and Castro after the revolution.[12]

When Allende arrived on 20 January 1959, Havana was a party. On the radio could be heard the notes and verses of Orquesta Típica Loyola's 'Guagancó miliciano' and Quinteto Rebelde's 'Que se vaya el mono' (Que se vaya el mono/no lo quiero ver/porque todo' en Cuba/estamo' con Fidel! Hey blondie, you gotta go/I don't want to see you no more/'cause here in Cuba we're all with Fidel!). Pablo Neruda, whose book of poems *Canto General* Che Guevara would carry with him everywhere, dedicated 'Canción de gesta' and 'Pasaron los años' to the victorious revolution. In the streets, the effervescence caused by the defeat of the dictator Batista was still very much alive.

On the afternoon of his arrival, Allende got a phone call from Aleida March, Che's lover and secretary. 'Comandante Guevara wants to see you. He's going to send a car to pick you up,' she said.[13] The historical encounter between these two men took place at the military headquarters of La Cabaña. Allende himself described the scene in cinematographic detail to the French writer and philosopher Régis Debray:

> When I arrived Che was lying on a campaign rollaway, he had only his fatigue trousers on. Naked from the waist up he was trying to recover from an acute asthma attack with the help of an inhaler. I sat on the bed, beside him, and waited for him to regain his breath. 'Comandante,' I began to say, and he interrupted me: 'Allende, you see, I know very well who you are.'[14]

In January 1952 a twenty-three-year-old Ernesto Guevara had heard Allende speaking during the perilous presidential campaign that he, La Negra Lazo and other leftists undertook during a time of persecution. Then a medical student in Buenos Aires, Guevara set off from the Argentinian capital with his friend Alberto Granado astride a 1939 Norton 500cc motorcycle, which they had named 'The Mighty One'. 'This isn't a tale of derring-do,' wrote Guevara in his memoir of the trip. 'It's a chunk of two lives running parallel for a while, with common aspirations and similar dreams.' Their exuberant plan was to cross into Chile and make it all the way north to Peru, where they would spend a few weeks working as volunteers at the San Pablo leper colony on the banks of the Amazon River.

It was to become an inner journey of huge importance, a coming-of-age story as much as one of coming into consciousness, an existential odyssey as well as a quest to the farthest reaches of the continent and back. 'In nine months a man can think a lot of thoughts, from the height of philosophical conjecture to the most abject longing for a bowl of soup – in perfect harmony with the state of his stomach,' Guevara said.[15]

In February 1952 the two friends travelled from Bariloche to Temuco, the place of Pablo Neruda's childhood that was also the ancestral home of the People of the Land in the Chilean south, the legendary indigenous Mapuche. Upon entering Temuco, the young men introduced themselves to a local newspaper called *El Austral* as internationally renowned physicians. The journalist in charge wrote a glowing article, which helped them score a few meals and a bed here and there as they made it to the desert up north.[16]

On the way to the copper mine of Chuquicamata, Ernesto and Alberto met a couple; they were workers, communists escaping persecution. 'By the light of a single candle we used to drink mate and share some cheese and a piece of bread,' Ernesto wrote of their encounter. 'The pinched features of this humble working man gave off a mysterious and tragic air . . . the couple, frozen stiff in the desert night, hugging one another, were a live representation of the workers anywhere in the world.' For the first time in his life,

Guevara came across a living image 'of the proletariat of any part of the world', not in books but in the small town of Baquedano at the height of persecution against the people of Chile. By candlelight, the husband told them about his three months in jail, praised his wife, who had stuck with him through cold and hunger, and the neighbours who generously offered to take care of their children. He spoke of his futile pilgrimage through cold ice and fiery desert looking for a job, and of the fate of his friends and comrades mysteriously disappeared, 'it is said, thrown overboard into the sea'.[17] This was the day Guevara's consciousness was born: 'They didn't even have a miserable blanket with which to cover themselves,' he wrote. 'So, Alfredo and I gave them one of ours and used the other to cover ourselves as well as we could. It was one of the coldest evenings I've spent in my life, but also the one I felt somewhat closer, bonded by feelings of fraternal love, to this, until then, strange species of humanity.'[18]

To the young Guevara, the misery of this couple, most probably of mestizo peasant or indigenous origins, was made far worse by the fact of their persecution; all because they had dared to ask 'In reality, what am I?' and found in socialist militancy an answer. To them, it was not merely about realising some utopian future, but most of all about finding a voice in the present, and a place for themselves in a story that could sustain their belief that in the end they did count. Furthermore, that they counted for everybody. To find this voice and a place in the story was a question of justice and hope. To occupy their place in history and realise their beliefs here and now was a matter of courage.[19] He wrote of the militant husband and wife:

Setting aside whether or not leftism is a peril for the good health of a society, the 'communist worm' gnawing at their entrails was no more than a natural longing for something better as well as a protest against ever-present hunger and destitution, translated into love for this singular conviction whose doctrinal essence they might never grasp but whose practical translation 'bread for the poor' were words they understood and, moreover, changed and gave substance to their existence.[20]

Overcome by the cold night of the Chilean desert, Guevara encountered what Jean-Paul Sartre thinly disguised through his fictional characters in his play *The Flies* and the novel *Nausea*. The revelation was this: portrayals of raw individual experience make little sense if cut off from the lives of others – the total foreigners, the 'inhuman' others – but such lives are never completely alien to ourselves. On the contrary, such images, portrayals and stories about the lives of others constitute the building blocks of our innermost feelings and existence. Unlike Sartre, Guevara found this revelation staring back at him in the face of a native peasant and his wife.

The fullness of their souls and the thinness of their dark bodies made a stark contrast with the sturdy presence and impertinence of their fair-haired masters, and the power of that image would become engrained in the heart of the young traveller. 'This mine is no tourist attraction,' the mine administrator told Ernesto and Alfredo in his broken Spanish. 'I'll give you a guide who will explain to you the efficiency of our installations in a half-hour; then you will leave us alone, for we have much work left to do.' 'Stupid gringos, they are ready to lose thousands of dollars per day because of a strike instead of giving a few cents more to a poor worker. All that is bound to change!' said the guide to both friends. And a poet miner told them: 'This is the famous staircase going deep into the bowels of the earth, so we can penetrate it and extract all the copper that still remains. People like you often ask questions about how we can make the work more technical and efficient, but few ask how many lives have been wasted in the process. I can't answer that question. But thanks for asking.'[21]

These anecdotes can be read as iterations of the same contradiction between slavery and liberty encountered before. The contrast between the gringo masters and the dark couple corresponds to the opposition between slavery and liberty at the heart of modern conceptions of law, democracy and humanitarianism. But such opposition would be too facile, as Manichean as the Cold War's ethics of enmity. So the guide and the poet miner stand for various degrees of complexity. It is not clear, for instance, whether the change called for by the guide would benefit the owners or the workers. The guide invoked the ambiguous figure of the populist politician Carlos Ibáñez as the saviour who would bring back law and order to the mine. At the time, Guevara would be sensitive to the problematic character of a figure so similar to that of Juan Domingo Perón in his native Argentina. Rather than solving the contradiction, the appeal to messiah figures like Ibáñez or Perón, coming from the middle managers standing for the middle classes of Latin America, further complicates things. And the poet miner? He corresponds to a figure already familiar in this story: the popular intellectual, the prophetic voice that in this case literally cries in the wilderness. He has no answers, only questions.

The passage in Guevara's diary can be interpreted as the prescient description of a conflict yet to come, setting the messianic saviours and inquisitors against the lonely prophet. The stage for such a conflict would be the global market. At the global level, the conflict between slavery and liberty would be experienced as a clash between the forces of salvation and purification by fire (a Christian theme related to the inquisitorial procedure) and prophecy, or the promise of a new consciousness and a new man. The dawn of the 'New Man' (Guevara's embodiment of historical creation), if it ever happened, would occur in the midst of disaster.

This means that rather than reading Guevara's *Motorcycle Diaries* as the Latin American version of Jack Kerouac's *On the Road*, we should interpret it as the beginning of a theory of the apocalyptic fantasies of late capitalism. Other Chilean poets of the time, for instance Alejandro Jodorowsky, were doing something quite similar: imagining the copper mine at Chuquicamata as a desert monster at the centre of an imperial war over resources with religious overtones.[22] Such imaginings reflected on the reality of places like Chile in the 1960s and 1970s, dependent on the fate of their natural resources in the global market and the decisions made by global state and non-state powers, such as multinationals and their local beneficiaries or opponents, battling against each other with a ferocity of conviction over the absolute righteousness of their own cause and the absolute error of the enemy's.

Chile produced over 20 per cent of all the copper in the world. The metal's value had risen in the 1950s due to its importance to the weapons industry at a time of growing tension between the superpowers and within America. Guevara speaks of 'pre-war'.[23] He was talking about the Cold War. US General Curtis LeMay, the notorious mastermind behind the terror firebombing of Japanese cities in the Second World War, had declared in 1948: 'We are at war now!' LeMay was not talking about fascism; he had communism in his sights.

In *The Motorcycle Diaries*, the young Che Guevara began to reflect upon the way in which the rising stakes at the international level, especially within the US and in relation to Eastern Communism, could impact Latin America. Thus, for example, he made the connection between the hike in the price of copper and the global situation with local Chilean debates concerning the fate of the workers in the copper mines. 'There is in this country a political and economic battle between those who advocate the nationalisation of the copper mines, including nationalists and the Left,' he observed, 'and on the other side those who, based on the ideal of free enterprise, prefer to have efficiently run mines (even if they are in foreign hands) to the uncertainty of having them managed by the dubious expertise of the state.' To the climate of 'pre-war' – Guevara's term for the looming conflict between the powers of the Cold War era, and the escalation of hostilities at the global level – corresponds an economic and political battle at the local level mirroring, in a distorted and uneven manner that included warped perceptions of status and race, the battle lines between the capitalists and the various forms of protest on the left.[24]

At the time of Guevara's journey through Latin America, global tensions, warped perceptions and paranoid fears within the US and abroad had literally reached the point of madness. 'The Russians are coming!' shouted the former US Secretary of Defense and fierce anti-communist James Forrestal, before jumping, 'out of his mind', from the sixteenth-floor room he occupied at Bethesda Naval Hospital in 1949.[25] Two weeks after US President Harry Truman announced his insane decision to build an even deadlier hydrogen bomb on 31 January 1950, Albert Einstein appeared on Eleanor Roosevelt's television show to warn: 'if these efforts should prove successful . . . annihilation of all life on Earth will have been brought within the range of what is technically possible.'[26] In February that year, the little-known Wisconsin senator Joseph McCarthy told the Ohio County Women's Republican Club he had a list of 57 to 205 names 'known to the Secretary of State as being members of the Communist Party' who had infiltrated the federal government, making explicit the way in which tensions abroad had triggered another wave of Red-baiting and hatred in the USA and elsewhere. By the time McCarthy and FBI director J. Edgar Hoover were done, the US Left had been decimated, labour unions, popular movements and cultural associations that proved crucial to the reforms of the New Deal in the 1930s and 1940s were eviscerated, and many − for instance, the American trade union movement − would never recover. Other bodies, such as the African-American Civil Rights movement, were put under sufficient pressure as to feel forced to expel civil rights pioneers such as Paul Robeson and W. E. B. du Bois, who were joining all the dots, at home and abroad. Du Bois was purged for having supported the campaign of the progressive candidate Henry

Wallace and called for the UN to address racism in America.

Under the guise of that most sacred word in our political lexicon, 'security', and in tune with the Red Scare, government agencies in the US also purged gays and lesbians from federal offices and extended their persecution into the private sector.[27] With the invasion of South Korea by North Korea on 24 June 1950, and the entry of the Communist Chinese into the conflict (provoking the frantic retreat of General Marshall's US forces in November), war by proxy between Soviets and Americans, and between Eastern Communism and America and its Western allies, became a reality, drawing at least one Latin American country, Colombia, into the cauldron. In his December 1950 Nobel Prize speech, the writer William Faulkner cautioned: 'There are no longer problems of the spirit. There is only the question: When will I be blown up?'[28]

This was the mad reality that the young Guevara summed up under the term 'pre-war', in connection with the battle lines being drawn in Chile in the 1950s. It is also in the context of such economic and political battles that he referred to Salvador Allende's position at the bottom of the pile in the 1952 Chilean presidential campaign. Allende was 'supported by the communists, whose electoral base has been reduced by 40,000, the number of names struck from the electoral register because of their militancy in the party', he wrote. He was referring to the political consequences of the Damned Law, a direct result of America's anxiety.[29]

'I know very well who you are,' a grown-up Che Guevara would say to an already seasoned Salvador Allende during their encounter after the triumph of the Cuban Revolution in January 1959. 'I heard two of your speeches during the presidential campaign of 1952, one of the speeches was very good, and the other very bad. So we can talk without qualms, in confidence, because I have a very clear opinion of who you are.'[30]

During his childhood, Guevara had helped out refugees fleeing persecution from Republican Spain and stood up to pro-Nazi teachers and professors. In December 1953, having completed his motorcycle journey through South America, Guevara arrived in Guatemala to breathe in the feverish atmosphere described by Gore Vidal in his novel *Dark Green, Bright Red*. There, he began to act following his newly made-up mind by working as a 'barefoot doctor' among the peasants. One of them was an elderly washerwoman, to whom he wrote a poem that evokes the image of the couple in the Chilean desert. In the poem, Guevara made 'a promise to fight for a better world for all the poor and exploited', similar to the one made by Allende during his father's funeral.[31]

He fell in with other young rebel souls seeking refuge from lost battles against the dictatorships of Somoza, Trujillo and Batista. Among them were some exiled Cubans who had participated the previous July in the failed but already famous attack led by Fidel Castro on the Moncada barracks. Castro had been arrested and put on trial. A lawyer, Castro defended himself. He pronounced the now famous claim: 'La historia me absolverá'. Together with the group of exiled Cubans was Hilda Gadea – the first female secretary of the economy of the Executive of Peru's Alianza Popular Revolucionaria Americana (APRA), another refugee escaping to Guatemala from the dictator General Odría. Guevara read Einstein in English with her, along with Russian psychology, Lenin and Marx.

Hilda schooled Guevara in the Marxist literature that he had so far paid only scant attention to, preferring Freud instead. The real lesson came in late January 1954 when word leaked out that the US, which had propped up all the other dictators in the Latin American continent on the pretext of forestalling a communist takeover, was now training an invasion force bent on overthrowing the democratically elected government of Jacobo Árbenz. Árbenz, handsome and charismatic, who had declared that 'all the riches of Guatemala are not as important as the life, the freedom, the dignity, the health and the happiness of the most humble of its people', was for his words and his sins branded in the American media a communist, even before he had the time to implement his reform agenda. His words we know, and for those the *New York Times* decried him in June 1951 as 'The Guatemalan Cancer'. His sins consisted in having had the courage to challenge the almighty United Fruit Company, called 'the Octopus' by Guatemalans, which controlled the country's economy.

In an extraordinary turn of events, Edward Louis Bernays, the nephew of Sigmund Freud, one of the real-life Mad Men, founding father of the discipline of Public Relations and author of *The Engineering of Consent*, who also sat on the US Committee of Public Information, launched a campaign to brand Árbenz a communist in all major American media. It was in the context of such efforts, and in reference to the United Fruit Company's sway over the corrupt governments that previously ruled in Guatemala and other Central American countries, that the term 'banana republic' originated.[32]

On the heels of their success in 1953 in overthrowing the government of Mohammed Mossadeq in Iran, accused of being both a communist and a Jew after nationalising British oil interests and confronting economic warfare, CIA director Allen Dulles launched 'Operation Success' against Guatemala. It helped that Allen and his older brother, Secretary of State John Foster Dulles, had written United Fruit's agreements with Guatemala through their law firm, that Assistant Secretary of State for Inter-American Affairs John Moors Cabot – whose brother Thomas had been president of the company – was a major shareholder, and that the head of the National Security Council (NSC), General Robert Cutler, had been chairman of the board. After Árbenz handed power to a military junta led by the US-trained Colonel Carlos Castillo Armas, Dulles declared that the country had been saved from 'communist imperialism'. He drew the lesson that after Iran and Guatemala it had been proven that covert operations could be used to topple popular or democratic reform governments with little cost to America's reputation.

Che Guevara drew a very different lesson: Árbenz had made a major mistake. 'He could have given arms to the people but he did not want to. Now we see the result,' he wrote to his mother at the time. He would not make the same mistake when it came to protecting the Cuban Revolution a few years later.[33] Allende, in turn, observed:

> From an economic point of view [military governments such as the one installed in Guatemala] are convenient to the interests of those in charge in America, because such governments are the more ready to hand over their countries' resources, and are the most anti-patriotic of all. These dictatorships are the most corrupt and anti-national phenomenon.[34]

Here lay the origins of the so-called Allende Doctrine of 'geo-economic sovereignty' and self-determination. Later on in life, a promulgation of that doctrine to justify the nationalisation of copper in Chile, and avoid the payment of compensation over excess profits to American owners, would profoundly impact the shape of human rights and international law, and change the course of Latin American history for ever.[35]

Together with Hilda and his Cuban friends Guevara left Guatemala for Mexico, where he joined Fidel Castro. Thereafter, they sailed for the Cuban Sierra Maestra on board the boat *Granma*, and on New Year's Day 1959 they made their triumphant entry into Havana. Guevara was now a revolutionary combatant. He would later write that a true revolutionary combatant must be willing to turn himself into 'a cold killing machine'. The Bay of Pigs invasion, prepared by the Eisenhower administration just like the coup in Guatemala, and bequeathed to John F. Kennedy, was launched against Cuba and failed in 1961. It would confirm Guevara's belief that only an armed people and the coldest willingness to kill and be killed could withstand the Furies loosed by Washington. Allende begged to differ. On 27 July 1960, just before the Bay of Pigs debacle, he told the Chilean Senate:

It is time everyone acknowledges that the lesson of Guatemala has been learned. The United States must realise that Latin America has now been changed and revitalised after the Cuban Revolution. With other tactics, diverse methods and different strategies, in accordance with the characteristics and the situation of each one of our countries, we shall move towards one and the same goal of dignifying our own lives and securing the economic independence of our countries.

In another dark twist, Guevara would reconsider his position after the events of 1962. Between 1965 and his ill-fated departure from Cuba in 1967, he would dedicate his energies to solving the problem of how to allow for an institutional and legal transition to socialism and a transformed, decolonised economy, while at the same time responding to the persistence of the old ways even after the revolution. In contrast, there would come the time for Salvador Allende to risk his life in battle. In the wake of Vietnam, Guevara would once more call for one, two, many Vietnams. Cuba would in fact have its successful Vietnam in Angola, but Guevara's military failure in Bolivia would push an entire new generation of Latin Americans to reconsider not only armed struggle but also the crucial question of the day after. Some, like the Argentinian critic León Rozitchner, went back to Freud in search of a different Marx; others, like the author Ricardo Piglia, would look to China for inspiration. In Bolivia, Silvia Rivera Cusicanqui and Álvaro García Linera would later renew the exploration of the misunderstanding between indigenous and socialist rebellious rationalities as two diverse forms of political dissidence – one steeped in the past, the other overtly modernist – that were not always compatible and at times ignored one another, even though they both wrote their own scripts for modern resistance, learnt from each other and considered the achievement and transformation of political power in the present. Yet others, like Beatriz Allende, would reaffirm their commitment to social justice and transformation no longer by seeking to withdraw from, but rather by engaging with politics, law and the state.

This is where today's protest and occupy movements reconnect with those days, in the search for new economic answers in the face of crisis in the Americas and elsewhere. They all became, in their own way, new women and new men. For they all persevered, and none of them gave in to the paralysing grasp of complacency, guilt or melancholy.

'Che and I were close. I could say, I believe, that I was for him a friend,' Allende told Régis Debray. Expressing for Guevara the kind of affection a father would harbour for a son, Allende said: 'I loved him, respected him. Let me show you this photograph of his, dedicated to my daughters Carmen Paz, Isabel and Beatriz, "with the heartfelt feelings of the Cuban revolution and my brotherly love". You see, he was the object of this family's affection, and he knew it just as he knew my daughters.' Allende told Debray that his relationship with the Cuban revolutionaries, and with the new generation of Latin Americans that reflected on the impact of that event, was deep and powerful. 'I want to share with you something exceptional that I keep as a treasure, something that is priceless to me,' he said, as he reminisced about the meeting with the leaders of the Cuban Revolution in January 1959. 'There was this copy of *Guerrilla Warfare* on top of Che's desk that day. It must have been the second or third copy because, I guess, he gave the first one to Fidel . . . He wrote a dedication, there you have it, which reads thus: "to Salvador Allende, who searches for it, the same as me, through other means. With love, Che".'[36]

Were Guevara and Allende so different? Che's dedication referring to their different choice of means and Allende's constant emphasis on the diversity of their tactics and strategies suggests so. Their temperaments seem diametrically opposed. Guevara could never stay in one place long enough, always looking for the next battle; he belonged to a generation that after tasting victory came to think that history always sides with the nobler cause. Allende lived, on the contrary, a regular life, made regular choices and regular mistakes. He stayed in one country, settled into family life, cheated on his wife, kept up appearances and so on. At twenty-nine years of age Guevara was leading a guerrilla front in the mountains and had escaped death more than once; when he was twenty-nine Allende was taking up his post as congressman, by thirty he was a minister, then a senator, and when their paths crossed for the first time Allende was a presidential candidate. Guevara believed it was a mistake not to arm the people; Allende believed it was a mistake to arm them. From that perspective, their lives could not seem more different.

Ryszard Kapuscinski thought otherwise. According to him, Allende wished most of all to preserve a kind of ethical and political honesty, and 'Guevara behaves in much the same way'.[37] Kapuscinski, like the American philosopher Michael Walzer and many others, observed that the Cuban guerrilleros were continually capturing enemy soldiers and cutting them loose. In terms of military tactics it is a mistake, wrote Kapuscinski: 'the prisoners take no time to divulge the location of Castro and Guevara's men, their numbers and weapons. Yet Guevara does not execute any one of them.'[38] Now we know that was no longer the case by the time they entered Havana. In La Cabaña, under Castro's orders, Guevara oversaw the summary trial and execution of key members of Batista's dictatorial regime. And even if the same could be said of the judgements at Nuremberg or the trial of Adolf Eichmann in Jerusalem, this was in any case a classical example of victor's justice.[39] The tendency to apply victor's justice and resort to show trials would continue in the coming years, as threats of invasion from the US, assassination attempts and opposition from within and without became all too real.

Allende appears, in contrast, legalistic and attached to constitutional 'bourgeois' institutions. After all, for Chileans, as for many Latin Americans since at least the 1930s, democracy and socialism were the same thing: the fight for the right to vote was indistinguishable from the fight for welfare, education, health, land reform and the right to economic self-determination. This was especially the case in Chile, where a motley crew including socialists, communists, anarchists, Christian leftists, indigenous activists and other anti-fascists, together with the popular movements, pushed for the rights of people, a people's government and popular power. 'No one represented better the unclean mix of electoral and economic democracy than Allende . . . Appointed minister of health in 1939, he helped increase pensions for widows, provided free lunches for schoolchildren and prenatal care for women and introduced workplace safety regulations.'[40] Afterwards, when – bowing to pressure from a US already driven to the brink of anti-communist insanity – the Chilean government set about repressing the Left and the grassroots movements, obliging people like Pablo Neruda to flee, Allende stayed, worked hard to get national healthcare enacted in 1952, stood up against intervention and persecution in his own country, and denounced it elsewhere, in Guatemala and Cuba. Literate women did not get the vote in Chile until 1949, which means that in all probability the peasant woman who conversed with the young Guevara in the Chilean desert could not even vote but was still being persecuted, as were a great number of illiterate or barely literate activists. In 1957, a few months after Guevara and Castro launched their campaign in Cuba, Allende and his colleagues in the Senate passed legislation establishing a secret ballot for the first time in Chilean history.

Literacy restrictions on the vote meant that left-leaning democrats like Allende had to push harder for greater education: his speeches, which Guevara heard while in Chile in 1952 and judged between the very bad and very good, were part of a sustained effort to run 'each campaign like an extended consciousness-raising session'.[41] This included the creation of new forms of popular and folk music, poetry and imagery in pamphlets, muralist painting and photography, as well as the novel use of radio, cinema and new media including, in time, computing and networking. Here lay the other origins of today's network revolution.[42]

5

A Long Cold War

One significant parallel between the lives of Salvador Allende and Ernesto Guevara is the extent to which they were both documented in photography and film, and their words recorded and reproduced electronically. They are closer to us precisely because they have lived on, captured and, with time, greatly enhanced by electronic media.

Crucially, Allende and Guevara considered the power of these new technologies as central to the creation of new spaces of personal and individual liberty as well as to making personal freedom possible for the majority. Very early in the development of information technologies, scientists and sociologists identified birth control, divorce laws, the enfranchisement of younger sectors of the population, feminine control over their own choices, women's participation in the workforce, more meaningful participation of workers in creation and production, and a revolutionary conception of laws and regulatory systems, as preconditions of what we now know as the Internet way of life – characterised by horizontal hierarchies, consensus and deliberation within multiple networks, collective problem-solving, and weaker commitment to vertical authorities.[1]

People like Allende and Guevara, together with the younger generations of activists and creators of the 1960s and 1970s, sought to realise that potential through their desire to reinvent the state and its institutions as well as to bring about a new humanity and a new society. They saw the future made possible by these new forms of

expression, media, technology and imagination in an entirely different light from their opponents, who conceived of them only as tools
to enhance their military and commercial interests. In that sense they
offer us a glimpse of a future that might have been and never was –
our present – but which lives on, for instance, in the so-called
'network revolutions' that rocked the world in 2011 and in the struggle of young people today. People like Aaron Schwartz and the
Anonymous group of hacktivists defending the Internet against priva-
tisations and enclosure, Bradley Manning, Edward Snowden and the
digital whistle-blowers WikiLeaks, Camila Vallejo and the Chilean
student movement that achieved global recognition after 2011 for
their stance against the wholesale privatisation of higher education, or
the nameless gamers, hackers, Tweeter-feeders, OWS occupiers and
the other 'networked individuals' that populate today's political landscape and fire the imagination of contemporary literature.[2]

There is a key link to be made here between the narratives that
emerged in the late 1940s and early 1970s, of which Pablo Neruda's
Canto General and the films of Luis Buñuel, Tomás Gutiérrez Alea
and Patricio Guzmán are apt examples, inspired by the aesthetics of
the early twentieth century in which the protagonist role swings
between the unnamed masses and the few rebels determined to live
life to the fullest, come what may, and the central question of
whether technology, and the political institutions and regulatory
systems we use to manage it, can make individual freedom possible
for the many who do ordinary jobs 'at the heart of the industrial
machine'.[3]

An original place to begin making such a link would be the first
bi-monthly meeting of the Ministry of Industries in post-revolutionary Cuba, which Guevara led in January 1962. At it, he observed:
'We are entering the era of automation and electronics. We have to
think of electronics as a function of socialism and the transition to
communism . . . Electronics has become a fundamental political
problem . . .'[4] Guevara believed in the liberation of man as an individual and collectively by means of the machine. He witnessed how

advanced capitalist corporations used automated systems to maximise their economic and decision-making operations, and took the first steps towards harnessing that potential to reorient subjectivity, society and the economy on the basis of the common ethics of voluntary work entailed by the Spanish term *conciencia*,[5] and technological innovation, rather than solely by appealing to workers' self-interest and monetary incentives.

This specific objective would illuminate Guevara's approach to economic matters as the political economist and Minister of Industries in 1960s Cuba gradually replaced Che the guerrilla fighter, at least for a while. It also helped to highlight the mistakes he and others made while applying the guidelines of Raúl Prebisch and Regino Boti's Economic Commission for Latin America-inspired strategy for industrialisation and import substitution during the early stages of the revolution.[6]

Guevara and others believed that Cuba enjoyed an advantage, not only because of its relatively better levels of literacy and economic industry vis-à-vis the first socialist countries and China, but also thanks to the technical training and assistance provided by socialist bloc countries; however, Guevara felt that such technical assistance was hindered by the fact that too little investment was being made by socialist countries in improving civilian production in contrast with the high level of research and development taking place on military technology. This contradiction, a result of the imperatives imposed by Cold War ideology on both sides, seriously distorted the priorities as well as the choices that needed to be made concerning means as well as ends. Guevara would come to the conclusion that the mimetic principle operating at the heart of Cold War foreign policy – with one superpower imitating the other's search for bigger, deadlier weapons of mass destruction, and mimicking each other's militarism – was detrimental to the goals of the revolution.

Nothing exemplified this better than the constant attacks launched by Washington on the island of Cuba, and the

potential for total annihilation inherent in the policy of nuclear
deterrence pursued furiously by the US and the Soviet Union.
On 17 March 1960, President Eisenhower ordered the CIA to
organise a 'paramilitary force' of Cuban exiles that would invade
Cuba and overthrow Castro. During the coming months,
Eisenhower also authorised CIA covert operations to assassinate
the democratically elected prime minister of resource-rich
Congo, Patrice Lumumba, whom CIA director Allen Dulles
likened to an African Fidel Castro. Lumumba was murdered,
though the lion's share of the blame belongs in this case to the
Belgians. He was replaced by the CIA-backed Joseph Mobutu,
who ruled for over two decades 'as one of the world's most
brutal and corrupt dictators', becoming during that time the
West's most trusted ally in Africa.[7]

Parallel to the embrace of Third World dictators by the US, was
a drift towards dangerous reliance on nuclear blackmail to gain
advantage in the Cold War. It entailed adding ever more terrify-
ingly powerful thermonuclear weapons to the existing arsenal, a
behaviour mirrored by the Soviet Union's emphasis on and investment in military research and nuclear production.

The madness of these developments became all too real between
1961 and 1962. At first, the newly elected President J. F. Kennedy
inspired hopes of a new beginning between the US and Latin
America, in spite of his past profile as a Cold Warrior, a supporter
of Richard Nixon's Red-baiting campaign against a fellow progressive Democrat, and a critic of Eisenhower's 'tolerance' with Castro.
In March 1961 Kennedy proposed 'to complete the revolution of
the Americas' through a ten-year development plan called Alliance
for Progress.[8] The multi-billion-dollar programme would be signed
at an inter-American conference at Punta del Este, Uruguay, in
August 1961, with Guevara in attendance and Allende present at the
Anti-Imperialist Gathering taking place in Montevideo. Behind
closed doors, however, Kennedy proceeded with Eisenhower's
plans to have the CIA train an invading force of 1,500 Cuban exiles

in Guatemala. When Kennedy asked about the scheme's chances of success, Allen Dulles assured him the invasion would inspire opposition to Castro in the island to rise up against him. Three days before the invading force landed at Bay of Pigs in April 1961, eight US B-26 bombers destroyed half the Cuban air force. Two of the invading ships belonged to the United Fruit Company. Against the calculations of Dulles's CIA, on the day of the invasion the Cuban army easily subdued the invaders, and the promised popular uprising never came. One hundred and fourteen men were killed and 1,189 captured, among them four US pilots under contract to the CIA.[9]

The fallout would be damning, and would determine the shape of things to come in the Americas. In Cuba, a series of show trials and the execution of the 'traitors of Playa Girón' took place, signalling a hardening of positions and ideological severity that would lead to much closer military and not only technical collaboration with the USSR. The subsequent exodus of upper- and middle-class Cubans to Miami and the general climate of uncertainty about the future of the revolution were brilliantly captured in Tomás Gutiérrez Alea's film *Memories of Underdevelopment* (1968). In America, the *New York Times* declared that US 'hegemony . . . in the Western hemisphere is threatened for the first time in a century' as the Cuban Revolution offered a model for the rest of Latin America.[10]

Then, as soon as the post-mortems were done, Kennedy put his brother Robert in charge of the CIA's most crucial covert operations. In January 1962, Robert Kennedy told CIA head John McCone that overthrowing Castro was 'the top priority of the US government'.[11] Many in Latin America had interpreted the Alliance for Progress proposal as mere whitewash, aimed at repairing America's dented prestige. That is not strictly correct, given that Kennedy did seek to distance his foreign policy from the militarism of the Joint Chiefs 'sons of bitches' and 'those CIA bastards'.[12] But they were right in pointing out that the Alliance was a first step towards isolating Cuba from the rest of Latin America, stalling any leftist advance in the region, and part of a plan to wreck Cuba's economy and overthrow or kill Castro. The plan, set in motion as early as November 1961, was called Operation Mongoose. 'My idea is to stir things up . . . with espionage, sabotage, general disorder, run and operated by Cubans themselves,' observed Robert Kennedy when outlining the policy. By any conceivable measure, this was a terror campaign against Cuba under the auspices of the US government.[13]

In March 1962 the Joint Chiefs were asked by the CIA counter-insurgency expert Edward Lansdale, under Kennedy's orders, to provide a 'description of pretexts to justify' US intervention. Brigadier General William Craig produced a list of suggestions that gave origin to an operation code-named Northwoods. The plan drawn up by the Joint Chiefs of Staff contemplated a wave of violent terrorism to be launched in Washington, Miami and elsewhere in the US which 'could be pointed at Cuban refugees seeking haven in the United States' and included blowing up a US ship in Guantanamo Bay and blaming Cuba; hijacking a US aircraft and then attributing the consequences to the Cuban government; sinking 'a boatload of Cubans en route to Florida (real or simulated)'; staging the Cuban shooting down of an American civilian airliner whose passengers could be 'a group of College students off on a holiday'; and 'exploding a few plastic bombs in carefully chosen spots' on the US mainland that would be pinned on Cuban agents. These were some among a number of other similarly sordid schemes.[14]

Although none of the Northwoods schemes were activated, the suspension of Cuba from the Organization of American States (OAS), the April 1962 two-week military exercise involving 40,000 US troops, the October 1962 announcement by the US of Operation Ortsac (Castro spelled backwards), a mock invasion by US Marines of a Caribbean island ending in regime change, and other such actions convinced Castro, Guevara and the Soviets that an invasion was imminent. What followed, in the context of responses and counter-responses to perceived threats, has been dubbed with reason 'the most dangerous moment in human history'. The emplacement of Soviet nuclear missiles in Cuba was viewed by the Cuban leadership 'as a defensive measure', while the Soviets likened it to the US missiles placed on the USSR's Turkish border and in Western Europe.[15]

Castro and the Cubans feared most of all being left under a radioactive cloud after a US attack. General Curtis LeMay and the majority of the Joint Chiefs of Staff indeed favoured an air strike to destroy the missiles and he personally assured J. F. Kennedy there would be no Soviet response. Questioned by Kennedy, LeMay welcomed the possibility of not only overthrowing Castro but also obliterating the USSR. Kennedy worried that allowing the missiles to stay would have serious political consequences in Latin America and elsewhere, and confided to his brother Robert his fear of impeachment, or something worse, if he did not act decisively. They opted for a blockade, against the suggestion of the Chiefs and ex-President Eisenhower, who favoured a strike followed by an invasion. In fact, under international law both the blockade and the strike were acts of war, war crimes, and given the likely consequences, also crimes against humanity punishable under the Nuremberg principles.

The US and the USSR were heading inexorably towards nuclear war, soon their leaders would be unable to stop it, and Cuba and Latin America were right in the middle. The real madness of this scenario would be satirised a few years later by Stanley Kubrick's film *Dr Strangelove*.

On 27 October, all hell broke loose: a navy group led by the aircraft carrier USS *Randolph* dropped depth charges on a Russian *B-59* submarine, carrying nuclear weapons. Panic ensued. Commander Valentin Savitsky, unable to reach the general staff, ordered his crew to prepare the nuclear torpedo as the lights went dark and the air inside the ship became toxic. 'We're going to blast them now! We will die but we will sink them all – We will not disgrace our navy,' he shouted. His second in command, Commander Vasili Arkhipov, managed to calm him down and persuaded him not to launch.

Meanwhile, having received information that a U-2 spy plane had been shot down over Cuba, and thinking the Russians were trying to blind them, the Chiefs demanded authorisation for a strike and an invasion. Reconnaissance missions were drawing fire, and reports came that missiles were being placed on their launchers. Two hundred and fifty thousand US troops were mobilised and ready to invade Cuba, while American officials outlined plans for a new Cuban government.

Convinced that a strike would take place in the next few hours, Castro drafted a letter to Khrushchev asking whether he would respond and keep his word to defend the island at all costs, or wait until the US attacked the USSR. Castro has said that he, Guevara and the others were persuaded that the island was going to be obliterated and were prepared to die. In his memoirs, Khrushchev claims that Robert Kennedy sent him a desperate message through the Soviet ambassador: 'Even though the president himself is very much against starting a new war over Cuba, an irreversible chain of events could occur against his will . . . If the situation continues much longer, the President is not sure that the military will not overthrow him and seize power.' The next morning, the Russians announced they would withdraw their missiles from Cuba. The US had come 'within a hairsbreadth of invading Cuba', and the world within seconds of annihilation.[16]

For both Khrushchev and Kennedy this episode marked the beginning of a steep learning curve that would take them beyond the Manichean strictures of the Cold War. Kennedy remained ambivalent towards Cuba and the rest of Latin America, speaking of democracy, alliances for progress and reform while at the same time endorsing a new round of covert operations against Castro, and supporting a military coup in Guatemala as late as March 1963. After these turbulent months, progressive Latin Americans started to view Vietnam and Cuba, and by extension the entire region, as part of one and the same project of constructing a 'One World' under the auspices of US homogenising capitalism (or proto-globalisation).

While the ripples of the Missile Crisis were still being felt throughout Latin America, in November 1962 the Chilean government of Jorge Alessandri responded to a national strike called by the CUT union with the massacre of the José Maria Caro slum in the outskirts of Santiago. During the funerals, Salvador Allende observed: 'We live in a society that does not really exist as such, just as our democracy is purely apparent. People ask satisfaction to their basic needs, and the government responds with violence, repression and persecution.'[17] In this speech, Allende linked the fragile appearance of democracy in Chile – in which notions of peaceful coexistence between classes quickly gave way to the violent repression of the lower classes – to the merely apparent coexistence between the world's most powerful nations during the Cold War. He also referred to the limits imposed on peoples asserting their right to life and self-determination, such as Cuba and Vietnam, and to the undermining of democracy and revolutionary will in the increasingly militarised big powers, the US and the USSR.

For Allende, who had repeatedly defended Cuba from US aggression and hailed the revolution as 'a necessary event that could not wait to happen . . . yielding a different Cuban people, which today is the master of its own destiny',[18] the lesson of 1962 was quite sobering: to a lesser or greater extent, the Cuban Revolution had lost the capacity it had so recently gained to shape its own history by reacting to the whims of the US government and the pressure of its anti-communist crusade. In an article published in August 1964, he argued that 'today nobody can deny that the Cuban Revolution has had to adapt its strategy and its tactics to the motivations of the US State Department.'[19] This reaffirmed the view he had expressed before, that 'those who believe they can simply transplant or imitate the Cuban Revolution make a huge mistake, just as those who believe they can ignore its actuality and future projection are stupid.'[20]

According to Allende, what followed from this was the need 'for the revolutionary transformation of each country', always in accordance with its own specific situation, but also in keeping with the reaction of the bourgeoisie and the US government. He concluded that, 'given the international situation . . . and the momentum achieved by the mobilisation of the popular movement', Chile was approaching its own crossroads.[21] While directly acknowledging the crucial role of the 'revolution from below', Allende now linked it to the increasing belligerence of the anti-communist crusade that united the interests of the local 'Import-Export coalition' with the motivations of the US State Department and its security forces, and their capacity to respond with overwhelming force to perceived threats.

And just as Castro and Guevara had become disillusioned with the Soviet Union after the Missile Crisis, and sought to reduce their dependence on their erstwhile ally (even expressing a willingness to normalise relations with the US in April 1963), Allende's Socialist Party renewed its internal debate with the Communist Party about the role of the Soviet Union and the socialist bloc, as well as the need for a peaceful road to socialism. In response to these challenges Allende, already a presidential candidate for the 1964 elections on behalf of the Popular Action Front coalition (FRAP), began to downplay the tactical differences between the parties of the Left as a thing of the past.

Allende argued that such differences were tending to be superseded by the mobilisation of grassroots movements from below and the pressure exerted from above by the converging interests of conservative local elites and international counter-revolutionary crusaders. He proposed two answers: on the one hand, the thesis of an independent 'People's Government' responsive to the specifics of the Chilean situation, and on the other the doctrine of geo-economic sovereignty, as opposed to the Washington doctrine of geostrategic sovereignty or 'national security' that advocated the merging of security and development.

'Given the fact that both parties [socialist and communist] have agreed to accept the programme of the Popular Action Front

[FRAP], and the thesis of a People's Government,' Allende explained, 'which are neither socialist nor communist, but rather, the expression of thousands of independent Chileans', it made no sense to apply to it the kind of counter-revolutionary and fiercely anti-communist discourse coming from above.[22] 'First they have created a twisted image of communism, then they made the ill-intentioned suggestion that I'm the communist candidate, the representative of an absolutely distorted form of communism.'[23] To counter such distortions, the FRAP coalition's programme emphasised as its main proposals: agrarian reform – defended also by the centrist Christian Democratic party led by Eduardo Frei; a foreign policy independent of both the USSR and the US; the entrenchment and reform of welfare institutions, specifically health, education and pensions; and the regulation of industrial, commercial and financial monopolies, and in particular the nationalisation of extractive industries such as copper mining, iron and nitrates.[24] A further novelty was the creation of a series of organisations that made the link between the parties and the revolution from below: the Independent Committee of Allendista Women led by his sister Laura Allende, the Catholic Allendista Movement, the Civilian–Military Front, the Independents Commando and the Professionals and Technicians Commando.

Another crucial innovation of the FRAP coalition was the so-called Creative Front tasked with finding novel uses for existing media such as radio and creating new media to advance the message of the popular movements, and to overcome the virtual monopoly exercised by the old 'Import-Export coalition' over dominant media such as television, private radio stations and newspapers. The embodiment of such monopoly was none other than Agustín Edwards, a namesake of the man who in 1891 had financed the beginnings of the counter-revolution against President Balmaceda, and figurehead of the Edwards family, its bank of A. Edwards & Co., its light industries and its influential newspaper *El Mercurio*.

In 1891 the local and foreign press had argued, in relation to Balmaceda: 'There is in Chile a communist government, a despot or various despots who under the false name of Executive Power have overturned all the peace, all the prosperity . . . of the preceding eighty years.' In July 1964 *El Mercurio* declared, in relation to the FRAP coalition and their candidate Allende:

> Everywhere . . . they [the communists] have ended systematising abuse, suppressing the most elementary rights, and imposing hunger, violence and misery. The parties that support the candidate of the Popular Action Front [Allende] have dedicated their existence to fighting for Marxism and consequently promoting the dictatorship of the proletariat, the abolition of property, the persecution of religion and the suppression of the rule of law.[25]

The message in *El Mercurio*, consciously tying the defence of property and the domestic economy to the defence of religion, was particularly addressed to the urban and predominantly Catholic sector of middle- and upper-class women. It was intended to reinforce the stereotypical image of the feminine as policing the strict borders separating order from chaos, 'which must regulate such borders . . . in order to defend the social order and its legality whenever the fatherland [*la patria*] is supposedly threatened by mob-rule, sedition and revolt',[26] at a time when such sectors began approaching the Left in the context of the overtures brought about by Vatican Council II and Liberation Theology, which in Latin America had the impact of a veritable Reformation movement.

The Latin American Episcopal Conference (CELAM), formed in 1955, pushed the conclusions of Vatican Council II towards a more socially oriented stance that would result in the 'preferential option for the poor' adopted by Latin American churches at the Medellín Conference of 1968, against strong orthodox opposition. But the real power of these reorientations lay in the so-called Christian base communities, a bottom-up network of small groups especially active in urban slums and rural parts of Latin America, which placed a high value on lay participation, particularly among women. In Chile, for instance, women like Francisca Morales, who were active in the slums of Santiago where no male priests and no Church hierarchy were present in the 1960s, would be central to the development of a reading of biblical stories and images from the perspective of the poor and the people. It constituted a profound challenge to the established roles and political conventions of the time. Many of these groups coalesced around issues of land and agrarian reform, and the condemnation of all forms of colonialism and the nuclear arms race in places as far apart as South Africa, Haiti, Brazil, Colombia and Chile.[27]

According to the cultural theorist Nelly Richard, the mobilisation of conventional images of femininity in a situation of perceived chaos and disorder, identified explicitly with the rise of the popular movements and the Left, explains why so many middle- and upper-class women abandoned the 'law of bourgeois femininity according to which their traditional place is in the privacy of home and family' and became 'the most zealous protectors of the established order' and the current laws, in the specific circumstances of the 1960s and 1970s.[28] In this way, says Richard, they could carve out a place for themselves in a social pact and the legal institutions that in principle relegated them to home and family life. She suggests that assuming the persona of the staunch guardian of the status quo was these women's way out of home and into the streets and squares where politics take place, without overturning the social pact.[29] Something similar may have happened in other parts of the world, in 1970s England for instance. It helps to explain the significance of figures like Margaret Thatcher, who helped usher in a more militant, counter-revolutionary kind of conservatism better attuned to the emerging global pact between militarism and economic progress along liberal lines.

But it is important to consider the fact that other women – Francisca Morales, Carmen Lazo, Laura and Beatriz Allende, among many others – were at the same time pushing the boundaries of the social pact and breaking free from it. They mounted a

challenge from below to the patriarchies of Church and fatherland, the impact and significance of which has not been properly
assessed. In doing so, they helped transform the political landscape
of countries like Chile in ways that male politicians and patriarchal
institutions did not expect and were obliged to adapt – or over-
react – to.

It is worth noticing in this regard, the nearly all-male make-up of
the anti-leftist reaction emerging in Chile, from the fascist paramilitary movement aptly named Fatherland and Freedom (*Frente
Nacional Patria y Libertad*) to the membership of the civilian–military
conspiracy against Allende's coalition and the Vatican hierarchy that
was sympathetic to them.

In this respect, referencing the subordinate role played by women
in the anti-leftist reaction in Chile, Nelly Richard points out the
way in which, historically speaking, fascism 'played with the drives,
desires and sexual fantasies of women – the male sublimation of
domination and command, the eroticisation of the rule of authority –
leaning on the pro-family, moralist and Catholic ideology of the
capitalist bourgeoisie predominant at the time'.[30] She observes the
prominence of the language, iconicity and attitudes of religious
veneration and Canon Law accompanying, or activating, stereotypes of subordination: the mother and wife in relation to such
iconic figures as the head of the family or the fatherland, and the
canonical images of patriarchal economic and military might. Such
languages, rules and icons were prominent in the public arena and
the media of the time, echoed for instance in the July 1964 article in
El Mercurio cited above, or captured by the filmmaker Patricio
Guzmán.

The result was a veritable war of words and images, played out
on radio, television, city walls and new media. These conflicts
pitched, on the one hand, the distorted images of communism that
Allende complains about and the icons of social, political and religious subordination and order, against, on the other, the images
created by muralists like Roberto Matta, Víctor Jara's folk and pop

music, Neruda's poetry, the narrative comics and *fotonovelas* accounted for in Ariel Dorfman's pioneering analyses of popular culture, the popular religiosity of Christian base communities and Liberation Theology, cinema and even more daring experiments with new media and computer technology. Not by accident, the contradiction between the popular militant women of the slums of Santiago and their middle-class counterparts in the 'Pots and Pans Protests' against Allende's coalition, the images of better-off women shouting at the camera '*Afuera con esos comunistas de mierda!* (To hell with those shit communists!)', would come to hold a prominent place in the new media created to express the novel expectations and dilemmas of the time. A particularly apt example is the documentary cinematography of the period, the so-called 'Third Cinema' that inherited the concerns and imagery of earlier creators such as Luis Buñuel, Eisenstein, Tarkovsky, the muralist painters and Neruda, as can be seen in the definitive portrayal of these years, Patricio Guzmán's film *The Battle of Chile*. Similar questions concerning the role of femininity vis-à-vis predominantly patriarchal politics, including the remnants of machismo in the Cuban Revolution, are posited in Tomas Gutiérrez Alea's *Memories of Underdevelopment*.

All this explains the arc opened up by the creation of the Creative Front within Allende's Popular Action Front coalition in 1963 and the development of Project Cybersyn in 1971. This was a scientific project to help the economy adapt quickly to changes in the national environment. It involved the construction of a computer-based network, an operations room, and a wider system of telecommunications equipment linked to the nerve centres of Chile's new economics and society during Allende's years.

It was created to assist Allende's government implement its vision of socialist change. The designers and creators of the project expected that high-ranking members of the government would use the operations room to make rapid decisions in connection with other users – mainly the non-virtual networks of workers that at the time were taking control over factories and supply chains, as part of the revolution from below and the creation of the 'social' sector of the economy in the wake of nationalisations and agrarian reform. Based on current data and an expanded focus over the whole of national economic activity, the technologists and their partners in government hoped it would be possible to establish an entirely new regulatory system of society and the economy, one less hierarchical, more horizontal, and far more deliberative and consensual.[31]

In that sense, Cybersyn was also an innovative experiment in participatory democracy and regulation as collective, networked, problem-solving, backed by the latest advances in technology and the science of 'effective' organisation and self-regulation. But it could also serve as an effective communications system, helping Allende to respond to the anti-leftist propaganda machine run by the private media – owned by the most important and powerful business conglomerates and tycoons of the country, such as Agustín Edwards and the Edwards and Matte families, with powerful connections in the US – during the years of Allende's rise to power and the increasing momentum of the revolution from below in the 1970s.

Back in 1963, Allende's answer to Chile's dilemma – caught between distorted images of socialism and the norms of conservative order, and the creative imagination of the social movements – took two main forms. First, to highlight the momentum and diversity of the 'revolution from below', as the driving force of the Popular Action Front. Second, to display the pluralism of the social movements and the Popular Action Front, as a guarantee to the fiercely anti-communist local and international interests that 'the Left', narrowly defined as socialist or communist, would not come to dominate and impose its view over the conduct of a future People's Government. Allende's message was that such a government would not constitute a threat 'to the formal aspects of our predominant civic habits', meaning democracy and the rule of law.[32]

In the coming years, the lessons of Cuba in 1961 and 1962 would lead Allende to emphasise the need 'for a more flexible politics of wider alliances', even against the influential views within his own party that advocated it put itself at the head of the revolution from below, confront head-on an increasingly hostile bourgeoisie, and avoid all compromise. Allende consistently opposed such calls, pointing out that 'it was obvious that a party that proclaimed armed struggle as a means to take power would not be able to broaden its political front.'[33]

Crucially, the creation of a broader political front entailed the invention of new media, and technologies able to express and enhance the new languages and images of freedom emerging from below. New ideas such as 'popular power', 'people's government', the 'social economic sector', or 'now we're dreaming reality', which sought to reform, eliminate or replace the old exclusive legal and political regulations dating back to the conservative Portales Constitution of the nineteenth century, and its basis in the protection of tradition (meaning Christian values and Hispanicist culture), family and property.

This was not simply a question of propaganda, or of setting the record straight against the distortions spread by old media bent on defending vested interests. It was also an existential question, in the sense that there was an emerging subjectivity from below crying to be heard. It required, as Ariel Dorfman would put it in the 1970s, 'a new language', new narratives and new images.[34] A new voice also means different institutions that would not play it down, and new norms to shape such institutions. It also entails a level of technology adequate to make newly felt and expressed longings for freedom accessible to the many, as well as the individual and collective spaces where such freedom can be realised.

At stake here is the question of individual liberty, which would have been recognisable to any good Marxist then as now. Only the most advanced and imaginative technologies, and institutional, managerial and organisational forms, no matter whether or not they have been created within capitalism, can serve as the basis of the project to deliver a classless society in which wealth can be distributed according to need. You cannot withdraw from the existing state and its institutions, just as you cannot return to the past or expect that outdated technologies and techniques will be up to the tasks of the revolution.

To people like Guevara and Allende in the early 1960s, among many others, including the younger economists and scientists going beyond the old recipes for industrialisation in Latin America, and the base theologians warning that dependency was not only economic but also intellectual and spiritual, the contradiction between investing so much in military production and capability and so much less in civilian production – a contradiction at the heart of the Cold War imperative and the anti-communist crusade – threw into relief the issue of individual liberty. Capitalism was heading in the direction of globalisation, automation and large enterprises – the 'multinational vampires' that Julio Cortázar would write about in the 1970s.[35] These people were searching for ways to take control of such big beasts – global finance, extractive industries, agribusiness, the military–industrial complex, the media – that given their head would sacrifice the individual liberty of the many to satisfy the greed of the very few. Only then could the alienation, invisibility and servitude at the heart of human existence be addressed.

Their goal was not 'the dictatorship of the proletariat' or 'universal tolerance' and 'class' or 'multicultural' solidarity as much as the liberation of individual human beings and the completion of the projects of independence of peoples and nations. They often referred to this goal in the language of the time as bringing about 'a new man' and 'a new humanity', thereby expressing very conscious feelings of interconnectivity quite different from the image of the individual with his or her human rights alone against the world. They come closer to the image of the 'networked individual' more familiar to today's interconnected youth: the more he or she has a project of freedom or autonomy, the more he or she interconnects, and the more autonomous he or she becomes in respect of the current rules and institutions. Hence the need for new ones.[36]

In many ways, the tragedy of these men and women of the 1960s and 1970s is that, unlike us in the twenty-first century, they did not have the kinds of technologies that would allow for the sustainable creation of such spaces of personal and collective freedom. But as we will see, at least in some cases they invented them.

First, however, they had to escape the strictures of their time: the straitjacket of Manichean anti-communism, the stranglehold of the multinational vampires over their wealth and resources, the increasing militarisation of society and even the narrow-mindedness of many who declared themselves on the side of the revolution, leftists and centrists alike.

One example of such narrowness was the 'Revolution in Liberty' launched by the Christian Democrat Eduardo Frei after his victory in the 1964 elections, aided and abetted by the distortions of *El Mercurio*, the electoral support of the anti-leftist camp, and the funds provided by the United States to guarantee the defeat of Allende's coalition.

The CIA and the American government had been meddling in Chilean affairs since at least 1958. In 1963, according to a statement made to the *Washington Star* by a friend of his, the Belgian Jesuit priest Roger Vekemans received ten million dollars from the American Kennedy administration earmarked for Frei and anti-communist think tanks and unions in Chile and Latin America. Vekemans was close to the Christian Democrats and provided intellectual support from the Centre for Latin American Economic and Social Development (DESAL) think tank that he directed. He was also connected to the Catholic hierarchy in Europe, which was growing concerned about the advancement of Liberation Theology and the increasing closeness between sectors of the popular church, popular movements in the slums and rural areas, and the Left. They were also providing generous funding. In 1964 the CIA helped Frei defeat Allende, and over the next few years the US spent millions more supporting anti-communist groups and some $163 million in military aid, placing Chile second among all Latin American states.

Meanwhile the United States trained some four thousand Chilean military officers in counter-insurgency methods on military bases in the mainland and at the notorious US Army School of the Americas in the Panama Canal Zone. Among them was the now Major Augusto Pinochet.[37]

As Frei took his first steps to nationalise the copper industry and redistribute some fertile slopes in the south of Chile to Mapuche peoples and landless peasants, some of whom were part of the Christian base communities, he appeared to many in Europe as the South American figurehead of a brand of moderate left-wing reformism favoured by the likes of Harold Wilson, who became British prime minister in the same year. In 1965, Frei visited Britain and was described by one English paper as 'the de Gaulle of Latin America'.[38] During the visit, the purchase of twenty-one Hawker Hunter combat jets by the Chilean government was arranged and made effective a year later. These aircraft had become the emblem of a very specific kind of warfare, 'the bombing of guerrillas and other small groups putting up stubborn resistance against superior forces',[39] since the mid-1950s after seeing action in Suez, Borneo, Cyprus and Pakistan.

But by 1968, the year of global revolution, Frei's land reform had made him enemies among the old landowning aristocracy, while limited nationalisation – or 'Chilenisation', as he preferred to call it – angered the 'Import-Export coalition' and encouraged the Left to demand more. The perennial difficulties of controlling inflation, which Andy Beckett links to the tendency to luxury consumption of the middle- and high-income classes, identified earlier by Nolff, gave the unions good reasons to go on strike demanding better wages. The 1969 congressional elections confirmed the Christian Democrats' downturn: they managed to obtain only 29.7 per cent of the vote, against the 20 per cent of the right-wing Partido Nacional that combined conservatives, nationalists and some liberals, and the upward tendency of Communists and Socialists who – riding on the wave provoked by the revolution from below –

together obtained 28.1 per cent (with the Communists almost four points ahead of the Socialists).

The 'revolution from below' continued to gather momentum, taking advantage of the overtures made by social Christians in government and novel political configurations. Five days after the congressional elections a group of some seventy families of landless peasants and indigenous people occupied the wetlands near Puerto Montt. On Sunday 9 March 1969, the Christian Democrat government, represented by Minister of the Interior Edmundo Pérez Zujovic, sent 220 agents of the Carabineros force armed with machine guns and tear gas. The forces opened fire on the peasants, killing eight and wounding some twenty-seven, and burned their humble shacks. Allende was part of the massive funeral parade that accompanied the bodies of the murdered peasants and opened a congressional session to investigate the massacre. During the session, he responded to accusations by Edmundo Pérez Zujovic, that the Socialists, not the government, were responsible for the massacre because they had created a climate of violence and accepted armed struggle. Citing Lenin's *State and Revolution*, Allende said:

We aren't *golpistas* [coup makers] or adventurers. We do want a revolutionary transformation of the bourgeois state into a socialist republic. The path we follow to achieve it will depend on the actions of those who now have power and control the use of force. If they close for us the legal road, as they're trying to do using repression, threats, money and corruption, then we'll find a road of our own. Perhaps for the majority of Latin American countries there's no other way than armed struggle, we don't deny that. But we aren't inventing these facts, they emerge in realities where there aren't political parties, parliaments or unions. Can anyone believe those peoples could achieve power through peaceful ways? If the Minister of the Interior . . . and their Christian Democrat excellencies who have wrecked their so-called 'Revolution in Liberty' . . . believe it, that proves their ignorance. Similarly, can anyone believe that because of our declarations and debates in the past at Chillán, the massacres and nefarious events of La Coruña, Ránquil, San Gregorio, the Labour federation of Magallanes, Santa María, the north, José María Cano and El Salvador took place?[40]

Allende offered by way of disclaimer and counter-attack a brief history of the systematic use of force by Chilean governments, including the Christian Democrat administration of Eduardo Frei, every time the popular movements set about transforming the relationship between the people at the base and the state. He was denouncing the contradiction at the heart of modern law – slavery and liberty – joined in unholy embrace by the cement of force. The emerging voice of the popular movements needed to be heard, and the only way to allow it was to create new institutions, rules, techniques and technologies, including democratic institutions that did not reach for the gun every time the voices of a more genuine and deliberative popular culture, including the participation of the most disadvantaged, wanted to make themselves heard.

II

THE COUP

6

The Chilean Way Versus the Multinational Vampires

For Guevara the Missile Crisis and the events of 1961–2 confirmed that the Soviets' decision to place the emphasis on militarisation rather than civilian research was a mistake.[1] For it compromised the possibility of socialist development everywhere. According to Guevara, the biggest obstacles to 'fully developed humanism' under socialism were alienation and antagonism, which manifested themselves in the concrete conditions of global warfare, mutually assured nuclear destruction, and the transformation of our capacity to work and create into a privatised source of wealth for the few, and permanent crisis and emergency for the many.

The US and the USSR could have developed a partnership in the years after the Second World War to end imperialism everywhere and initiate much-needed reform at home. Instead, the US engaged in a worldwide anti-communist crusade that painted every desire for autonomy in the east and south of the globe as the enemy of Western civilisation and the foe of mankind.

From Vietnam to Indonesia, and from Cuba to Brazil and Chile, the crusade was fought in the name of Western and Christian values, including an individualistic view of production and property relations, which benefited mostly US corporations that thrived in the post-1962 business-friendly climate that would be shaped in places like Indonesia and Brazil, and elsewhere, with the help of US economic advisers and willing local clienteles, and safeguarded by brutal military regimes that crushed the slightest signs of creative dissent.

Looking back in 1970, US President Lyndon Johnson told the historian Doris Kearns that he had faced an impossible choice and ended up sacrificing his dream of becoming a great social reformer to pursue the anti-communist obsession of the hawks within the administration; but he also felt vindicated in the fact that, had he taken a different course of action, he would have been seen as both a coward and an appeaser. In the end, the choices made by him and others tipped the balance between democracy and security in America towards the path of imperialism and permanent war. 'I have lost,' he said, 'the woman I really loved – the Great Society – in order to get involved with that bitch of a war on the other side of the world'.[2]

Similarly, the socialist camp led by the USSR put the emphasis on defence. Threatened by NATO missiles in Turkey and Italy and the military might of the US and its allies, it gambled on developing technology almost exclusively dedicated to catch up and offset the military balance, for instance by placing Soviet missiles a few miles from Miami. The Cubans, certain that a US invasion was coming, consented and even urged the Soviet premiership to strike against the imperialists in the event of an attack on the island, before the USSR was also destroyed. The result of such a game of cat and mouse, with each side ready to point an even bigger weapon at the other, was a near-apocalypse.

The crisis was not over after the USSR acceded to US demands in exchange for a promise not to invade the Caribbean island and the removal of Jupiter missiles from NATO bases in Italy and Turkey in 1962. Throughout, the Americans were ignorant of the fact that there were nuclear weapons in Cuba. They knew about the Luna missiles, which could be nuclear or conventional, but did not believe these were nuclear. The arsenal also included 'some eighty FKR missiles with 12-kiloton warheads . . . and at least six 12-kiloton bombs' destined for the Cuban air force Ilyushin-28 bombers. Some one hundred thousand Americans would have died in the event of a strike on Cuba, and the US most certainly would have responded by obliterating the Caribbean island and its 7 million people. The world would have moved ever closer to all-out nuclear war – in the Japanese island of Okinawa F-100 fighter bombers armed with hydrogen bombs were readied for action, the most likely target being communist China – with the lives of hundreds of millions of people at risk, perhaps all mankind.[3]

The Chinese charged the Soviet premiership with cowardice for having caved in to US demands, as did several Soviet officials. In the US, the military chiefs expressed anger at the fact that the 1962 Missile Crisis had ended without regime change in Cuba. For them, and for the staunch anti-Castroite exiles still licking their wounds after the Bay of Pigs fiasco, the opposite happened: Castro's position was strengthened. Some, like General Curtis LeMay, stated that the US had lost and accused Kennedy of cowardice.

Both Khrushchev and Kennedy (and also Castro) made peace overtures, with Kennedy going as far as to speak of 'genuine peace', not 'a Pax Americana enforced on the world by American weapons of war . . . not merely peace for Americans but peace for all men and women'. In his June 1963 address at the American University, he called for a re-examination 'of our attitude toward the Cold War', and in a gesture that can only be interpreted as an overture to Cuba, the rest of Latin America and the other peoples seeking global justice, he linked the call for new international peaceful relations with remedial and hopeful economic justice for all men and women of all nations. 'The kind of peace that . . . enables men and nations to grow and to hope and to build a better life for their children' that Kennedy spoke of – that Khrushchev publicly supported, and that Guevara would respond to in his December 1964 address to the UN General Assembly, his March 1964 statement at the UN Conference on Economics and Development in the Third World, and his March 1965 'Socialism and Man' letter to the Uruguayan weekly *Marcha* – amounted to a common vision presenting a law of life as opposed

to the law of death that had so far dictated the terms of global relations. At this point in history, the three or four most influential men
in the planet held a common view on peace and global justice, and
were ready to act on it. They were about to change the course of
history. On 16 October 1964, however, the Soviet premier Nikita
Khrushchev was ousted, almost a year after Kennedy was assassinated and nearly three years later Guevara was murdered in Bolivia.

Castro was dining with the journalist Jean Daniel – who had
brought Kennedy's constructive message, and was getting ready to
go back to Washington and relay Castro's positive response – when
he was told about the US president's assassination. 'This is bad
news!' he exclaimed three times. 'They will blame us for it, you
wait and see.'⁴ Reportedly, Khrushchev broke down and cried.
Other men in America would pick up the torch – men like Nelson
Rockefeller, Dean Rusk, Thomas C. Mann, John Foster Dulles, his
brother Allen, George Bush Sr, Richard Nixon and Henry Kissinger.
The result would be disastrous, especially for Vietnam and Latin
America.

But also for the US: it has been said that America lost its soul in
the jungles of Vietnam and the mountains of the Andes, as the realities of napalm and torture replaced visions of peace and justice and
the law of life envisioned by Kennedy, Khrushchev, Castro and
Guevara.

With Kennedy and most of his Cabinet out of the picture, the
Americans drew the conclusion that willingness to go to war and
superior force had proved effective in taming the Soviets and
containing the advance of communism, and that if it had worked in
Cuba it would also work elsewhere, in Vietnam as well as the rest
of Latin America. The Soviets drew the opposite lesson: feeling
their prestige had been seriously dented by weakness, they embarked
on an even bigger build-up of atomic weapons and invested most of
their economic capacities in a hopeless race to match the US militarily. The Cubans, in turn, felt betrayed by their erstwhile allies.
Relationships between Cuba and the USSR would never fully

recover after 1962. To place too much trust in the Soviets, their allies and their model seemed unwise. Although forms of economic support and exchange continued, for many in Cuba and the rest of Latin America it became clear that an autonomous path towards socialism and economic independence was the only option. It also became clear to them that the US was ready to use overwhelming force to crush such ideals.

In fact, as a consequence of these events Castro and Guevara, among others, signalled a change of course. Guevara would deepen his criticism of Soviet-style plans and warlike economy. Instead, he emphasised the need to create new civilian institutions, new laws and new relations, a new economic management system aimed at harmonising two goals: production and consciousness, which must be fostered in parallel, for 'to build communism, a new man must be created simultaneously with the material base'.[5]

These were no abstract musings. At heart, they constituted a practical alternative to 'growth', 'development' and the regulation of international relations as defined by the modern tradition that extended from the 29 January 1949 declaration by Harry Truman that America 'should make available to the peace-loving peoples the benefits of our store of technical knowledge in order to help them realise their aspirations' to Johnson and Nixon's practice of many forms of warfare against any other than the liberal–capitalist notions of pluralism. Based on the idea of a 'new humanity', the alternative that began to emerge between the mid-1930s and the 1970s, it recognises the fact that social plurality remains a stubborn fact worldwide. And since it may not be wished away (nor pushed away by force, at the cost of permanent war and even the extinction of mankind), the task is always to construct what American philosopher John Rawls called a 'reasonable pluralism', but one that takes stock of other versions of peace and remedial justice beyond Euro-American liberal pluralism.[6]

Therefore, the starting point is to identify a wider plurality of existing conceptions of peace and global justice – composed even

before President Truman offered his single version of the relation
between development and pluralism. For instance, those advanced
by the multitude of peoples who have struggled to overthrow colonial and neocolonial impositions, coming up with narratives of
their own against plunder and predatory legalities, and making 'self-
determination the foundational principle for relatively autonomous
directed human and social development'.[7]

In the context of renewed crises and hostilities after 1962, Guevara
argued that the laws regulating the conduct of international and
economic relations not only operated 'in context', obliging nations
to adapt to the current order or perish, but actually set a context of
global inequality. To make self-determination a foundational principle, and a key to development, meant creating new contexts, new
solidarity alliances, new forms of reasonable pluralism beyond the
Truman–Nixon definition of a world divided between Euro-
American developers and 'irresponsible' developees living in a late
twentieth-century version of the state of nature: the wretched and
infinitely poor.

Crucially, the Truman-Nixon normative construction follows
the same logic as the 1601 Poor Law proclaimed by Queen Elizabeth
I: the poor (the underdeveloped or developing nations of today's
world) constitute a threat not only to themselves but also to other
prosperous people. Any duty to assist the wretched of the earth
emerges, in this mindset, not in terms of global justice but rather as
the foreign policy of rich powers and other 'well-ordered' hierarchical societies towards the "disordered' peoples of the world, out
of security concerns. Justice and poverty are reduced in this frame
of mind to a global security problem, and dealt with as such by
those with sufficient military power to do so.

This leads to the militarisation of international and economic
relations, governing both economic development and any attempt
to gain economic independence. In fact, it is not possible to speak
of, let alone achieve, genuine economic independence in that situation, since (outside of the Euro-kinship considerations that led to

the Marshall Plan of American economic assistance to Britain and others after the Second World War) there is simply no place here for any serious consideration of remedial equality or justice for the plundered and vandalised subject peoples, and those subjected to the torture chambers and killing fields of the Cold War.

In lieu of this, Guevara argued that without fully demonstrating solidarity and support for the underdeveloped world, the socialist countries would not only be appeasing the forces of reaction 'but would actually become accomplices to those forces'.[8] Growth, development and economic independence come to signify in this alternative framework a new international common sense, a 'consciousness' apt for the 'new man' and 'new humanity' of Guevara's parlance.

This is different from and much more than an ethic of sentiment or benevolence, which is what the Cold War pragmatism in the Truman–Nixon tradition appeals to in its understanding of development as a suite of strategic gestures – varying from subtle diplomacy to blunt military assistance and intervention – of American or largely Western largesse driven by self-regarding moral considerations.

In concrete terms, in the environment of the late 1960s and early 1970s, this meant that 'the socialist countries must help pay for the development of countries now starting out on the road to liberation . . . a change in consciousness resulting in a new fraternal attitude towards humanity.'[9] According to such a view, economic exchanges between countries bonded in solidarity should not include 'mutually beneficial trade' based on prices imposed on developing countries by the laws operating in the global market and the relations of unequal exchange that force the latter to sell their raw materials at world market prices and to buy at such prices the machinery produced in the automated factories of the developed world. Foreign investments from fraternal countries should involve no payment or credit, and 'the supply of marketable goods on long-term credits' to poorer countries could be 'one form of aid not requiring the contribution of freely convertible hard currency'.[10] Similarly, relations between fraternal countries would involve acquiring and sharing the latest technology without regard for the limits imposed by mainstream notions of patents and copyright.

These, and other related notions such as Frantz Fanon's idea that former coloniser and enslaver states must pay their due to plundered peoples in the global South just as Germany paid reparations to Israel after the war, constitute the precedent for current designs of concrete forms of remedial justice and equality as part of the reconstruction of human rights, and contemporary practices of solidarity economics between countries like Venezuela and Cuba or Nicaragua, just as they prefigured in their own time the development of new doctrines of compensation after nationalisation in international law. One example of such development would be the Allende Doctrine of 'excess profits', applied by the Chilean government in 1971 after the nationalisation of the copper industry in the hands of the multinational conglomerates Kennecott and Anaconda.

The practice of solidarity or 'proletarian internationalism', involving an understanding of economic and political norms entailing the possibility of creating one's future independent of the circumstances of the past and the current situation, an ethics of individual responsibility in global perspective, and a clear choice for the least favoured on the side of the law of life, richly informed the normative reconstruction of the idea of human rights as people's rights. It began in the late 1960s as a viable alternative to the human rights and militarised politics of the weak liberalism characteristic of the Truman–Nixon tradition, and closer to the strong liberalism of the Roosevelt–Kennedy tradition in North America. In the South this notion of rights as people's and human rights, followed from the histories of the specific struggles of the poor and the disenfranchised. Far from being a poisoned or phoney gift of the European Enlightenment, it constitutes in the opinion of the Indian human rights scholar Upendra Baxi 'a live legacy of their authorship by suffering peoples and communities in struggle'.[11]

Speaking in 1962, Allende described in very similar terms the experience of the Socialist Party:

> the Socialist Party was born in Chile thirty years ago in response to a specific social reality of evident inequality and disenfranchisement. This allowed us to gather an ample and diverse set of the sectors of society, principally workers, but also peasants and middle-class people in a movement responsive to our typical circumstances, in accordance with Chile's situation, and autonomous from any command from abroad. Rather, it has been oriented towards the notion that the Chilean people can achieve economic independence and social justice.[12]

Referring to what Guevara had called 'non-capitalist' or 'moral' incentives – which the latter had proposed since the early 1960s as a way to upset the primacy of individualist law, competitive logic and the use of consumer goods as a psychological moulder of consciousness – Allende observed: 'The Cuban people are today a different people, they're masters of their own destiny. They have gathered and fused together anew, around notions of work as a common task and a social duty, of emulation and voluntary labour.' Invoking an image from his teenage years, this time applied to the daily and perhaps unglamorous tasks of keeping the revolution alive, feed the people, clothe them, and allow them to benefit fully from their own efforts, Allende explained that in Cuba 'the university lecturer and the peasant, the student and the professional, the intellectual and the worker, are coming together in the crucible of [the moral transformation of] the nation.'[13]

After the Missile Crisis, Guevara became highly critical of the contradiction between militarised international relations and solidarity and investment in civilian production, particularly in the socialist countries that kept falling behind in terms of technological innovation for non-military purposes. He observed that: 'the error of not having acquired the highest technology at a given moment has cost a lot for some socialist countries; it has cost them in terms of development and in terms of competition in the world market.'[14] Before departing to the Congo in 1965, Guevara sent a letter to Fidel Castro outlining the main problems with the Soviets' 'New Political Economy', arguing for a completely different direction in Cuba. Chief among them, he explained, was the fact that the technological development and 'scientific progress made in the service of war and defence is not put to the service of peace, or only in a very limited fashion'.[15]

Guevara and his collaborators in Cuba since 1959, among them Jorge Ruiz Ferrer, were very enthusiastic about the impact of such novel approaches as cybernetics, systems theory, computer science and recent advances in the study of human physiology, psychology and the brain. As a physician himself, Guevara understood them better than most and suggested their application to transitional socialism in Cuba, arguing against the rejection on ideological grounds of such pioneering scientific fields in the Soviet Union and other socialist countries. His increasingly pointed criticisms of these attitudes in such a sensitive aspect of Cuba's revolutionary early life as the economy set him on a collision course with many in the international socialist camp and at home. It may have contributed to his decision to leave Cuba for good in 1967, a momentous choice mainly attributed to his stubborn desire to kick-start armed rebellion in South America, especially his native Argentina.

Another key factor in his decision was the turn for the worse taken by US policy towards Latin America. Two months before his assassination on 22 November 1963 in Dallas, President John F. Kennedy had responded to Castro's explicit wishes to explore the normalisation of relations between the two countries with an extraordinary declaration to the French journalist Jean Daniel:

From the beginning I personally followed the development of these events [in Cuba] with mounting concern. There are few subjects to which I have devoted more painstaking attention. My conclusions go much further than the European analyses. Here is what I believe.

I believe that there is no country in the world, including all the African regions, and any and all the countries under colonial domination, where economic colonization, humiliation and exploitation were worse than in Cuba, in part owing to my country's policies during the Batista regime. I believe that we created, built and manufactured the Castro movement out of whole cloth and without realizing it. I believe that the accumulation of these mistakes has jeopardized all of Latin America. The great aim of the Alliance for Progress is to reverse this unfortunate policy. This is one of the most, if not the most, important problems in American foreign policy . . . I approved the proclamation which Fidel Castro made in the Sierra Maestra, when he justifiably called for justice and specially yearned to rid Cuba of corruption. I will go even further: to some extent it is as though Batista was the incarnation of a number of sins on the part of the United States. Now we shall have to pay for those sins. In the matter of the Batista regime, I am in agreement with the first Cuban revolutionaries. That is perfectly clear.[16]

Kennedy told Daniel, who was about to travel to Cuba to interview Fidel Castro, that the Missile Crisis that pushed the world to the brink of destruction in 1962 and the escalation, '[Castro's] "will to independence", his madness or Communism', had been a consequence of 'sins on the part of the United States' and that 'the United States now has the possibility of doing as much good in Latin America as it had done wrong in the past; I would even say that we alone have this power – under the essential condition that Communism does not take over there.'[17] Kennedy also pointed out that the US would be ready to tolerate 'economic collectivism', as they did in the cases of Sékou Touré's Guinea and Tito's Yugoslavia, and that 'the continuation of the blockade [of Cuba] depends on the

continuation of subversive activities',[18] before inviting the journalist
to come and see him upon his return from Cuba. Daniel interpreted
this as meaning that 'John Kennedy had doubts, and was seeking a
way out'.[19]

Daniel went to Havana in October 1963 and found Fidel and
Guevara buried under a mountain of work as a result of Hurricane
Flora, which obliged them to revise the whole of their economic
programme.[20] On the evening before his departure, Castro came to
Daniel's hotel room and they talked into the early hours of the
morning. Fidel asked Daniel to repeat Kennedy's remarks against
Batista, as well as those concerning the crisis of 1962, three times. 'I
believe Kennedy is sincere,' Fidel told him. 'I also believe that today
the expression of this sincerity could have political significance . . .
I have not forgotten the Machiavellian tactics and the equivocation,
the attempts at invasion, the pressures, the blackmail, the organisation of a counter-revolution, the blockade, and, above everything,
all the retaliatory measures imposed before, long before there was
the pretext and alibi of Communism.' Then came his reply to
Kennedy's overture:

> But I believe that he inherited a difficult situation; I don't think
> that a president of the United States is ever really free, and I
> believe Kennedy is at present feeling the impact of this lack of
> freedom. I also believe he now understands the extent to which
> he has been misled, especially, for example, on Cuban reaction at
> the time of the attempted Bay of Pigs invasion. I also think he is
> a realist.[21]

Afterwards, Castro focused on the fact that the transnational
corporations that Julio Cortázar dubbed 'the Multinational
Vampires' were distorting US policy towards Latin America:

> For years and years American policy – not the government, but
> the corporate trusts and the Pentagon – has supported Latin

American oligarchies. All the prestige, the dollars, and the power was held by a class which Kennedy himself has described in speaking of Batista. Suddenly a President arrives on the scene who tries to support the interests of another class (which has no access to any of the levers of power) to give the various Latin American countries the impression that the United States no longer stands behind dictators, and so there is no need for more Castro-type revolutions. What happens then? The corporations see that their interests are being a little compromised, just barely, but still compromised. The Pentagon thinks the strategic bases are in danger, the powerful oligarchies in Latin American countries alert their American friends; they sabotage the new policy; and in short, Kennedy has everyone against him.[22]

Castro told Daniel that evening that the few 'liberal presidents who were chosen as instruments of the new policy are swept out of office', and offered as an example the fate of the writer and politician Juan Bosch in the Dominican Republic. At the end of the interview, Castro responded to Kennedy's gesture and pointed towards a possible way out. He told Daniel:

I have just talked to you as a Cuban revolutionary. But I should also speak to you as a peace lover, and from this viewpoint . . . I cannot help hoping . . . that a leader will come to the fore in North America – why not Kennedy, there are things in his favour! – who will be willing to brave unpopularity, fight the corporations, tell the truth, and most important, let the various nations act as they see fit. I ask nothing, nothing but peace, and to be accepted as we are! We are socialists, the United States is a capitalist nation, the Latin American countries will choose what they want . . . As far as we are concerned everything can be restored to normalcy on the basis of mutual respect of sovereignty.[23]

All this was said two days before Kennedy's murder. It staggers the mind to wonder what would have happened had Kennedy been allowed to complete his presidential term. Perhaps relations between the US and Cuba would have become normalised on the basis of tolerance and respect, as both he and Castro declared. And maybe Latin American nations might even have been able to choose what they wanted. As it turned out, they could not.

Effectively, less than two years after the interview in which Castro predicted his fall, the United States invaded the Dominican Republic and ousted President Juan Bosch, replacing him with the repressive regime of Joaquín Balaguer. Before that, on 25 November 1963, the new US president Lyndon Johnson met with CIA director McCone and made clear that his Latin American policy, much like his Vietnam policy, would differ sharply from Kennedy's. His Assistant Secretary of State for Inter-American Affairs, Thomas C. Mann, announced on 18 March to all Latin American ambassadors in Washington that from now on their countries would be judged on how they promoted US interests, meaning those of the multi-nationals and the military, not those of their own people. The US would aggressively protect the $9 billion worth of American corporations' investment in Latin America through an increase in military aid to Latin American armed forces and their leaders, whom Mann considered 'a pretty decent group of people'.[24]

In 1964, the US ordered the Brazilian president João Goulart to impose economic austerity on his citizens, already suffering as a consequence of one of the financial crises that were as common in those days as they are in ours. Instead, Goulart opted for land reform and foreign capital controls. Like his predecessor, he also made the mistake of recognising Cuba and offering assistance and protection, and took steps to legalise the Communist Party. Brazil was the fifth-largest country in the world, a resource powerhouse and continental giant occupying an area larger than the continental US. That sort of behaviour would not be allowed. The US cut off aid in an attempt to strangle Brazil's economy. Inflation skyrocketed. On 27 March,

McCone and other top US officials were told to back the Brazilian army chief General Humberto Castelo Branco and 'help avert a major disaster . . . which might make Brazil the China of the 1960s' in South America.[25] The CIA went to work in the shadows in league with calls for counter-revolution from influential politicians, landowners, businessmen, media moguls, the Church and a sector of the middle classes in Brazil. Soon enough Goulart was out, exiled in Uruguay.

The ousting of the Brazilian president and the beginning of a military dictatorship that would extend well into the late 1980s provided others in Latin America with a model to follow: the infamous 'National Security' doctrine. It happened at the same time the CIA was funding to the tune of $20m more than half the cost of Eduardo Frei's election in Chile. It also financed and promoted a virulent anti-leftist propaganda campaign during the 1964 Chilean presidential elections that made massive and unprecedented use of the press, radio, film, pamphlets and posters showing images of Soviet tanks and planes bombarding La Moneda presidential palace in Santiago and Cuban soldiers trampling on families and children. The campaign, aimed most of all at women, reached its height when Fidel Castro's sister, Juanita, was flown into Chile to speak on radio and television warning Chileans that a victory of Allende's Left would mean the establishment of a Cuban-style system, which she described in the most frightening terms.[26] According to Mario Amorós, the 1964 presidential campaign and the vicious anti-leftist propaganda marked the beginning of a period of extreme political and social polarisation in Chile way before Allende's actual rise to power, which would extend into the 1970s.

A few months later, the US, in collaboration with the armed forces of such Latin American countries as Brazil, Paraguay, Honduras and El Salvador, participated in the overthrow of Juan Bosch in the Dominican Republic. Bosch rejected Lyndon Johnson's assertion that 'Communist leaders, many of them trained in Cuba . . . took increasing control and what began as a popular democratic revolution [in the Dominican Republic] . . . was taken over . . . and placed into the hands of a band of communist conspirators . . . The American nations cannot, must not, and will not permit the establishment of another communist government in the western hemisphere,' and declared the intervention as immoral as the Soviet invasion of Hungary.[27]

The aggression was condemned by many among Latin America's civilian governments, among them Chile's Christian Democratic president Eduardo Frei. Allende too protested. On 5 May 1965, he read in the Chilean Senate a communiqué addressed to President Lyndon Johnson: 'The attitude of your government is an affront against the independence of the Dominican people, places in danger the existence of millions of them and humiliates the whole of Latin America. Out of respect for the heroes of American independence you must put an end to this aggression against the autonomy of the Dominican Republic.'[28]

In the first days of January 1966, Allende participated in the Tricontinental Conference taking place in Havana that, together with the 1964 UN Conference on Trade and Development (UNCTAD), marked the highest point in the emergence of a new voice in the international arena, aligned neither with the Soviet Union nor with the US. It grouped together the countries of Asia, Africa and Latin America and argued for the overhaul of the rules and institutions managing the production and distribution of the world's wealth. As a result of the action of these non-aligned countries in the General Assembly of the United Nations, the doctrine of 'Permanent Sovereignty over Natural Resources' entered the canon of international law. This meant that nationalisation was entrenched as a right recognised under international law. Permanent sovereignty over resources was associated with the main tenets of the UN Charter and the right to self-determination. These developments set the criteria to call for a New International Economic Order (NIEO) and the strategy of non-aligned countries for the elimination of apartheid in South Africa.[29] Allende warned the UNCTAD conference that 'the Johnson Doctrine' constituted for 'the Chilean people as well as for all Latin American countries, an explicit declaration that the imperialists' would not hesitate 'to oppose violence to any popular movement that in our continent may be in a position to achieve power'. By imperialists he meant not the US in general, but rather what Castro had described during his interview with Jean Daniel as the emerging alliance between 'the [American] trusts . . . the Pentagon . . . the powerful oligarchies in the Latin American countries [and] their American friends'. Allende added: 'In the case of Chile's popular movement, which has contributed to the widening and deepening of democracy in our country, this means we now know, with pristine clarity, that the United States will impede by force any democratic access to power.'[30]

Guevara may well have drawn a similar lesson, and decided that the time had returned for guerrilla warfare against the actual and impending attack of the Multinational Vampires and 'their American friends' on the popular movements of Latin America. This is not to say that he abandoned his concerns with institutional invention, technological innovation and behavioural and economic experimentation. After all, such concerns had been there from the very first day after the revolution. We know that after January 1959 Guevara's reading became more focused on the search for practical solutions: he studied Marxist classics as well as recent developments in political economy and economics, but also management theory from the corporate capitalist world, mathematics and advanced set theory, had lessons in probability and theories of information and handed out copies of a book about linear programming to his colleagues at the Ministry of Industries' Management Council, complaining that 'you are not thinking about the future. Hell, you're not even thinking about the present.'[31] The potential inherent in such a novel approach remained unrealised in Cuba after his departure, but what happened in Chile during Allende's presidency was a different story.

The final years of Frei's Christian Democrat 'Revolution in

Liberty' were not exactly peaceful. As the revolution from below continued to gather momentum, with *tomas de fundos* (land take-overs) by indigenous peoples and landless peasants happening more often in the south, as well as workers' strikes breaking out in the mining north, the government fell back on the default position of authorising armed repression. On one occasion it instructed Augusto Pinochet, who had expressed sympathies for the Christian Democrats and had risen from major to brigadier in the three years after his return from the United States in 1965, and from division commander in Iquique to deputy military governor in the far north, to put down a strike at the El Salvador copper mine. He did so, literally. His soldiers opened fire on a crowd of protesting workers and their families, killing six miners and two of their wives.

Episodes like El Salvador and the massacre at Puerto Montt provoked an internal schism within a Christian Democratic Party (PDC) already divided between Freístas, so-called *terceristas*, looking for a third way between the rightist Frei and leftist rebels, chief among them a group of young students associated with the Christian Democrat Youth (JDC) and social Christian sectors more or less close to the Church and the Christian base communities.

In May 1969 Eduardo Frei himself had to intervene during the national party conference of the PDC to prevent the majority view favourable to an electoral alliance with the FRAP coalition from becoming the PDC's official position. This would have paved the way for a much wider coalition between the Christian Democrats and the leftist parties against the conservative coalition led by Jorge Alessandri and his right-wing nationalists. Frei also had to act to contain the rebel sector within his own party that advocated the 'non-capitalist road to development'. As a result, the PDC senator Rafael Gumucio and PDC leaders Julio Silva Solar, Alberto Jerez, Jacques Chinchol and Vicente Sotta resigned their PDC allegiance, together with some militants and a significant number of students and university academics from the JDC who went on to form the Movimiento Popular de Acción Unitaria (MAPU) in order to work for 'popular unity' and 'join the people's struggle for justice, democracy and revolution, towards a new society, communitarian and socialist'.[32] The internal division of the party of government would greatly weaken its options for the coming presidential elections.

To make matters worse, the PDC's fears of a possible military coup were realised on 21 October 1969 when General Roberto Viaux started a rebellion at the Tacna regiment in Santiago. Allende – who had made no secret of his fears that pressure from the Pentagon and the CIA, and the influence of the officialdom trained in America and the Panama Canal Zone, might in time push elements within the Chilean military to break with their tradition of constitutionalism and non-intervention – went to La Moneda with the other leaders of the Left to express their support for Frei's legitimate government, democracy and the Constitution. The CUT workers' union took to the streets in defence of civil liberties and democracy, although they would neither forgive nor forget the government's repression against their colleagues in the north and the south.

The crisis was averted, for now, but the PDC found itself under siege from all sides: internally divided, without support from the right wing and its resurgent authoritarian and counter-revolutionary nationalism embodied in Alessandri's National Party, violently repressing union activity and the gathering momentum of the revolution from below, responding to a more and more popular Left critical of the government's recourse to violence, and confronting a counterculture that extended far beyond the established trade unions and the traditions of industrial militancy.

The burgeoning counterculture was in part distinctively Chilean. It emerged from below, with the new generation of young workers described by Peter Winn in his classic study of activism in the Yarur textile company, and with university students. It responded to renewed Mapuche activism, and to the uneven encounter between Christians and Marxism among socialists, communists and members of the important MAPU and the Guevarist Movimiento de Izquierda

Revolucionaria (MIR), as well as in the Christian Left and the movement Cristianos por el Socialismo. But it was also inspired in part by events in Paris, Berkeley and Mexico City. The result was a counterculture as plural and diverse as those of northern countries.[33]

There is little doubt that the renewed climate of activism was driven by the energies of a younger generation, able to reinvent the legacy of almost a century of popular politics. As Winn observes, the rise of the Left in Chile during the two decades leading up to the presidential election of 1970 coincided with the coming of age of a new generation of *jóvenes* going to school and university or to work. This youth was much more radicalised than the previous generation of workers and activists. The young workers had developed a negative image of Yarur, the work environment, and society in general during childhood, as they grew up listening to their parents' complaints about the factory, its owner and the wider situation, and witnessed the impact that such a situation had on the daily lives of their families.

The new generation was opposed to the factory's system of social control and the new techniques of management that basically reinforced spying and informing on fellow workers or neighbours who were perceived either as work-shy, as freeloaders manipulating the syste, or as spreading leftist, unionist propaganda on the factory floor, in the classroom, in the neighbourhood committees and so on. Since this new generation had no personal recollection of previous crucial events such as the Yarur strike of 1962, they were much more willing to take risks than their counterparts among the *viejos*.[34]

The value of Winn's focused study of the Yarur younger workers is enhanced by the fact that he used tools of oral history research that dated back to the 1930s Depression, when many unemployed historians in the US were put to work interviewing former slaves in the American South. The goal then was to explore the precise effects of slavery and unemployment on the individual and the process of transition to a free labour market. The use of such techniques in America and Chile ties in very neatly with the longer tradition of autobiographical storytelling and existential memoir that in the Americas is particularly strong among peoples of African and indigenous origin.[35] It is thus no surprise that the story told by Winn about the young Yarur workers resonates with that of the younger generation of Mapuche indigenous leaders, and university students.

Historians using similar or associated approaches have pointed out that the agrarian reform of 1962–1973 in Chile was paralleled by a new phase in the historical struggle of the Mapuche Indians, moving away from the attempt to achieve goals through recognition and 'respectful integration' into Chile's predominantly white settler culture and society, and towards a new approach based upon protests and direct action in response to dispossession. Land redistribution, focusing and deepening the mechanisms inherited from the Frei administration, was a major pillar of the political programme set out by the left coalition in the late 1960s and intersected with the new trajectory of indigenous political activism. The main issues from the latter's perspective were the recovery of usurped reservation land and reform of deteriorating living conditions. There was an overlap, even a common cause, with leftist and peasant groups, even if at times the indigenous perspective was not taken seriously enough by sectors of the Left whose Marxist rhetoric often amounted to a kind of lower-key racism advocating a dose of Marxist enlightenment and paternalism.

This was the case particularly in the mix-ups and encounters between Mapuche activists and MIR militants. The MIR had been founded as a semi-clandestine group inspired by Guevara-style guerrilla tactics, including the idea of the 'small engine' or *foco* – an enlightened vanguard igniting in a localised area a wider rebellion against a centralised government. Crucially, that tactic clashed with the older and far more entrenched strategies of the indigenous movements of Peru, Ecuador, Colombia, Chile, Brazil and Bolivia advocating common conflict-resolution and decision-making institutions, mass mobilisations and occupations based on traditions of pre-colonial and colonial politics and collective voluntary work such as the *tinku*, a form of collective problem-solving, and *minga*, voluntary collective labour.[36] As the 'Chilean Way' advocated by Allende and the parliamentarian Left gained ground, the extra-parliamentarian Left represented by the MIR began to organise an undisguised revolutionary mass movement focused on unorganised peasants, rural migrants and indigenous peoples. This gave the chance to many young *mestizo* urban students to come into direct contact with indigenous activists, and to discover they had more in common in terms of family histories and grievances than they first thought.

It is true that the external image projected by the MIR through its fiery rhetoric and militant imagery reinforced the notion of revolutionary violence peddled by the 'Import-Export coalition' and their American friends to persuade Chilean television viewers and the readers of *El Mercurio* that revolutionary confrontation was an inherent and inevitable threat, but it would be a mistake to conclude from this that the relationship between the young MIR militants and Mapuche or peasant activists was purely strategic and manipulative. The Mapuche were never the passive or naive recipients of leftist recipes, and the parliamentarian and extra-parliamentarian Left was not merely manipulative or ignorant of Mapuche circumstances. The story of younger indigenous activists like Rosendo Huenuman paints a much more interesting picture.

Born and raised in a Mapuche community near the coast, Huenuman became a well-known union activist in La Lota coalmines during his early life in the 1950s. The intense violence and cruelty employed by the Carabineros and the landowners when responding to workers' action – the mines employed large numbers of indigenous mineworkers – or expelling them from their reservations convinced him that not only class prejudice but also race was a problem. The legal framework that had been in place since 1927 and further entrenched by the 14.511 Act of 29 December 1960 condemned

Mapuche land and their community to disintegration. Right from the start, and until the 1960s and 1970s, the political practice of the Mapuche nation opposed such moves towards the further colonial fragmentation of its people. Resistance remained their priority, first under the leadership of more traditional organisations such as the Corporación Araucana and leaders like Venancio Coñuepán, and then through the Frente Único Araucano, leaders like Huenuman, the Confederación Nacional Mapuche, the National Federation of Indigenous Students and the Federación de Campesinos e Indígenas (FCI) of the 1960s, connected to the Socialists and the Communist Party, which in 1967 evolved into the Confederación de Campesinos e Indígenas Ránquil, so called in honour of the dead and the disappeared during one of the worst mass killings in Chilean history, which took place in June 1934 near the city of Temuco – Chile's equivalent to the massacre at Wounded Knee in the US.[37]

On 6 April 1964, the then presidential candidate Salvador Allende signed a document known as the Cautín Pact with representatives of the Mapuche nation in a ceremony at Cerro Ñielol near Temuco, Neruda's homeland and the same site where the Mapuche signed the peace treaty that put an end to the Indian Wars of the late nineteenth century. From then on, the convergence between indigenous and leftist organisations grew, while the former shifted from resistance to mass mobilisations in an attempt to recover the land of their ancestors, reconnect with their roots and reconstitute community space. People like Rosendo Huenuman and Reynaldo Mariqueo were part and parcel of a veritable indigenous renaissance. But they did not see this as incompatible with left-wing militancy. Huenuman's story illustrates such cases of dual militancy. He went on to become a member of the Communist Party, and part of Allende's coalition as a Congressman in the 1970s. Other younger activists would join forces with the MIR and the Movimiento Campesino Revolucionario (MCR) led by revolutionary students in Cautín province – which excitable journalists began comparing to the Cuban Sierra Maestra.[38]

The MIR, which counted among its sympathisers Allende's daughter Beatriz, not only focused its efforts on organising transient workers and collaborating with indigenous land takeovers or *tomas*, but also, according to Andy Beckett, carried out unsuccessful bank robberies and aircraft hijacks at a time of heightened tensions and youth militancy. Bombs were detonated at the US consulate and the tomb of a conservative president, fights broke out between rock fans and squares at a fancy ice-cream parlour in Santiago, and more lastingly, a protest movement coalesced creatively around a number of folk-rock musicians, muralist painters, new media designers, writers and filmmakers such as Víctor Jara, Roberto Matta, Gui Bonsiepe, Ariel Dorfman and Patricio Guzmán.

Equally indelible has been the mark left by student activism. The powerful Student Federation of the University of Chile (FECH) is over a century old, while the National Association of Catholic Students was formed in 1915, the Federation of the University of Concepción (FEC) in 1920, and in the late forties the Federation of the Universidad Técnica del Estado (FEUTE) and the Federation of High School Students of Santiago (FESES), which by 1973 included all the secondary schools of the metropolitan area.

Education and popular politics go hand in hand in Chile: on the one hand literacy has been perhaps the most constant demand of leftist parties and popular movements seeking to extend their electoral base. On the other, the plea for education as a social entitlement and a right has constantly been made from below. This resulted in a gradual increase in school and university education after 1940 that would achieve its highest point during the 1960s and 1970s. On 25 May 1961, a declaration by the students of the Universidad Técnica del Estado established, among other measures: representation of the student community in the design of education policy and the appointment of authorities, freedom of thought, teaching and learning, and academic autonomy. The process would gather further momentum after the student takeover of the School of Architecture at UC-Valparaíso on 15 June 1967, making possible a qualitative leap in teaching, research and international exchange as well as opening the doors of the university to a whole new generation for the first time. The extent of student and youth involvement in the political awakening of those years is demonstrated by the fact that those between the ages of twenty-one and thirty would bear the brunt of counter-revolutionary repression. But it is no surprise that Chile's universities constituted one of the main political battlegrounds, setting a precedent for today's generation of young activists and student movements.[39]

One of those who benefited from Chile's progress in education and international exchanges was a young law student from Leeds named Jack Straw. Having returned to Britain after a six-week stint in Chile, the then aspiring left-wing politician published a substantial article on the Chilean situation for the Labour Party newspaper *Tribune*. He argued: 'The entire underlying trend to Chilean politics is a burning desire for reform. At the last election, Chileans decided they would prefer this reform to be brought about by the more moderate Christian Democrat Party. Now, party loyalties in Chile are very tenuous.' Though perhaps wrong about party loyalties – these were tribal and fierce in Chile compared with Britain, as would emerge in what was to come – Straw was right about one thing: as Frei's reformism stalled and the revolution from below in all its forms – peasant, Mapuche, workerist, extra-parliamentarian, militant, student and countercultural – kept gaining momentum, the Left and Allende appeared as 'the only choice left'.[40]

But nothing guaranteed that Allende would be the left coalition's candidate for the 1970 elections. The leadership of the Socialist Party was sceptical about yet another Allende candidacy; even Allende joked that his epitaph would be 'Here lies the next president of Chile'. To cap it all, in September 1969 the Communist Party proclaimed as its candidate the most admired and world-famous of its leaders, Pablo Neruda. Neruda, who in private was less keen than most about Castro and Guevara, who confronted the revelations about Stalinism as a personal tragedy, sang about 'the [revolutionary] wind from Asia', drank copious amounts of whisky and fine wines, and challenged Jean-Paul Sartre's perceived disgust with the world around him, was a formidable rival.[41] He had fought all previous elections on behalf of Allende, even though he did not think much of his friend's oratory skills; he shared Allende's love for Mexican muralist painting and pre-Columbian art, and was as pleased and surprised every time Allende recited stanzas he himself had forgotten as by Allende's profound knowledge of his *Canto General*.

Although he thought it unlikely that everyone could be rallied around a Communist, Neruda told a crowd gathered below 'the balcony of the headquarters of the Communist Party's Central Committee' in Teatinos Street that he accepted the nomination, for 'I have never conceived my life as divided between poetry and politics.' As Feinstein says, his candidacy made the headlines in Santiago's newspapers, and some abroad. He went on the campaign trail and was 'caught up in the excitement', as he himself put it.[42] The candidacy was, however, conditional on the achievement of an ample and plural coalition, as were those of all the other parties and movements, which for the first time would include not only the Marxist parties but also the centrist Christian Democrat splinter group MAPU and the liberal Radical Party. When Neruda was told that they were withdrawing his candidacy in order to achieve that objective he felt sorry, yet supportive. The various movements had come together around Allende's name under the banner of a Popular Unity coalition (UP). In time, Neruda grew concerned that the fears expressed by the powerful of Chile about an eventual Allende government might turn into active paranoia and violence. As New Year 1970–1 arrived, Neruda told friends he was afraid that Allende, whom he had declared 'the greatest Chilean President since . . . Balmaceda', would suffer the same fate as the Second Spanish Republic.[43]

He had good reasons to be afraid. According to Gabriel García Márquez, as early as 1969 a group of three generals from the

Pentagon had considered the prospects of Allende's victory during a dinner in a house in the suburbs of Washington with five Chilean military officers. The hosts were Lieutenant-Colonel Gerardo López, assistant air force attaché of the Chilean Military Mission to the United States, and members of other branches. The guest of honour was the new director of the Chilean Air Force Academy, General Carlos Toro Mazote. The eight officers dined, García Márquez says, on 'fruit salad, roast veal and peas and drank the warm-hearted wines of their distant homeland to the south, where birds glittered on the beaches while Washington wallowed in snow'. Over dessert, one of the Pentagon generals asked what would happen if someone like Allende were elected. General Toro Mazote replied: 'We'll take La Moneda Palace in half an hour, even if we have to burn it down.'[44]

The mere possibility of Allende's victory and its geostrategic implications were shaping the US agenda in Latin America. According to García Márquez this was not simply a matter of protecting corporate economic interests, even if that was precisely what the Chilean industrialist and media mogul Agustín Edwards had in mind when he travelled to America on the eve of Allende's election. On 14 September 1970 he talked to President Nixon and Henry Kissinger, thanks to his American friends in the corporate world, especially Donald Kendall, then president of PepsiCo. During the meeting at the White House, Edwards appealed for US intervention in Chile.

Like García Márquez, the historian Tanya Harmer downplays the role of the multinational vampires, but she explains the whole affair as a consequence of the fact that Latin America was the US back-yard, an area commonly perceived as underpinning America's superpower status.[45] García Márquez speaks instead of 'much deeper reasons of world politics'.[46] This can be understood as a reference to the counter-revolutionary anxieties that plagued the American mind at the time, the fallout from the situation in Vietnam and Cuba, and the veritable metaphysics of Allende-hating that the current version of the Red Scare had spawned among corporate trusts and their Pentagon friends, as Fidel Castro had explained. But all those things were the ultimate consequence of a much older view of the world according to which some peoples made history and others merely suffered it.

Rather than amounting to a fact, as Harmer says, there was a metaphysical and philosophical construction underlying the idea that the peoples south of the Rio Grande inhabited some sort of no-man's-land or *terra nullius* that could be declared 'the US back-yard'. Few expressed this metaphysics better than Nixon's foreign policy adviser Henry Kissinger. Back in 1969, the grand master of twentieth-century geopolitics told Chile's foreign minister Gabriel Valdés that history had never been made, and would never occur, in the South. The moral implication was that America's historical mission was to make sure history continued to move in the right direction: 'The axis of history starts in Moscow,' Kissinger pontificated, 'goes to Bonn, crosses over to Washington and then goes to Tokyo.'[47] In such a worldview, inherited from the metaphysics of conquest developed in Europe during the Age of Empires, the only place for South America and the Caribbean in world history was no place at all.

The key term in the above assertion is 'no place', a rough translation of the term *terra nullius*. The term refers to a narrative fiction created by sixteenth-century Spanish jurists, Roman Catholic theologians and Genoese financiers on the basis of ancient Roman Law, fragments of Aristotelian philosophy, and the Bible, read from the perspective of their own profit interests, to justify the dispossession of the lands and resources of the indigenous peoples of the Americas as well as their alleged incapacity for government. That fiction was reinvented in the late nineteenth and early twentieth centuries. The American 'Manifest Destiny' doctrine is an example of it.[48]

Buried deep within that fiction is a philosophical problem that concerns on the one hand the ambiguous combination of some old and deep-seated cosmological assumptions about the impact of geography and climate upon the relative advancement of different peoples around the globe, and on the other, some modern ideas about the movement and circulation of commodities. Strung together they created a narrative according to which there were two kinds of peoples in the world: first, the thrifty peoples who shall inherit the earth, last the rest who shall be damned. The tragedy of the native civilisations of the Americas between the sixteenth and the nineteenth centuries, and beliefs about where history happens such as those voiced by Kissinger in 1969, can be understood as consequences – geopolitical and legal, as well as existential – of that shady union between old geographical stereotypes and modern economics.

Geopolitics, as practised by politicians like Kissinger, is a direct late modern successor of the ambiguity that infuses any assertion of place as politically determinant. This is why the Western tradition of international law and the ideas of development and comparative advantage are so central to classical and neoclassical economics.

We know that geography and politics have been closely allied. Originally, they were the two sides of an old cosmological tradition that imagined the globe as a machine, working by more or less mechanical rules that could be discerned rationally and applied as part of a system of Natural Law. The idea of place was crucial to such a tradition, which witnessed and theorised the encounter between Europeans and the native peoples of the Americas.[49] It also informed a newer sense of the accumulation of wealth, of the special worth of (Western) institutions created at the time, as well as the idea of a connection between relative levels of wealth and the location of diverse peoples north and south of the globe. This was oftentimes translated into notions of backwardness and race.

For men like Francisco Pizarro, the Spanish conquistador of the Inca civilisation, geography was not merely a tool for locating and describing the allegedly uninhabited parts of the globe. It also justified violence as higher truth, as the means to bring true civilisation to those who, from that perspective, suffered from a lack of it. There

are echoes of a not too dissimilar sense of moral duty and geography
in Kissinger's 1969 commentary about the lack of history in the
South, or his quip that he saw no reason why a country like Chile
should be allowed to 'go Marxist' merely because 'its people are
irresponsible'.[50]

As explained before, in Greg Grandin's words there was 'a metaphysics of Allende-hating in Washington that went beyond issues of
national security and economics'. Allende, 'horn-rimmed, jowly',
looking a little too dandyish to be a revolutionary, as Grandin says,
'an avowed Marxist who was also an avowed democrat', conformed
neither to the US administration view of a bipolar world nor to
Kissinger's 'axis of history' thesis. An aide at the National Security
Council in those years has declared that no one ever fully grasped
the extent to which Kissinger and most of the relevant officials in
the Nixon government saw Allende as being a far more serious
threat than Fidel Castro.[51]

All kinds of events were happening in and around Washington in
the 1970s, from war in Vietnam to social and racial unrest at home,
and after June 1972 the Watergate scandal that would engulf and
eventually destroy Nixon's political career and legacy. But according to the NSC aide cited by the historian Greg Grandin, 'Chile
scared him' more than anything else.[52] The source of his anxiety was
a more sophisticated version of the Red Scare of the 1940s and the
public image of the popular intellectual: the possibility that having
won the 1970 election, at the end of Allende's term the political
process would work and he would be voted out of office in the
1976 election. Such an outcome would prove that democracy and
socialism were not polar opposites, and that the former could
cohabit with the latter. Thus, Allende was a threat to the US administration not simply because he was a socialist or a communist, but
because he defied such a principle and the very context of the Cold
War and market economics.

Allende was a revolutionary and a democrat, an avowed Marxist
radical reformer, but also a statesman who believed in law and

democracy rather than force. In the eyes of the powerful corporations and their friends in the Chilean military and the Pentagon,
Allende was a silver-tongued liar as effective as the devil himself,
who boasted that he trusted the people's judgement more than that
of any self-appointed vanguard. That kind of combination was too
rare, too strange, too perilous to be allowed to appear possible from
the viewpoint of Cold War politics.[53]

As it turned out, the impossible would happen: on 1 September
1970 Salvador Allende closed his presidential campaign with a
gigantic demonstration that gathered over a million people from
Plaza Italia to Plaza Bulnes in downtown Santiago. As it went on,
the most important voices of the Chilean New Song movement
performed the music of the revolution: Víctor Jara, Inti-Illimani,
Isabel and Ángel Parra, and the world-famous poet Pablo Neruda.
In closing, a chorus of a million voices sang 'Venceremos', the
anthem of Popular Unity. Victory was at hand.

7

The Revolution Will Be Televised

Television played a central role in Chilean electoral politics for the first time in 1970. On Sunday 24 May, the conservative presidential candidate Jorge Alessandri, PDC candidate Radomiro Tomic and leftist nominee Salvador Allende appeared in the programme *Decisión '70* to debate their positions in front of a national TV audience.

At the time, polls published by the influential newspaper *El Mercurio* – owned by the Edwards family – and other mainstream media gave Alessandri an advantage of ten to fifteen points over his rivals. Alessandri's National Party, which included old nationalists with ties to the *nacista* party (the pro-Nazi National Socialist Chilean Movement of the 1940s) and the new young conservatives who were merging the legacy of Francoist Spain with a renewed emphasis on entrepreneurial freedom, had rekindled the 'terror campaign' of the presidential election of 1964. Their TV, radio and press adverts warned the middle classes and the well-off that a victory for Allende would entail the imposition of a Stalinist dictatorship.

The main streets and newsstands of Chile were flooded with images of a weeping Virgin Mary, captioned '*Virgen del Carmen, Queen and Patron of Chile, Deliver Us from Communism!*' Others featured a Soviet tank or a line of red-starred combat jets ready to strike La Moneda presidential palace. These were signed by such organisations as *Acción Femenina de Chile* (Chile's Women's Action), Poder Femenino and Chile's Youth. Later on, a group of young leftist activists entered the offices of a prestigious advertising agency in Santiago and found a cache of documents proving that the agency had received generous funding for these and other parts of the 'terror campaign' from some well-known sources.[1] Chief among them were the multinational Anaconda copper mining corporation, Bank of America, the First National City Bank and Agustín Edwards's newspaper *El Mercurio*. The papers also demonstrated a close link between the 'terror' ad campaign, the fundraisers and Alessandri's men, in particular Sergio Onofre Jarpa, president of the conservative candidate's National Party, successor to the National Action Party that Onofre had founded in 1964 together with former National Socialist Chilean Movement's Jorge Prat Echaurren, also a strong supporter of the Spanish fascist caudillo Francisco Franco.

The damning papers, filed with the parliamentary commission led by the PDC congressman Bernardo Leighton that investigated the campaign, showed that in the space of three weeks the agency had placed adverts in forty radio stations, twenty-two newspapers, over a million billboards in the streets and on the walls of Chile's main cities and towns, distributed a hundred thousand pamphlets by mail, and edited and distributed nine issues of the magazine *Idea*, addressed to middle- and upper-class households, members of the intellectual elite and captains of industry.

In contrast, Allende's campaign relied mostly on the graffiti and muralist brigades, led by the Chilean surrealist painter Roberto Matta, among others, and on the voice of the poets and the folk-rock singers of the burgeoning countercultural scene. This new form of Chilean politics and culture that combined leadership 'from above' with participation 'from below' was a true successor to the creativity displayed on the campaign trail by Carmen Lazo and others during the years of persecution in the late 1940s, and the imagination of the wild young poets and artists of the 1950s such as Alejandro Jodorowsky and Nicanor Parra.

Allende's Popular Unity manifesto spoke of the creation of 'a new culture and a new person', not by decree, but rising 'from

154 STORY OF A DEATH FORETOLD

mankind's struggle against individualism . . . for the people's access to art, literature and means of communication . . . against their thorough commercialisation'.[2] Echoing Guevara's 'new man', the programme linked the transformation of law, the state and social relations with the creation of a new person, a new consciousness and culture. At the heart of such a project of construction and creation was the intricate relation between the city, its public spaces and local places, new forms of communication and regulation, and legal as well as political change. The muralist brigades or *Brigadistas* seized upon this connection, challenging distinctions between high and low culture, between rules of property and what traditional Chilean society considered proper or decent. They claimed the city's streets as sites of social transformation as well as self-realisation, and recognised in tele-technologies the potential to enhance such spaces of freedom, legality and life, from below, here and now.

'I decided to work with these guys because, if things are going to change,' said Roberto Matta, 'the very idea of the museum', of memory and the rules of culture, 'has to change . . . the streets have to be the museum.'[3] For Matta and the other members of the muralist brigades, the given rules of property and decency associated with commerce, capitalism and the images of patriarchal religiosity threatened those public and imaginative spaces in which memory is tied to everyday places, objects, images and gestures with fragmentation, obliteration and oblivion.

This mattered in so far as people – displaced indigenous peoples, migrant peasants and slum-dwellers – orient themselves through their relation with such places, images and objects, and without them are left disoriented. The essence of such relations – horizontal rather than hierarchical, deliberative rather than imposed from above, mediated through the community rather than exclusive – was depicted by Matta in the 4 x 24-metre mural *The First Goal of the Chilean People*, painted in collaboration with the Ramona Parra muralist brigades, one of the most creative groups associated with Allende's UP. The mural portrays the relation between the people and their landscape, as well as between them and Allende, not in the iconic style of the guiding father orienting the childlike masses, which evokes the figures and rules of patriarchal traditional religiosity in society. Rather, in a series of vignettes reminiscent of the style of popular comic books, frolicking naked figures intertwine as if making love in order to give birth to the new man. Accompanying captions read: 'Let's give each other a hand, instead of a fist,' referring to the trauma of conflict and contrasting the violence of the right-wing shock troops active at the time with the declaration of the peaceful option of the people in the pledge for transformation 'within the law' made with Allende, or, as in other works: 'Let's become an inner guerrilla to procreate the new man.' These images declared the urban landscape also an inner space of transformation. They spoke to a new conception of law and regulation, but of memory too, which transcended the notion of limits and normal boundaries to embrace a sense of the new distribution of the elements of society, as well as remedial equality balancing the wrongs of the past.

Searching for memory in the fragmented, war-torn, nuclear-bombed, post-apocalyptic landscapes of our contemporary urban and industrial world (think of the hole in the earth that is the Chuquicamata copper mine, surrounded by workers' ghost towns and prison camps) is 'nothing more than an attempt to master the perceived loss of one's history', as the historian Pierre Nora observes.[4] For Matta and the others, however, we are left with the possibility of new directions: the need and creative ability to read the signs of culture in places marked by the vestiges of the past, ruins remembered in the vicissitudes and struggles of the present, and invested with the intensity of an emerging consciousness that reimagines better futures and new rules out of the urgency of today. The Chilean *Brigadistas* – together with the designers, students and young technophiles riding the countercultural wave of the era, people like Gui Bonsiepe or the young MAPU activist and engineer Fernando Flores – claimed urban landscape in all its forms, including emerging tele-technologies of the image as well as mural painting, graffiti, spoken word and folk music, as a central pillar of political participation and new forms of communication and regulation.

Together, they conceived of the emerging urban landscape of communication as a deeply democratic, consensual and deliberative space for collective problem-solving. Those within it cut across class, race and gender barriers to become politicised, participatory and conscious people who engage with left-wing and right-wing messages and other media output, but always with the aim of sorting out new rules, new laws, and a different order that redraws the lines of separation between political citizenship and activism, militancy and identity, belonging and participation.

Between May and September 1970, the muralist *Brigadistas* launched the initiative 'Amanecer Venceremos' (At Dawn We Shall Triumph), combining text-based messaging and, later on, an elaborate and ephemeral visual language of colour, word and image turned into a potent means of artistic and political communication, part art and part agitprop. Seizing walls originally built to demarcate private property, *Brigadistas* like Matta and the graffiti artist Alejandro 'Monkey' González – working together with non-artists, designers, science and humanities students, militants and so on – stole and 'borrowed' styles with which, according to González, 'we build a language. We reinvent and we work this language into a new context, into a new reality with our own commitments' and new rules.[5]

'I want art that comes from below rather than an art that is imposed from above,' declared Matta to the journal *Ramona*, produced by the brigades.[6] This meant, among other things, that the muralist brigades and the organisations pushing the 'revolution from below', linked to the UP coalition, would fight against right-wing groups, most notably the violent Fatherland and Freedom and the paramilitary ex-Cadet Commandos, for control of public spaces and mass communications.

Originally created in the 1960s in response to the 'terror campaign' activated by the far-right nationalists and their paramilitary groups, the Ramona Parra Brigades and other groups on the side of the left-ist coalition became established during 1968 and 1969, as worldwide student protests and anti-Vietnam war marches made their mark in Santiago de Chile and Valparaíso. They took the initiative during the 1970 presidential election, as the right-wing 'terror campaign' was reactivated. Not only did these and other young activists help uncover the deep connections between the 'terror campaign', foreign money and multinational capital, and the ultra-nationalist parties gathered around the figure of Jorge Alessandri, but they also helped create a network of communication between the movements from below and the leadership above, which would prove decisive during the crucial junctures of Allende's years, especially in 1972. This larger network and framework of meaning and activism provided a fertile soil for some of the most striking experiments in the use of technologies and new media in the service of the transformation of law, state institutions and the public and economic sphere into a shared political community.

The 24 May televised debate before the 1970 election proved disastrous for Alessandri and the right-wing parties. 'Alessandri had just returned from the campaign trail, and against the better judgment of his advisers decided to participate without sufficient preparation,' wrote an American academic observing the 1970 Chilean election who witnessed the TV debate. 'His answers were disconnected, his language lacked articulation, and his habitually coarse personality was on full display, contributing to create the image of an old and ill-tempered man.' In contrast, Allende appeared affable, charming and persuasive. Tomic looked passionate, but perhaps a little too impetuous. 'Allende won the televised debate hands down, even though few of his followers would have a TV set at the time,' Professor Michael J. Francis observed.[7]

On Friday, 4 September 1970, 3.5 million citizens would cast their votes to choose between the economic programme of Alessandri's right wing, the PDC progressive centre, and Allende's left alternative. Alessandri's was a rehashed version of the small-state, private-sector, liberalising policy he had pursued during his 1958–64 first term as president, which had failed disastrously (in spite of that, the historians Collier and Sater call him 'a good manager' who 'did his best').[8] The policy had been given a more radical ideological twist in 1970 by the young conservatives Sergio de Castro and Jaime Guzmán, members of Alessandri's fiercely anti-communist close circle, inspired by the 'liberalising' Falangism of Franco's Spain. The latter was combining, since at least the 1950s, ultra-Catholic ideas about the autonomy of professional medieval guilds with the libertarian–individualist creed of the modern Austro-German school of economics, scepticism about meaningful democracy, and staunch anti-leftism, thereby paving the way for the monetarism and 'shock therapy' economics to come. The ill-tempered image that Alessandri projected on television found its more concrete political expression in his austerity economic policies and law-and-order, furiously anti-communist, stance.

Allende, on the left, promised the people of Chile not merely 'to improve and maintain the regime and the system. We want to change the regime and system and construct a new society on a completely different social and economic foundation.'[9] His pledge was not simply to reform the law so that more things were permitted and wider choice was available to those in a position to choose. Rather, he was pledging a revolutionary use of the law, focusing not just on what is prohibited and allowed but on the law of what is meant by the possibility of a law, that is, the kind of pluralisms it accepts as possible, the kinds of people it counts as participants and fully engaged subjects, and the sorts of spaces it constructs for such people.[10]

In short, Allende was not promising to tinker here and there with the given set of options, but to reorganise all the elements of society into a new set that would seriously take stock of the principle of remedial equality, which argues that something more should be expected of surviving beneficiaries whose unjustly acquired gains continue to appreciate in value generation after generation, even after the perpetrators of past evil are defeated or gone. In the case of Chile in 1970, these beneficiaries were people like Agustín Edwards or the Matte family, but also the copper-mining multinationals and the financiers, who were the current inheritors of the families and conglomerates that had taken possession of natural wealth and resources back in the nineteenth century, on the back of state and privatised violence and plunder, and benefited almost exclusively from them.

As happened in the case of Chile in the 1970s, people like Agustín Edwards may be capable of activating the security and intelligence apparatus in the hands of their far more powerful American friends. This means that they were and are not merely passive satellites, even though their relation was and is hierarchical. It is also the case that, for all its might, its nuclear weapons and investment banks, America cannot simply 'switch on' its friends in Santiago, people like Edwards, or individuals among the politicians and the military, and oblige them to march to its tune.

Power relations are always much more nuanced and complicated than that. According to the philosopher and historian Michel Foucault, who delivered some important lectures on the subject in Latin America during the 1970s, power relations are ultimately about persons, not just systems or abstract structures. Power relations are about subjecting oneself to others, as well as to places, images and objects, becoming a person in solitude, and retreating from certain subjections and ways of being with others.

Similarly, law and politics, which act on persons at an intimate level in so far as they choose some and relegate others, always deal with force or violence of a certain kind – state or police violence, the force exercised by intelligence services and investigative security agencies – which is, strictly speaking, lawful violence (even when laws and rights are suspended, as in the 'states of emergency' of our age of anxiety and terror), in that it 'contributes to the creation of that which it is used against [and] . . . which it captures'.[11]

This subjective conception of law and power relations is much closer to the understanding of the muralist *Brigadistas* and creative activists engaged in the politics of Chile in the late 1960s and 1970s. They understood their relation with city streets, walls and public spaces, but also with communication, as an inner space as much as an external landscape. The 'new man' and the new political culture they sought to bring about, together with Allende, was in this sense not only interpersonal but also infra-personal and extra-personal. In other words, their aim was to produce a new collective assemblage, a new set, and a subjectivity that would be both more human and more than human. This concept is the key to making sense of the fascination that the emerging sciences of automation and self-regulated activity – for instance cybernetics, the study of self-regulated artificial, biological and social systems, and the exploration of the concurrent forms of behaviour evident in the activity of larger groups – exercised in the minds of many among those engaged in the Chilean Revolution, including Allende. This is the new subject depicted in Matta's *The First Goal of the Chilean People*. It is also the wider conception of subjectivity, law and revolution encapsulated in Guevara's notion of the 'new man', which Allende made his own and placed at the heart of his promise to the Chilean people.

Concretely speaking, Allende's promise meant: meaningful agrarian reform; full nationalisation of various industries – for instance mining and finance, but also the media – that since the nineteenth century had been exclusively in the hands of multinational corporations and their local beneficiaries; and the re-articulation of social as well as foreign relations (including economic relations) in terms of solidarity and remedial or reparative global justice. His Christian Democrat opponent in the 1970 election, Radomiro Tomic, standing on behalf of an exhausted governing Christian Democratic Party, ran on a platform that according to Greg Grandin was 'not dissimilar to Allende's'.[12]

As a result of this convergence between Allende's and Tomic's programmes, almost 2 million Chileans, 64.1 per cent of the electorate, voted to raise the minimum wage, to increase spending on education, healthcare and pensions, to distribute large haciendas and *fundos* or landholdings to their original indigenous custodians and to peasants, and to deepen participatory democracy both within the state and at the level of communication and economic production, which included nationalisation as well as the overhaul of the rules of international and economic relations, compensation and so on, as well as the creation of new spaces of deliberation and expression. Out of that wider support for the programme of change, Allende obtained 36.3 per cent of the vote, and Tomic 27.8 per cent.

In a reversal of the situation in 1958 – when Alessandri had won by a slim margin of some 30,000 votes – this time Allende came out ahead of the right-wing candidate by almost 40,000 votes. Allende won in the areas of the country with the highest concentration of workers and peasants, with high percentages in Tarapacá (48.8 per cent), Antofagasta (45.9 per cent), Concepción (48.3 per cent) and in the traditionally indigenous area of Arauco (55.7 per cent). He lost in the two biggest cities: to Alessandri in Santiago, and to Tomic in Valparaíso. His weakness was the female literate vote: he obtained only 30.5 per cent of the women's vote, compared with 41.6 per cent among men. But Allende's overall support was consistent: only in the Cautín province did his vote fall below 29 per cent.

Did Allende misinterpret his mandate, launching too radical a programme for reform without wider electoral support? One way of answering this question is to compare it with the British situation. Today's ruling party in Britain, the Conservative Party, obtained in the last general election of 2010 only 36.1 per cent of the electoral vote, slightly less than Allende did in 1970. And yet, in the opinion of many, it is carrying out a programme of reform more radical than that put into practice by Margaret Thatcher. It is also the case that during the two most recent general elections in British history, the parties allowed to form a government have done so with an average support of only a third of the electorate. In 2005, for instance, the Labour Party had obtained 35.2 per cent of the vote against 32.4 per cent for the Conservatives.[13]

Under the rules of the British Constitution, if none of the parties obtain a clear majority they must prove their capacity to gather wider support in the House of Commons, and subject to the approval of the monarch they may go on to form a government. Hence the current coalition government, which comprises the Conservative winners in the election and the Liberal Democrats who had come third in 2010 with 23 per cent of the vote. Something similar happened under the rules of the Chilean Constitution in 1970. Given that none of the parties obtained a clear and absolute majority, and in the absence of a monarch, it falls to the National Congress to establish which of the two parties with the highest support – in this case Allende's UP and Alessandri's Nationalists – may form a government, rule the country, and legitimately carry out its programme until the end of the constitutional term. In Chile, the conventional rule commands that the candidate who has gained the majority of popular votes should be allowed by Congress to form a government, just as in the most recent British general election it was widely accepted that the Conservatives who had gained the majority of the votes should have the first crack at forming a government. Nevertheless, it was crucial for the UP to obtain the support of the twenty Senators and fifty-five Congress deputies of the PDC to secure Allende's designation as president.

On 5 September, the third contender and PDC candidate Radomiro Tomic visited Allende in his residence, and recognised his victory and legitimacy in writing. In the afternoon, Allende gave a press conference expressing his gratitude for Tomic's support and his recognition of the UP's victory and legitimacy to form a government. This seemingly symbolic act can be interpreted as an analogy with the British conventions that guide the conversations, visits and expressions of support between party leaders after a 'hung parliament' leading to the formation of coalition governments; these constitutional conventional rules are non-enforceable and therefore could be said to be symbolic. What matters is the fact of recognition by other parties in Parliament or Congress, often meaning the third contender, and that fact is considered sufficient to justify forming a government, and applying the political programme established in the relevant manifestos. Something similar happened in Chile in 1970.

Another answer to the question concerning Allende's legitimacy to put into practice his programme for reform is to point out that an absolute majority of the voters supported the very similar programmes put to them by Allende and Tomic, and that effectively more than 62 per cent of the electorate voted for radical reform. This is Greg Grandin's position. According to him 'by 1970, electoral democracy in Chile meant socialism'.[14]

In the end, an agreement between the Christian Democrats and Allende's Popular Unity paved the way for Congressional recognition and the designation of Salvador Allende as the legitimate president of Chile. The PDC rejected calls to form an anti-leftist coalition with the right-wing Nationalists, and on 21 October ordered its Senators and deputies in Congress to give Allende their full support. On 24 October 1970 the votes of 195 parliamentarians resolved the impasse: Salvador Allende gained 153 votes, Alessandri only 35, and there were seven abstentions (*voto en blanco*). At 11:48 a.m. that day, PDC congressman Tomás Pablo proclaimed Salvador Allende as president of the Republic for the term beginning 3 November 1970 and ending 3 November 1976.

But in the interregnum between election day and Allende's confirmation, the spectre of political violence reared its head. The director of public relations for the multinational telecommunications corporation ITT (today's ATT), Hal Hendrix, wrote to the company's senior vice-president E. J. Gerrity warning:

unless there's a move on the part of elements within the Chilean military in a week or so, the consensus in Santiago is that Salvador

Allende will be designated President of the Republic by Congress on 24 October . . . The possibilities of a coup are unclear, but exist . . . the key person is General Roberto Viaux.[15]

Hendrix, as well as the other multinational giants with interests in Chile, feared that the Allende administration would harm their businesses and that the economy would collapse in the following months, wiping out their investments and future profits. A branch of ITT in Peru had been nationalised recently. The telecommunications behemoth had been running Chile's telephone network since 1930, and by 1970 its assets and investment interests were worth some 150 million dollars. The stakes were as high for ITT as for the other US-based multinationals.

Within eleven days of Allende's electoral victory in Chile the president of the Pepsi Cola Company, Donald Kendall, who had given Richard Nixon his first corporate account as a young lawyer in New York, discussed with Agustín Edwards (who would work as vice-president of PepsiCo until 1973), David Rockefeller of Chase Manhattan Bank, the directors of ITT and Nixon's security adviser Henry Kissinger the fate of Chilean democracy.

On 15 September 1970, Kissinger, Director of Central Intelligence Richard Helms and Attorney General John Mitchell met with Richard Nixon in the Oval Office.[16] Nixon wanted to prevent Allende taking office, and if that should happen he made it clear that he wanted the Chilean president out by any and all means necessary. 'Not concerned risks involved . . . No involvement of Embassy . . . $10,000,000 available more if necessary . . . Make the economy scream,' read the notes taken during the meeting by CIA director Helms.[17]

Given the task of overseeing the operation, Henry Kissinger moved fast to implement Nixon's directive under the code-name 'Track II'. 'Track II' designated the blunt approach now chosen by the American president – aimed at provoking a military coup, ultimately by backing a violent putschist plot against Chile's legally minded commander-in-chief of the army, General René Schneider, in order to clear the way for an interventionist role on the part of the armed forces together with some ultra-nationalist civilians. The declared goal was to establish a military regime. Any notion that the Americans hoped for a quick return to democracy or an interim liberal government, but could not have predicted that the violence unleashed by Track II would get out of control, as alleged for instance by the historian Mark Falcoff, is both historically false and in any case does not clear those involved of either legal or ethical responsibility.

Peter Kornbluh's *The Pinochet File* and Tanya Harmer's *Allende's Chile and the Inter-American Cold War* have shown, with ample and meticulous documentation, that Washington 'wanted authoritarian rule patterned on Brazil's dictatorship and a war against the left as the only remedy to reverse' what US officials saw as the inevitable damage done by an Allende administration in the region.[18] Nixon's and Kissinger's fingerprints can be seen all over: a mass of leaked and declassified documents show that they wanted a coup, funded a coup, and worked with Chilean nationalist politicians to derail Allende's confirmation or overthrow him, and with young, fanatically anti-communist activists connected to Alessandri's National Party as well as to the paramilitary Fatherland and Freedom, and members of the military and the media, to stage a coup. In general, they gave Allende's opponents a critical push, a 'little edge' as Nixon's top diplomat in the region put it, albeit hidden from view.[19] As Kant would say, the fact that it was hidden makes them all the more responsible. They set in motion a chain of events whose lethal outcome redounds on them, even if there is no brief memo from, say, Kissinger to General Viaux or his friend Pinochet with the words 'kill them all' scribbled on it.

Track II, subversion and violence, did entail a distinction from the more subtle procedures of diplomacy, or 'Track I', which involved using embassy channels to persuade members of the Chilean Congress, especially the Nationalist conservatives, to act within the framework of the Constitution to compel PDC support and confirm Alessandri. At some point, this plan included Alessandri's commitment that upon his designation he would not take office and new elections would be called, in which the nationalists and the PDC would present a common front under a PDC candidate.

The distinction between Track I and Track II is, however, wafer-thin. The fact is that the civilians effectively involved in Track II through their contacts in the Chilean military belonged to paramilitary groups such as Fatherland and Freedom that were also hand in glove with Alessandri's National Party and with the young conservatives who were part of Alessandri's inner circle, such as Federico Willoughby – who had been Alessandri's adviser since 1958, and throughout the campaign – and Jaime Guzmán. Their activities connected with Track II, including the use of terrorist tactics and force, would therefore reach straight to Track I, which involved getting Alessandri confirmed by Congress.

From their perspective, if not that of the Americans in Washington, Track I and Track II were the two sides of a plan in which the means were effectively indistinguishable – as was also clear from the US presidential directive to use each and every means of violence, from direct force to financial violence. The different timetables were complementary and shared one single aim: oust Allende. According to Greg Grandin, Nixon's CIA told its operatives in Santiago to use 'every stratagem, every ploy, however bizarre', to induce a coup. They were also told to 'play up' Cuban and Soviet involvement in Chile.[20] At best, the only real difference between Tracks I and II is that in the latter case the American government kept its own embassy in the dark.

From the American perspective, the distinction between Track I and Track II also reveals the different reading of the Chilean situation by the US State Department, which thought intelligence about Allende's imminent victory was exaggerated, and the CIA, which viewed the State Department's stance on Chile and the threat that the Eastern socialist bloc would pose to the US in the case of the birth of another Marxist state in the Americas as at best naive and in any case ignorant. As it happens, they were both wrong: Allende did win the 1970 election, but neither was Allende's Socialist Party a client of Moscow, nor would the Eastern bloc led by the USSR exert any significant influence over its government; it would most likely be perceived as a 'Titoist' or independent socialist state, as Kissinger himself had recognised. Such disagreements between the US State Department and the CIA would characterise American operations in Chile until at least 1973. But they all agreed on one thing: Allende must go.

The prevailing, condescending, view among the members of the US government was that Americans not only were wiser and more capable of governance but had a duty to save the irresponsible, reckless and vulnerable Latin Americans. Secretary of State Dean Acheson had asserted: 'we must concede that harsh governmental measures of repression may be the only answer; that these measures may have to proceed from regimes whose origins and methods would not stand the test of American concepts of democratic procedure.' The State Department's George Kennan saw Latin America as a hapless blend of Indian populations, barbarous Spanish conquistadors and 'Negro slave elements', all of which proved to be 'handicaps to human progress' and contributed to 'create the illusion of desperate courage, supreme cleverness, and a limitless virility where the more constructive virtues are so conspicuously lacking'. When Allende won, the US Foreign Intelligence Advisory Board – and especially Nelson Rockefeller, Kissinger's former boss – could not understand why they had failed to 'arrange the election'.[21]

On 15 October 1970, Henry Kissinger was informed that General Roberto Viaux, a Chilean army officer with ties to the far-right Fatherland and Freedom group in Alessandri's National Party, would be willing to take on the job of removing General René Schneider, commander-in-chief of the army at the moment of the presidential election of 1970. Schneider was a constitutionalist – one of many members of the armed forces respectful of the Constitution, and adamantly opposed to any prospect of a coup. As such, he was perceived by Viaux and his friends as an obstacle to any attempt to pit the armed forces against the democratically elected president.

Brigadier General Roberto Viaux, chief of the army division of the northern city of Antofagasta, had come to notice a year earlier. On 21 October 1969 he seized command of the Tacna regiment in Santiago de Chile after being accused of plotting against the Christian Democrat government of Eduardo Frei. Viaux was a good friend of General Augusto Pinochet. After his experience as director of the Pisagua Camp (where prisoners thought of him as a man of democratic convictions, doing his job but not particularly obsessed with communists), Pinochet went to Ecuador as part of a diplomatic mission, and taught geopolitics at the War Academy in Santiago. Upon his return from the US in 1969 he was promoted to brigadier general and interim head of the Sixth Army Division posted in the northern city of Iquique. It was while holding the post of military governor of the region that he clashed with communist student activists. Pinochet visited General Viaux several times in Antofagasta and stayed in his residence prior to the events of October 1969.

Arguably, Pinochet knew about his friend's intentions in October 1969, though in his memoirs *The Road Travelled (El camino recorrido)* he barely mentions the incident. Conveniently, at the time of Viaux's attempted coup in 1969 Pinochet had withdrawn to Santiago, and not even his subordinates in Iquique knew where he was. In an interview published posthumously, Pinochet stated: '[Viaux] wanted to get me on board marching southward to take over the government. "You're talking nonsense," I said . . . "there are two thousand kilometres to Santiago and on the way they can tear us to pieces . . . forget it."'[22] Thus, on 21 October 1969, Pinochet, the former camp director with a keen sense for opportunity, simply dropped out of sight.

Viaux's actions at the time were motivated not by ideology but economic interest. The situation of the Chilean military had deteriorated markedly during the 1960s, and showed no great improvement during Frei's centrist government. Only after Viaux was promised that officers' salaries would be raised and after the commander-in-chief resigned, did he surrender; the 1969 putsch might have failed but Viaux gained respect and recognition. Following the agreement between Frei and Viaux, the latter was discharged and General Schneider designated commander-in-chief of the Chilean armed forces, mainly because of his known and well-respected constitutionalist stance.

A few hours later, Pinochet reappeared in Iquique. Thereafter, Pinochet withdrew once more into the background (in his memoirs he says he defended his friend Viaux after the failed coup, but there's no evidence of any complaints on his part), followed orders, continued to make his way up the military ladder by being most favoured under Allende's administration, and kept a careful watch on the direction of prevailing winds. His friend Viaux, on the other hand, stayed firmly set on a collision course.

On 27 September 1970, the CIA sent four 'false-flag' officers to Chile, tasked to get in touch with Chilean military officers – a mission too problematic, if discovered, for local CIA operatives.[23] They contacted at least twenty-one officers in the military as well as the Carabineros police force, who were given assurances 'of strong support at the highest levels of US government'.[24] Of these, the CIA maintained communications with General Viaux, 'who has a certain mystique within the Army', according to US ambassador Edward Korry, and two serving officers, General Camilo Valenzuela of the Santiago garrison and General Vicente Huerta of the Carabineros.[25] The CIA concluded that Viaux had 'extensive support among non-communists and junior officers'. The 'non-communists' referred to here are in fact the fanatically anti-leftist core of Alessandri's National Party, former *nacistas* and younger ultra-Catholic supporters of the Franco regime in Spain.

Another CIA memo observed that since Chile's armed forces were led by a man who respected the constitutionality and legitimacy of Allende, those opposed to the president-elect lacked a serving senior officer to centralise the plot and 'looked to General Viaux for inspiration'. The general, and his friends in Fatherland and Freedom, were 'in touch with active duty army officers who may or may not decide to move'. In noting that a plan led by Viaux would not succeed without the active involvement of the army, and furthermore that the leadership of General Schneider prevented such involvement, the CIA false-flaggers were at the very least suggesting the way forward for 'Operation Fubelt', as Track II was now formally called.[26]

Fearing that a coup led by Viaux might not yield the desired results, and knowing that the Communist Party of Chile had agents of their own infiltrated among Viaux and his agitators, the CIA operatives turned to General Valenzuela.[27] He arranged a meeting with General Schneider on the evening of 16 October, in a last-ditch attempt to persuade the constitutionalist leader of the army of the need for the military to intervene in order to oust Allende. By then, the CIA had concluded that 'the Viaux solution' was the most viable option, though the most likely outcome would be the division of the armed forces, perhaps civil war, and the evidence of US involvement coming to light.

'You have asked us to provoke chaos in Chile. Thru Viaux solution we provide you with formula for chaos which unlikely to be bloodless. To dissimulate US involvement will clearly be impossible,' read a cable sent from Santiago to Langley on 10 October 1970. 'Station [CIA] team, as you know, has given most serious consideration to all plans suggested by HQs counterparts. We conclude that none of them stand even a remote chance of achieving [US government] objective. Hence, Viaux gamble, despite high risk factors, may commend itself to you.'[28] The cable establishes that the CIA had opted for the Viaux plan, in spite of its shortcomings, but also makes it clear that his position vis-à-vis General Schneider's leadership made it unlikely the outcome would be as secret and clean as Washington would prefer.

What transpires from the CIA cables of the period is the

realisation that although Viaux was willing to act, and kept trying, the major problem he confronted was 'a sure way of containing the high command', especially Gen. Schneider in the early hours of a coup attempt. The cable also mentions the difficulty of finding a 'method of controlling the pro-Allende mobs which very probably would swarm through downtown Santiago in the event of a coup attempt'.[29] In short, the US-sponsored Operation Fubelt aiming to thwart the will of the Chilean electorate confronted two problems: Schneider's presence and Chile's people.

For a coup to succeed, then or later, two things were necessary: a coup before the coup, one that would neutralise General Schneider and those within the armed forces who could oppose the idea of a military intervention against the Constitution; but also a method to contain or at least immobilise the people. Silencing the people, instilling fear in their souls, and inducing despair and uncertainty in their everyday lives – for instance, by strangling Chile's economy and specifically its ability to provide the most basic supplies and foodstuffs – would do the trick. The design for getting rid of Allende was complete even before he had a chance to mismanage the economy or let the momentum of the revolution from below spin out of control.

The meeting between General Valenzuela and General Schneider 'turned out [to be] a complete fiasco'.[30] What came later reveals what this meant: not only must General Schneider have refused to take part in the coup, but now that he knew about Track II and most likely also about the US involvement, he had become a liability. The following night, Valenzuela sent one of his men to meet up with the US defence attaché in a back alley in Santiago to put his plans for direct action in motion. Like Viaux's, it involved kidnapping Schneider, provoking Frei's immediate resignation and exile, and forming a military junta that would dissolve Congress until further notice. The fact that General Valenzuela was at pains to convince his fellow plotters that this would be 'their only unconstitutional act', as a CIA cable put it at the time, shows how uncertain it was that the entirety of the armed forces were ready to abandon their commitment to respect the Chilean people.[31] However, the CIA's cable glosses over a no less significant fact: that given the level of support for Allende among the people of Chile, any action by the military and the nationalists to rob him of the presidency would inevitably result in the repression by draconian means of a significant percentage of the Chilean population. To suggest that there could be a bloodless coup is sheer bad faith. This was to be no bloodless intervention, no mere attempt at kidnapping, followed by a frictionless transition.

Christopher Hitchens is right in pointing out that the kidnap plot was really a hit, organised murder. No one asked what would happen to General Schneider after his kidnapping (supposedly he would be flown to Argentina, which cuts no ice: he knew too much), but no one would be naive enough to misunderstand what they were supposed to do if Kissinger's spooks came up with hand grenades and untraceable machine guns.[32]

In May 1970, Schneider had told an interviewer from *El Mercurio* that the army would respect the constitutional process, and would make no attempt to intervene or interrupt it.[33] After the election results gave Allende a lead over his political rivals, Schneider stated at a meeting of the Chiefs of Staff that 'the armed forces are not a road to political power nor an alternative to that power. They exist to guarantee the regular work of the political system and the use of force for any other purpose than its defence constitutes high treason.'[34] A few days later, on 19 September 1970, Schneider reiterated his position in favour of the constitutional route in his public address to the military during the army's annual celebrations: 'There are no options that would invite the armed forces to undo what the politicians had wrought in Chile.'[35] And on the evening of 16 October he flatly refused General Valenzuela's invitation to do the opposite. His moral consistency, and respect for law and democracy, set him on a collision course with Washington's designs.

According to Hitchens's version of the events of the evening of

17 October 1970, the US defence attaché met in secret with two Chilean armed forces officers linked to Fatherland and Freedom and General Viaux, who was aware of the plans drawn by General Valenzuela. As it turned out, their plans were exactly the same. They informed the agent that the move on General Schneider would happen in the next couple of days and asked the US attaché to 'furnish them with eight to ten tear gas grenades (. . .) and three 45 calibre machine guns ("grease guns") with 500 rounds of ammo each', as stated in a CIA cable sent to Kissinger's Track II group from Santiago on 18 October 1970.[36] 'We are being watched by Allende's supporters. They suspect us. Now it's the time to move,' the Chilean officers said. 'That's fine by us,' replied the US attaché, 'but we need assurances that you have widespread support.' One of the Chilean officers had come late to the meeting that night, having taken evasive action to shake a couple of taxicabs with dual antennas that were tailing him. He said that communist agents were on to him.

The army men informed him they had no co-conspirators in the air force. The CIA had been trying to bring on board Chilean Air Force General Gustavo Leigh; no luck so far, but it kept on trying. 'Unless they act now they are lost,' the CIA Santiago station told Kissinger's Track II group in an 18 October cable.

> Our reasoning is that our asset is dealing with active duty officers. We cannot tell who is the leader of this movement but strongly suspect it is Admiral [Deleted]. Hence it is important that our asset's credibility with [armed forces officers] be strengthened by prompt delivery of what they requesting. Request headquarters agreement by 1500 hours local time 18 Oct on decision delivery of tear gas (. . .) request prompt shipment three sterile 45 calibre machine guns and ammo, by special courier if necessary. Please confirm.[37]

The CIA spooks did not have to wait long for a reply. A cable dated 18 October confirmed: 'sub-machine guns and ammo being sent by regular [deleted] courier leaving Washington 0700 hours 19 October due to arrive Santiago late evening 20 October or early morning 21 October.'[38] The weapons were delivered at 0200 hours on 22 October.

On the evening of 19 October an attempt on General Schneider was thwarted when he decided to leave the dinner party he was attending in a private car rather than use his official vehicle. General Viaux, his protégé Captain Arturo Marshal and Fatherland and Freedom were behind the attempt, aided by members of the Valenzuela group. This prompted a telling cable from Washington to the local station in Chile 'asking for urgent action because [CIA] Headquarters must respond during morning 20 October to queries from high levels [meaning Kissinger, as confirmed by CIA cover operations director Thomas Karamessines later on, during his deposition before a senatorial committee].' Payments of $50,000 each to General Viaux and his chief associate were then authorised on condition that they made another attempt.[39]

On the evening of 20 October they tried and failed again. At last, on 22 October 1970, the 'sterile' machine guns put by Washington in the hands of General Roberto Viaux and his gang ended the life of General René Schneider. This time, General Schneider used the official car. The vehicle was intercepted at a crossroads in the capital Santiago. The attempted kidnap came to nothing when General Schneider drew his army-issue gun to defend himself and was shot at point-blank range several times in the chest. He was taken to hospital and died of his wounds the next day. As far as the Chilean military police was concerned, this was, as it had been planned from the very beginning, a hit.

The CIA Santiago station was unsure whether the assassination had been premeditated or constituted a botched abduction, but they knew that Valenzuela, Viaux and their associates had been 'fully clued in'.[40] The CIA did worry that the weapons it had given to Valenzuela and Viaux were the ones used to kill Schneider. These were 'sterile' guns, meaning they had been made untraceable, unlike the army-issue weapons that the Chilean army officers and the Fatherland and Freedom thugs had access to. What would be the purpose of making guns untraceable if they were not meant for use in a murder? At the very least, even if the aim was not spelled out, the idea that to kidnap an armed and experienced soldier carried no risk of killing him is disingenuous. The sole grounds for doubting whether the CIA's weapons did not, in fact, kill Schneider are the assurances of the CIA Chilean asset, who may or may have not been among the perpetrators, that the machine guns and the grenades were still in '[name deleted]'s home and never given to anybody'.[41]

However, according to Hitchens, after the killing Colonel Paul Wimert, the US defence attaché in Santiago and chief CIA liaison with the Valenzuela group, retrieved the two payments of $50,000 that had been paid to the Fatherland and Freedom thugs and the three 'sterile' weapons. Taking his car he drove at full speed to the coastal town of Viña del Mar, and once there, he threw the machine guns into the ocean.

It has been alleged that Washington did not mean Schneider to be killed, and that in fact it 'turned off' General Viaux after a meeting on 15 October. A directive was issued that:

the Agency must get a message to Viaux warning him against precipitate action. In essence our message was to state: 'We have reviewed your plans, and based on your information and ours, we come to the conclusion that your plans for a coup at this time cannot succeed. Failing, they may reduce your capabilities for the future. Preserve your assets. We will stay in touch. The time will come when you with all your other friends can do something. You will continue to have our support.[42]

Whatever the alleged intentions hidden between the lines of what was said during the 15 October meeting in Washington and communicated to the CIA station in Chile, the fact of the matter is that General Viaux's people were incited by it to redouble their efforts to provoke a coup. The point, as the memorandum of that day's meeting and the 20 October cable sent to Santiago confirm, was to discourage Viaux 'from acting alone', and 'to encourage him to join forces with other coup planners so that they may act in concert either before or after 24 October'. Rather than to 'turn off' the plot, the aim was to spur the military rebels to bring on board more sympathisers.[43]

Did Track II fail? Yes, but only if measured against the immediate aim of stopping Allende from taking office. However, that was not its main goal. The main goal was to provoke a coup. And here as we have seen there were two key obstacles: Schneider's presence, and the will of the people of Chile. The first obstacle had been removed. The next step was to remove the second, to break the will of the Chilean people to rally behind Allende.

How? Recall the instruction given to CIA director Helms in the Oval Office on 15 September 1970: 'make the economy scream'. It was now time to silence the vibrant voices and the imagination of the people – captured in the murals of the streets of Santiago and Valparaíso, and in the experiments of the young scientists and designers inventing new forms of self-regulation with new technologies of communication, as well as in the actions of the revolution from below, all of them hopeful and capable of 'dreaming reality'.[44] The next move of the plotters was to instil fear in the souls of the people, induce despair and uncertainty in their everyday lives, and replace the hopes of 1970 and 1971 with fear and scarcity.

For instance, by strangling Chile's economy and specifically its ability to provide the most basic foodstuffs and materials for labour. And if the people did not heed the message, if they were to respond and behave badly and disruptively, then some corrective violence would be necessary.[45] That inquisitorial brutality could only take place in the name of slaying an evil creature: namely communism. It is a matter of persuading people that this violence is necessary, inevitable, like the absolute peace of terror or deterrence, or in any case, the lesser of two evils. It would operate against an unspecified enemy: 'communism', the 'Jewish–Masonic–Bolshevik plot', the 'atheist cabal' conspiring against Christian civilisation, unnameable 'terrorists', and the 'South' or the 'Third World' in which history does not take place.

This would all be done for the sake of law and political order. Law and politics become then, to invert Clausewitz's formula, the continuation of war by other means: the moment when technology stops making individual freedom possible for the mass of the population, unleashing instead the limitless power of total war and emergency regulation to raise up some and relegate others.[46] The trick is to persuade a country like Chile, to beat it into people's heads, as Ariel Dorfman put it, that if no real peace and security await at the other end, then at least organised insecurity and programmed catastrophe do. Once persuaded, 'too many people tend to shrug their shoulders' – looking the other way while their leaders unleash the Furies of violence in the name of stability and security.[47]

In The Flies, his 1943 adaptation of the Greek legend of Orestes, Jean-Paul Sartre described exactly this situation. Orestes the exile returns to the city to incite revolt among the people whose apathy has enabled the crimes of its leaders. In Sartre's play, the flies represent the Furies; their intervention is part of the process, a trial by fire. Such was the process that would begin in Chile with the October Strike of 1972.

8

The Flies, Act I

By the end of 1971, a year into Allende's presidency, the fears expressed by the powerful 'Import-Export coalition' to their American friends about the imminent collapse of the Chilean economy under a leftist government had not materialised. If anything, the opposite was happening: unemployment had fallen from 8.3 per cent in September 1970 to 3.8 per cent in November 1971, when Allende celebrated his first year in government before a gigantic popular rally in Santiago's National Stadium. In Santiago alone, only 5,000 unemployed remained of the previous year's 87,000. In terms of wealth redistribution, the income of working households had risen to 59 per cent of the national income, while inflation fell from 33 per cent in September 1970 to 15 per cent. Industrial production grew 12.1 per cent, the highest percentage in a decade. Mining production had increased around 10 per cent, while agriculture had grown between 4 and 5 per cent. Chile's Gross National Product soared by almost 8.3 per cent, compared with its average 2.7 per cent between 1967 and 1970.[1]

Together with the control of inflation and an important reduction in unemployment, these advances along the *via chilena* 'had won the Popular Unity a rapid increase in popular support', according to Peter Winn.[2] This was reflected in the improved political position of the UP by the end of 1971. In the municipal elections of April 1971, the UP coalition obtained 49.7 per cent of the electoral vote, nearly two points more than the opposition. Unfortunately for the UP, the boundary distribution of constituencies as well as the legal complexities of the electoral system in place meant that this victory would not translate into an improvement in the UP's position in Congress. It continued to control only one-third of the Senate and two-fifths of the lower Chamber. However, the electoral strength of the UP did impress the centrist Christian Democrats, whose leader Radomiro Tomic proposed that the UP and the PDC should field a common candidate for the Valparaíso by-election. Allende accepted, but was overruled by his own coalition. Allende also missed the opportunity to push legislative proposals to reform Congress, strengthen the presidency, replace the at best outdated electoral system, and even call for a plebiscite convoking a constitutional 'People's Assembly' tasked with reforming the Constitution, all of which were part of the UP manifesto. Given its electoral momentum, it might well have won such a plebiscite. In the end he did not go ahead with it. As Collier and Sater say, it was a serious miscalculation.[3]

The most spectacular gains took place in the so-called 'Social Area' of the economy, which included expropriated industries managed by the workers themselves. Allende considered as priorities of his government such legal measures as the nationalisation of resources controlled by American capital, finance, the expropriation of public utilities and monopolies, the establishment of a minimum wage (equal for workers, peasants and employees), the elimination of unemployment, and genuine agrarian reform. Nationalised resources and expropriated industries would constitute the Social Area of the economy co-existing with the privatised and state-owned sectors. Another goal of his administration was to pave the way towards the 'full exercise of power' by workers and popular sectors in the management of the production units of the Social Area, and – especially for the Socialist Party – the construction of a new system of self-regulation known as 'Popular Power'.

At the time, the concrete shape that such 'Popular Power' could take was not altogether clear. This lack of clarity disclosed the problem that Guevara, among others, had criticised back in 1965: the lack of a blueprint for the management and non-capitalist operation of the economy, as well as a regulatory framework appropriate for the tasks of the revolutionary transformation of law, society and the state.[4]

The problem was not the absence of a 'theory of the state' in the corpus of Marxist political philosophy, as some thinkers of the Left believed at the time. After all, countries like Great Britain seemed to do pretty well at governing themselves as well as others without the need for anything resembling a theory of the state. The English do not have a written constitution defining the form of the state, complete with a narrative of its origins and goals, as other countries do (for instance, the US), but they have developed workable principles of government, which can be added to or removed according to circumstances. The issue was how to develop principles applicable to the tasks of socialist transformation − 'transition', in the parlance of the time. If the creation of a Social Area of the economy was to become a viable reality, it would require 'a qualitative change in property relations and a redefinition of social relations . . . and this process has a human, political and economic significance', as Allende put it.[5] This entails a sense of urgency as well as a 'high degree of responsibility' on the part of the workers, which was all the more urgent given the hostile environment in which socialists in government found themselves.[6]

On 28 January 1971, Allende alluded to this urgency when he remarked that 'the political parties of the left and the workers must take stock of the fact that they are now in government; they must confront reality, and in particular take into account the historical lesson according to which those who exercised power will not let it go willingly.' He was referring to the violent events of late 1970. Allende said: 'this morning in Santiago, a team of forensic investigators reconstructed the scene of the crime that resulted in the assassination of the Commander-in-Chief of the Army, General René Schneider. We must understand the meaning of such an event.' Allende explained that, in the short run, Schneider's murder had strengthened the constitutionalist view in the armed forces and isolated the reactionary sectors of Chilean politics, facilitating the UP's confirmation. But in the long run, it meant the assassins' goal was to do away with the people's government. 'I was the target, I'm the one who should have been murdered,' he said. In such a situation, discipline, realistic expectations, in short, the mentality of being a government, was crucial.[7]

Constructing Social Area of the economy would be the main task of government. It would comprise the giant copper-mining industries, nitrates, iron and coal, the finance sector, commerce and trade, strategic monopolies, and the economic activities that conditioned social and economic development, such as energy and oil, construction, communications, paper and transport. To operate this sector alongside an area of private property and another one of mixed property was a daunting task. It required, as the Chilean jurist and Allende's chief adviser Eduardo Novoa Monreal put it, 'the invention of new blueprints for development geared towards the construction of socialism'.[8]

The fact that a lawyer was one of the main architects of the Chilean Way in government is not without reason or consequence. The creation of the Social Area was to be done through the exercise of existing domestic legal powers, in keeping with the relevant rules of international law at the time.

Beginning with the epoch-making UN Declaration on the Granting of Independence to Colonial Countries and Peoples in 1960, the declared near-equivalence between independence (or self-determination) and human rights – or solidarity between peoples seeking independence for the sake of a new humanity beyond the confines of national borders – centred on issues of development and economic independence.

That is why it is possible to speak of at least two fundamentally opposed traditions of human rights and internationalism emerging out of the post-war context of the first half of the twentieth century: on the one hand, the position maintained in the 1950s by colonial and neocolonial powers that they could bind themselves to human

rights in a legal covenant without fear that this would mean that the
UN, especially its more pluralistic General Assembly, could inter-
fere in their affairs. As a Belgian delegate put it at the time, in this
light human rights 'presuppose a high degree of civilisation . . .
often incompatible with the ideas of peoples who had not yet
reached a high degree of development'. In such a statement, rights
become the exclusive province of developed – that is, colonial and
neocolonial – countries, and to allow their use by underdeveloped
peoples, for instance against their status as subjects of empire or
economic dependence, would be 'to lead them abruptly to the
point which the civilised nations of today had only reached after a
lengthy period of development'.[9] The link between development
and rights in this view matches the narrative that maintains there are
two sorts of people in the world and only one of them should inherit
the earth and prosper from its riches. It keeps the relevance of
human rights and economic independence or self-determination
out of the picture, out of empire, or any meaningful discussion
about the principles of government.

Although this was the position shared by many of the original
iconic drafters of the Universal Declaration of Human Rights
(1948), for instance Eleanor Roosevelt or the French jurist René
Cassin, it did not prevail. A second position, beginning in the
second half of the twentieth century, linked economic independence or self-determination with discourses on rights in a bid to take
nineteenth-century ideas of the Rights of Man and the post-war
construction of Human Rights in a more radical direction: to bring
about a new and more inclusive humanity, which would count
among its number the peoples who had for so long been considered
backward, or not to have reached a high degree of development.
This second position built on nineteenth-century examples of wider
legal universalism such as those present in the 1804 Haitian
Constitution, after the slave revolution of 1801. More specifically, it
drew on the experience common to the majority of peoples in the
world, that 'under the rule of powers which regarded themselves as

qualified to teach others lessons, the world had known oppression, aggression and bloodshed,' as an Afghan delegate put it during the heated debates in the UN General Assembly on this issue in 1952.[10]

A corollary of this position, developed by rights theorists and anti-racism or decolonisation activists in the 1960s such as Frantz Fanon, was that past and present colonial and neocolonial powers had a duty to pay reparations to plundered peoples, and the latter a corresponding right to apply forms of remedial justice and equality in relation to the local and global transfers of capital that had resulted, and still result, from the more or less overt use of violence by such powers. At bottom, this was a reversal of the position taken by beneficiaries of slavery and neo-colonialism during the long nineteenth century, who sought compensation for the 'loss of property' caused by the application of abolitionist and egalitarian measures. In the case of Chile, slave-owners and big landowners denounced abolitionist measures taken between 1811 and 1823 as a 'threat against property rights and law', insisting they should be paid compensation. The wives and mothers of these elite families argued for the repeal of such measures with a degree of hostility that was condemned by the Chilean Senate of the time. They set a precedent for the marches and demonstrations of the better-off women against egalitarian measures taken by the UP government during the Allende years.

In the 1960s and 1970s there was widespread recognition that the rules generally imposed by global powers upon the peoples of the world, and in particular the rules of post-war reconstruction applied to Germany and Belgium after 1948, were detrimental to the objectives of economic autonomy and self-determination of most of the peoples of the world.

Although historians of post-war reconstruction tend to focus on the importance of the Bretton Woods conference of July 1944 on global monetary and financial policy, which created the IMF and the World Bank, a no less significant development took place in the Anglo-American zone in Germany. In April 1948 the Scientific

Council formed by the two Allied powers to work alongside the German economic administration presented a report that laid down the following principle: 'The Council is of the view that the function of the direction of the economic process should be assured as widely as possible by the price mechanism.' It called for the immediate deregulation of prices in order to bring them in line with world market prices.[11] A few days later at a meeting of the Council in Frankfurt, the economic administrator of the Anglo-American Zone, Ludwig Erhard, made explicit the conclusion to be drawn from the principle of no price controls and deregulation: 'We must free the economy from state controls' because 'only a state that establishes both the freedom and responsibility of the citizens can legitimately speak in the name of the people'.[12]

On the one hand, this is to say that a state that encroaches upon the autonomous activity of individuals and associations in the economic realm violates their liberty and therefore forfeits the right to represent them. On the other hand, it means to say that if a state guarantees the free exercise of economic liberty by individuals and their associations, the mere fact that they exercise it implies their adherence to such a framework and therefore the legitimacy of the state. In this case, there is no need to trace the state's legitimacy back to previous constitutions, the succession of monarchs, or international law. Put simply, an economic regime produces legitimacy for the state: economic development and economic growth produces sovereignty, 'the economy creates public law'.[13]

In the context of post-war Germany – a country defeated, outlawed and under occupation – this was a clever way of rejecting the previous Nazi state as non-representative of the German people because, retrospectively speaking, it had violated the most basic rights of individuals and thus it did not act in their name. At the same time, it reasserted the sovereignty of the new German state as a matter of economic governance and the guarantee of owners' interests. From this perspective, a strong currency, a satisfactory rate of growth, higher purchasing power, low inflation and a favourable balance of payments constantly manifest and reinforce the founding consensus of the state.

Since the late 1940s, if not before, Spanish intellectuals sympathetic to the Franco regime had come in contact with the ideas that inspired Erhard and the Scientific Council in Germany. The problem of how to link together the legitimacy of a state and the freedom of economic partnership, while accepting that the second must found the first, had already arisen at the time of the European crises of the 1930s in the German Weimar Republic as well as in the Spanish Second Republic. It was a thinking of crisis, designed to grapple with the plight of states whose legitimacy was constantly being called into question, and that had to struggle to keep up with serious economic challenges. Chief among those who inspired these ideas in the German context were people like Wilhelm Röpke, who during the Second World War wrote a book titled *The Social Crisis of Our Time*, the Jesuit economist Oswald Nell-Breuning and someone whose career and trajectory would be important in the delimitation and influence of this school of thinking, the Austrian jurist Friedrich von Hayek. Hayek visited Barcelona and Madrid in 1949, where he contacted the Catalonian anti-Keynesians Salvador Millet i Bel, Joan Sardá and Lucas Beltrán.

The Spaniards were working on their own versions of crisis thinking on the basis of medieval notions concerning the autonomy of professional guilds, inspired by the legal and economic thought of the Jesuit School of Salamanca of the sixteenth and seventeenth centuries, the ideas of St Thomas Aquinas, and Christian theology. Chief among such ideas was the assertion that it was a Catholic duty to rebel against a state that encroached upon the autonomous liberty of individuals and their associations.

In the 1930s, such ideas were defended by theologians like the Jesuit Aniceto de Castro Albarrán and the Carlist ideologue Juan Vázquez de Mella, as justifications for the violent overthrow of the Spanish republican government. According to them, the reaffirmation of the working class, the application of wealth-redistributive measures and secularism violated the liberty of individuals and made the republican government tyrannical and oppressive. Therefore, it had forfeited its rights of representation. For these and other conservative intellectuals close to the Spanish Right, this was part of a Jewish–Masonic–Bolshevik plot against economic liberty. According to Vázquez de Mella, the Jewish communists and the liberals, in union with Muslim hordes and other elements of the undesirable masses, were out to destroy Christendom and Western civilisation, and oppress individual liberty. These people were part of an intellectual milieu that the historian Paul Preston has described as 'theorists of extermination'.[14]

After Hayek's visit in 1949, Millet i Bel published an influential article defending individualism as 'an attitude of humble humility before the impersonal and anonymous character of the economic-social process'. According to the sociologist Pinilla de las Heras, this assertion amounts to 'the identification of Adam Smith's invisible hand, with the inscrutable mysteries and secret plans of Divine Providence'.[15] These, and other Spanish intellectuals like Gonzalo Fernández de la Mora and Rafael Calvo Serer, helped to merge Catholic corporatism and individualist economics after the over-throw of the Second Republic and during the dictatorship of General Francisco Franco. Joan Sardá would become the architect of Francisco Franco's 'liberalising' Falangism, in the 1950s, includ-ing the Stabilisation Plan of 1957, and Beltrán the most spirited populariser of the Austrian School and a permanent feature in the neoliberal cradle, the annual meetings of the Mont Pelerin Society.

Their ideas circulated widely among the young students of law and economics at Catholic schools and universities in Chile, from at least the 1950s. Out of these intellectual and political milieux, espe-cially those sympathetic to Franco and Francoist Spain, and close to the National Party of Onofre and Alessandri, emerged the young conservatives who would play a central role in the events of the 1970s and beyond. They renewed conservatism at a time of crisis. Using the Catholic theology of the right to rebellion, together with the assertion of the link between the legitimacy of the state and the liberty of economic partners, they would contest the juridical as well as political legitimacy of Allende. This assertion also allowed them to bypass constitutional law, and to undermine the constitutionalist position within the armed forces, strengthened in the wake of the assassination of General Schneider. According to them, the legalism espoused by Novoa Monreal and the other legal and economic advisers of the Allende administration who appealed to the Chilean Constitution and international law in order to justify nationalisation, income redistribution, price controls and state intervention in industry and transport – that is, the construction of the Social Property Area of the economy – violated the liberty of individuals and their associations. It was, therefore, in their eyes, an oppressive law that did not bind the Chilean people.

In fact, from this perspective the construction of the Social Area retrospectively stripped the Allende government of its right to represent the people, while leaving intact the sovereignty of the Chilean state. Hence, it was both right and a (Catholic) duty to engage in the violent overthrow of the government. The same distinction between representation and sovereignty, and the link between legitimacy and the liberty of economic partners, would then allow for the restoration of the state under the assumption that the second must found the first. From then onwards, a strong currency, low inflation and expanding purchasing power, together with the guarantee of individual liberties, rather than the desires and aspiration of the common will of the people as expressed in the Constitution or the rights of peoples, would enable the structures, mechanisms, commands and justifications of power to function. The economy would produce the public, and public law, not the other way around.

The architect of such a vision in Chile was the young conservative jurist Jaime Guzmán Errázuriz. He was part of a group of young conservatives who formed the inner circle of the ex-president and leader of the right-wing National Party, Jorge Alessandri. Prominent with Guzmán in that circle were also the economist Sergio de Castro and Federico Willoughby. Together they would be responsible for the renewal of the Chilean Right in the 1970s. Guzmán studied at the School of the Sacred Heart in Santiago, where he was exposed to the main tenets of Francoism and Hispanism – the view of Spanish culture consolidated, after the fall of the republic, around Catholic tradition, patriarchal family values and conservative politics, conceived as the bulwark of civilisation against its barbaric enemies.

In the School's journal, which he edited, Guzmán published an early essay titled 'Viva Franco, Arriba España!' The essay, whose title alludes to the name of the Spanish Falangists' daily newspaper *Arriba*, shows the early influence of José Antonio Primo de Rivera and the theorists and theologians of the rebellion against the Second Republic.[16] One of the main tenets of such Hispanic conservatism was the association of the Left with Jewish Bolsheviks, Freemasons and Moors, depicted as lying fraudsters or savages lacking spirituality and civilisation, conspiring together against Christian mores to impose tyranny.

Arriba claimed, for instance, that the 'Judaic–Masonic International is the creator of the two great evils that have afflicted humanity: capitalism and Marxism.'[17] As happened in Germany after the writings of Werner Sombart,[18] in Spain, too, capitalism was conceptualised as having produced the mass, depriving individuals of their natural community and reducing them to atoms lacking in spirituality. From this perspective, Marxism and Nazism attempted, in their own way, to fill the vacuum left in society through an intensification of the standardising and normalising that capitalism had brought about through a multiplication of signs, rituals and spectacles that created an illusion of belonging, for instance, in the party, the cadre or the Latin American guerrilla *foco*. This was why according to this view Marxism and Nazism were, in diverse ways, forms of creed or religions. But they were fake religions, which nevertheless pointed at a symptom of the true malaise in modern society: its spiritual lack, made concrete in the inability of the state to accept the natural responsibility and duties of individuals.

Primo de Rivera shared with other Spanish rightists – like Vázquez de Mella, whose views were introduced into Chile by one of Guzmán's most influential teachers, the theologian Osvaldo Lira – a belief that violence was legitimate against a state that he perceived as influenced by Jews and Freemasons. Like Sombart, however, Primo de Rivera did not take on the full weight of the racial theories of National Socialism, and concerned himself with Jewishness mainly in the case of Jewish Bolshevism and Freemasonry supposedly influencing the masses.[19] This would also be the case in the rightist position forged by Guzmán and his friends in Chile.

Like his Falangist intellectual mentor Primo de Rivera, Guzmán would begin his career in the torrid climate of student politics. In August 1967, by then a law student at the Catholic University of Santiago, he witnessed the student occupation of the university. He abhorred it, and interpreted the student mobilisation as 'the first sign of the Christian–Marxist alliance' that would lead in the 1970s to such important phenomena as the split of MAPU from the Christian Democrats, the emergence of *Cristianos por el Socialismo*, and the experience of the Christian base communities linked to the revolution from below and the UP coalition.[20]

In 1968, Guzmán created the *Gremialista* movement. Directly inspired by Primo de Rivera and Vázquez de Mella, the theological underpinnings of Francoism and the assertion of the economic foundation of public law, the *Gremialista* 1968 Declaration of Principles advocated the autonomy of mid-level sectors of society, individuals and associations of individuals such as the professional, industrialist and merchant guilds (known as *gremios*). It also defended the notion that any encroachment of the state's action on to the autonomous areas of entrepreneurial, corporatist or *Gremialista* activity entails the violation of basic individual rights and natural law. The state now forfeits its claim to be representative, and its laws no longer bind the people in whose name it acts. They and their associations are entitled to rise in violence against it. Here, the 1968 Declaration of Principles of the *Gremialista* movement created by Guzmán follows the prescription of the apologists for the military uprising in Spain, as well as that of the 1948 German Scientific Council declaration cited above reacting to the state of crisis of the previous years.

Guzmán called this the Principle of Subsidiarity. The principle according to which state action is secondary to or subsidiary in respect to the activity of economic partners in society leads directly to a minimalist conception of the role of the state. It follows that any state that fails to conduct its activities in accordance with the principle may be deemed illegitimate, and its laws void or at least unrepresentative of the liberty of individuals and economic partners. The principle turns on its head the initial formula of liberalism according to which we accept an area of free market enterprise and private property defined by law and the state, and keep it under the supervision of law and state: private property and the free market become the organising principle and regulatory norm of the state. Evidently, this precludes the regulatory frameworks invoked by the Allende government in 1971–2 to construct the Social Area of the economy and carry out its nationalisations, or take redistributive and remedial measures. In fact, it turns such legal measures into the very reason that justifies the violent overthrow of the government, regardless of constitutional or democratic niceties.

Among such measures are the domestic constitutional framework, any 'statist' legal framework, be it liberal, Christian progressive as in the case of Tomic's PDC, New Deal as in the years of F. D. Roosevelt in the US, Keynesian, national socialist or socialist, but also international law as produced, for instance, in the 1960s by the UN General Assembly in the name of decolonisation and the self-determination of the Third World 'underdeveloped' countries. In 1962, the UN General Assembly had adopted one such resolution, providing that states and international organisations must respect the permanent sovereignty of peoples and nations over their natural wealth and resources, in accordance with the Charter of the

United Nations and the rights proclaimed by the resolution. These included rights to exploration, use of resources, the sharing of profits, rules of foreign investment, and the right of nationalisation and expropriation. The UN Commission on Human Rights had noted at the time that the right of peoples to permanent sovereignty over their natural wealth 'formed a basic constituent of the right to self-determination'.[21] It was on the basis of this kind of international legality that the Allende government developed its programme of nationalising copper and other industries in the early 1970s.

Here we find, in sum, the justifications for the plot to overthrow Allende in the 1970s, provided by those who took part in the conspiracy and helped carry it out. Here also, among the apologists of the post-Nazi German state and Franco's Spain in Berlin, Vienna, Salamanca, Comillas, Barcelona and Santiago, rather than solely in the classrooms of the University of Chicago or in the writings of the Scottish legal and moral philosophers (which in fact defend a totally opposite view of liberalism), lay the bases of the constitutional and economic edifice built in Chile after 1973, which has come to be known nowadays, misleadingly, as neoliberalism.

Guzmán, De Castro and Willoughby – who also got involved in student politics in the late 1950s, and like Guzmán and De Castro was a member of Alessandri's inner circle and the National Party – advanced the views that turned the veteran of the National Socialist Movement Jorge Prat Echaurren, Jorge Onofre, Alessandri and the other grandees of Chilean conservatism into firm believers in small government and the withdrawal of public investment in infrastructure and local industry, which they thought would allow the private sector – the autonomous guilds or *gremios* of medieval theory – to lead the way in creating wealth and employment, spurred on by bespoke 'liberalising' measures.[22]

The renewal of the Chilean right wing in 1972 was possible thanks to a fusion between the authoritarian nationalism represented by Prat and Onofre and the new legal and economic naturalism advocated by Guzmán, Willoughby and De Castro, inspired by

Francoism, Catholic ultra-orthodoxy and German–Austrian anarcho-capitalism. If the former originated in the old Chilean aristocratic tradition going back to Diego Portales and the rightist position in the Spanish Civil War, the latter interpreted such a position in a way that allowed for a new mystique that could also reach the urban middle classes, by linking the defence of the right to property and individualism with a return to Catholic orthodox philosophy and values (vis-à-vis Christian Democrats or socialists) and an apocalyptic discourse of security against misrule, specifically reformist or revolutionary uses of law and democracy (against socialism and communism).

This explains why, at first, the Chilean rightists reacted fiercely against the Christian Democrats' reform of article 10 of the Chilean Constitution during Eduardo Frei's administration, which paved the way for Agrarian Reform. In their view, 'it constituted the most emphatic step towards the destabilisation and destruction of our middle class, to abolish liberty and open the door to Marxism.'[23]

The next step was taken by the restored Right in 1972, after the failure of the plot to stop the confirmation of Allende, the assassination of General Schneider, the evidence of the strength of the constitutionalist view in the armed forces represented by General Carlos Prats – designated commander-in-chief in place of the martyred Schneider – and the positive economic and electoral results of the first year of Allende's government. Here there were two aims. The first was to react against reformist/revolutionary uses of law by Allende's state – for instance, against legalising forms of unionisation and political organisation among peasants and indigenous peoples, which the neoconservatives interpreted as the symptom of a rot threatening the health of the entire social organism, the stability of its established hierarchies, and in particular the autonomy of owners, professional and industrialist guilds. The second aim was to sow discontent and mobilise wider sectors of the urban middle and upper classes in order to convince the armed forces (at least the fiercely anti-communist sections within it, for instance that represented by the naval officer José Toribio Merino, another student of the School of the Sacred Heart and fervent Francoist) of the need to bypass the constitutional loyalists and intervene to stop the illegitimate Allende government from further damaging the economy with inflationary measures and spreading Jewish–Masonic–Bolshevik atheism. It should not be too hard to paint Allende as a fraudster and an atheist out to destroy Christian civilisation and *chilenidad* (Chile's Hispanism). After all, he was both a Marxist and a Freemason. He was also of Jewish origins, on his mother's side.

The third and final step was counter-revolutionary violence. Faced with the radicalisation of the revolution from below during Allende's presidency, the Right radicalised its response, especially as workers began to get ahead of the timetable set by government and took over factories that refused to produce out of fears of expropriation or because existing supplies had run out (the US blockade of credit and trade imposed unilaterally by the Nixon administration made it harder and more expensive to buy replacement parts and raw materials). All the while, peasants and indigenous movements outpaced agrarian reform by occupying lands mostly in peaceful ways (at times also spurred on by the Guevarist-inspired rhetoric of the MIR and other sectors on the far left), and discussions began to take place about the possibility of replacing state institutions increasingly unhappy about 'popular power' and 'people's assemblies'.

In rural and urban areas, the merging of old nationalism and new Francoist law and security rhetoric within the Right boosted its slide from traditional conservatism to counter-revolutionary reaction. Now the rightist alliance would turn not only against Allende but against democracy itself. Thus, for instance, the death of a farmer named Rolando Matus during a confrontation with landless peasants in the course of a land occupation served as pretext for the formation of the Rolando Matus Brigades within the nationalist youth of Alessandri's National Party in 1971. Together with Fatherland and Freedom and the ex-Cadet Commandos, the Rolando Matus Brigades constituted a new breed of neo-fascist paramilitary organisations with links to nationalist officers in the navy, the army and the CIA.[24] They clashed with Allende's sympathisers and leftist groups like the Ramona Parra muralist brigades in the streets of Santiago, sabotaged power lines, bombed railroad tracks and pipelines and attacked key factories, damaging the economy and stirring up further violence.

At about the same time, Federico Willoughby began using his contacts in the National Agriculture Society, which contained most of the big landowners in the country, in order to put together a list of friends and relatives in the Chilean security forces who 'knew themselves to be a reserve that could act without great risk . . . We introduced them to one another, people in different branches of the armed forces, and put them together.'[25] Always the man of action, Willoughby facilitated contacts between Guzmán and his friends in the National Party, business and landowners, the armed forces, especially the navy, and the US diplomatic corps.[26] Until 1966 Willoughby had been chief press officer of the US Information Service (USIS) in Chile, with access to the information-gathering network of the US embassy in Santiago, and thereafter, until 1972, the public relations officer of the Ford Motor Company, which many at the time viewed as part of the front of covert operations of the US government in the country.[27] In parallel, they set up the *Gremialista* Action Commandos, which helped to turn the old 'Import-Export coalition' into an insurrectionary war machine.[28]

De Castro and Guzmán met each other at the time of the foundation of the secretive Cofradía Náutica del Pacifico Austral (Naval Brotherhood of the Southern Pacific) in August 1968, if not before. Among the members of the Cofradía were the naval officers José Toribio Merino – who had been contacted by the CIA during the meetings that, as part of the Track I/Track II plot, resulted in the assassination of General Schneider – Patricio Carvajal and Arturo Troncoso Daroch, as well as the former navy officers Roberto Kelly and Hernán Cubillos. Among the civilian members were Sergio de Castro, Arturo Fontaine, *El Mercurio*'s editor René Silva Espejo and

its owner, the magnate Agustín Edwards. It was thanks to the dona-
tions from Edwards's bank, *El Mercurio*, the Matte group, the Bank
of Chile and other benefactors with ties to the Cofradía that the
Catholic University Economic Science Foundation acquired a new
campus in 1967. De Castro was the Dean of the Faculty. Members
of the Cofradía and economists from the Catholic University –
many of whom had benefited from an exchange programme with
the University of Chicago – would be decisive in the drafting of an
economic programme that would provide the foundation for the
legal and political restoration of the state in the event of Allende's
overthrow, along the lines designed by Jaime Guzmán.

Like Merino, Guzmán too had played a role in the plan to stop
Allende's confirmation as president in 1970. Although he might not
have kept in close contact with General Viaux, according to declassified documents 'he actively participated with his group of religious friends in the *Gremialismo* of the Federation of Students of the
Catholic University . . . He had been tasked with planning the
occupation of the Catholic University and TV Channel 13 after the
kidnapping of General Schneider.' According to the same document, Guzmán was one of the founders of the Movimiento Cívico
Patria y Libertad (Fatherland and Freedom Civic Movement, the
civilian wing of the Fatherland and Freedom Front mentioned
before) in 1971, though not a defender of old-fashioned nationalist
views.[29] Both Merino and Guzmán had studied at the School of the
Sacred Heart, the former in Valparaíso and the latter in Santiago.
Willoughby was also a fervent Catholic, and like Guzmán, a member
of Alessandri's inner circle with ties to Fatherland and Freedom.[30]

The armed counter-revolution would surface during the 'Pots
and Pans Protests' and the 1972 October Strike. The 'Pots and Pans
protests' were a series of demonstrations by middle- and upper-class
women of Poder Femenino, with links to the National Party, against
declining supplies of imports and locally produced goods. In the
marches, female demonstrators of Poder Femenino would bang
pots and voice their fierce opposition to the UP government with

renewed nationalist fervour, using religious and patriarchal images
and incendiary rhetoric, always flanked by armed members of
Fatherland and Freedom. The protests began in December 1971 and
became more frequent during October 1972, as scarcity hit stores
and the Right, through the industrial *gremios* and trade guilds, raised
the stakes of the political game.[31]

In early 1972 Orlando Saenz, the president of the Society for
Industrial Development, contacted Benjamín Matte, president of
the National Agriculture Society, and Jorge Fontaine, of the
National Confederation of Production and Commerce, also a relative of *El Mercurio*'s Arturo Fontaine. They agreed that it was time
to 'back Allende into a corner, beginning with a massive publicity
campaign to turn popular support away from government, and
afterward overthrow him constitutionally'.[32] They were reacting
not only to Allende's measures to construct the Social Area of the
economy, but mainly to the increasing momentum of the revolution from below. In 1970, the last year of Frei's government, peasants and Indians had recovered or occupied 365 farms; in the first
eight months of 1971 that figure had climbed to 990, an average of
four takeovers per day. The same was happening in industry, where
the number of takeovers of factories by workers had jumped from
133 in 1970 to 531, an average of over two a day, in 1971. 'We no
longer care whether the requisition to take the factory is legal or
not,' said a Yarur textile factory worker in an interview with *La
Nación*, after the takeover was declared illegal by the Controller
General. Yarur Textile Company was at the heart of an economic
conglomerate that included finance, chemical and food industries,
owned in part by Chase Manhattan Bank. 'The UP government has
given us the opportunity of making decisions in our factory. Our
aim is to keep moving forward, even if we have to bypass the law.'
He was referring to the fact that Allende had made a promise not to
use the security forces to enforce legal measures against the workers,
effectively uncoupling law from force.[33]

The 1972 October Strike saw the first public appearance beyond the enclave of the Catholic University of Jaime Guzmán's *Gremialismo*, decisive in reaching the middle classes and attracting some of them to join the ranks of the counter-revolution. Significantly, to set the anti-government offensive in motion, the trade guilds relied on the economic effect of price controls, wage rises equal to inflation, and the mobilisation of national production to full capacity. The price freeze allowed quasi-monopolistic manufacturers a reasonable profit margin, but impacted severely on small and medium-size businesses whose costs of production were higher due to their smaller scale. Similarly, once full-capacity production was reached, without a parallel accrual of capital, a scarcity of goods due to excess demand and the resulting rise in black market prices threatened to return control of wages and salaries to the owners.

Allende's solution was to set up the Social Area, which would change the structure of production, making shortages easier to avoid and setting prices at the level of production costs in small and medium-size businesses. The surplus profit received by the large industries of the social sector, like mining, no longer in private hands, could be reinvested in the economy as capital growth and social welfare, improving the living standards of the least privileged. The UP government also used the surplus it had inherited from Frei's administration – a result of high copper prices in the world market – to subsidise imports for consumers. But due to the decline in global copper prices in the early 1970s, and the subsequent decrease in export earnings, Chile's foreign reserves dwindled by 90 per cent, making it impossible for Allende's administration to continue to underwrite the consumer economy.

Since the price freeze had already pushed small and medium-size businesses to the verge of bankruptcy, and private businesses in general had restricted their capital growth (11 per cent at the end of 1971), the effects of scarcity became widely visible and the impact of black market prices more severe.[34] This was interpreted by the *Gremialista* conservatives and the trade guilds, along the lines of Guzmán's Principle of Subsidiarity, as a violation of basic individual

rights and natural law and liberty, and therefore as a sign that the
state had forfeited its claim to be representative. In their view,
Allende's government no longer acted in the name of the Chilean
people: the trade guilds (and the military) could overthrow the
government 'legitimately', destroy Allende and 're-found' a state
based on economic freedom and nothing more.

At that point, relations between the UP and Frei's PDC were
deteriorating. On 8 June 1971, members of the ultra-leftist VOP
(Organised People's Vanguard) had killed Edmundo Pérez Zujovic,
held responsible for the massacre of Puerto Montt. Zujovic was a
former PDC minister and a close friend of Frei. Although Allende
condemned the murder in no uncertain terms, repercussions quickly
ensued when the PDC broke the agreement to co-preside over
Congress and its candidate defeated Allende's adviser Eduardo
Novoa Monreal in the elections for the rectorship of the University
of Chile. Allende hailed the 'exemplary attitude' of the chief of the
Santiago garrison, General Augusto Pinochet, who stopped his
soldiers from intervening in the combat between members of the
Carabineros forces and the VOP, in which two members of the
latter were killed. It was in this heated climate that the former PDC
presidential candidate Radomiro Tomic proposed to Allende that
the UP should give its support to a candidate of the progressive
wing of the PDC in the Valparaíso by-election (after the National
Party withdrew its candidate and supported the PDC). If Tomic
and Allende came to an agreement they could neutralise the
approach made by the National Party to the right wing of the PDC.
Allende consulted his coalition, but was overruled by the leadership
of the UP and especially his own Socialist Party.

As a consequence of the resulting closeness between the nationalists and the right wing of the PDC, members of the progressive
wing still within the latter broke away to form *Izquierda Cristiana*
(Christian Left). Not only did this weaken the progressive side of
the PDC in favour of its more conservative tendency; ultra-
Catholics like Guzmán saw it as a decisive step towards cleansing

Christian values of the polluting influence of Marxism and Liberation Theology.

Frei, leader of the conservative wing of the PDC, was recruited to present a constitutional amendment bill for consideration by Congress, to scale down the construction of the Social Area. At the same time, the *Gremialista* Commandos launched a campaign to attract support from medium-size and small businesses affected by price controls against expropriation, something they had no reason to fear since expropriation was targeting big businesses exclusively. No less significantly, they would intensify the propaganda concerning 'the failure of socialism' and the 'mismanagement of the economy', and push hard against the emerging network of popular organisations supporting state price controls, production control and supply distribution, which were at the heart of the revolution from below and linked up with the leadership from above, branding them as examples of 'Marxist dictatorship' that aimed to strangle democracy and replace it with a proletarian tyranny based on 'popular power', 'people's assemblies' and Cuban-style 'popular courts'.

According to the Chilean author Robinson Rojas, some of the 'constitutionalist' and 'reformist' officers in the armed forces, such as Orlando Urbina and Augusto Pinochet, had conveyed to Saenz, the trade guilds and the *Gremialistas* that if they wanted to impeach the executive or provoke regime change in keeping with the Constitution, for instance via a plebiscite, 'we won't get in your way'.[35] Hardliners like Admirals Merino and Carvajal were already on board. All that was needed would be to ensure a deepening of chaos and scarcity, in order to sap the hopes of Allende's supporters and secure a defeat of the government in the event of a plebiscite or, in any case, pave the way for military intervention. This was the objective of the Pots and Pans Protests, which forced Allende to declare martial law in Santiago for several days, coinciding with Fidel Castro's visit in late 1971 following the re-establishment of diplomatic relations with Chile, and the October 1972 strike organised by the trade and transport guilds.

On 10 October 1972, in response to an initiative announced by Allende to form a state transport and trucking company in Magallanes province, the president of the Truck Owners Association, León Vilarín, invited associates all over the country to blockade roads and stop all movement of goods and resources 'as a sign of protest against the Marxist state dictatorship'.[36] In the following days, the Confederation of Retail Merchants (led by one of Frei's Christian Democrats), the transport guild of private owners of microbuses and taxis (also close to the PDC) and, significantly, Saenz's Society for Industrial Development, the National Confederation of Production and Commerce, the College of Lawyers, the private commercial banks and the National Agriculture Society (with ties to the National Party), private businessmen (like Edwards and Matte) and most other professional and small sector guilds joined the protest. It was the first time Allende faced the combined strength of large and small guilds, businessmen and both nationalist conservatives and Christian Democrats – the concrete face of the *Gremialismo* that Guzmán had theorised – aiming to break the will of the Chilean people who supported the government, and openly calling for anti-government revolt.

Furthermore, the strike relied on the direct and violent intervention of right-wing shock troops: Fatherland and Freedom and the so-called ex-Cadet Commandos, formed after the director of the Bernardo O'Higgins Military School, Colonel Eduardo Labbé, refused to present the military salute to Fidel Castro when the latter visited Chile in December 1971. Labbé was a hardliner opposed to the constitutionalists within the armed forces. Together with other officers, he began to plot a military coup in March 1972, was found out and sent into retirement. According to Robinson Rojas, the conspirators' 'main contact with the US Embassy was Federico Willoughby'. Willoughby was contacting members of three branches of the armed forces, 'putting them together', by his own admission, and also had strong links with the National Agriculture Society.[37] Members of the Agriculture

Society, especially the big landowners from the south, were in turn closely connected to Fatherland and Freedom. Willoughby had strong links with the Agriculture Society, and as a journalist collaborated with the National Agriculture Society radio station in Santiago which was put in the service of Fatherland and Freedom, according to Rojas. He asserts that the Agriculture Society's president, Benjamín Matte, was one of Fatherland and Freedom's leading members.

The industrialists, for their part, contributed to the good offices of the Society for Industrial Development's president, Orlando Saenz.[38] Fatherland and Freedom was founded by a lawyer, Pablo Rodríguez Grez, who had been a member of Alessandri's campaign committee in 1970 and was once the director of Forestry Industries (Industrias Forestales S.A.), linked to the Matte group and the Edwards family. Rodríguez Grez acted as defence counsel for General Roberto Viaux when the latter was put on trial for the assassination of General Schneider. According to the newspaper *Última Hora*, Fatherland and Freedom had support within the navy and the army, especially from Lieutenant Colonel Oscar Haag Blaschke, 'who allowed them to smuggle in arms from Argentina and Bolivia', and in Santiago Colonel Roberto Souper Onfray, who commanded the Second Armoured Regiment in the city.[39]

President Allende ordered General Herman Brady to contain the chaos provoked by these groups, intervene with the Santiago transportation guild that had brought the city to a halt, and restore order. Though the president kept his promise not to use force against the workers, whose actions were noticeably non-violent, he was ready to confront the violence and disorder spread by Fatherland and Freedom and the ex-Cadet Commandos as the latter attacked workers and drivers who defied the strike called by the owners, bombed the energy infrastructure and sabotaged the economy. Brady responded that he would have to put one soldier in each microbus to protect drivers from Commando sabotage, and this would mean leaving the city vulnerable without a military garrison.

As the strike held out against efforts to break it, the shortage situation worsened. As can be seen in Patricio Guzmán's documentary film *The Battle of Chile*, long queues became the order of the day in Santiago and elsewhere as people struggled to obtain basic goods like flour or toilet paper, and found it increasingly hard to get around town. To survive, Allende's government needed to find a way to maintain distribution of basic goods and foodstuffs throughout the country. Struggling to solve the crisis, and to find a response in terms of progressive uses of law and regulation to the challenge posed by the *Gremialista* assertion of the economy as the basis of public law, the government decided to use the telex and computer network that had been set up as part of an experimental initiative known as Project Cybersyn.

The technological network would allow the Allende administration to communicate with and coordinate its actions together with the so-called industrial belts (*cordones industriales* – first formed in Santiago's industrial districts in June 1972 to fight right-wing sabotage), the people's stores, union organisations, neighbourhood cooperatives, mothers' networks, and supply and price control boards. These groups demanded that the government departments in charge of distributing consumer goods supply them such goods to sell directly to the people and bypass the private distribution system. In this way, for instance, a union cooperative would be able to sell its members a kilo of flour four times cheaper than the neighbourhood supermarket. Similarly, as factory managers stayed home, organised workers became worker-managers, engineers and administrators, fighting to keep factories and the whole country going. This entailed the emergence of concrete forms of decision-making, self-regulation and collective problem-solving, with the potential to extend and deepen democracy and progressive uses of legality and regulation.

First built as an experiment to help manage the growing Social Area of the economy, the Cybersyn network was expanded by the government beyond the industrial sector in the context of the 1972

October crisis. Although its computing power could not be compared with that of an iPhone, Cybersyn was also to send messages quickly and reliably from one end of Chile's unique geography to the other, from Arica to Punta Arenas, so as to give an edge to the government and the emerging network of social movements from below, and a new way to respond to the impact of the owners' strike.

At the centre of Project Cybersyn was an eccentric British character named Stafford Beer.[40] He has been described variously as 'a cross between Orson Welles and Socrates', a 'swashbuckling pirate of a man', a charlatan and a fool, a self-made entrepreneur who at one point drove a Rolls-Royce and smoked cigars – he was one of the first people in the history of the IT revolution to make a fortune out of the application of computer and cybernetic principles. Together with a group of young Chilean scientists, artists and designers, activists and members of the UP government, he was the protagonist of one of the most fascinating stories of technological and political creativity to take place in the late twentieth century. Later in life he gave up most of his possessions and ended up living in a small cottage in Wales without central heating or a telephone line. All the while, Beer decisively shaped the technological era, counterculture, cognitive science and contemporary rock music through his influence on musicians like Robert Fripp and Brian Eno.

In July 1971, Beer received a letter from a young Chilean engineer named Fernando Flores, who was also an activist working on new frameworks of development for the newly elected Allende government. Flores had got to hear of him while working as a consultant for a job that Beer's firm in Europe, Science in General Management (SIGMA), was doing in Chile in the 1960s. SIGMA was trying to apply the principles of operational research and new management thinking to improve the productivity of Chile's steel industry. Flores told Beer he was familiar with his writings on computer technology, management and the emerging science of cybernetics.

The early cyberneticians, most of them specialists in physics and mathematics, laid the groundwork for what we now know as cognitive science, the science of mind and brain, of the organisation and self-regulation of biological, technological and social systems. They were armed with a battery of concepts that were new at the time but now form part of the everyday vocabulary of Internet users and developers: the information 'data highway' (a phrase coined by Beer), connectivity, feedback (the notion that connected items or terms relate to and affect one another in a causally circular manner), complexity, systems and, above all, the neural network.[41] What they mean by these terms is that certain complex systems – which may be biological, artificial or social – can simulate or mimic through their behaviour what we often interpret in terms of purpose, will, or even finality and intention. For them it was not particularly important whether a piece of hardware was part of a natural physical or an artificial physical system, the point was to identify the imitative behaviour, the ability to simulate, or the causal circular organisation that they displayed, which would yield the same effects of purpose and intentionality.

The applications of this insight can be quite significant. For instance, it can help demystify the concept of money. Fiat money, the paper currency we all use, has true value according to this perspective only because we all falsely believe that it possesses true value. In this respect, there is no essential difference between a dollar printed by the Federal reserve and a simulated or counterfeit dollar. Why does only the former work? Because we all accept it as valuable. Something similar happens with prices in the global market and, crucially, with state laws, regulations and even with our sense of selfhood and identity. We are all the time confusing essence with appearance, say cyberneticians, but that does not mean that everything is illusory. Rather, appearances do matter if we treat them as if they had objective value, as inventions. These inventions help us to frame objective reality, which never appears to us in all its full glory and transparency.[42]

What does this have to do with the Chilean situation in 1972? The self-proclaimed owners of Chile, the people behind the 1972 October Strike, thought they held all the cards and would bring down the people's government of Allende by withholding them. They believed that by sowing chaos they could provoke a simple response from the Chilean people in the direction they wanted, treating the people as they had always done, as if they were the dog in some Pavlovian psychological experiment. But once people stopped believing they could only go on if things went back to normal, and began to invent forms of communication, problem-solving, regulation and distribution of their own, they also began to create new spaces for democracy, self-regulatory sites, more power-ful political subjectivities, as well as objective ways to confront the world and one another. In doing so, they discovered they could go on without having to depend upon the 'normality' imposed by the 'owners' of Chile. Rather than behaving like Pavlov's dog, they began inventing or 'dreaming reality', as a slum-dweller in Santiago told Ariel Dorfman in the early 1970s.[43]

Flores, one of the young intellectuals at the Catholic University who in 1969 had broken with the PDC, created MAPU and joined the UP coalition, had become after 1970 general technical manager at the Corporation for Development and Production (CORFO) in charge of the nationalised Social Area of the economy. He told Beer he 'was now in a position from which it is possible to implement on a national scale . . . scientific views on management and organisa-tion', and apply them to the nationalised sector of the Chilean economy.[44]

A small team in the Chilean government, led by Flores in collab-oration with Beer, believed the challenges involved in setting up and managing the Social Area, compounded in 1972 by the October Strike and the violent action of Fatherland and Freedom and the ex-Cadet Commandos, could be addressed through the use of computer and communications technology. They set out to create 'a new system for industrial management in collaboration with a group of British technologists'.[45]

Initially, Beer was called to help confront that challenge, but his involvement with Chile went far beyond a mere crisis-management operation. It became part of Chile's experiment with a deeper sense of democracy. In a 1970 address to the Conference on the Environment organised by the American Society for Cybernetics in Washington, Beer spoke of something he called the 'Liberty Machine'.[46] The Liberty Machine simulated 'a sociotechnical system that functioned as a disseminated network, not a hierarchy', and treated the information gathered by the network as the basis of individual and collective problem-solving and action. It could operate in real time, or close to real time, thereby facilitating faster decision-making, and taking advantage of forms of collective behaviour that allow a group to advance together and disperse almost at will (what strategists call 'swarm tactics'). This is what London student protesters did in 2011, when they used their smartphones to tweet or text information about police movements in streets and squares, and managed to outpace them.

According to Beer in 1970, the Liberty Machine might allow for a more adequate balance between centralisation and individual freedom. Effectively, he was hinting at the possibility of principles of government that could be more appropriate to the tasks of progressive transformation. Unlike the 1940s Germans and the 1950s Francoist Spaniards, he was not suggesting deregulation, but rather people's self-regulation. Later on, he would speak of a new people (as in Guevara's 'new man') and of 'the will of the people'.[47] Beer envisioned his 'Liberty Machine' as a series of operation rooms in which people would use computers to get wired to a cloud of real-time information coming from different sectors of society and the economy, run simulations, and focus their collective energy on generating hypotheses about future behaviour and solving problems, especially in situations of crisis in which old models of information-gathering and communication, forecast and mainstream probabilistic simulations tend to be useless. He coined the term 'data highway' to designate this virtual space of cloud-like, networked information, while developing new media of communication, information and image transfer through computers, at least twenty years before terms like 'information highway' and 'cyberspace' were borrowed from speculative fiction novels by high-tech pundits and universally adopted to describe the Internet.[48]

In connection with the work that the Chilean scientists Francisco Maturana and Humberto Varela were developing in the 1970s, Beer added some key ideas about how systems, from single biological cells to large collective groups, survived and thrived by regulating themselves internally and externally. That idea, which he presented as 'the viable system model', resonated with other philosophical concepts being developed at the time, for instance Jean-Paul Sartre's notion of 'totalisation', or Ernesto Guevara's call to harness the potential of automation and psychological behaviour for the purposes of transformation and progress.[49]

Unlike Allende or Guevara, Beer was not a Marxist, and yet his enthusiasm and his conviction that technology was profoundly aligned with freedom both reflected and benefited from the main tenets of the Chilean Way towards socialism. Put together, these ideas framed the design of the technological system that became Chile's Project Cybersyn: a combination of networked telex machines, computers, information, image and file transfer, collection, and processing through mainframe technology. This network would be run from one or more operations rooms. Together they embodied in practice what Beer had described before as the Liberty Machine.

On 12 November 1971, Beer met Salvador Allende at La Moneda presidential palace. He explained to Allende 'the whole damned plan and the whole Viable System Model in one single sitting'. Beer discussed with Allende and acknowledged the difficulties that government was facing as a result of the US economic blockade, the increased hostility of the owners of Chile and their direct action groups, as well as the challenges brought about by governmental decisions on the economy and the momentum of the revolution from below. They talked about the problem that lack of access to cutting-edge technology in foreign markets would create for the project, and about Chile's limited resources, but Beer confirmed his conviction that the team could 'accomplish feats deemed impossible in the developed world'. In turn, Allende insisted that the socio-technical system should behave in a 'decentralising, worker-participative, and anti-bureaucratic manner'.[50]

When Beer finished the presentation of his model with an explanation of the last and most encompassing level of simulation and collective problem-solving, Allende exclaimed: 'At last, the people!' According to the historian Eden Medina, this reflected the presidential view that equated political leadership with the rule of the people themselves. The words also chimed with Beer's belief that, essentially, his Liberty Machine did not consist of one person controlling all others alone, in the manner critically portrayed by George Orwell as Big Brother in his novel *Nineteen Eighty-Four*, but behaved as a multi-nodal horizontal network.[51]

Beer was communicating an insight shared by most pioneers of the Internet, one that has only come to be fully understood in our time: peer-to-peer communication in real time produces, among other things, a free dose of personal well-being. This would be something like the feelings of solidarity and camaraderie shared by the members of a group, expressed in the everyday use in the 1970s of such terms as *compañero* (Salvador Allende, for instance, was referred to by most people as *Compañero Presidente*). But in the case of technological social networks, this affective experience is multiplied over a thousandfold by the number of nodes or participants in the network.

As the pioneers of the Internet suspected, and as millions of young activists and users of social media have confirmed in practice today, the effect can be quite revolutionary. The network effect allows for a specific form of collective problem-solving, consensus-making and consensus-breaking, or the ability to know when to swarm and when to break up, but also to be ahead of the curve. In an oft-cited 2003 study of Catalonian Web-users, the sociologist

Manuel Castells confirmed and developed this intuition. He observed that Web use did produce new attitudes and behaviours beyond the computer interface among the subjects of his study: 'The more an individual has a project of autonomy (personal, professional, socio-political, or communicative), the more he or she uses the Internet, [and] the more autonomous she becomes vis-à-vis societal rules and institutions.'[52]

This potential was realised and tested at least twice in Chile during Allende's presidency: first, during the October 1972 block-ade planned and executed by industrialist *gremios*, truck and trans-port owners, and violent right-wing groups. And then again in August 1973 when the same groups coordinated their action with mainstream media, the opposition in parliament and members of the military, with foreign support, in order to create the conditions that would bolster a military coup against Allende.

On Sunday 15 October 1972, Mario Grandi and Fernando Flores, the key people pushing for Project Cybersyn in Allende's circle, proposed applying what they had learned about social networking and socio-technical management 'to manage the [industrialists'] strike'.[53] The proposal included setting up a 'situation room' similar to the one used by Churchill's Cabinet during the Second World War, but enhanced following the futuristic model of Cybersyn's operations room, which could also include the heads of the coali-tion parties and representatives of the National Labour Federation. They could reach out to the networks of decision-makers and prob-lem-solvers in their home institutions and grassroots organisations, such as the workers' industrial belts, the Mothers' Centres, the people's stores and the price control boards, using specialised command centres dedicated to transportation, industry, energy, banking, agriculture, health, logistics and the supply of consumer goods, interconnected via the telex machines already in place for Project Cybersyn.

Project Cybersyn's telex room, housed at the time in Flores's Corporation for Development and Production (CORFO), served

as the presidential command hub during the 1972 October blockade. These machines transmitted messages about shortages, distribution problems such as the location of available trucks to carry raw
materials and spare parts needed to maintain production in worker-
run factories, communications from sector committees, and the
networked revolution from below, in almost real time. This allowed
Allende's government and the movements from below to address
problems and needs almost immediately. In addition, Flores and the
Cybersyn team created a telephone network of eighty-four numbers
linking government, the coalition parties, the Labour Federation
and grassroots union organisations, and through them neighbourhood cooperatives and supply community boards. This allowed
government to respond to requests coming from these groups to
allocate resources and consumer goods to sell and distribute directly
to the people. Also, those in the network could learn exactly how
many trucks were needed and were able to request replacements
whenever a transport was lost due to the blockade or an attack by
the right-wing Commandos. Records could be kept, mistakes were
corrected, and they could track developments on the ground as they
were happening. The Cybersyn network was kept in use throughout the remainder of Allende's presidency.

An estimated two thousand messages were transmitted daily
through Project Cybersyn's network during the 1972 October
Strike. Even Stafford Beer, who was in London at the time, remained
in contact through the network.

According to Eden Medina, the network enabled the Cybersyn
team 'to create an overview of national production based on a closer
approximation to real-time data than any government had been
able to assemble in the past'.[54] She says the networked tele-
technologies of Project Cybersyn 'extended the reach of the social
network that Flores had assembled in the presidential command centre,
and created a sociotechnical network in the most literal sense'.[55]

Factories kept producing, collective supply networks replaced
those formerly in private hands, and now workers held meetings to

discuss challenges and find possible solutions together. This show of coordinated strength on the part of the people prompted considerations about extending the revolution from below to the legal and institutional apparatus, as well as to the economy and the state monopoly over use of force. 'How long are we going to give the *momios* [reactionaries] to come to work?' asked workers in these meetings, as cited by Robinson Rojas, and in others declared: 'We should organise in armed people's brigades to overthrow our enemies permanently . . . the military are helping the bosses by not acting . . . We have to solve the problem ourselves.'[56] The security services received intelligence about these discussions and reports on the 'people's mobilisation'. Recognising the fact that the country was functioning without owners and managers, some senior officers in the armed forces expressed their admiration: 'the rabble can do it . . . The Allende government deserves respect. It has pulled off quite a stunt.'[57] Beer put it thus: 'we absolutely defeated [the October Strike] by using computers and telex machines, of all things.'[58]

It would be wrong, however, to distinguish too sharply between the swarm mobilisation tactics used by the people during the strike and the role played by networked tele-technologies. As we have begun to understand in the wake of the Arab Spring and the twenty-first-century student protests in Britain, Europe or Chile, the human-centred bias that commentators, human rights and legal scholars, political scientists and historians often display when analysing such situations betrays a poor understanding of transformative action in the technological age, if not a philosophical prejudice about the essence of human nature. In fact, there is no essence of human nature that could be sharply distinguished from the prosthetic technologies we humans have created for ourselves. Our relationship with these technologies is no one-way street: they affect us, and decisively transform our nature. This is a fact with profound implications for current understandings of human rights, law, philosophy and politics.

The implication is neither pessimism nor scepticism about human nature or the human condition, and the limits of law and democracy. On the contrary, examples such as Chile's in 1972 demonstrate that humans can develop forms of self-determination and notions of group rights beyond what is often considered possible, and make them operative in practice thanks, among other things, to far more constructive technological inventions. It shows that consensus is not only about a set of techniques, with people behaving solely as consumers content with responding to the signals sent by the self-proclaimed owners of the economy.

The example of 1972 Chile suggests that it is wrong to understand human nature in terms of an assumed ability or inability to perform cold rational calculations born of the power to issue and follow commands. If so, we must rethink our ideas about truth, law and human rights. Consider the alternative: we can ascertain that there is truth, law and right, provided we take into account the lesson taught by Socrates, Diogenes or Anacharsis: that truthfulness and reasonableness come first. This is the attitude that presents one as never in possession of the truth, and as never being in the position to tell others to shut up and do as they are told. The opposite attitude – which was the attitude of the self-appointed owners and legislators of Chile in 1972 – lands one in the false position of believing one owns the truth, that one has some exclusive monopoly over the power to think, reason and issue commands, or that some create reality while others merely study it. Socrates and his followers reacted against such an attitude and called it, simply, ignorance. And as we know, ignorance leads to impotence. In contrast, 'knowing is always itself an ethical act'.[59]

Echoing such insight, Eden Medina observes that using networked technologies during the 1972 October Strike 'allowed the Chilean government to transform the nation into an information system', which top officials and grassroots movements could manage. Beer had designed systems that facilitated the reception and exchange of data between a peripheral node and a central point in a network in real time, and hoped this would help coordinate the different sectors

of the Chilean economy, often slowed by missing or delayed information. But in the concrete situation of the 1972 October Strike,
networked grassroots movements and government officials actually
exchanged information about blockades and lack of supplies almost as
these events were unfolding, assessed their environment, adapted to
survive and invented new sites of self-regulation and freedom. They
surpassed what was thought possible: the people thought and reasoned,
and acted to determine themselves. That kind of technologically
enhanced self-determination leads one to consider the notion of posthuman rights, in reference to the feats of self-regulation and the creation of 'the will of the people' that pioneers of the computer age like
Stafford Beer theorised and the men and women of 1972 Chile put
into practice. In doing so, they transformed themselves and their relations. In short, the rabble began to think and to reason, and the gentry
of Chile feared them all the more because of it.[60]

Another consequence of the strain that the October plot put on
all parts of Chilean society was the revelation that there existed in
the armed forces a group of officers who not only were constitutional loyalists, but were becoming convinced that the Allende
government was on to something. Chief among them was the
commander-in-chief of the army, General Carlos Prats.

Looking back over the 1960s and early 1970s, Prats concluded that:

> the government which has had a more reasonable and clearer
> conception of national security, and demonstrated in practice
> genuine interest for the problems of national defence and interest,
> was, precisely, the Allende government . . . The evidence shows
> that he has been the only President in forty years, to open a
> coherent path for the interests of national security . . . by devel-
> oping and sharing with others an innovative conception of geo-
> economic sovereignty.[61]

General Prats was making the point that self-determination,
which included independence from a local elite intent on defending

foreign interests as if these were the interests of the people of Chile, was a more reasonable path towards sovereignty. Sharing that conception, in practice, with the people who resisted the 1972 October Strike, Allende had shown that the cold rationality of economic calculation – which in fact boiled down to treating people like children, content to receive goodies and be told what to do – could not lay the basis of a strong republic. Rather, in 1972 the public acted as grown-ups, and kept going without their bosses and managers.

The historical experience of what actually does happen in a crisis demonstrates, as in the case of Chile in 1972, that even those who have not grown up in an environment of genuine sovereignty, self-rule and participatory democracy, if you take away guns and un-couple law from coercion, suddenly become not only quite reason-able but also extremely inventive. It is extraordinary what people do when they pull together in the face of crisis: they invariably invent new forms of cooperation, self-regulation and security, and often do so in ways that contrast with patriarchal habits of law and order.[62]

On 30 December 1972, Allende invited General Prats to see the secret weapon.[63] Cybersyn's Operations Room had been located in a downtown building owned by the National Telecommunications Enterprise (ENTEL). It was an interior courtyard, nearly 400 square metres of open space with no columns or partitions, in an edifice several stories high, wired for telecommunications. From the outside it seemed an inconspicuous building, but on the inside it was the stuff of fantasy. The setting seemed to come straight out of Stanley Kubrick's *2001* or Alejandro Jodorowsky's 1970 visionary designs for *Dune*. For Beer, the room recreated the spirit of Melquiades, the magus–inventor who arrives from a foreign island in Gabriel García Márquez's *One Hundred Years of Solitude*.[64]

When Allende and Prats arrived, they could hardly believe their eyes. Before them was a hexagonal room, illuminated by colour-changing lights that gave viewers the impression of being inside a spacecraft. A series of screens and electronic panels hung from the first wall to their right, displaying flow charts and Rama Sets, graphics inspired by Arthur C. Clarke's literature and the Indian epic *Ramayana*. In the middle of the room were seven white fibreglass chairs with orange cushions placed in a circle on a brown carpet.[65]

Allende and Prats learned that people in the room, and those connected to it from the outside through the network, constituted the brainpower. They were all served, as the brain itself is served, by a nervous system covering the totality of the body in question, in this case Chile's economy and the relevant social sectors. Daily information and sensory inputs came in via a software program called Cyberstride, together with binary codes of pleasure and pain signifying concrete achievements and challenges. Questions and requisitions were entered, distributed and solved simultaneously by the community of networked individuals.

General Prats and President Allende were invited to sit on the white swivel chairs. They pushed and tapped buttons, calling up information and providing feedback. To their left was a screen displaying a stylised model of the whole of Chile's economy and society, driven by an experimental and still unfinished computer that worked visually rather than on the basis of text. They were impressed. In mid-1973, Allende contacted Fernando Flores and asked him to move Cybersyn's Operations Room to the presidential palace. The president and the general did not grasp the digital logic behind the operations of the secret weapon that had helped them outwit the owners of Chile and survive the October Strike, but it worked. It was an astonishing advance.

9

The Flies, Act II

Throughout 1972, General Carlos Prats not only remained loyal to the Constitution but in the wake of Cybersyn and the government's victory over the October strikers came to share Allende's view of 'geo-economic sovereignty'. According to that view, freeing the economic and democratic potential of the Chilean people from the dictates of an elite that often acted as if the interests of foreign powers and corporations were identical with Chile's, which therefore prospered from its own subordination, was a reasonable path towards securing economic independence, geo-political as well as juridical legitimacy, and clout in the international sphere.[1]

The existence of a group of officers aligned with General Prats in the armed forces posed a serious challenge to those who had thought the Chilean military was of one mind. Between November 1972 and June 1973, US policymakers and intelligence analysts harboured serious doubts about any possibility of a military intervention against Allende. The chief of the CIA Santiago station, Ray Warren, opined that the main obstacle to a successful coup lay within the military itself. He was referring, especially, to the fact that the military was divided.[2]

Moreover, constitutionalist officers like Prats seemed to be moving closer to Allende's view. On 2 November 1972, President Allende announced a Cabinet reshuffle that further stressed the image of governmental strength and support within the armed forces after the October crisis: General Carlos Prats became the new Minister of the Interior – a post that carried the same rank and legal attributes as a vice-president; Rear Admiral Ismael Huerta was named Minister of Public Works; and Air Force General Claudio Sepúlveda headed the Ministry of Mines, overseeing the 'wages of Chile' that came from the recently nationalised copper and nitrate industry.

Air Force General Alberto Bachelet, a constructive critic of Allende's economic policy who had devised a plan to keep the supply of consumer goods in reach of the majority of the population, also a friend of the hardliner Air Force General Gustavo Leigh, was appointed Secretary of National Direction of Commercialisation and Supplies (DINAC). DINAC, together with the Ministry of the Economy led by the civilian Orlando Millar, had the all-important task of supervising the supply and price control boards (Juntas de Abastecimiento y Control de Precios: JAP) and the people's stores. During and after 1972, these had become a key part of the networked movement linking government to the revolution from below, which continued to gain momentum at the grassroots level in spite or because of the continual attempts by the owners of Chile to block the supply of goods and production, as well as the US-sustained economic aggression. In turn, the young technophile responsible for the use of the Cybersyn network during the 1972 October Strike, Fernando Flores, was appointed by Allende as the new Minister of Finance.

Confirmation of the Allende–Prats doctrine of geo-economic sovereignty came on 30 September 1972, when the multinationals Anaconda and Kennecott acted on their threats of economic retaliation against Chile. These had been made after the nationalisation of their assets in the mining industry, and Allende's decision on compensation. Allende made a case for copper nationalisation based on UN General Assembly Resolution 1803/1962 on the right of peoples and states to a 'Permanent Sovereignty' over their natural resources. It recognised their right to recover and use such basic resources, allowing for compensation rules to be set in accordance with the laws of the state making the nationalisation, and establishing the courts of that country as the appropriate place in which to settle any resulting conflict.[3]

This was a vexing question for Allende, as it threatened to provoke the wrath of the multinationals and the US government abroad, or else bitter disappointment among UP sympathisers at home who expected Allende to stand up for Chile's interests. Allende's daughter Beatriz, for instance, challenged her father to ignore the multinationals' demands. In an anecdote she told some years later, Beatriz described that occasion: 'My father loved painting. I had this painting by Portocarrero, which he loved. I told him I would give it to him the day he nationalised copper. But only if he did not compensate the Americans.'[4]

Allende's doctrine of excess profits was declared under Decree 92 of 28 September 1971. It solved the question of compensation by appealing to legal arguments concerning restitution and remedial rather than redistributive justice. Basically, the argument was that while multinational corporations and their local beneficiaries *have* property, Chile and the majority of Chileans – since their fate has always been tied up with that of their natural resources – *are* property. In that sense, the former amassed wealth or stored surplus to the detriment of the latter, thereby doing them damage. An 'excess profits' doctrine attempts to remedy such kinds of historical wrong, while also entailing that the property of some is always limited by the interests of all (or others). Since the nineteenth century, British and American copper- and nitrate-mining companies had operated in Chile under little or no regulation, mostly occupying a quasi-monopolistic position. Profits were sent abroad for the most part, and their investments in the country were rarely proportionate to their gains. Historically speaking, therefore, the 'wages of Chile' had been paltry in comparison with the cumulative gains of these companies and their direct beneficiaries. Since this imbalance was the result of colonialism or neocolonialism, which excluded certain peoples in the domestic context, these cumulative gains could be seen as unjustified.

Although it would be hard to put a figure to these companies' excess profits from the beginning, the Chilean Copper Department had kept records of profits made and taken out of the country since at least the 1950s. These data could be used to calculate a sum in excess of which profits might be deemed 'excessive'. The surplus would be subtracted from the amount of compensation owed to the former proprietors of nationalised assets. In some cases, this would mean that the former owners actually owed a debt to countries like Chile, not too disimilar from Holocaust-related claims of financial and economic spoliation, which Germany paid to Israel after the Second World War and the 1951 Claims Conference. In other cases, the compensation owed by Chile would be much lower than expected. Allende's doctrine was in many respects ground-breaking, but it was legal: it addressed the circumstances in which rewards of past injustice have accumulated, those originally or directly harmed may or may not survive, and it seems difficult for individual victims to prove losses on the scale of the cumulative gains derived. Creatively, the Allende government construed such historical grievances as permanent features in a global market economy, which the beneficiaries ignore or under-value, and which give the victims of past history an option to demand payback now rather than in some receding future.

After Allende issued his 'excess profits' doctrine, US-based multinationals such as Anaconda and Kennecott and the US government, which expected full compensation to be paid for assets taken over, reacted by cutting off most sources of credit to Chile, or threatening to block the sales of copper extracted from El Teniente and other Chilean mines. The crux of the matter, however, is that the aggressive financial and economic blockade launched from Washington was not caused by the nationalisation and compensation measures; it had been decided on way before these were passed, when Nixon instructed his foreign, security and intelligence services to 'make the [Chilean] economy scream' in September and November 1970.

Nevertheless, a month after the nationalisation of copper, the president of the Export and Import Bank (Eximbank) warned Chile's ambassador to the US, Orlando Letelier, that the country would not obtain loans or financial guarantees unless it satisfactorily compensated Anaconda and Kennecott. If in 1969 Eximbank had loaned Chile some $28.7 million, in 1971 that amount shrank to zero; in 1972 – as the international price of copper fell in the wake of the hike in oil prices and the sale of US stocks, and with it the much-needed reserves to buy consumer goods made scarce by the owners' strike and other economic factors – it was $1.6 million, and in 1973 it rose to a mere $3.1 million.

On 13 September 1972, Kennecott asked a French tribunal to stop payments to the Chilean State Copper Corporation and embargo a shipment en route from El Teniente mine to the port of Le Havre. In solidarity with the Chilean revolution, French port workers refused to unload the cargo and stopped it from being taken over by Kennecott. Kennecott extended its court offensive to Sweden and West Germany, obliging Chile to suspend several shipments to Europe. This derailed ongoing credit negotiations between the country and European banks. *Time* magazine compared the multinationals' offensive to a military campaign.[5] Their hostility, together with US economic aggression and the downturn in the international price of copper, had a disastrous effect on Chile's economy.

In 1971, Allende had told the workers of the mine at Chuquicamata: 'Now it is a fact that Chile owns the mines, and we must be conscious of what this means. This is the main source of wealth for Chile.' Speaking at the Union Theatre in Norte Grande, he explained: 'I've put it this way. Copper revenue amounts to the wages of Chile. Eighty-three per cent of the reserves in hard currency available to Chile come from copper exports. Such commerce represents 800 million dollars out of the 1,150 million dollars of all Chilean exports. Twenty-five per cent of the national budget is funded with the income of the copper industry.' Turning to the political significance of the mines, Allende observed that:

'Many would like to provoke a confrontation between the mine workers and this government, a conflict between an industry that now belongs to the workers and the people and the people's government.' He was pointing out that even if Chile managed to obtain other sources of revenue and hard currency, the impact of any blockade on copper exports would be felt mainly at the level of relations between government and the miners: it would render the conditions for the renegotiation of wages more difficult than they were in the past. It would also harm its capacity to underwrite the consumer economy in the face of renewed efforts by the guilds to stop the flow of consumer goods, and to respond to economic dislocations as well as to the US embargo on imports needed for production and credit. Allende told the miners: 'Among the workers of Chile you have the biggest responsibility.'[6]

Between November 1971 and early 1973, the Chilean government approached the US government and its creditors in an effort to maintain reasonable relations and clarify its position. In a public letter to the US government, Allende wrote:

[The] internal process of transformation that our country requires in order to overcome such harsh realities as hunger, ignorance, and misery . . . is possible only with external support on the solid principles of self-determination, non-intervention, and dialogue between countries at the international level. We have followed that line consistently. However, we have been subject to constant attacks, either overtly or through covert means, from opposed interests and forces. There has been a campaign to distort who we are and what we want.

Having referred to the efforts of the Nixon administration to block the meeting of the Third UN Conference on Trade and Development (UNCTAD III) in Santiago in 1972 – which had become one of the main global forums for the unification of the voices of the Third World – its intervention in the credit restructure negotiation with the Paris Club of finance creditors, and the economic blockade from financial institutions, Allende told Nixon:

> The nationalisation of the copper mines was not a whim of the Chilean government. It has been a sovereign decision of our people, approved unanimously by the National Congress, and incorporated as an amendment in the text of our Constitution. Our Congress, Mr. President, has been elected by universal suffrage, secret and direct, and the majority of its membership belongs to the opposition parties.[7]

In spite of such efforts, the US government flatly rejected Chile's suggestion for a meeting aiming to resume normal relations between the countries. The US State Department had closed off that avenue even before Ambassador Letelier approached US Ambassador Davis, on the basis that such a meeting would only help to raise Allende's international profile.[8] According to Tanya Harmer, while the US, Soviet and Chinese leaders had agreed to disagree across the Pacific, the US would simply not listen to any attempt at an explanation from Chile's leaders and dismissed any idea of a reasonable disagreement. The implication is that such agreements were considered possible, from the point of view of the recently re-elected Nixon administration, between East–West big powers but never along the North–South axis, and clearly not in the area that the US considered its 'backyard'. As Nixon's adviser Henry Kissinger had told Chile's previous ambassador, the assumption underlying US–Latin America relations was that history simply did not happen in the South. South of the US border were peoples 'without history'. 'While the Nixon administration refused to countenance any financial settlement with Santiago to ease its balance-of-payments deficit,' Harmer observes, 'it also continued to exacerbate the UP's challenges back home, actively subverting Allende's parliamentary opposition, and sympathising with military plotters.'[9]

Salvador Allende and Pablo Neruda at a rally of the Unidad Popular during the 1970 presidential campaign, San Antonio, Chile.

President Salvador Allende during the inauguration parade, 3 November 1970; General Augusto Pinochet salutes in the background.

Front of a leaflet explaining the significance of the nationalisation of copper to the Chilean people, 1971.

President Salvador Allende signs the constitutional amendment nationalising copper, 11 July 1971.

Salvador Allende and Fidel Castro, during Castro's visit to Chile in 1972.

The October 1972
Truck Owners' Strike.

Allende with female leaders of the Mapuche indigenous people whose
role was central to agrarian reform, 1971–2.

Pinochet in 1973 with Allende, weeks before the coup.

Richard Nixon and Henry Kissinger in the early 1970s.

General René Schneider, constitutionalist and commander-in-chief of the army, was murdered on 22 October 1970 by members of Fatherland and Freedom connected to the CIA as part of a plot to stop Allende's confirmation.

Project Cybersyn
Operations
Room, visited by
Allende and new
commander-in-chief
General Carlos Prats,
30 December 1972.

First thought to
have been taken
on 11 September
1973, this iconic
picture of Allende
at La Moneda is
now agreed to
have been taken
during the 29 June
coup attempt.

One of a number of demonstrations in support of Allende between June and
September 1973. The banner reads 'Create Popular Power'.

The Chilean army moves into position on the morning of 11 September 1973. Armed junta units are pictured here moving a gun into place in front of the Cuban embassy in Santiago.

Allende addresses the Chilean people over the airwaves from his office at La Moneda, 11 September 1973.

The aerial attack by Hawker Hunter combat jets on La Moneda, around 11.55 a.m., 11 September 1973.

The dictator, General Augusto Pinochet Ugarte, 1973.

Santiago's National Stadium, which was turned into the first of many prison camps after the 1973 coup. Thousands were tortured and killed.

Troops detaining government supporters on the streets of Santiago. By December 1973 1,823 people had died. The official victim list accepted by the Chilean government in August 2011 totalled 40,018.

Popular folk singer Víctor Jara, tortured and killed in the National Stadium a few days after the 1973 coup.

General Carlos Prats, former commander-in-chief of the Chilean Army and a convinced constitutionalist, was murdered with his wife in a car blast by Pinochet's DINA agents in Buenos Aires, 30 September 1974.

Federico Willoughby, photographed at the funeral of Spanish caudillo Francisco Franco, November 1975.

Henry Kissinger greets General Augusto Pinochet, President of the Chilean Military Junta, during a visit to Santiago, June 1976.

The remains of Orlando Letelier's car after it was bombed by Pinochet's DINA agents in Washington, DC, 21 September 1976.

Writer Julio Cortázar at home in Paris, France, 27 November 1978.

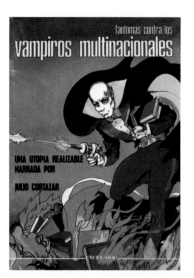

Cover of Cortázar's graphic novella *Fantomas contra los vampiros multinacionales*, based on his experience as a member of the Second Russell Tribunal (1974–5).

Nearly forty years later a new generation of Chileans becomes radical: protests led by the Chilean student movement, September 2011.

Camila Vallejo and Francisco Figueroa were among student leaders who made world headlines as they ushered in a new era of Chilean politics, inspired by Allende. Pictured here during the 2011 Santiago Book Fair at an event moderated by Víctor Hugo de la Fuente (*centre*).

All this meant, in the eyes of Chilean armed forces officers like Carlos Prats, that Chile's position of ineluctable dependency – which underpinned the US overt financial aggression and covert intervention, as well as its attempt to subvert the opposition in and out of parliament, but also the hawks within his army – was the real threat to national security. If so, then moving towards 'geo-economic sovereignty' appeared completely reasonable. In that situation, it would be crucial to form international alliances independent of the big power games. Forums like the UN General Assembly, the G-77 coalition of developing nations seeking to enhance their joint negotiating capacity vis-à-vis developed powers, the UNCTAD conference, and the Non-Aligned Movement of countries that had not formally sided with any of the Cold War power blocs since 1961, were propitious to that purpose.

Together, the non-aligned countries have come to represent nearly two-thirds of the UN's members and more than half of the world's population. In their diversity, both political and economic, these countries also represent the position that in a healthy cosmopolitan world it is unreasonable to expect to be able to convert our opposite numbers completely to our viewpoint. From this perspective, domestic as well as international relations and regulations must be based on genuine consensus, and the ability to listen well enough to understand views that may differ fundamentally from our own, and then try to find pragmatic common ground without imposing our own position. It is in this sense that the purpose of alliances like the Non-Aligned Movement was defined as 'ensuring national independence, sovereignty, territorial integrity and security . . . [and] to struggle against imperialism, colonialism, neo-colonialism, racism, and all forms of foreign aggression, occupation, domination, interference or hegemony, as well as against great power and bloc politics'.[10] It would be senseless, and a gross mistake, to reduce the diversity of these perspectives to the oversimplified and paranoid binary logic of the Cold War's formulations – for instance, communism versus the free world – just as it made no sense to present the

diversity within the UP coalition or the Chilean government as
'communist', 'socialist', and so on.

Allende was a socialist and a Marxist, but he was also a democrat
and a legalist who thought guerrilla warfare or civil war would only
destroy his country. Although respectful of Castro and Guevara, he
did not put his country on the path of becoming a one-party state
like Cuba. In turn, Castro acknowledged that in countries like Chile
the 'electoral and legal path' was possible, although fraught with
difficulties because of the dogmatism of old-school Cold Warriors.
And Prats was neither a socialist like Allende, nor a revolutionary
like Castro, but became convinced that Allende's doctrine of geo-
economic sovereignty was more reasonable for countries like Chile
than continued dependence on the rules imposed by the big powers.
That three men from such different political, social and historical
backgrounds, as well as women like Beatriz Allende, Miriam
Contreras or Carmen Lazo, could find common ground, in the
same way in which the Non-Aligned nations struggled to find a
common purpose, is a testament to the fact that a diversity of
perspectives, even a radical one, while it may cause difficulties, can
also be a source of creativity. After all, a group of people who tend
to see things the same way is much less likely to come up with new
and challenging ideas.

The problem, in 1972 and 1973, was that US officials and a hard
core of Chilean society did not see things that way. President
Nixon's officials plainly told Santiago representatives that they had
developed the best economic and political system worldwide, and
although they would not impose it on others, at least not openly –
with the obvious and glaring exception of Vietnam – they expected
others to follow their example. The Chileans told them that
although they were committed democrats, they did not think it
reasonable to believe that Americans were in sole possession of the
truth or could tell others what was best for them. After all, history
is full of examples of powers thinking they could tell others what
was best for them and ending up by oppressing them. For example,

the notion that capitalism is the best system there is, or can be, assumes an idea of development tethered to the notion that the global North owes no obligations of remedial justice to the peoples of the global South. According to Upendra Baxi, this assumption makes it clear beyond doubt that 'the past victimage costs of Euroamerican "success" stories of development remain entirely inconsequential for the Global North institutionalised conceptions of development aid and assistance as forms of North-favoured regime acts of largesse,' or for their prescriptions of self-reliance and entrepreneurial initiative.[11]

When Allende left Chile at the end of 1972 on an international tour that would take him from Bogotá and Mexico City to Havana, via New York, Algiers and Moscow, he appealed to the idea of the Third World not as an oppositional but as a self-positioning entity in world affairs and global history. He hinted also at a different story of globalisation: rather than observing the logical evolution of the old Westphalian arrangement of international conduct, which prescribed non-inteference between recognised sovereigns in Europe, while allowing for imperial competition in the rest of the world, the 1970s saw the eventful emergence of Third Worldism. This was a living and creative project of resistance against the notion of a 'One-World' model imposed from above by big world powers. Borrowing Pablo Neruda's phrase that described what was happening in Chile as a 'silent Vietnam',[12] Allende denounced the agression of mining multinationals and such corporations as ITT against his country, during the UN General Assembly meeting of 4 December 1972. He accused the multinationals of trying to provoke a civil war, after recalling their role in the assassination of General Schneider. 'The aggression of these capitalist corporations aims at impeding the liberation of the popular classes,' he said. 'It represents a direct attack against the economic interests of the workers.'[13]

Emphasising the political maturity of the people of Chile, Allende explained that the problems facing Chilean society fell squarely within the remit of the UN Charter and the attention of the General

Assembly: 'the struggle for social justice and liberation, the effort to achieve welfare and further intellectual progress, the defence of our dignity and identity'.[14] His message was not meant directly for the US and the USSR, whose priority at the time was to defuse tensions between them as the Vietnam War drew to a close, but rather, and mainly, for the majority of the peoples and nations of the UNGA that gave shape to the very idea of the Third World.

This idea continues to provide a rich repertoire concerning notions of development and justice, far in advance of those limited ideas of justice, humanitarianism and development that focus on largesse, charity or military intervention. The latter remain tethered to geopolitical military and economic assumptions, and contribute to the militarisation of humanitarian considerations that originated in the Manichean worldview of the Cold War and continue to inform today's defence of military intervention against the much richer tradition of human rights, the rights of peoples and international law.[15] In contrast, the political histories and juridical legacy of Third Worldism, of which Allende's voice was part and parcel in 1972, helped install at the heart of post-war international law the principle and language of self-determination as a collective human right of the colonially vanquished peoples. According to Upendra Baxi, Third World languages contributed remarkably to the UN Charter's rejection in international law of possession by conquest – whether of peoples, resources, territories, or even of nature.[16]

This was the progressive language of the times, voicing a history of self-affirmation and positioning in history and world affairs, even if, or precisely because, the big powers were, as they remain today, not ready to listen. Allende confirmed this sad fact of international relations during his visit to Moscow and his last-minute meeting with the US ambassador to the UN, George H. W. Bush, future director of the CIA and forty-first US president. Face to face with Allende at the Waldorf Hotel in New York, Bush told the Chilean president that Americans 'did not consider ourselves imperialists and that we still had a deep conviction that our free enterprise system was not selfish but was the best system'.[17] He also told Allende that, in spite of 'excesses from time to time', this system did not bleed people when it was exported abroad. Owing to such deep conviction, Bush said, 'the people, the government, and the system' were 'interlocked'. There is nothing to indicate that Allende intended his arguments in this regard to persuade US officials of the error of their ways and push them into making concessions or relaxing their economic stranglehold. In fact, he responded to Bush's requirement that Allende should withdraw the most damning passages from his UN speech with a firm refusal, pointing out that he hoped to highlight the global responsibility of the CIA and the multinationals.

Legally speaking, Allende was right. If, as Bush would have it, the people, the government and the system were 'interlocked' in their convictions when, as a result of acts committed by government officials abroad, others were harmed, then it would not be possible to apportion responsibility and to hold such officials culpable for illegal actions committed in 'defence' of their 'system'. But this would strike at the very heart of the Nuremberg Principles that allowed for the trial and condemnation not only of Nazi leaders, but also of civilian lawyers, bureaucrats and industrialists 'following orders' or acting on the belief that they were defending a system they too considered the best during the Second World War. After Nuremberg, individual responsibility cannot be melted back into some wholesale 'deep conviction'. If Nuremberg could be seen as only a partial success because it did not result in the mass prosecution of the 'good Germans' who stood by as the Holocaust happened, looked the other way, or were, as Daniel Goldhagen put it, 'Hitler's willing executioners', then the standard of responsibility thus laid down stands as a challenge that the post-war world has yet to meet.

According to Robert Meister, at the time of the Vietnam War many protesters in the US against the actions of the Nixon administration read Nuremberg (through the lens of the trial of the Nazi war criminal Adolf Eichmann) as an argument that bureaucrats, legal advisers and ordinary soldiers should be held to account for the crimes of their government, and that 'US citizens must make an existential choice between resistance and complicity'.[18] In 1968, Bertrand Russell and Jean-Paul Sartre interpreted Vietnam in the light of Nuremberg. Russell convened a citizens' International War Crimes Tribunal, arguing that the principles applied in the Nuremberg Trials also applied to the victors in the war and still powerful countries such as the US. Sartre stated that US military strategy in Vietnam amounted to a strategically staged genocide. He also pointed out that this strategy was being applied with the intention of imposing a one-world model in the interests of big world powers.[19] In doing so, Sartre was extending Nuremberg Principles to the case of crimes committed against human rights in the context of colonialism and neocolonialism.[20] 'The ties of the "One-World" model on which the United States wants to impose its hegemony, have grown tighter and tighter,' he wrote. 'The group which the United States wants to intimidate and terrorize by way of the Vietnamese nation is the human group in its entirety.'[21] The relevance of Nuremberg to Vietnam would be reaffirmed by the US chief counsel before the Nuremberg Tribunals. In his 1970 book *An American Tragedy*, Telford Taylor measured the success of the trial at Nuremberg by the extent to which it had become a precedent in ordinary prosecutions not only against the defeated at war but also of those whose human rights abuses were committed on behalf of still powerful states.[22]

In recasting the events taking place in Chile as a 'silent Vietnam', Neruda and Allende were hinting at a powerful philosophical and juridical argument with a very strong precedent. If collective and individual responsibility, ethics and politics are inseparable, if 'deep conviction' that our system is the best there is cannot be used as a pretext to avoid responsibility for the violation of human rights and the rights of peoples, and among such rights the right to development must be included, then Allende's speeches in late 1972 and early 1973, before the UN General Assembly and elsewhere, amount to something more than outdated rhetoric or misplaced tactics. For they argued that the deliberate causing of 'maldevelopment' through a range of concerted efforts by states, multinationals, international finance institutions and client national elites, such as Kennecott's 'military campaign', US economic aggression, or its intervention in favour of subversive domestic opposition groups like Fatherland and Freedom – which according to Patricio Guzmán, among others, received military training by CIA operatives in Chile – should be treated as ordinary war crimes.

If so, then they could be construed as having risen to the level of genocide because the final and willed goal of such overt and covert tactics and strategy would not only be regime change but to show to all others – to humanity as a whole – that if they resisted 'They will be crushed the way we are crushing the first'. Allende and Neruda, especially during the Third UNCTAD Conference, the international tour of late 1972, the Twenty-Seventh UN General Assembly sessions and at least two meetings of the Non-Aligned Movement, the last of which took place in July 1973, were in fact working towards a ground-breaking notion of financial violence and crimes against self-determination, economic independence, the right to development and participatory democracy.

The arguments rehearsed by Allende and Neruda, among others, between 1968 and 1973 would be picked up in 1974 and 1975 by the Second Russell Tribunal, convened in order to consider the case of Latin America. In its verdict, the Second Russell Tribunal explicitly referred to the role of multinational corporations (MNCs) in this vein. The criminal acts hinted at in the literature of the period, and the duties to desist from such acts through effective acts of legislation and legal administration, could easily be extended to the actions of public–private partnerships fostering pathological regimes of development. For instance, as in later cases like Bhopal, Ogoniland, Bechtel–Aguas del Tunari in Bolivia, and BP's *Deepwater Horizon* oil spill in the Gulf of Mexico. Or in a different but related manner, the case of the banks and financial institutions – public and private, local as well as global – responsible for the 2008 financial collapse, and the protracted suffering of thousands if not millions of people from the Americas to the south of Europe. This remains a hitherto uncharted field for law, politics and human rights, but one much more promising than the empty statements about self-regulation or the 'social responsibility' of ethical multinational corporations inscribed in such texts as the Global Compact and other UN-driven MNC guidelines.[23]

For the duration of Allende's international tour, almost a month, General Carlos Prats assumed control of the Executive Office's domestic functions, in his capacity as minister of the interior and vice-president of the Republic. As such, he welcomed Pablo Neruda on 5 December 1971, as the poet returned for good to Chile having led its diplomatic mission in Paris, and having won the Nobel Prize for Literature. Prats also learned first hand about the effects that the 1972 October Strike and the continuing campaign, both domestic and international, to strangle the Chilean economy were having on the political stability of the country. During this time, Prats reaffirmed his conviction that the country was sharply divided between two sectors with irreconcilable political differences. But he also believed that the majority of the population would accept the transformative process led by government, if it took place within the law and with full democratic guarantees.

Throughout 1972 and at least until late 1973, Prats remained persuaded that the participation of loyalist members of the armed forces in government could contribute to the achievement of a political compromise with the opposition to support the Executive in its efforts to overcome skyrocketing inflation, restructure the commercial and financial domestic and international set-up of the country to offset the effects of the US blockade and intervention-ism, and neutralise the hawks within the Chilean military. All the while, he assumed, such political compromise would help moderate the expectations of the more radical sectors within the UP and the population, bringing the process closer to the progressive centrist position in the PDC. 'It is clear that our participation in the Cabinet did not entail the politicisation of the armed forces or their commitment to one of the sides in the political spectrum,' he wrote. 'Rather, its foundation lies in the difficult situation that the country was going through and in the urgent need to restore some sense of public normality.'[24]

In November 1972, General Prats declared, presciently, to a magazine associated with the PDC:

There are some Chileans who seem to think that only a violent and forceful solution would do. They are not the majority. Such a solution has no future. For where would it lead us? To a dictatorship. It would have to be an implacable, ruthlessly repressive dictatorship. To behave as such, the military would have to turn itself into a specialised, secretive political police. And this would mean transforming the people into 'tupamaros', guerrilla fighters and enemy combatants all of them. The next week, having applauded the self-appointed dictator, the most embattled political sides would be shouting at us: Gorillas! And asking for a transition to electoral democracy . . . The workers represent a real social power. They are organised. There is a dignity in this country that extends to all of its sectors. Political leaders in this country move the masses because they truly relate to them. Our mission as military personnel is not to replace civilian power, and we cannot entertain that idea.[25]

Washington begged to differ. As US policymakers stalled negotiations with Santiago, concerning its financial and economic blockade of the country, the US government continued to subvert Chile's democratic process. The CIA defined its overall goal for 1973 as 'slowing down the socialisation of Chile', and in this regard Chile's upcoming congressional elections of March 1973 were widely considered as a red line: either the opposition would gather enough strength in Congress to constitutionally impeach Allende, or else only a military solution and even civil war would remain possible.[26]

During the five months leading up to the elections, the US government committed $1.6 million to promote the opposition, while the CIA station in Santiago led an 'effective and outstanding' effort to help the opposition fight an 'optimum campaign'.[27] That campaign included a repeat and playing up of the media 'scare campaign' of the previous years, for instance through the Agriculture Society radio station where Federico Willoughby and others ramped up their anti-government rhetoric, but also more focused support to the organised militant Right, especially to Jaime Guzmán's *Gremialismo*, and the militant shock groups. These had proven successful in their attempt to recruit wider sectors of the Chilean middle classes to the cause of overthrowing Allende, providing contacts between civilian politicians, industrialists and hardliners within the armed forces from within the right-wing National Party as well as rightist sectors of the PDC.

These elements were also in charge of keeping up the pressure on Chile's economic infrastructure, shifting attacks on the government from the halls of Congress to the streets of Santiago, creating a climate of violence and then pinning it on the government and on those masses that Peter Winn called 'the revolution from below'. From Allende's perspective, these elements and their foreign patrons had declared 'war against Chile inside and outside the country'.[28] Yet Allende tried to cool down the political scene, building bridges to the PDC, as well as responding to the economic consequences of the *Gremialista* strike and US blockade, and the government's own mistakes. At the initiative of General Prats, the ministers of the economic area, Millar and Flores, among others, prepared a new legislative bill concerning the Social Area. This legal proposal contemplated nationalising only fifty out of the ninety companies listed for inclusion in the Social Area. The others, and the rest of the industries taken by the workers in the wake of the 1972 October Strike, would be returned to their owners. Something similar would happen with land appropriations of less than eighty hectares. This would mean a clash between the actions and expectations of the revolution from below and the political survival instincts of the UP government. It was a clear message that the government was prepared to pull the handbrake on the increased momentum and speed of the revolution from below.

According to Winn, the key to the revolution from below and the opposition's charge that the Executive was forfeiting its rights to represent good Chileans was Allende's pledge, unlike his predecessors, not to use the security forces and the force of the law against the people.[29] Although the government bill did not break that pledge, it certainly put a strain on the relation between the leadership from above and the revolution from below. During an encounter between Allende and the industrial belts of Santiago, the president tried to persuade them to support the so-called 'Prats–Millar' legislative project. In February 1973 the industrial belts, together with the community commandos and the National Organisation of Builders, had issued a declaration calling for the construction of a socialism 'from below' and 'the struggle to establish a worker's management in all of the industries of the socialised sector'. Parallel to such demands were efforts to create concrete political and self-regulatory institutions outside those of government and the existing legal and political architecture, such as people's assemblies and community boards. In a sense, the revolution from below had arrived at a turning point, after which it would begin to transform itself into a self-regulated body that in many ways made some of the existing institutions of law and state superfluous, or at least announced their withering away.[30]

It is difficult to say whether the experience of the Chilean people at this point was that of the effective withering away of the state, or its transformation into a state that relates to the people at its base in a wholly different manner. What is clear, however, is that the opposition sectors were alarmed by these and other related developments. The deputy director of the Edwardses' newspaper *El Mercurio*, Arturo Fontaine Aldunate, also a member of the secretive Cofradía society that included Sergio de Castro and hardline navy officers José Toribio Merino, Patricio Carvajal and ex-officer Roberto Kelly, claimed that this was yet another step towards the establishment of a 'rigorous socialist apparatus'.[31] He was referring, especially, to the announcement made by finance minister Fernando Flores concerning the further development of the supply and price control boards (JAP) into popular support networks and the rationing of up to thirty products, yet to be decided, according to the needs of the population. In response to right-wing criticism of the entrenchment of the networked movement from below and rationing measures, a slum-dweller woman from the Nueva Habana camp, organised in conjunction with MIR militants, stated: 'They talk about rationing as if the word would scare the people off. Don't they realise that we always lived under a system of rations? Rationed because of the salaries the wealthy would pay us. For instance, I started work when I was eight, so my education was rationed . . .'[32]

Everyone's attention, however, was focused on the electoral contest of 4 March 1973. In Santiago, for instance, the leader of the conservative wing of the PDC, Eduardo Frei, clashed with the president of the National Party and co-founder (with *nacista* Jorge Prat) of Acción Nacional Sergio Onofre Jarpa, and the Communist leader Volodia Teitelboim, of Jewish origin. Frei stated that the election was 'a plebiscite on Allende, and the most important in Chile's history in this century at least'. On 28 February, Frei made explicit that the choice that faced the people of Chile was one between the 'democratic' surrender of the UP and brute force. 'We are for a democratic solution that would rebuild the country, with peace and jobs,' he said. 'We do not want the country to be pushed to civil war and confrontation.'

Frei's solution was no solution at all. On the one hand, it called for the UP government to surrender if it was defeated, the assumption being that such a defeat would translate into Allende's impeachment. Certain of his triumph, Frei was already looking forward to the reconstruction of the country after the havoc allegedly caused by the UP. On the other hand, ominously, the message was that if the people did not vote Allende out by giving the Nationalist–PDC opposition – which for the first time appeared united in the election – the two-thirds of the congressional seats it needed in order to impeach the president, then the only option was military force. Frei said he wished to avoid that option – as most reasonable people in Chile would have, for civil war is the worst of all options, or no solution at all – but in fact he was telling the people of Chile just the opposite: give us your vote, or violence comes next. At best, it was political blackmail, a forced choice. At worst, it meant the right wing had already chosen for – rather than with – the people of Chile: victory or war.

When the first electoral results came out in the evening of 4 March, and with 40 per cent of the ballots still to be counted, the odds seem to favour the opposition. Impatient, the women of the Poder Femenino, escorted by the shock troops of Fatherland and Freedom and the ex-Cadet Commandos, took to the streets of Santiago, together with a caravan of cars in the better-off sectors of the city, to celebrate their victory and the end of the UP government. Asked for a response before the camera of Patricio Guzmán, a sympathiser of Poder Femenino in dark glasses, soon to be the trademark of the patriarchs in charge of restoring 'law and order' to Chile, ranted about how 'the filthy communists should leave the country immediately, or be taken away!'[33]

But the celebratory mood promptly gave way to feelings of shock and disappointment as the right-wing opposition and US officials learned that not only had the UP not lost the election and its congressional seats, it had actually picked up two additional ones in the Senate and six in the lower Chamber. Given the expectation on both sides of the opposition that the economic stranglehold over the people of Chile would force a conditioned response on their part, which would translate into Allende's defeat, the result could not have been more surprising. After twenty-nine months of administration, political killings, errors, economic blockade and covert subversion from Washington, high inflation, a transport blockade and overt violence from the powerful of Santiago, a terror campaign in the media and a shortage of consumer goods, the UP government increased its popular electoral support to 43.4 per cent of the electorate, while the recently formed right-wing *Confederación de la Democracia* (CODE), which contained, among others, the National Party and the PDC, obtained 54.7 per cent. The PDC saw its support reduced to 29 per cent, six points less than in 1969. In contrast, the Nationalists achieved a sizeable 21 per cent. Although not being representative of even a third of the electorate, it became clear to Guzmán and the other young conservatives that the move from traditional conservatism to a more overt counter-revolutionary stance was bearing fruit.

But the most important result of the election became immediately apparent to US false-flaggers and agents on the ground. The CIA station in Santiago now urged its superiors in Washington to 'keep all options open . . . including a possible future coup'. The station's chief Ray Warren argued that from then on support for political parties, private businesses and the media in which Federico Willoughby and Jaime Guzmán played a central role – which in fact also meant direct support for the right-wing parties' paramilitary troops – should focus on creating 'an atmosphere of political unrest and controlled crisis'. The ultimate goal would be to 'stimulate' military intervention.[34]

Washington hesitated over the outcome of a coup, fearing that after Allende and the Chilean people had demonstrated being far stronger than previously thought, to push them further might result, at best, in a PDC victory in future elections with a strong 'socialist communitarian' component, and at worst, all-out revolution. US officials considered what would be the best and safest way to go about it, if required, while the CIA continued to gather information that could be valuable to military plotters in the event of a coup – arrest lists, intelligence about government installations, UP contingency plans to resist a military challenge – and also to work in close collusion with members of the opposition and young conservatives with links to the armed forces, the media, the captains of industry and the paramilitary troops. To 'wait and see', as instructed by Washington, meant finding a solution on the ground to what Warren considered the real problem: for him, the main obstacle to a successful coup lay within the military itself. That meant the constitutionalist officers and those who seemed to share some of Allende's views. Chief among these was Carlos Prats.

On 30 December 1969, Prats had written a report titled 'Analysis of the political situation from a military standpoint'. In it he predicted quite accurately that Allende would win the election (he gave Allende 38 per cent of the vote; Allende gained 36.4 per cent) and observed that '80% of the personnel of the armed forces belong to "the left-of-centre tendency, not openly Marxist or leaning towards it". The other 20% could be divided into two groups: a right-wing faction constituted by high- and mid-ranking officers, and "another infiltrated by Marxist propaganda", constituted by officers and low-ranking NCOs.'[35]

A study of the political make-up of the armed forces carried out by Arnoldo Camú in 1973 estimated that there were two tendencies splitting the military into two: one group committed to the defence of the Constitution and another group of *golpistas* in favour of a coup, inspired by the Brazilian example of 1964 – possibly with active support from the military regime in Brasilia, which Nixon had brokered and secured personally. The latter were quite strong, but could not break the chain of command on their own. Later on, Colonel Fernando Reveco confirmed this appreciation of the situation in the military: 'according to him in 1973 between 25% and 30% of the officers were with the Allende government, out of respect for the Constitution, rather than because they were Marxist or socialists. Only between 10% and 15% were openly in favour of a break with the constitution.'[36]

These numbers confirm CIA chief Warren's concerns. If only up to 15 per cent of the members of Chile's armed forces were in favour of a military intervention in 1973, then for a possible coup to succeed a massive purge within the military would be required. This meant staging not one coup but many. The coup against Allende, which after the results of the March 1973 election everyone in the hard-line opposition wished for and actively sought, required a previous and quite brutal coup within the coup, a purge within the military. At this point, a coup against Allende also meant a coup against the law and democracy. One could argue that the purge had begun before 1973, with the assassination of General René Schneider. It can also be argued that the coup within the coup went well past 1973, as implied by General Prats's observation that in the event of a coup the military would have to turn itself into a political police and the people into its enemy. Hence the fourth and deadliest coup, the genocidal measures aimed at the people.

Admiral Patricio Carvajal summed up in one phrase the reasons for the coup against Allende: 'Allende is the devil reincarnate.' He was talking about one of the meetings he attended with the president as part of the High Council for National Defence, in charge of Chile's national security. After the failure of the 1973 March elections, the owners' guilds and Jaime Guzmán's *Gremialistas* resumed their blockade and strike campaigns (which now included a small but powerful sector of the workers of El Teniente copper mine against the majority of the mine-workers position and, according to Patricio Guzmán, founded and supported by the *Gremialistas*), including a transport strike in the capital. Fatherland and Freedom, the ex-Cadets, Poder Femenino and the other paramilitary groups with ties to the *Gremialistas* and the nationalists launched an even fiercer campaign of violence, disorder and bombing, which also targeted the industrial belts. Allende himself would lead the sessions of the High Council. According to Carvajal:

They were never really council meetings. Instead, Allende would give us a pep talk. He would tell us that national security was in peril because of the CIA and other reactionary elements within Chile, who were behind the transport strikes. I could tell he was lying . . . and he lied extraordinarily well, as did his ministers. Nothing could be believed. Allende certainly could lie diabolically well.[37]

Admiral Carvajal deserves more credit than historians of the Chile coup allow him. Because of his initiative, the so-called Committee of Fifteen was instituted on 30 June 1973. Unlike the Cofradía Náutica, the Committee of Fifteen did not act behind a veil of secrecy. General Carlos Prats agreed to its formation, taking on board Carvajal's initiative and the advice of his two colleagues in Allende's Cabinet, Admiral Raúe Montero and General César Ruiz Danyau, enlisted by Allende to help to stabilise the country. Five high-ranking members of each branch of the armed forces would make up the Committee. Their task would be 'to establish where the situation is going, and find some common ground'.[38] Now the minority group of conspiring generals and admirals, who had been meeting in secret, could express their views in the open, and from a position of command.

Carvajal made his proposal after the failure of an attempted coup on 29 June 1973. It had been crushed by the loyalists within the armed forces, Prats and others, but revealed the existence of an internal split in the military, as well as its darker side. On 29 June Lieutenant Colonel Roberto Souper attacked La Moneda presidential palace with the tanks of his Second Armoured Regiment. Prats and, eventually, garrison chief Augusto Pinochet put an end to the conspiracy. Accompanied by Lieutenant Colonel Hernández Pedreros and other officers, General Prats got one tank driver after another to surrender. Towards the end, one of the tank drivers, Lieutenant Mario Garay, pointed his sub-machine gun at General Prats and told him he refused to give up. Major Osvaldo Zavala, Prats's most trusted soldier, reacted quickly: he pulled out his gun and pointed it at Garay's head. Garay gave up. Around midday, Colonel Souper took refuge back at his headquarters with the remaining three tanks. Seventeen soldiers and five civilians died that morning, including an Argentinian journalist named Leonardo Henricksen who captured the moment when a soldier turned towards his camera and shot him down. The cameraman filmed his own death.

According to Patricio Guzmán, who included the entire shot in his documentary *The Battle of Chile*, he also revealed the darker face of the Chilean army.[39] In the afternoon, five leading members of the right-wing paramilitary group Fatherland and Freedom sought refuge in the Ecuadorian embassy. They assumed full responsibility as the alleged instigators of the military's revolt. Souper had been recruited by the group earlier on, but was not the only one in the military with strong ties to the group, which also had links among the *Gremialistas* and members of the National Party close to ex-President Alessandri. The Fatherland thugs argued that the coup had failed because they had been betrayed. The incident also revealed that civilian combatants, including terrorist organisations such as Fatherland and Freedom, which had had previous dealings with the CIA and took part in the murder of General Schneider in 1970, were conspiring with members of the army.

In turn, the plotters within the armed forces confirmed the lesson first learned by CIA chief Warren: no coup would succeed if they did not get rid of the chiefs of command who continued to abide by the 'Schneider Doctrine' of respect for law and the Constitution. Most of all, Carlos Prats. A year after the events of 29 June, General Sergio Arellano would reveal that several other units in the armed forces were in fact prepared to follow the Second Armoured Regiment that day, undeterred by legality. What stopped them? Seemingly, a blunder by the right-wing lawyer Sergio Miranda Carrington, a member of the National Party close to Alessandri's circle, like Guzmán, Willoughby and De Castro. His indiscretion alerted Prats to the plot.

Certainly, in June 1973 there was no consensus among the officers of the armed forces about the coup. A considerable number of them, under the leadership of the commander-in-chief, actively opposed any such idea. Which leads to the conclusion that the coup Admiral Carvajal was helping coordinate since at least June 1973 was not the work of the Chilean armed forces as a whole: rather, it would be carried out by a faction within. According to the historian Jorge Magasich-Airola, the little-known story of the law-abiding members of the forces who refused from the outset to take part in any such coup 'destroys the myth of the unanimous uprising of the Chilean military', which has been one of the dogmas of contemporary Latin American history.[40]

Before Carvajal proposed his initiative, on 28 May 1973, a number of ex-High Command officers sent a public letter to Allende declaring that the armed forces would consider themselves free to take action should the government 'violate the constitution'. This rightist perception was motivated by two significant developments. The first was the number of debates that ensued on the left after the creation of a 'People's Assembly' in the city of Concepción. Five thousand people and over a hundred organisations of workers, slum-dwellers, peasants and students gathered in Concepción to decide whether to proceed towards the establishment of an alternative 'popular power' that would in time replace Congress, the judiciary and other institutions of 'bourgeois law and democracy', or to lend further support to the UP 'people's government' programme through such organisations, especially in conflict areas such as workers' participation and the entrenchment of the economy's Social Area.[41]

The second development was a legislative proposal for educational reform known as ENU (National United Education system), presented by the Allende administration in mid-March 1973. The bill was the result of a consensus achieved during the 1971 National Congress for Education, backed by the government's significant achievements on literacy and recommendations by UNESCO. The

Right focused its criticism on the leftist wording of a leaked document connected with but not part of the bill. In spite of assurances
by Education Minister Jorge Tapia that the bill guaranteed freedom
of thought, teaching and conscience, that it respected the 1971
consensus and followed not Marxism but the advice of UNESCO,
Guzmán's *Gremialistas* in the National Party branded ENU an
attempt by a Marxist government to impose a cultural internationalist tyranny contrary to the values of *chilenidad* and to indoctrinate
children against Christianity.

The second incident was much more serious than the first, in
spite of the heightened rhetoric about 'forming popular power' to
the left of Allende after the 29 June attempted coup.[42] This is
because, for the first time, the UP government was not only
confronted by right-wing nationalists but also faced a strong reaction from the Catholic hierarchy and explicit criticism from top
levels of the armed forces; some of these officers branded Allende's
a 'Marxist government', thereby implying its foreign and illegitimate character. The education bill incident made clear the extent to
which high-ranking officers had aligned themselves with the most
extremist views of the right-wing opposition.

Crucially, there was a historical precedent. In 1933 the Spanish
Republican government presented a reform bill that sought to secu-
larise education. Carlist landowners, rightist National Action politicians and ideological pundits appearing before the Women's
Association for Civic Education immediately construed the Spanish
draft law as 'a satanic plot by the Freemasons to destroy the Catholic
Church', and 'the work of foreigners, just like the sects and the
Internationals'.[43] Even though the Chilean 1973 reform did little or
nothing to exclude religious education, and in spite of the fact that
Santiago's Cardinal Archbishop Raúl Silva Henríquez highlighted
the reform's positive aspects, it was successfully construed as Marxist-
inspired and anti-Christian, like its Spanish predecessor. The Chilean
1973 equivalents of the Spanish rightist organisations of 1933, the
Carlist-inspired *Gremialismo* of Jaime Guzmán, the National Party,

ideological pundits with access to the media like Guzmán and Willoughby, and Poder Femenino, successfully used the incident as a pretext for popularising and extending far-right clichés of Masonic–Jewish–Bolshevik conspiracies into good Christian middle-class Chilean homes.[44]

To their eyes, Allende's policies and growing electoral support, riding on the back of the growing momentum of the revolution from below (now shifting into 'popular power'), confirmed the evil nature of his Masonic manipulative ways, his wicked influence over the working class, and how far through the nation's political body the populist cancer had spread. On the occasion of the proposed educational reforms, Rear Admiral Ismael Huerta, one of the military members of Allende's Cabinet, stated: 'We cannot accept that future soldiers arrive at the barracks converted into Marxists.' Huerta's statement not only belies the alleged apolitical status of the conspirators within the armed forces; it shows them assuming the role of a public force organised for the suppression of the revolutionary movement of the Chilean people working along-side the UP government. The faction of the armed forces repre-sented by Huerta, Carvajal, Merino and the former members of the High Command was way ahead in the process of abandoning tradi-tional conservatism to become part of a counter-revolutionary war machine.

From their shared viewpoint, Marxism came to signify nothing more and nothing less than the lurker in the dark, the stuff of night-mares. In *The Battle of Chile*, Guzmán places this transition, and the use of a heavily charged language, in the context of the Cold War 'battle of ideas'. 'Since 1950, more than four thousand officers have been on training courses in the US and in the Panama Canal area,' says the narrator in Guzmán's film. 'Over the two and a half years of Allende's government the Pentagon has given them forty-five million dollars in military aid. That is more than a third of all the aid received in the last twenty years.'[45] In that situation, concrete conflicts and specific positions, but also real people like Allende

himself, end up acquiring mythical meaning. Hence Admiral
Carvajal's allusion to 'the devil reincarnate'.

Some time later, Admiral Merino confirmed the extent to which
the rightist clichés of Francoist Spain had been combined with the
anxieties of the Cold War to shape the views of Chile's 1970s new
Right. Asked by a journalist: 'You have said that Marxists are
"humanoids", what do you mean?' the good Admiral replied: 'A
human with no conscience and no soul.'[46] Apparently, this was
intended as a joke. Replace the word 'Marxists' with, say, 'Jews',
and a joke it is not. Questioned by a more sympathetic journalist in
his *Memoirs* to give his views on 'the devil we all carry inside',
Merino, a devout Catholic, gave the cartoonish reply that he always
had an angel on one side, 'and on the other side this Negro [*este
negro*] making damn sure things go bad'. Thereafter, the journalist
proposes replacing 'the Negro' with 'the Red', meaning a Marxist.
The admiral does not object.[47]

Whether meant as racist or not, Carvajal and Merino's crude
language reveals a common feature among those who participated
in the 1973 coup in Chile, military as well as civilian: these were
men who shared the sort of colonial arrogance and religious fervour
that Paul Preston identifies among the *Africanistas* and their ultra-
Catholic anti-leftist supporters during the Spanish Civil War.
According to Preston, they enacted 'a transference of racial prejudice which would facilitate the savagery carried out by [Franco's]
Army of Africa during the Civil War', and peddled the idea of a
sinister alliance of Jews, Freemasons and leftists.[48] Just as in 1930s
Spain, the civilian and military men involved in the 1973 Chilean
coup were landowners or had contact with the political conservative parties representing the traditional interests of the big landowners (endorsed by an assumed right of conquest) and fanatically
defended tradition, family and property. Their outrage at the sheer
effrontery of landless indigenous peoples, workers and peasants in
daring to take part in the revolutionary upheavals of 1964–73
reflected their sense of social and cultural superiority over those

who worked their estates, manned their mines, and supplied domestic near-slave labour for the middle- and upper-class houses of the suburbs of Santiago and Valparaíso.

Similar clichés helped justify the coup within the coup. From this point of view, otherwise intelligent, even heroic people like Prats, Admiral Montero or General Ruiz Danyau could not resist the siren song of Allende's voice. His words were represented as poisonous as a snake's tongue. The closeness between the constitutionalist generals and Allende was portrayed as the result of a Faustian pact. This also meant that their decisions, though the result of free will, were not free at all. In this way, the Chilean generals and soldiers who said no to the coup were dispossessed of their own free will, their agency and their ability to say no. To arrest them and judge them as traitors to the fatherland would be justified, but not nearly enough. They would have to be tortured, exiled or killed, and their names erased from memory and history. For what was needed went beyond the confines of a martial court. As far as the military hawks and their civilian pundits were concerned, Chile needed an Inquisition.

In this respect, it is useful to remember Walter Benjamin's statement that not even the dead are safe from the fury of the victors. Just as Kissinger considered the Chilean people who elected Allende to be no more responsible than children, so Admiral Carvajal, Admiral Merino, Jaime Guzmán, Federico Willoughby and the other conspirators came to think of their constitutionalist colleagues in the armed forces – Prats, Montero, Ruiz Danyau, Bachelet, etc. – and the people in general, as no better than the hoodwinked audience – Dorothy, the Tin Man, the Lion and the Scarecrow – of an all-powerful Oz. And just like the characters in the 1939 film *The Wizard of Oz*, the generals too had been duped by a liar.

We know that in one reading of *The Wizard of Oz* the story and the characters created for children also serve as a representation of the problematic relation between money and politics during the time of the Great Depression. The villainous or heroic characters in the children's story referred also to real-life villains, generalised poverty, oppression and the struggle of a people to smash the bureaucratic–military machine.[49] Similarly, we can ask in relation to the story told in Patricio Guzmán's *The Battle of Chile*, what does it mean for an unarmed people to smash the state's bureaucratic and military machine? Allende answered this question in the aftermath of the failed coup of 29 June 1973. In another scene captured in Guzmán's documentary at the time, Allende responded as follows to the call by the people gathered in Plaza Constitución to abolish Parliament: 'We shall make all revolutionary changes showing respect for pluralism, democracy and freedom. This does not mean to show tolerance to those who are against democracy. We must never tolerate fascists! But you must also understand the position of this government. It would be an absurd contradiction to be against fascism and then close Congress. I won't do it.' Almost silenced by the deafening hissing and booing coming from some of the demonstrators, who expected this to be the moment when the leadership from above would take control of the revolution from below and force a revolutionary break, Allende explained: 'I have advocated respect for law and democracy. But if necessary, I will call for a plebiscite and let the people resolve this question once and for all!'[50]

Rather than contemplate the possibility of destroying Parliament and forcing a violent break, Allende's answer was to take stock of the fact that workers, peasants and slum-dwellers could actually organise themselves as the class in government and 'win the battle of democracy'.[51] Allende did not indulge in utopias. Only the experience of the mass movement would provide an adequate answer to the question concerning the specific form that the organisation of the people as a class in government would assume, and how it could be combined with the most complete and consistent victory in 'the battle of democracy'.[52]

In the case of 1970s Chile, the specific form was the plebiscite. After he announced the move to call for a plebiscite in June 1973, Allende tried to convince the Popular Unity, and some sectors of the opposition, that the only way to fight the coup was to extend democracy rather than withdraw from it. Here, perhaps for the first time, one of the actors in this historical drama managed to break away from the repetitive, tragic cycle of violence that seemed to have been accepted by all others as if it were an imperative of history. While his enemies left and right called for fire to fight fire, Allende found a way to escape the vicious circle of reciprocal violence.

During the last three months of his mandate he fought tirelessly to persuade the UP coalition and the PDC sector of the opposition that this was the only way to sever ties with the state war-machine that was being used to crush the Chilean Way by force. The working class could not simply lay hold of that ready-made machine and wield it for its own purposes.[53] The uphill struggle to persuade people on both left and right during these months confirmed to Allende that in the end he would have to fight this battle on his own. The parties in the UP would not listen. For many of its leaders, motivated perhaps by the strength of the revolution from below but carried away by their own utopian fantasies, it was time to stop talking and start acting. As far as they were concerned, the Left should take the fight to the enemy on the enemy's own terms. Like the military, they too fell prey to the apparent cathartic powers of fighting fire with fire, a common theme of tragic narratives and sympathetic magic. In doing so, rather than stopping the coup, which was their purported aim, they helped to bring it about.

They all failed to realise that the difference between ancient tragedy and modern tragedy is that in the latter the innocent are always made to pay. Or, to borrow the appropriate terms from *The 18th Brumaire*, the Left that began to lose its way and the Right that never found one forgot the crucial difference between ancient and modern tragedy. In antiquity, the working classes lived at the expense of society. This was the case in the Greco-Roman world because the great productive mass of the population, namely the slaves, 'formed the purely passive pedestal' for the combat between the free rich and the free working poor, often solved by the sacrifice of a guilty scapegoat. In modern times, however, capitalist societies live at the expense of the working classes and those barely existing, if at all, in destitution. The sacrificed are always the many.

Coming to the end and realising his isolation, Allende appealed to the most organised of all the parties of the left, the Communist Party, for they shared the conviction that smashing Leviathan also entailed having something to replace it with: further democracy and a principled refusal of the violence that until then everyone had thought was inherent to all revolutions. The tactical value of that position, made concrete in the 1973 call for a plebiscite, was to stop or derail the coup plans being laid by the conspirators. The strategic value of that position was to part company with an essential staple of anti-revolutionary propaganda since at least the English, French, Haitian and American revolutions of the pre-communist era, namely the notion that oppressive violence is necessary to bring about major social change.

The aim of the initiative for a plebiscite was to pull the rug from under the conspirators by robbing them of their main justification: that by staging a successful coup they would be saving Chile from plunging into a much more costly civil war. Allende actually contemplated the real possibility of losing the plebiscite, and said he would resign if he did. His promised resignation in the event of defeat would have made the coup effectively redundant, while at the same time proving that democracy and Marxism were not incompatible. The plebiscite would have been an unprecedented intervention by the people. It would have forced the Parliamentary doors open, allowing the revolution from below to become a neo-Jacobin movement, following the example of the Jacobin club and the French National Convention of the 1790s. Such would be a new, deeper and extended democracy, complete with new rules of its own. According to such rules, Marxism and popular self-regulation become part of the democratic game, rather than constituting an exception that must be eradicated.

What such new rules would disqualify is what jurists and political philosophers call a 'state of exception', which suspends the rules of democracy for the purposes of fighting by all means necessary an alleged existential enemy. As modern legal and political history has shown time and again, particularly during the twentieth and twenty-first centuries, the problem with declaring 'states of exception' is that they tend to grow so thoroughly normalised that the outcome is not to enhance the ability to defend society from its enemies, but, as Carlos Prats foresaw, to transform the state into a secretive political police, a war machine, a 'national security' state and the people into its hardened enemy.

On 8 September, General Prats and Fernando Flores informed Allende they had irrefutable evidence that members of the military would launch a coup before 14 September. Allende's plan, whose details he shared with Prats among other members of his close circle before 11 September 1973, would have made redundant not only the conspiracy of the Chilean military, Guzmán and Willoughby and their CIA backers, but the very framework of the Cold War as well. Seen with the benefit of hindsight, Allende's plebiscite proposal was game-changing and genuinely revolutionary. According to Greg Grandin and the Pulitzer Prize-winning investigative journalist Seymour Hersh, Henry Kissinger may have understood this very well. In Grandin's words:

> Seymour Hersh, drawing on a conversation with another NSC [US National Security Council] staffer, wrote that what Kissinger feared most about Allende was not his winning the presidency but that at the end of his term 'the political process would work and he would be voted out of office in the next election.' Socialism, much less Marxism, could not be seen to be compatible with electoral democracy.

'We cannot endeavour to ignite the world if Chile itself is a placid lake,' Kissinger had pointed out. 'The fuel for the fire must come from within Chile.'[54]

At 10 a.m. on Sunday, 9 September 1973, Allende met with the leaders of the Chilean Communist Party (PCCh). He pleaded with them to accept his proposal for a plebiscite. Given the information he had received from General Carlos Prats and Fernando Flores the day before about the imminence of a coup, he knew the initiative could not be deferred. He also remarked that, whatever their decision, he would go ahead at once with his proposal. The leaders of the PCCh conceded, and promised to issue a written statement next day on the content and implications of the plebiscite.

However, given the circumstances that had brought the Chilean state to a grinding halt, the call for a plebiscite required additional support. Allende and his advisers, such as Carlos Prats and Joan Garcés, had to consider the political blockade mounted by the National Party/PDC alliance in Congress, the *Gremialistas*, a sector of the middle classes, and the radicalised counter-revolutionary faction of the armed forces and the rightist paramilitaries. The situation had changed since June 1973. Back then, the support of at least a part of the army, the UP coalition and the networked movements from below was sufficient. Now, in view of their deeper division, Allende also needed an explicit commitment from the armed forces. In order for the plebiscite to succeed, their unconditional support, their agreement to allow the vote to take place and their willingness to stand by the result of the elections were required.

To make matters worse, Allende could no longer count on the strength of General Prats within the army. On 22 August 1973, the coup within the coup had claimed the constitutionalist commander-in-chief as its last victim. The plotters succeeded in removing what CIA chief Warren had deemed the main obstacle for military intervention. Using as a pretext an incident involving General Prats and a woman named Alejandrina Cox, whose insults in the street Prats responded to by shooting at the tyres of her vehicle, a subsequent protest in front of the general's house including at least six wives of his high-ranking officers weakened Prats's resolve. According to General Guillermo Pickering, commander of the military institutes, it was a staged protest. The next day, the majority of Prats's colleagues in the High Command made it clear that his loss of control meant they could no longer trust him. Due to overwhelming pressure from his fellow officers and the media, Prats resigned, citing health reasons, and was replaced by General Augusto Pinochet Ugarte as the new commander-in-chief of the army. On 22 August, General Pickering resigned too. Later on, Pickering stated he knew a plot was in the making, with which he could not agree. He also questioned the responsibility of those civilians who declare their allegiance to democracy 'when it serves their interests, and break it when it doesn't.' Pinochet was perceived by all sectors, as a constitutionalist.

According to Joan Garcés, it was because of the imperative need to secure the armed forces' support for the plebiscite that on 9 September 1973 Allende sent for General Pinochet and the inspector general of the army, General Orlando Urbina.[55] This was not the first time that the two generals had been summoned in a hurry to go to the presidential residence at Tomás Moro. Early on in August 1973, General Pinochet had just arrived at his house in Laura de Noves Street when he was startled by a phone call from the president's secretary, Miriam 'Payita' Contreras, demanding his presence at Tomás Moro. On that occasion, Pinochet was so nervous he decided to take his wife, Lucia Hiriart, and his two younger children, sixteen-year-old Marco Antonio and fifteen-year-old Jacqueline, to the Los Dominicos residence where his older daughter Lucía lived with her husband Hernán García, an agribusinessman who managed the import of cheese and dairy products for the Empresa de Comercio Agrícola, part of the National Agriculture Society.

After taking a break to take care of her two little ones, three-year-old Hernán Augusto and one-year-old Francisco Javier, Lucía Pinochet Hiriart had returned to university and studied children's education at the Pedagogical Institute of the Universidad de Chile, one of the most politicised places in the country at the time.

Whenever her father, General Pinochet, came to visit, Lucía would tell him about the increasing polarisation of the youth of Chile.

Having left his family in safer hands, General Pinochet was driven by his chauffeur to Tomás Moro. Was he already a plotter, harbouring fears of being discovered? Most sources suggest that at this point no one seemed entirely sure where Pinochet stood, not even the general himself. When he entered Allende's living room, Pinochet found himself in the unexpected company of the civilian minister of defence, Orlando Letelier, the new secretary general of the government, Fernando Flores, PCCh secretary general Luis Corvalán and the director of Investigaciones, the Chilean FBI, Eduardo 'Coco' Paredes. General Orlando Urbina joined them a couple of minutes later. Urbina was third in command of the army and the only one in the High Command who had graduated in the same class as Pinochet. President Allende arrived last.

After a few moments in which Allende welcomed the generals and chatted politely with his other guests, the president spoke of the clash between government and opposition, the challenge to national security posed by far-right terrorist groups blowing up electricity grids and merchants blocking transports and the distribution of foodstuffs. He spoke of the media's alarmist campaign, and the presence of CIA and other foreign (mostly Brazilian) agents subverting the armed forces and providing training and weaponry to Fatherland and Freedom and the ex-Cadets. Allende asked the two generals how they felt about the pressure brought to bear upon the armed forces to abandon their non-political position and side with the opposition, the industrialists and the *Gremialistas* against the constitutional government.

As always, Pinochet held his tongue. He did not declare which side he was on. Either he already knew and proved to be a master of deception, or he did not know for sure, and preferred to wait for the critical moment to join whoever had the best chance of victory. Earlier in July, after his last-minute appearance to contain the failed coup of June 1973, Pinochet had been asked by Prats and Allende to review the outline of a security operation in case of widespread disorder – for instance, a coup. It was known as Plan Hercules. Initially designed in collaboration with Garcés and other security experts within government to contain a coup, according to General Carlos Prats the plan was transformed by Pinochet into a tactic to come out on top, whatever the outcome.

In any event, the fact is that Plan Hercules was circulated more widely than it should have been. It included a plan to take control of the rightist media in case of a coup, mainly TV, privately owned newspapers and the radio stations coordinated by the National Agriculture Society radio station that were ramping up their demonising war against the government. Federico Willoughby was contacted in order to review that part of the plan, probably by the army's telecommunications officer, Colonel Roberto Guillard. At best this was a serious indiscretion, for Willoughby, together with his friend Jaime Guzmán and the other young conservatives, was fully involved with the plotters – as was Colonel Guillard. Together, they were able to design a blueprint for taking out the that part of the media communications network sympathetic to the government.[56]

Pinochet did make one important change to Plan Hercules: the reorganisation and unification of all intelligence services under the command of the chief of the armed forces, himself. Seen from the government's angle, this would enable a better control of the flow of information, and prevent the use of the intelligence services within the different branches of the armed forces for the purposes of a coup. But Prats's observation about Pinochet twisting the aims of Plan Hercules reveals that the plan could just as well be used to concentrate information and covert operations under Pinochet, and give him an edge over everyone else.

The other problem with the hypothesis that Pinochet had already chosen sides while revising Plan Hercules is that both Allende and Orlando Letelier were fully informed about the changes he made to the plan, and did not disagree. Although Pinochet would later recall the August 1973 meeting as a cunning attempt to probe his deep beliefs, an interrogation designed to reveal his secrets, the truth is there was nothing to discover.[57] Pinochet was not a schemer with a deep-laid plan, or an ideologue with firmly held beliefs – unlike future admirers of his in Europe, such as Margaret Thatcher. 'Pinochet's ideology was self-interest,' says Heraldo Muñoz in his political memoir about the general. 'In times of passionate commitments and causes, his policy was realpolitik: be pragmatic, appear neutral, and cultivate the trust of those with power and authority. Pinochet was above all a survivor. [But] for all his ethical and intellectual shortcomings, he possessed a remarkable instinct for power.'[58]

Pinochet was a hard-core Cold Warrior educated in the paranoid counter-revolutionary attitude predominant among the security forces of the Americas in a time of anxiety and reaction against the New Deal, Kennedy-like approaches and the student counterculture. He was also an admirer of the Spanish dictator Generalísimo Francisco Franco.[59] His sympathies may have not have been ideological in the narrower sense of the term, but he and Franco shared a common history of military experience in the desert – Franco in Morocco, Pinochet in Chile's Norte Grande. The dilemmas faced by both men in the desert were not whether to choose between classical economics, the politics of the commons, Keynesianism, mercantilism or free trade, but rather, how to impose their command and control. This was so because whether in the Moroccan or the Chilean desert, to rule was to behave more like an envoy of the Almighty sitting at the top of a loose confederation of interested parties, demanding their personal loyalty in a tussle between political and religious fidelity. In such cases the regime was strong, the state was not. If Franco was, according to some, 'the High Sheriff of Morocco in Madrid', Pinochet would become 'the Camp Director of Pisagua in Santiago', complete with an arsenal of legionnaire techniques, colonial arrogance towards the people they were sent to pacify in the desert, and resentment – that odd blend of admiration and envy – against those who sent them there.[60]

Did General Pinochet plan his moves so carefully that he managed to fool everyone, starting with Allende – so often portrayed as the arch-schemer – into believing that he stood for the Constitution, while in fact he was working behind the scenes on a plan to destroy it? Opinion seems divided on that point. To some, there was no evidence of Pinochet having created or being behind such a plan. They would point out that Admiral José Toribio Merino was the true leader of the coup. He pushed Pinochet to join the plot. Patricio Aylwin, leader of the right wing of the PDC, and the man who only a week before 11 September 1973 signed a congressional decree asking the military 'to help re-establish the rule of law' in the country, had this to say about Pinochet: 'He did not get where he did by a carefully planned design, but rather by taking advantage of favourable circumstances.'[61] Aylwin describes Pinochet as an opportunist. Others, Joan Garcés for instance, believe by contrast that Pinochet's role in the 11 September coup was far more pivotal.[62]

Be that as it may, the fact is that Pinochet's silence during the meeting at Tomás Moro in late August 1973 was interpreted by Allende and his people as a pointer confirming that he should replace General Prats as leader of the army. That was the point of the August meeting. Urbina, on the other hand, did talk: 'the government should seek a prompt solution for the crisis. For instance, by way of a plebiscite, or an agreement with the opposition; otherwise, violence will only increase,' he said. Urbina was clearly referring to the proposal Allende had made during his speech after the failed coup in June.

When the meeting ended, Pinochet and Urbina went home in the same car. As they travelled through the streets of Santiago, Pinochet recalled another 9 September. It was 9 September 1936, when the Spanish General Vicente Rojo, defending the cause of the Republic against the Francoist army, went back to the War Academy in the Alcázar de Toledo and asked his former comrades in arms to surrender.

Just as in 1930s Spain, there were manifest signs of crisis in 1970s Chile – soaring inflation, shortages, political paralysis and polarisation. And yet, as also in Spain on 9 September 1936, none of these signs meant that a military revolt or civil war was bound to happen. Political and economic instability were as real in the late summer and early autumn of 1973 in Chile as they had been in the spring of 1936 in Spain. But such reasons neither necessarily explain nor justify the insurrection of the military or the brutality of the dictatorship. Perhaps this is what Pinochet had in mind when he asked General Urbina on 9 September 1973: 'If the confrontation Allende talked about takes place, would you be our General Rojo?' Urbina answered: 'No. What about you?' 'Me, neither,' General Pinochet replied.[63] According to Ascanio Cavallo and Margarita Serrano, there is good cause to doubt that they trusted each other's answer.[64]

On the morning of 10 September, having taken up his position as chief of the High Command after Pinochet's promotion, General Orlando Urbina travelled south to Temuco and spent the night there, with the Tucapel Eighth Infantry Regiment. Pinochet was relieved to learn that Urbina was away from the centre of action in Valparaíso and Santiago, given that the coup plotters had expressed strong reservations about the army's second in command. On 10 September 1973, having finally caved in to Admiral Merino's and Air Force General Leigh's pressure, Pinochet committed himself to the cause of the insurrection. He told the conspirators that if anything should happen to him, General Oscar Bonilla, rather than Urbina, was to take command of the army. Bonilla was sixth in the line of command, which means that Pinochet was in fact authorising an internal coup against Urbina and the remaining four more experienced men in the army.

Cavallo and Serrano describe General Urbina as thin, austere, and extremely professional, a constitutionalist who abhorred getting involved in political deliberation. Speaking as he did during the August meeting in Tomás Moro, Urbina may have given Allende and Pinochet a signal that he could be the General Rojo of his day. He may have disliked Allende's politics, but kept that dislike to himself. He shared that attitude with Pinochet, which is why at different times in this story both of them came under suspicion by the conspirators. But Urbina, unlike Pinochet, expressed his agreement with Allende's initiative to put an end to the political paralysis that beset the country.

There were other reasons why the conspirators would be more wary of Urbina than of Pinochet. Back in 1970, as commander of the Second Division and military judge in Santiago, Urbina had passed severe sentences on those implicated in the assassination of General René Schneider. Since the murder had caused widespread disgust, legal sentences had to be exemplary. Urbina obliged. In 1972 he was designated vice-president of the commission in charge of the organisation of the Third UN Conference of Trade and Development (UNCTAD III) and became the spokesperson of an event that the opposition viewed as pro-government propaganda, and the Americans as an echo chamber for Third World–leftist standpoints in the North–South debates of the early 1970s.[65] Come 11 September 1973, the chief of the army's High Command and second in command after Pinochet 'was one of the few generals who did not know that the armed forces [were] about to mobilise their heavy war machine'.[66] Unsurprisingly, Urbina seemed stunned when during his meeting with Pinochet and Allende on 9 September, the president announced he was going to follow the path Urbina himself had suggested in late August.

According to Joan Garcés, 'in this last encounter was decided the fate of the Popular Unity government and of the political system it was an integral part of.'[67] It was here, according to Garcés, that the coup against Allende fully transmuted into an attack on Chilean democracy itself. The conversation between the three men that day quickly turned to the situation inside the armed forces, the strikes led by the *Gremialistas*, and the measures taken to contain them. Pinochet reiterated the analysis of the situation he had shared with Urbina and the president back in August: there were worrying symptoms everywhere. Without making any explicit references to the conversation he had had with General Prats and Fernando Flores the day before, Allende compared the information he had with what Pinochet was saying. Then he told the generals: 'In the next hours I am going to make a public call for a plebiscite allowing the Chilean citizenry to choose which way we shall go.'

On the following day, Allende described the generals' reaction to Joan Garcés: 'Their eyes were bulging.'

Pinochet asked: 'But, President, Sir, is this resolution to allow for a vote definitive and resolute?'

'Yes, General, it is,' replied Allende.

'Well, that changes everything, Mr President. Now it is going to be possible to solve the conflict with the opposition in Congress, and that should dissolve all tensions.'[68]

Allende concluded that he could count on Pinochet's support and that the coup could still be averted.

10

The Flies, Act III

When General Pinochet left the Tomás Moro presidential residence on 9 September 1973, he realised that the plot to topple Allende by 14 September had been thrown into disarray. That at least is the opinion of Joan Garcés, one of Allende's closest advisers and privileged witness to those events. According to him, the *golpistas'* original plan relied on a sizeable provocation coming from the increasingly vociferous militants on the far left of Allende's coalition. In that way, Chile's officialdom could come across as galvanised and forced into action from without, rather than as the traitors they were. 'But this never happened, the tipping point never came, leaving all the responsibility for the unleashing of the violent Furies to fall squarely on the shoulders of the military.'[1]

Allende's call for a constitutional referendum during the week commencing 10 September would have opened up a non-violent, democratic path to solve the political paralysis threatening Chilean society. According to Garcés this explains Pinochet's sudden anxiety. In a hurry to assess the changing situation, Pinochet attended a meeting with Air Force General Gustavo Leigh and the Valparaíso conspirators that same afternoon.

It has been ascertained that the origins of the 11 September coup lay in the navy. In mid-August 1973, Admiral José Toribio Merino, poised to lead the overthrow of Allende, sent his friend in the Cofradía Náutica and former naval officer Roberto Kelly on a secret mission to Brazil. Kelly was to wait at a hotel in the capital Brasilia,

where he would be contacted by Brazilian intelligence. Merino
wanted reassurances that the Peruvian government, seen as sympathetic towards Allende, would not take advantage of the coup to
occupy the disputed Chilean–Peruvian border. Merino and the
other plotters looked to the Brazilian military regime as a model,
hoping for their support against the fifteen thousand foreign 'armed
extremists', led by the Cubans, who they imagined would ally with
the Chilean Left in the event of a coup.[2]

The Brazilian regime of General Emilio Garrastazu Médici had
taken the initiative in proposing to Richard Nixon that Brasilia and
Washington coordinate efforts to contain the leftist tide in the western hemisphere. 'President Nixon took great interest in this proposal
and promised to assist Brazil when and wherever possible,' according to a CIA memorandum dated late 1971.[3] Brazil, along with
Argentina, Paraguay and Bolivia, actively supported Chile's
Gremialistas as well as the paramilitary Fatherland and Freedom in
the weeks before the coup. In mid-1973, one of Fatherland and
Freedom's military leaders, Roberto Thieme, had returned to Chile
after contacting Paraguayan, Bolivian, Brazilian and Argentinian
supporters, and vowed to launch urban warfare against Allende. US
officials constantly drew parallels between the looming conflict in
Chile and the Brazilian coup of 1964 and stressed the potential
benefits of Brazilian involvement. On 8 September 1973 Nixon's
Interagency Group on Chile recommended that equipment to help
the Chilean plotters to carry out the overthrow of Allende be chan-
nelled through or obtained in Latin American countries, mainly
Brazil. At the time, while negotiating with Allende at the behest of
Cardinal Silva Henríquez, PDC leader Patricio Aylwin confided in
an American diplomat with ties in Brasilia that Chile now needed a
'Brazilian solution'.[4]

Happily for Merino, Kelly, Thieme and the Cofradía plotters,
Brasilia provided the required reassurances. After his encounter
with the Brazilian agents, Kelly boarded a plane back to Santiago.
Once there he reported the good news to Navy Admiral Merino

and the other members of the Cofradía, including the industrialist Agustín Edwards, economist Sergio de Castro and his young conservative friends Jaime Guzmán and Federico Willoughby. If they managed to unite a significant group of military officials behind their plans, the coup they had been plotting for so long would finally become a reality.

In contrast, the plot in the air force had begun no earlier than 20 August 1973. On that day, 120 air force officers gathered to express their discontent with Allende's decision to remove their commander-in-chief, General Ruiz Danyau, from the Cabinet and the force. The crisis had broken out a week before when Ruiz, a loyalist, presented his resignation to Allende nine days after his appointment. Ruiz had been unable to solve the stand-off with the transport owners who had been striking regularly since 1972. He also disagreed with the president's decision to ask the metropolitan intendant of Santiago to get the trucks and buses back on the streets by all means necessary. Allende asked Ruiz to resign from the air force too, but he refused. It was a political blow to Allende, and created unnecessary additional tension within the armed forces.

On the night Ruiz Danyau resigned, Allende was supposed to meet with Patricio Aylwin, leader of the PDC, at the behest of Cardinal Silva Henríquez. The cardinal believed there was still time to avert a confrontation if the PDC and the UP government came to some sort of agreement. To that end, he persuaded Aylwin to visit the cardinal's residence in Santiago for a private conversation with Allende. 'I need to ask you a favour,' Cardinal Silva Henríquez told Aylwin on the phone. 'Have dinner with me and the president. Only the three of us.'

Aylwin wavered. 'What is the point of that?' he replied. Cardinal Silva Henríquez said it was Allende's initiative, and that he believed it was necessary that the two most powerful politicians in the country should reach an understanding.[5]

Aylwin resisted: it was an initiative he neither liked nor expected. 'I've told my party there would be no secret meetings, no backdoor negotiations,' he said. 'You are asking me to attend a secret meeting. That puts me in an awkward position. I would be breaking a promise I made in public.'

In a calm but firm tone of voice, the tone that he had used in his sermons before the generals and the captains of industry, the tone of voice priests rehearse until their unique mixture of humility and thunder becomes second nature, the cardinal insisted: 'You do not want to assume the historical responsibility of not having done enough to correct the mistakes of the government and avert a military coup. I'm sure you do not want that responsibility to fall upon your party either. I'm asking you a personal favour.'[6]

The cardinal was persuasive. He was, after all, the Vatican's representative, and the Vatican was the spiritual home of the Christian Democrat Party. Aylwin acceded.

Patricio Aylwin's car stopped in front of Cardinal Silva Henríquez's house in Simón Bolívar Street right on time. 'Go home,' he told Sotito, his driver. 'Come and pick me up around one in the morning.'[7] Aylwin's driver stood outside the car until the PDC leader entered the house. Then he drove away. On the road, he passed a car parked a few metres from the cardinal's house. 'Allende's men, GAP presidential guards [Grupo de Amigos Personales] or policemen,' the driver concluded.[8]

President Allende had sent a message to Cardinal Silva Henríquez, apologising for being late. He had been held up by General Ruiz Danyau's sudden resignation. Allende arrived alone, without his guards. 'I'm late, I'm sorry,' he told Aylwin and the cardinal. 'Things happen . . . Ruiz Danyau has resigned.' Allende explained he had told General Ruiz from the outset that it would be better if he took the Ministry of Land and Agriculture, in charge of the process of land reform that had started during Frei's administration. General Ruiz insisted on being named minister of transportation. Allende had thought General José María Sepúlveda from the Carabineros force was better placed to deal with the truck owners' strike, but Ruiz had said he would not accept a ministry of less importance than that held by a member of the Carabineros. 'To make things worse, he said he wanted to leave the ministry of transportation but remain as commander in chief of the air force,' observed Allende. 'I told him that wasn't possible. That's why I'm late. It was a long conversation, but I have his letter of resignation here.' Allende now put the letter in the right-hand pocket of his jacket, having made sure that Aylwin could see it. He wanted to show the leader of the PDC he was still in control of the situation.[9]

Allende was a veteran politician, a tenacious worker who never slept more than five hours a night, a strategist who had been to every corner of Chile and knew deep down that it would take a very long time to change the relationship between the state, the law and the workers and peasants whose lives had touched him during his travels. The world was imperfect and static. Communist socialism, on the other hand, was a movement inscribed in the here and now, as well as a strategic anticipation of the day after, not only an idea or a concept.[10] He took pride in his tactical and strategic ability, and would boast about his powers of political manoeuvre.

When challenged, Allende could be intimidating, even aggressive. 'I'm here because I'm a Catholic and His Eminence the Cardinal asked me. There's no other reason, Mr President,' Aylwin told Allende. Then he challenged the president: 'You must choose: either [Carlos] Altamirano' (the controversial leader of the Socialist Party who was calling for armed resistance against the coming coup) 'or the navy. You cannot befriend both. You cannot be both for armed struggle and democracy. Choose.'

Allende turned to the cardinal, who until then had kept silent, trying hard not to betray his role as neutral arbiter. 'Cardinal, don't you find it difficult at times to keep your people in line? Take Christians for Socialism. Aren't they acting against your judgement? If it happens to you, in spite of your high moral authority, why wouldn't it happen to me?' Allende insisted he was against armed struggle, wherever it came from, as it would not solve but rather worsen the conflict. 'I will never allow the people of Chile to take to the streets with arms in their hands to defend the government,' Allende replied to Aylwin. 'But,' he said, turning once more to the cardinal, 'doesn't the Gospel say that the good shepherd would leave his flock behind in order to look for the sheep that lost its way? That's why we're here. That's why I asked Monsignor, the highest moral authority in this country, to receive us in his house.'[11]

Addressing Aylwin, Allende asked: 'What steps would you take to break out of this difficult situation?'

The conservative leader of the PDC answered: 'First of all, approve a constitutional amendment concerning property and the economy.'

'That would create an impossible situation for the Executive,' said Allende. He explained that allowing such an amendment would create a dangerous precedent: with a simple and rather slim majority, Parliament could impose its position on the president, paving the way for a constitutional reform that could shorten the Executive's term in office or prevent him from exercising some of his crucial preroga-tives, rendering the president powerless. Aylwin understood:

> Mr President, I can guarantee the PDC would not support an interpretation of the constitution or even an additional clause to the amendment establishing the need for two thirds of the members of Parliament to vote for a limitation of presidential powers, a shortening of his term in office, or any other measure that could result in the augmentation of the powers of Parliament and an imbalance in the equilibrium of powers.[12]

Aylwin told Allende that his minister of the interior, Carlos Briones, could work with him on a strategy that would satisfy Parliament and the Executive. 'However,' said Aylwin, 'there's another problem that needs solving: armed gangs.'

'We're working on it,' said Allende. The president was referring to the Law of Arms Control, which had been in force but remained dormant since its promulgation in 1972. The Law had been reactivated and firmly applied by the armed forces, all of a sudden, after the failed coup of 29 June.[13]

Allende had never been against the application of the Law of Arms Control. On numerous occasions he had proposed it should be applied with severity in order to stamp out the armed groups wreaking havoc on the infrastructure of the country – Fatherland and Freedom, the ex-Cadets and the Rolando Matus Brigades. Allende's firm intention not to allow groups outside the security forces of the state to carry and use weapons was one thing. The draconian manner in which the armed forces, particularly the air force, used the Arms Law against the community groups and the *cordones industriales* was another. It exasperated him. When General Leigh assumed command of the air force, following Ruiz Danyau's resignation, the air force used the Law of Arms Control to launch a series of raids against worker-occupied factories, slums and *cordones*, testing the strength of the networked movement from below while at the same time conditioning ordinary soldiers to turning their weapons against the ordinary people of Chile. Under the pretext of searching for hidden caches of weapons, these soldiers began using force against the lower levels of the population. Arms were never found, but the severity displayed by General Leigh's men upset those factions within the UP coalition already convinced that the military were plotting against them. It also threatened to unravel Allende's commitment not to allow the use of force against the people, and to divorce force from law.

On 8 July 1973, three air force helicopters descended upon a graveyard in a poor quarter in the outskirts of Santiago, allegedly to carry out a raid in search of weapons. Some two hundred air force soldiers jumped out of the choppers, secured a perimeter and proceeded to dig up graves and break down the gates of mausoleums supposedly hiding 'Cuban weapons'. They found none. 'This is unbelievable,' said a woman from the slum to the interviewer in Patricio Guzmán's film *The Battle of Chile*. 'Look at these "mummies". What are these reactionaries doing? It's happening every day. Why would anyone dig up the dead? How do they come up with the idea that the dead have bullets or anything? They're dead already, why would they kill them? Imagine digging the poor things up! All they could do was throw their bones at them.' The woman declared on camera that any day now the armed forces would send more planes and kill them all, 'because we're defenceless here.' Asked by the interviewer if the people should be armed, the woman, carrying in her arms a little girl, firmly replies: 'Yes, of course! The government has to do that, very soon.'[14]

Another incident demonstrating how the use of the Arms Law by the military was pushing the application of the rule of law into illegality took place in the Lanera Industrial, a textile company taken over by the workers in Punta Arenas.[15] A joint operation between the air force and the army descended into chaos, ending in a shoot-out that killed one of the workers. On the evening of 7 September, another air force unit raid on the worker-run Sumar textile factory also resulted in a shoot-out. According to the workers, the air force soldiers used excessive force against them. The soldiers argued they had been surrounded by a mob and feared for their safety. Next day, Allende ordered General Leigh to stop the raids against factories and *cordones industriales* unless they were authorised personally and directly by the civilian minister of defence, Orlando Letelier. Allende's nomination of Leigh to replace Ruiz Danyau had surprised everybody. Leigh was known to be a hardliner who lost no opportunity to criticise the president harshly during the meetings of the Committee of Fifteen.

On 20 August, clamorous discussions among air force officers in the theatre of the air force base at El Bosque put an end to the supposed political neutrality of the armed forces. After 7 September, Allende told Leigh that the director of Investigaciones, the socialist Alfredo Joignant, would be in charge of the questioning of soldiers and officers in the investigation concerning the events at the Sumar factory and alleged links with paramilitary groups. The Executive and the air force were unofficially at war with one another.

'You see Mr Aylwin, there are also armed groups on the right,' Allende told the PDC leader during the meeting with Cardinal Silva Henríquez. He would agree to control armed groups on the left and to apply the Law of Arms Control, but warned Aylwin he would not tolerate further contacts between the truck owners, *Gremialista* activists, opposition party members, the military and fascist groups like Fatherland and Freedom.

'As far as I know, none of the owners belong to Fatherland and Freedom,' was Aylwin's reply. The two men kept talking into the early morning of the next day. They considered a formula to end the truckers' strike that was leaving empty shelves in shops around the country. They discussed how to resolve the occupation of the University of Chile's TV Channel 9 by MIR activists and its return to the university's hands. They agreed to convene a collaborative team that would review the price controls on paper, which affected the economic interests of the powerful Edwards and Matte media-owning families, and the implications of price controls for freedom of expression – the freedom of expression of the private opposition media, that is.

At half past one in the morning, Allende and Aylwin left the house of Cardinal Silva Henríquez. An agreement between the two parties seemed possible, one that would have cleared the way for a plebiscite and changed the conditions favourable to a coup. But the tide was already moving in a different direction.

The third and final act of the Chilean tragedy began on 11 September with a secret operation named Silence. In years to come, the name given to this operation would acquire a wider meaning: that of an act of plunder. At first, it referred solely to the tactical and strategic move on 11 September 1973 to silence the enemy and erase his radical words and ideas from memory. Later on it would signify something else, a new kind of battle: the conservative appropriation of the enemy's radical language. Words like 'liberation', 'new man' and 'revolution' would now denote only the freedom of the market, the capacity of economic man to compete and adapt or perish, and the revolutionary power of money as universal leveller.

One of the main architects of Operation Silence on 11 September, and of its later becoming the 'Silent Revolution' hailed by *El Mercurio* as the beginning of a new era, was a journalist: none other than the young conservative Federico Willoughby. Among the so-called 'civilian generals' of the coup, he alone participated not only in the planning phase but also in the execution. Unlike his friend and co-designer of the Silent Revolution Jaime Guzmán, who was content to play the role of backstage mandarin, Willoughby preferred the limelight.[16]

He was, after all, a man of action. Early on, Willoughby and other landowners compiled a list of friends and relatives in the security forces who 'knew themselves to be a reserve that could act without great risk . . . We introduce them to one another, people in different branches of the armed forces, and put them together.'[17] In parallel, they had set up the *Gremialista* Action Commandos.[18] His contacts in the US Information Service (USIS) in Chile and the Ford Company made him particularly valuable to those preparing the coup.[19]

Willoughby played a central role in the National Agriculture Society's radio station, which made no apologies for voicing its opposition to Allende's government as an illegitimate Marxist dictatorship. Together with Guzmán – who became widely known as a pundit in an anti-government television show – the young conservatives became notorious, announcing the catastrophe that would befall Chile if the *rotos* were allowed to keep taking control of factories and land holdings.

Through their appearances in the media controlled by the Edwards family and other private interests, people like Willoughby and Guzmán acquainted wider audiences with the main tenets of the counter-revolution, and first of all that Allende embodied a threat against the very foundations of the nation, its *chilenidad* – which they identified with *hispanidad*, a view of Spanish and European culture centred exclusively on the defence of patriarchal family values, individual property and Christian tradition, as defined by Jaime Eyzaguirre, the rightist anti-republican Acción Española group of Menéndez y Pelayo and de Maeztu in 1930s Spain, and Osvaldo Lira, the Francoist theologian and Jaime Guzmán's mentor.[20] The Chilean counter-revolution also defended various other last-ditch positions: the benevolent influence of the Church versus the evils of secularism 'afrancesado' ('Frenchified': an oblique reference to the historical echoes of the Haitian and French Revolutions, which resonated with Allende's plebiscite proposal); the restoration of order (which meant, according to the Catholic intellectual Plinio Correa, 'Christendom . . . Christian civilisation defined by austerity and hierarchy; fundamentally sacred, anti-egalitarian and anti-liberal') and of moral law against impurity and revolt, 'which lead men towards revolution';[21] the absolute right to property (according to the legal naturalism of the jurist Julio Philippi);[22] and the traditional role of the aristocracy and the elite as determining the 'historical physiognomy' and the fate of Chile.[23]

Willoughby understood, however, that theory needs practitioners and propagandists. He was happy to oblige. When the armed forces asked him to join the army's telecommunications officer Roberto Guillard in order to introduce a series of changes in the so-called Plan Hercules, he designed the basic outline. 'I realised, when the going got tough, what it was actually for,' he said later on.[24] The aim was to set up a clandestine communications network that would spring into operation on the day of the coup, while at the same time destroying the government's media.

The coup d'état launched on 11 September 1973 against Salvador Allende was Inquisitional. It hoped to achieve purification through fire. Like most acts of violence of this type, shaped in the mould of religious and ritualistic trials, it started by punishing inanimate objects. Antennas, transmission cables, telex lines and recording equipment were destroyed first. The goal of Operation Silence was to make sure that dangerous words would not travel through the airwaves and reach the masses, which, if tempted or inspired, might mobilise against the coup just as they had done back in 1972.

According to the Venezuelan essayist Fernando Báez, those who engage in acts like these know what they are doing: their aim is to intimidate, 'demoralize, enhance historical oblivion, diminish resistance', and, above all, paralyse the many by fomenting self-doubt.[25] The guiding light in such actions is the idea that control is not established unless there is a conviction involved. The self-appointed inquisitors assume a heaven for themselves and their police forces, a burning hell for the transgressors. In the case of the Chilean conspirators of 1973, the ritualistic manifestation of religious and political beliefs about fire as salvation met the more mundane needs of military strategy.

In the early hours of 11 September 1973, Willoughby launched Operation Silence. He destroyed the cable network of the radio station of Universidad Técnica del Estado, which might help government reach the people if the bigger stations were rendered useless. Then, after changing clothes and warning his wife not to send the children to school 'because the coup is happening', Willoughby met Navy Admiral Patricio Carvajal, Pedro Ewing, Nicanor Díaz and Roberto Guillard. He was tasked to elaborate a system of encrypted communication between the coup command centres, but his most important job was to prepare the broadcasts to be made as the coup progressed on behalf of the plotters. These would lay the groundwork for the extirpation of communism and the erasure of every material object that could offer a reminder of emancipation.

Chile's original Declaration of Independence from Spain would be destroyed that day. Perhaps no one at the time understood the premonitory and indelible meaning of such a contingent act. Neruda's library was burned, and his pre-Columbian art smashed. The same would happen at the Tomás Moro presidential residence. These were the first of many such acts to come. Five million books intended for Cuba were pulped at the state-controlled Quimantú publishing house, which in its time ran editions for popular audiences of up to an astonishing 50,000 copies, an achievement unparalleled before or after. Works by Neruda, Jorge Edwards and Ariel Dorfman or texts on Allende would suffer a similar fate. And there was a remarkable echo of Ray Bradbury's 1953 novel *Fahrenheit 451*: twenty years after its publication, those sympathetic to Allende would be forced to burn or bury their own libraries in order to escape persecution.[26]

Such acts are not symbolic. They announce the torture chambers and the killing fields. To attempt to explain or justify them as a step, unpalatable but necessary, towards restoring economic progress or secure law and order is both erroneous and immoral: 'When man destroys by fire,' Báez observes, 'he plays God.' The goal of the violence unleashed on 11 September 1973 was revenge and eternal punishment: to silence those who dared to see things differently and to erase every trace of their voices and images for generations to come. *The First Goal of the Chilean People*, the mural painted by Roberto Matta and the muralist brigades in 1971, would be painted over with sixteen coats of thick white paint on the orders of the chief inquisitors. The aim was the mass murder of memory. That some people would have to fall in the slaughter was perceived as incidental, for in any case those people were always seen as disposable, fallen into mortal error and sin; less than human. After all, as Admiral Merino put it, communists have no soul.[27]

Willoughby's most emphatic recommendation to the coup leaders was to make sure that Allende did not become a heroic example of political consistency for future generations. It would not suffice to get rid of the man. His words must not be heard, his image must be tainted. No narrative other than that allowed by the censor should be written or recorded. The myth must also die.[28]

If that was their longer-term aim, then there is no doubt that Willoughby and the coup leaders failed to achieve it. Even though Operation Silence did cut off Allende from almost all available means of communication, and although his orders to move Cybersyn's Operations Room to La Moneda palace and link it with the communications network were not followed, his voice was heard and recorded on 11 September 1973.

In fact, Allende wove a careful first-person account of events as they happened, pregnant with messages for the future. If not a myth, this was an example of autobiographical narrative, the tale of a death foretold as well as a seed for the resurgence of memory. Not just in the sense of a factual account that runs against the grain of the misconceptions woven into the official story told by the victors. But also one that stands as a deeply affecting record of man's inhumanity to man and appeals to our imagination in the form of an allegory, a counter-narrative that does more than criticise the present situation; it inspires action to change it.[29]

The explicit aim of this sort of storytelling – of which Allende's broadcasts on 11 September are an example – is to connect today's resistance to an earlier one. This is memory as creation and invention in the face of catastrophe. Not nostalgia for the lost object, catharsis, or merely an antidote against oblivion and widespread habits of denial. The point of invention and imagination, in practice, is to give meaning to and draw legitimacy from human experience. It is to provide others with a treasure-chest full of the proper tools with which to reconstruct and found a fuller and more equal community. In that sense, stories like this are fundamental, not marginal. So are memory, oral history, allegory and the ghostly presence of the disappeared, truth and reconciliation, hope, and moral images of freedom.[30]

This sort of storytelling pertains to what Hegel called 'philosophy of right' and universal history, as well as to contemporary accounts of human rights. For a different definition of history and the human emerges here: 'It is in the discontinuities of history,' writes Susan Buck-Morss in this regard, 'that people whose culture has been strained to the breaking point give expression to a humanity that goes beyond cultural limits.'[31] This is why the story of Allende and Chile's tragedy constituted a turning point for the world human rights movement, in time providing new meanings to notions of genocide, disappearance, truth and universal jurisdiction. It helped to disseminate such terms as an international vocabulary and a new common sense, after galvanising organisations such as Amnesty International or the Washington Office on Latin America (WOLA), and to motivate individuals like Joan Garcés, the Spanish judges Carlos Castresana and Baltasar Garzón, Carmen Lazo and many others. For many around the world who learned about the events of 11 September, this was a moment of moral growth and awareness. And for many more among the younger generations of Chile and elsewhere, and those to come, Allende's story of a death foretold stands as an inspiration to change the way things are.

At 7:55 a.m. on 11 September, the voice of Salvador Allende reached the people of Chile over the airwaves:

> This is the president of the republic. I speak to you from La Moneda palace. We have confirmed earlier news that a sector of the navy has occupied the city of Valparaíso; the city is now isolated from the rest of the country. This is a revolt against the government and its legitimate authority, protected by law and by the will of the citizens of Chile. Under these circumstances, I call upon you the workers to mobilise and occupy your factories and labour posts, but also to keep calm and act with serenity. Up to this moment the movement of troops in the city of Santiago appears normal, and the regiment's commander has informed me that the military will stay in their quarters. Whatever the case may be, I will remain in the presidential palace, where I am now, ready to defend the government that I represent in accordance with the people's mandate. I ask the workers to remain vigilant, to follow these events, and to avoid being provoked. Let us see first how the soldiers of Chile respond. They have sworn to protect the government that is the expression of the will of the people and should follow the tradition of loyalty that has given such high standing and prestige to Chile and its armed forces. In these circumstances, I am certain

that the soldiers will know what their obligations are and how
to comply with them. But whatever the case, the people, and
most of all the workers, must act and mobilise in the workplace,
attentive to the call and to the instructions that their *compañero
presidente* may give them.

This was Allende's first radio broadcast on the morning of 11
September. From the outset, his words seemed to invite a shift in
the understanding of their intended audience. The two cornerstones
of the speech defined the meaning of Allende's actions that day.
They were restraint and defiance. It was a strange mixture. In politics, we are told, if you are attacked you should strike back. The
'paranoid style in politics', according to Hofstadter, dictates that you
emulate the enemy and respond to his attacks in kind: an eye for an
eye, a tooth for a tooth, and fire with fire.[32]

If so, what could be the meaning of restraint and defiance? In the
answer to that question lies the particular electricity of Allende's
speech. It did not serve a tactical or strategic purpose. In terms of
military tactics 'restraint and defiance' were useless, even disastrous.
Rather, Allende's aim was to shift the understanding of his audience, specifically the popular sectors of Chile and those engaged in
the revolution from below.

In his first radio broadcast on 11 September, Allende confronted
the consequences of the defeat of the leadership from above. Far from
concluding that this was the end, he presented it as the opportunity of
a new beginning for the revolution from below. The lesson of that
day was not that dreaming the impossible was to invite the fury of the
powerful. Rather, the lesson was that the powerful live in constant
fear of people daring to expand the range of what is possible. Such
fear and paranoia, the tendency of the wealthy and powerful to resort
to violence, reveals their fundamental impotence. Responding to
such violence with an equal measure of violence could not be the
answer. It would only serve to escalate things. And in the case of an
escalation of hostilities, civil war, the people had much more to lose.

In an interview with Peter Winn, Salvador Allende had explained his view that 'millions of people in the world want socialism, but do not want to pay the terrible price of civil war in order to obtain it'.[33] According to Winn, despite the final image of Allende firing the AK-47 rifle Fidel Castro had given him − defending his burning presidential palace alone against an entire army, according to García Márquez's harrowing description − Salvador Allende remained on the path of the Chilean Way until the day of his death. He remained faithful to its notions of peaceful and democratic revolution acting as restraint on the tendency to emulate the enemy and engage in reciprocal violence.[34]

In the end Allende acted as the Chilean president who believed civil war was the worst disaster that could befall a nation, not as the revolutionary vanguard willing to sacrifice the people for his cause. As Winn observes, rather than risk the evil of civil war, the evil of imitation and the paranoid emulation of the enemy, Allende chose to risk his own life.[35]

Allende's choice showed two things: first, that the moral and political choices of the peoples of Chile were not exhausted by external conditions such as the imposition of 'law and order' by force, US intervention or the might of the powerful. The fact that I can choose death as a possibility means that I can always choose my future, and that there is no such thing as fate. Since fate was not the issue, it can be said that the Chilean Revolution was not doomed to failure and therefore remains an open road to us in the present and the future. Allende's words can be understood in this sense as a reaffirmation of the fundamental freedom of the Chilean people and of the possibility of hope in the most hopeless situations. Allende's choice also showed that for the revolution to continue in the midst of defeat, the people of Chile needed to shift their attention: to turn away from the father figure, Allende as icon, or his obverse image, that of the guardians of order, and focus instead on the enemy brothers. That is to say, people needed to concentrate on overcoming the rivalries as well as the historical and intellectual differences of the various sectors of the Left and the revolution from below. To do that, the people of Chile needed to understand that Allende's example is significant for the community not because of the particular identity of the victim, but because of his role as a unifying agent, and the fact that such a role could in fact be played by any member of the group.

On the one hand, this could be interpreted as a prescient warning about the kind of violence that would come later, under the pretext of the restoration of law and economic order: anyone and everyone could become an embodiment of the 'cancer' spreading through Chile, from generals and Nobel Prize-winning poets to the humblest slum-dweller, student, folk singer or Mapuche Indian. On the other, it was a call to set aside historical differences and gather around a common goal: that no sacrifice is necessary or sufficient, neither the sacrifice of the people for the revolutionary cause nor the sacrifice of the many for the prosperity of some in an economy of supposedly constant growth. That such sacrifices are unnecessary means that past wrongs are unjust, and must be remedied. Allende's words were an appeal to remedial justice.[36] Later that day, during his last conversation with Beatriz Allende, Allende would return to that theme: the need for 'a unity of thought and purpose' and the urgency of justice.[37]

Allende's first broadcast from La Moneda palace reveals how his attention shifted from the stage of immediate conflicting interests and conspiratorial politics to that of universal history, open access to politics and man's inhumanity to man. History stepped into his life, changing his perspective, allowing a new dialogue to commence, just as had happened to the slum-dweller of Dorfman's story during the three years of the UP government.[38] And just as Dorfman concluded on that occasion, the new perspective required a new language to express it. Building on that notion, we can conclude that Allende's radio broadcasts on 11 September invented a new language with which to voice a change of standpoint on the issues of political direction and remedial justice, in dialogue with the people of Chile.[39]

Rather than push the country into the abyss of civil war, Allende was ready to risk his own life. This gesture would validate his life as a democratic revolutionary: his fidelity to the work of the revolution from below, realising the impossible without having to sacrifice itself in the name of the cause. That gesture would also deny legitimacy to the ambitions of the conspirators' violent counter-revolution, namely to refound the state on the basis of sacrificial violence, to complete a ritual of purification by fire.

The battle Allende faced on 11 September raised a further question: how to ensure that the people of Chile did not forget how to be ready for miracles to happen. Crucially, for the impossible to happen, for the slum-dweller to 'dream reality', fantasy must first be traversed.[40] In the case of Chile in 1973, the fantasy that framed the reactions and responses of the Right and the military, as well as some sectors of the Left, was violence. To an extent, this was part and parcel of the disinformation campaign that hinged on the image of 'child-kidnapping communists' and violent *guerrilleros*. This is the sense in which it can be said that the coup began even before Allende was named president, during the 1970 presidential election, with the logistical and financial help of the CIA. Back then, ads had been run in which frightened children stared at a closed door over a caption reading: 'When communists come to power, fathers disappear.' As Peter Winn points out, it was when the anti-communists came to power that fathers really did disappear in Chile. Although a revival of that campaign of terror throughout the 1970s did not remove Allende or the revolution from below, the fantasy of revolutionary terror remained in use and served as a basis for counter-revolutionary conspirators to strike at the sincerity of the Popular Unity's proclaimed commitment to 'peaceful change'.[41]

As the feared disappearance of fathers and children failed to materialise during Allende's administration, Guzmán, Willoughby, Merino and the other rightists shifted tactics: they began to accuse the revolutionaries of provoking mutiny in the armed forces, causing food shortages through economic mismanagement, and creating a general climate of violence, scarcity and polarisation in Chile. Key to that strategy was a concentrated attack on the legal and political conditions that allowed workers, peasants and slum-dwellers in Chile to 'dream reality'. Guzmán argued against the legal measures taken to continue Frei's agrarian reform, to reform education, to regulate and nationalise, and, crucially, to uncouple authority and force from law and democratic consent (Allende's commitment not to use the security forces to repress the people, avoid violence, and seek support from the opposition for a plebiscite), which formed the backbone of the UP's negotiations with the PDC under the auspices of Cardinal Silva Henríquez.

For Guzmán and the young conservatives, the Church ought not to lean towards progressivism or mediate between the UP and its opponents in order to stave off the inevitable confrontation between the revolution and the counter-revolution. Rather, it should return to its traditional sources in the Hispanic tradition and the teachings of St Thomas Aquinas. In effect, Guzmán's position reaffirms in no uncertain terms the commitment of the members of the Church to unquestionable authority. As far as he was concerned, the Church should never attempt to 'Christianise and offer impetus' or sanctuary for the revolution.[42]

The legal measures blocking the use of force to contain the increased momentum of the revolution from below, and the attempts to reach a political agreement with the Christian Democratic opposition and the Church, were construed by Guzmán and the others as proof of their claim that Allende was pushing Chile into the abyss. In this context, the failure of the conversations held between Allende, PDC party leader Patricio Alywin and the Church intensified the climate of polarisation. It also meant that from now on the opposition would act as a bloc in Congress to stop any governmental initiative, and in the last instance to declare Allende in violation of the constitutional order on 23 August 1973.

Allende's response to the shifting strategies of the counter-revolutionaries at the level of communication was twofold: on the

one hand, to emphasise the fact that the programme of nationalisation and agrarian reform took place in strict accordance with domestic and international law; on the other, to distance the government
from the heated rhetoric of the *Miristas* (MIR activists) and sectors
within the UP calling on him to take control of the revolution from
below, organise the people into actual militias and force a revolutionary break. In this way, Allende was responding to what he
considered misguided notions on both right and left.

To many in Allende's close circle, calls for 'revolution' instead of
'reformism' were extremely damaging to the aims and survival of
the Chilean Way.[43] From that perspective, the posturing of the
MIR via the Revolutionary Squatters Movement projected an
image of hostility – the *Miristas* would parade through the main
streets of Santiago shouting: 'People! Rifle! MIR!' even though
these guns were made of wood and cardboard. It reinforced the
image of revolutionary violence exploited by the counter-revolution to persuade the middle classes that such an imminent threat
needed to be pre-empted and contained by all means. The nightmare scenario concocted by the rightist media was of hundreds of
thousands of *rotos* – filthy armed slum-dwellers – ready to raid and
violate the neighbourhoods of the better-off. The air force and the
marines would use similar fears to abuse the Arms Control Law, and
aggressively persecute the industrial belts and other networked
elements of the revolution from below.

The truth is that neither the Revolutionary Squatters Movement
nor the industrial belts had any arms. Occupations did occur in rural
areas, led by Mapuche Indians and landless peasants, and they did
increase in number after Allende's election. But 'they were generally nonviolent occupations of empty lands and lots',[44] not unlike
those that had grown common in Chile in the wake of the rural
migrations of the late 1950s. Certainly, nobody invaded the affluent
quarters of Santiago or Valparaíso. There were no show trials,
massacres or summary executions in Chile, as had occurred in the
American, French, Russian and Cuban revolutions. In fact, when

conspirators and right-wing terrorists and assassins were discovered, captured and tried in court, their sentences, though intended to set an example, were generally lenient. Neither the US economic blockade nor the resulting crippling economic crisis and the errors of government led to the radicalisation of the Chilean Way and the embrace of revolutionary terror as had happened in earlier revolutions. Only the national majority obtained by the candidates of the UP in the 1971 municipal elections, when support for the government rose close to 50 per cent, led to added momentum for the revolutionary process.

In short, Allende did not take advantage of any of the pressures on his government to radicalise the revolution and mobilise and arm its supporters. The key fact is that he chose not to, and imposed that choice on his partners. Not only did he refuse to play the opposition at their own game – revealing to them and to anyone the obscenity of military men betraying their oath – he asked the people not to resort to the violence the Right had chosen, even if that meant sacrificing the cause itself. Allende was challenging the revolution from below not to withdraw from the state and the law, but to continue making the state work differently, and peacefully. After all, between 1971 and 1973 the revolution from below had managed to set about transforming its added momentum into 'popular power', creating new forms of democracy and self-regulation, because Allende was in the palace.[45]

Days before Operation Silence was launched, Allende told his daughter Beatriz that in the event of a coup he would face the rebels from La Moneda. Allende had made up his mind from the start that he would confront military intervention as the democratically elected and constitutionally legitimate leader of his country. 'I shall defend this Chilean Revolution, and will defend the People's Government, because this is what I have pledged to do,' he said back in 1971. 'That is the mandate I've received from the people of Chile. I have no other alternative. Only if they riddle my body with bullets will they break our will to carry out the people's programme.'[46]

This was no rhetoric: Allende had staked his life on the revolution. Luis Fernández Oña, Beatriz's husband and the main contact between Allende and the Cuban embassy, rated it a military disaster.[47] As far as he and the Cubans were concerned, in the event of a military strike, the GAP guards protecting Allende would take him to the outskirts of the Santiago, where workers and slum-dwellers had begun organising themselves as resistance fighters. To that effect, the GAP began stockpiling automatic weapons and bazookas at Tomás Moro.

The Grupo de Amigos Personales had been a creation of Allende's daughter Beatriz. On 14 September 1970, she and Miriam Contreras arrived in Havana on a mission to secure Cuban support for the formation and training of a small group of bodyguards. Their task would be to protect the life of the president at all costs. Beatriz was already well known to the Cubans. She had met and befriended Che Guevara in 1960. After being introduced by some Cubans as 'Allende's daughter', she replied assertively: 'No, I am Beatriz.'[48]

In the wake of Guevara's death in 1967, Beatriz had become the leader of a support network linked to the Bolivian ELN, an involvement she did not conceal from her father and that he respected as her own. Nevertheless, he had reservations. The Cubans refused Beatriz's repeated requests to receive intensive military training between 1967 and 1970, because of her father's position. Still, she learned to handle weapons and radio equipment. After 1967 Beatriz organised radio transmissions between Cuba and the Chilean branch of the ELN, and controlled the secret codes for communications between Santiago and Havana before the re-establishment of full diplomatic relations between the two countries in November 1970.

At the time, Beatriz wanted Castro to provide the president-elect with a proper armed personal escort, different from the rag-tag group of socialists armed with eight pistols and no means of transportation who protected him during the campaign. Her fears were well founded. Salvador Allende told Régis Debray that at least two attempts on his life had been foiled. There was a constant sense of apprehension, and rumours were rife about CIA plots and shadow games within the police and the armed forces.

If anyone in Latin America understood how well founded such rumours could be, it was Fidel Castro. He had survived his share of CIA-planned assassination attempts. Perhaps that is why he presented Allende with an AK-47 Kalashnikov rifle. The inscription on the gunstock read: 'To Salvador, from a comrade in arms, Fidel.'[49] Castro insisted on responding to the request made by Beatriz cautiously. Three Cuban agents were sent to Santiago to assess the situation. One of them was Beatriz's new husband, Luis Fernández Oña. Departing from Cuba almost immediately after Beatriz and Miriam left Havana, the Cubans arrived in Santiago as part of a science conference delegation. It took a while for them and Beatriz to get to work on assembling the group that became known as GAP. The initial group of bodyguards were ill prepared for combat compared with the right-wing paramilitary groups intent on killing Allende.

Hoping that the GAP would benefit from the experience of the MIR militants (one of them was Allende's nephew, Andrés Pascal Allende), Beatriz Allende had asked its leaders to join the group. Later, the Cubans began to supply proper weapons, while members of the Cuban *Tropas Especiales* that included members of Castro's personal guard offered logistical training. These efforts nearly collapsed after it was discovered that the *Miristas* were using the weapons and training for their own ends. Salvador Allende himself complained to the Cubans. For a while, relations with Cuba suffered, and to solve the crisis required Castro's personal intervention. The MIR were excluded from the GAP, and only a group of Socialist Youth members were left behind to receive training and weaponry from the Cubans under the leadership and care of Beatriz.

At twenty-seven years of age, Beatriz Allende was a seasoned activist who had been associated with Che Guevara's Bolivian guerrillas, a trained physician like her father, Allende's close adviser and fierce critic. She was also, together with Miriam Contreras

(Allende's secretary and lover), one of the leaders of her father's GAP security group.

As promised in his radio address, having learned that a group of navy marines had rebelled in the city of Valparaíso, Salvador Allende left the presidential residence for his office at La Moneda early in the morning of 11 September 1973. He was accompanied by a handful of his guards. The GAP guards were armed with machine guns and an RPG-7 rocket launcher. Some of the bodyguards stayed behind at the Tomás Moro presidential residence; others took combat positions at the adjacent building of the Ministry of Public Works. A few young militants made it to the buildings on the other side of Plaza Constitución. Beatriz put a gun in her handbag and, disobeying her father's orders, together with her sister Isabel promptly made her way to La Moneda.

So did Miriam Contreras. Ominously, on her way to the palace Miriam and those accompanying her were stopped at a military checkpoint. She managed to slip through, but her son was detained. She was never to see him again.

At the palace, President Allende made several attempts to locate General Augusto Pinochet, but all efforts were in vain. Tactically, Operation Silence had been a success. Unknown to the president, Pinochet and the other conspirators had occupied their various command posts in the early hours of 11 September.

All the while, the coup within the security forces was still going on. Admiral Raúl Montero, the navy's commander-in-chief, was arrested. Admiral José Toribio Merino appointed himself in his place. The head of the Carabineros, General Sepúlveda, would be sidelined in the course of the morning.

Air Force General Alberto Bachelet, who served in the government and did not agree with the coup plotted by his personal friend General Gustavo Leigh, was arrested and tortured.[50] 'I was arrested and remained incommunicado during 26 days. I was tortured 30 days . . . and finally sent to the FACh [Chilean Air Force] hospital with a pre-cardiac arrest,' he wrote later on.[51] 'They broke me inside; they cut me open, also spiritually. I never knew what it was to hate anyone. I've always believed that humans are amazing creatures and should be respected as such. But I found comrades in the FACh, people I've known for over 20 years, students of mine, who treated me like . . . a dog.'[52] General Bachelet died as a result of his torturers' treatment. Their names were Édgar Ceballos and Ramón Cáceres Jorquera, both of whom went on to achieve the rank of colonel in the armed forces.[53]

Even Pinochet's personal assistant was arrested on the morning of 11 September. After the two of them arrived together at Command Post Number One, late, as it happened, Pinochet revealed the true purpose of their presence there. His protégé refused to take part in the coup.

Back on 27 July, Allende's navy aide, Captain Arturo Araya, had been shot dead on his own balcony. Almost at once the rightist media pointed the finger at the Cubans and the GAP. In his documentary film, Patricio Guzmán suggests that the purpose of this assassination was to sabotage the negotiations between Allende, Alywin and Cardinal Silva Henríquez. Another possibility is that this was the 'provocation' that the plotters were looking for, fabricated by them to put the blame on the Left.[54] Given the extent of the coup within the coup, Allende had good reason to fear that his general might be out of action: 'Poor Pinochet. He must be under arrest,' Allende told Joan Garcés and others back at the palace. According to the journalist Carlos Jorquera, who was present that day, Allende's concern for the commander-in-chief of the Chilean army was sincere.

It is clear from Allende's initial radio broadcasts that day that he had concluded that, from a military standpoint, the workers' organisations would be in no condition to act if all connections with the armed forces were severed. His messages conveyed that notion very precisely: the army – or at least those sections that had remained loyal – should be able to defuse an internal revolt within the armed forces as it had done in the past. Early in the morning, the coup seemed confined to the navy in Valparaíso. In case the army and the Carabineros needed support to put down the rebellion, the workers' industrial belts could act as a back-up force, but in no way could they ever replace them.

'Problems with your navy again, Captain,' Allende had told his navy aide-de-camp, Captain Jorge Grez, when the latter arrived in La Moneda palace.[55] After the broadcasts, Allende and his colleagues continued their efforts to re-establish the link between the popular organisations, the palace and loyal units of the state's security forces. A key part of that effort was to regain control over the means of communication. A phone call was placed to the house of the vice-president of the Central Workers' Union, the Central Unitaria de Trabajadores (CUT), Rolando Calderón. Allende instructed him to silence the radio stations of the Right and the newspaper *El Mercurio*. But lacking the sort of network that had successfully helped popular action against the 1972 October Strike, mobilising the people's organisations would prove an impossible task.

Thereafter, under-secretary of defence Ramiro Valenzuela, a constitutionalist, gave Allende the first clear news about the situation inside the army. 'I come from the Ministry [of Defence]. I tried to get in but they wouldn't let me . . . it has been taken over by the army,' he said. The mood inside the president's office immediately changed. Allende knew the civilian secretary of defence, Orlando Letelier, had made his way to the Ministry of Defence building at seven in the morning. They had not heard from him since.[56]

The telephone rang, interrupting their conversation. The president's air force aide-de-camp was on the line. Allende picked up. The others heard him say: 'Tell General von Schowen that the president of Chile does not escape.'[57] From the Ministry of Defence, the air force chief of staff, General von Schowen, had offered Allende an aircraft to go into exile. Unwilling to do it in person, von Schowen sent the message through Allende's aide-de-camp. Until then, Allende had remained relatively calm. Now his mood changed.

General Sepúlveda entered the president's office and contacted the chief prefect of the Carabineros of Santiago. 'General Parada, what is your information about the situation? . . . What do you mean "Let's wait and see"? Carabineros have always been and will always be on the side of the government! We're here to stay until the end, whatever it takes! And I am the director general of Carabineros!' Effectively, he had been sidelined.[58]

Activities at the Ministry of Defence had started very early on 11 September. At 4:30 in the morning Colonel Julio Polloni contacted the ministry in order to coordinate Operation Silence with Federico Willoughby and Admiral Patricio Carvajal. Soon afterwards, Willoughby arrived in the building. Admiral Carvajal received Willoughby in his wood-panelled office located on the upper floors. 'We must issue a statement and keep the spirits up. Create a certain mystique, if you will. Let's use the media and in particular the radio stations,' Carvajal told Willoughby. 'There'll be no television today, with the exception of Channel 13. Colonel Polloni is in charge of that; he'll be here soon. Let's hope this is not too bloody. Would you like a cup of tea?'[59]

Willoughby settled across the admiral's office, in the workplace of air force general Nicanor Díaz Estrada. The desks were filled with maps, papers, coffee thermoses and combat gear. At the end of the corridor in a small cubicle, Colonel Roberto Guillard was seated in front of a microphone connected to an AM antenna. Willoughby grabbed a chair and sat in front of him.

The radio in the president's office was tuned to Radio Agricultura, Willoughby's National Agriculture Society station. It was transmitting from the small cubicle at the end of the corridor in Admiral Carvajal's office at the Ministry of Defence. Now, it was effectively operating as the equivalent of Orwell's Ministry of Truth. From the little desk where Federico Willoughby sat in front of Colonel Guillard, the words turned into radio signals travelled the distance separating the cable from the AM antenna at the back of the building of the Ministry of Defence. It was a makeshift procedure, necessary because one of Operation Silence's air raids had mistakenly hit the transmission equipment at Radio Agricultura's station. The martial music of the national anthem of Chile served as prelude. Because the repairs were not finished, the national anthem had to be played once again. Guillard and Willoughby grew impatient. Finally, the voice of the coup – written by Willoughby and spoken by Guillard – was heard on the radio in the office of the president at La Moneda palace:

Taking into account:

First, that the country has fallen into the gravest state of social and moral crisis.

Second, the incapacity of the current government to manage the ensuing chaos, and bring it under control.

Third, the constant increase in the number of paramilitary forces trained by the parties of the Popular Unity, which will plunge the country into an inevitable civil war; the armed forces and the Carabineros decide:

First, that the president of the republic give up his investiture and position in favour of the armed forces and the forces of Carabineros of Chile . . .

Signed by the Military Junta of Government, constituted by the commanders in chief, General Augusto Pinochet Ugarte and General Gustavo Leigh, together with Admiral José Toribio Merino and General César Mendoza, in charge of the Navy and Carabineros.[60]

As Joan Garcés confirmed to Allende that his trusted General Pinochet had signed the statement just read out on the radio, the president looked up to the sky through the window of his office in La Moneda palace in disbelief. Down in the streets, army tanks began to surround the palace. Allende leaned on his desk and began to tap on it with his right hand. He looked up again and said: 'Three traitors, three traitors.'[61]

The rebel officers did not dare communicate their intentions personally, not even by telephone. 'The names of those taking credit for what is about to unfold appeared for the first time,' remembers Garcés. 'Though they do not show their faces yet, and their own voices are not being heard, now, at long last, we know.'[62]

At 8:45 a.m. on 11 September, Allende once more addressed the people of Chile:

> The situation is now critical. We face a coup d'état launched by the majority of the armed forces . . . I have not sought this. I am not a martyr. I have struggled for social justice and to do the job that the people asked me to do. But let them understand this very well, those who wish to roll history back and disavow the will of the majority of the people in this country . . . I have no other alternative. Only with bullets will they stop me from realising the project of the people of Chile. But if I die, the people will keep going, with the only difference that perhaps things will get a lot harder, a lot more violent, because this would have been the clearest and most objective lesson for the masses, that there are those who stop at nothing to protect their own interests . . . I will remain in La Moneda, even at the price of my own life.[63]

Radio Magallanes and Radio Candelaria retransmitted the address. These stations, sympathetic to the cause of the people, had escaped Operation Silence. Allende's voice sounded broken, metallic, then it went off air. The presenter at Radio Magallanes picked up the transmission. 'The President of the Republic is in his office at the presidential palace . . . He keeps fighting . . .'[64] The crackle of interference interrupted his words in mid-flow. It was replaced by distortion and atonality as the consonants and syllables dissolved into broken patterns of half-repetition. Just when it seemed as if some logic were about to emerge, the broadcast reverted to bursts of noise interspersed with silence. 'T-t-t-s-s-s- . . . R-r-t-t-s-s . . . This is Radio . . . They won't scare us . . . S-s-k-r . . . k-e-e- . . . keep transmitting . . .' It was as if the Furies were entering this world through the silences of the radio. Then the voice returned:

They won't scare us . . . we will keep transmitting because we are the voice of the people. We will remain on air for as long as the nation keeps marching forward into the future. The president is Salvador ['El presidente es Salvador,' which also translates as 'the president is our saviour']. The workers have said it on countless occasions. So say we all. We made our voice heard loud and clear last 4 September, when over a million peasants and workers took to the streets of Santiago to reassert once more that the only legitimate authority of this country is the one elected by the people. President Allende said it moments ago, and you, the workers of all Chile heard him: 'A group of *golpistas* have betrayed their patriotic allegiance to the laws and the constitution. They're traitors who hide behind their medals and their uniforms. History will judge their betrayal, for they have broken their oath of fidelity.' This is Radio Magallanes, transmitting to the workers of Chile.[65]

In downtown Santiago, battle had broken out in earnest. The Second Armoured Regiment under the command of General Javier Palacios clashed with loyalist snipers and fighters near the Ministry of Defence, the hub of communications of the conspirators situated on the other side of The Mall, La Alameda, just behind Plaza Libertad and the presidential palace. The duel was fierce; machine guns and rifles crackled, their deafening sound interrupted only by the roar of the air force helicopters circling above.

Finding his regiment under sniper fire from the neighbouring Entel Tower, General Palacios ordered a tank to move forward. Earlier on, Palacios had told General Pinochet he could not guarantee that the tanks would operate properly. Their guns might not work through lack of maintenance. For all the talk of military preparedness, Pinochet's army was actually quite unprepared for the coup on 11 September.[66] Luckily for General Palacios, this time the tank worked. The shell it fired shattered the main door of the entrance to the Ministry of Foreign Relations across The Mall, part of the architectural complex of La Moneda palace. It would be the first of many explosions in the presidential palace, caused by heavy artillery and bombardment that day.

Meanwhile, a few blocks from the palace, ex-president Jorge Alessandri peeped out into the street from one of the windows of his branch office in Plaza de Armas. What the nationalist mentor of Guzmán and Willoughby saw left a lasting impression. Units of the army and Carabineros had engaged a group of young socialist resisters who had taken up positions in the towers of the Cathedral. The soldiers shot at the Cathedral from the trees and the monuments of the square, while the small group of resistance fighters responded with rifle fire from on high. Bullets whined, shells exploded, windows shattered. Soon, the walls of Alessandri's office were showing the scars of battle, while workers and cleaners ran for cover, shrapnel flying in all directions. One of the cleaners put her head through the window to see the duel up close. Alessandri shouted at her to come away. Too late. A bullet went right through her head.

As another presenter of Radio Magallanes repeated the statement published in the leftist newspaper *El Siglo* that morning, its director, Guillermo Ravest, tried desperately to find a cigarette in his office. At six that morning, the engineer Lucho Oliva had woken him with the news that the coup had begun and that he would come straight to collect him to go to the radio station, located on the sixth floor of Estación 235. An hour and a half later, after avoiding several military roadblocks, the two men arrived at Estación Street and Plaza de Armas.

The radio station buzzed with activity. The journalists listed for the afternoon shifts had decided to come earlier to back up their colleagues in the morning. At times there were up to three radio controllers in the studio, frantically trying to keep their transmission on air together with Radio Corporación in order to broadcast the president's words to the nation. The two stations would sometimes link up under the name Voice of the Nation in order to boost their signal and counteract, no matter how slightly, the greater kilowattage of the many stations in the hands of the conspirators. Willoughby's Operation Silence had taken off the air the University of Chile and the Technical State University radio stations, as well as the workers union's Radio Recabarren.

Meanwhile, led by the National Agriculture Society radio station, transmitting from the Ministry of Defence with Willoughby in charge, the national network of the Chilean armed forces constantly broadcast martial music and proclamations in an attempt to legitimise the military coup. Together with the only TV channel broadcasting that day, Channel 13, also in the hands of the *golpistas*, they dressed up the violence now engulfing downtown Santiago in the guise of the purifying wrath of God. The Furies were unleashed on the back of radio signals and televised images. They worked their peculiar magic, feeding the hearts and minds of those whose righteousness needed confirmation from on high. Their colder hearts grew brutal.[67]

Ravest realised they were on their own. Radios Corporación, Portales and Candelaria had been silenced. He was frightened. For a couple of hours now, a law decree issued by the *golpistas* had been threatening radio stations that refused to submit to their orders with combined attack 'by ground and air'. His radio station was located a mere five blocks from La Moneda. Although he knew they could be raided at any minute and maybe killed, all he worried about was the fact that not one cigarette could be found in his office.[68] The wind-up telephone rang. It was operated by a handle and communicated directly with La Moneda. 'The iron', as they called it, rang twice. Ravest picked up. On the other end of the line he heard the unmistakable voice of Salvador Allende.

'Who's this?' asked the president.

'It's Ravest, *compañero* . . .' he replied.

'I need you to put me on the air immediately,' said Allende.

'Give me a minute so I can set up the recording equipment,' Ravest replied.

'No my friend. It has to be now. There's no time left,' said Allende.[69] It was 9:10 a.m.

Without taking the handset from his ear, Ravest shouted at Amado Felipe, his radio operator, to fit a tape on the recorder and to Leonardo Cáceres, the producer, to announce President Allende. Felipe decided to roll over Cáceres's voice the first notes of the national anthem, leaving the ambient mic open. In the original tape one can hear Ravest yelling at the top of his voice for some *huevón* (lazy bastard) to shut the door. This also explains the background noise in the original recording, provided by the *golpistas*: bullets shattering windows, shells fired from Sherman tanks, British-made Hawker Hunter jets flying at low altitude over the roofs of the terrified people of Santiago. That was the soundtrack to Salvador Allende's last words:

This will surely be the last time I speak to you. The air force has already bombarded the communication towers of Radio Portales and Radio Corporación. My word carries no resentment; it speaks only in disappointment and will be the judgement and moral punishment of those who have betrayed their oath of allegiance: soldiers of Chile, titular commanders, Admiral Merino, who has appointed himself the navy's commander in chief, and Mister Mendoza, an abject general who only yesterday declared his fidelity and loyalty to the government and today has also appointed himself general director of the Carabineros forces. Faced with their betrayal, all that remains for me to say to the workers is this: I shall not surrender! Placed at a historical crossroads, I shall pay with my life for your loyalty, the loyalty of the people. And I tell you with complete certainty, that the seed I put today in your hands and plant in the untainted soul and the worthy memory of thousands upon thousands of Chileans will not be uprooted ever. They are strong, they can defeat us, but the movement of society cannot be stopped by either crime or force. History is ours, and the people make it. Workers of Chile: I thank you for your fidelity, the trust you have placed in a man who was merely an interpreter of your deep yearnings for justice, who pledged his word to defend the law and the constitution, and who has kept it. In these final hours before my voice is silenced, I want you to learn this lesson: foreign capital, imperialism, together with the forces of reaction in this country, created the conditions for the armed forces to break with the tradition bequeathed to them by General Schneider and reasserted by Commander Araya, victims of the same fraction of society that today will be at their homes waiting to recover, through a hireling, the power to keep on defending their rents and privileges. I wish to speak most of all to the humble women of our land, to the peasant women who believed in us, to the working women who gave everything to work more, to the mother who knew of our concern for her children. I speak to the professionals of our country, those who kept working in spite of and against the sedition encouraged by the professional guilds, elitist institutions out to defend the advantages a capitalistic society grants them for their own ends. I speak to the youth of Chile, those who sang and gave their joy and their spirit to the struggle. I speak to the men of Chile, the worker, the peasant, intellectuals, all of whom will be persecuted; because an insidious form of fascism has been operating in our country for some time. It is evident in their acts of terror, blowing up bridges, cutting railway lines, destroying oil and gas pipes, all done in the face of the silence of those who had the obligation to pro—

At this point another voice imposes itself on Allende's, making the president's voice inaudible – Ravest's perhaps. Then the president continues:

... they had an obligation; history will judge them. Radio Magallanes will soon be silenced and the calm tone of my voice will no longer reach you. It doesn't matter. You will continue to hear it. I will always be with you, and you will remember me as a dignified man who was loyal ... the workers. The people must defend themselves, but not sacrifice themselves. They should not let themselves be destroyed nor demolished, but they should not let themselves be humiliated either. Workers of my land, the land of our fathers, I believe in Chile and its destiny. Other men shall overcome this grey and bitter moment in which treachery claims the upper hand. You will keep going, knowing that sooner rather than later the great avenues will open up once more, through which free men will walk on, to build a better society.

Long live Chile! Long live the people! Long live the workers! These are my final words. I am certain that my sacrifice will not be in vain. I am certain that, at the very least, it shall serve as a moral judgment on the felony, cowardice and treason that lay waste to our land.[70]

Allende spoke with his sights fixed on the future. His words were left to those who would hear them forty years later.

11

A Death Foretold

From the early hours of 11 September, Admiral Patricio Carvajal supervised all communications between the different branches of the armed forces from Post Number Five, located in the building of the Ministry of Defence. The building was located in downtown Santiago, a few blocks away from the presidential palace, where Allende and his small band of men and women prepared for combat after their arrival at 7:30 a.m.

At that time, Allende still believed that at least a portion of the armed forces would abide by their historical tradition of respect for legality and the Constitution. Having in mind the example of constitutionalists like General Prats, General Mario Sepúlveda and General Guillermo Pickering, the UP government expected that a significant part of the army, led by General Pinochet, would act to defend the Constitution. After all, as recently as 10 September General Pinochet had boasted in public about his democratic convictions, his admiration for and loyalty to both General Prats and President Allende, and his determination to keep his oath as a soldier to defend the Constitution and the president until the end. Seven days before the coup he said: 'There is a group of lunatics here, arguing that the armed forces should make their mind up and act against the president, even at the cost of a hundred thousand deaths if that avoids a million more in the case of a civil war.'[1] He also explained to defence minister Orlando Letelier that he was doing everything in his power to stop the lunatics within the forces, as instructed by General Prats, short of retiring them too quickly. 'To immediately retire the generals who make such arguments would make things worse,' he said. 'I need enough time to put the people I trust in charge of some units. If there is a revolt now, we run the risk of facing a united front within the armed forces, unlike what happened on 29 June.'[2]

Such protestations convinced Letelier and Allende that General Prats's influence over General Pinochet and other loyalists in the army continued. It was a guarantee that when the time came, they would act in defence of the Constitution, the Schneider Doctrine, and in accordance with the plans drawn up for such an eventuality. The action of the loyalist armed forces was crucial for the security plans devised by the High Command to defend the government against an uprising, and for those agreed with the UP coalition parties – the so-called Plan Hercules. According to such plans, militant sectors of the Left and the network from below would occupy their posts in factories, rural cooperatives and recovered lands, and streets around the country in order to resist. At least in some cases this could involve armed resistance, but in all cases their role would be to complement the actions of the constitutionalist sector of the army, as during the failed 29 June 1973 rebellion led by Colonel Souper and Fatherland and Freedom. This meant that only if and when the loyalist sector of the army acted against the plotters within would the workers and leftist militants be able to mount viable resistance.

By 11 September, however, the loyalist officers were gone. Prats had been forced to resign. Generals Sepúlveda and Pickering, responsible for the two most important operational units in the army, also resigned, convinced that their departure (and Prats's influence over Pinochet) would make it easier for Allende and the new commander-in-chief of the army to retire the officers involved in the *golpista* plot. What neither of them knew was how differently Pinochet felt about Prats. General Prats was well respected by his former junior officers, many of whom had been students of his in the Geopolitics and War Law course at the War Academy. According to the findings of Juan Cristóbal Peña and the results of an investigation recently published by investigative journalism blog CIPER Chile, Pinochet, on the other hand, secretly harboured feelings of intellectual jealousy towards the former commander of the army that turned into resentment.[3]

Pinochet fancied himself as an authority in global geopolitics. While Kissinger modelled his views on geopolitics and strategy on Klemens von Metternich, the nineteenth-century foreign minister of the Holy Roman Empire who engineered a European détente that included the marriage of Napoleon to Archduchess Marie Louise, and who was also the architect of the war that would send Napoleon into exile, Pinochet sought to model himself on Napoleon. Throughout his life, Pinochet got his hands on every book he could about Napoleon and kept a collection of busts of the French military and political leader in his personal library at El Melocotón and his summer house in Los Boldos. Importantly, like Napoleon, Pinochet saw himself as a revolutionary rather than a reactionary. Perhaps this is what his plotting colleagues in the armed forces picked up, the source of their mistrust, as well as the source of the confidence that both Prats and Allende had in him.

It is safe to say that, like his Corsican idol, Pinochet hoped to spread the ideals of a liberal revolution, first in his country and then elsewhere, through legal reform, while at the same time restoring aspects of Chile's *ancien régime* discarded by the revolutionaries of 1964 and 1970. He studied Napoleon's military campaigns as well as his political manoeuvres, and lectured on them at the War Academy, even though, like Napoleon, he had not been the brightest of students himself and did not shine during the early days of his career. Similarly, he rose to prominence under the republican revolutionary period that started in the 1960s and was extended after 1970, especially during Allende's years. And just like the French general, Pinochet would join the coup of 11 September 1973 and install himself at the top of the Supreme Command of the Nation, even though he did not stage the coup alone.

It has been pointed out that the title of 'President of the Supreme Command', which Pinochet assumed, had no meaning or precedent within the Chilean constitutional tradition. The closest reference would be article 60 of the 1925 Constitution designating the president as the supreme head of the nation in charge of internal and external security. No specific powers came with the title. This has led some to argue that it was used in error due to haste.[4] But an equally likely and more enticing proposition is that the title of Supreme Command was in fact inspired by Napoleon's position as First Consul after the 18 Brumaire 1799 coup d'état. After all, under such a guise Napoleon acted as head of a more conservative, authoritarian and autocratic government in France, without entirely abandoning the legalist and republican tradition, and crucially, not declaring himself head of state. Napoleon was thus merely one among the members of a supreme executive, but this was not an equal status, since he would be first among those in the 1799 triumvirate. Similarly, Pinochet would be first among what was effectively a triumvirate composed of the heads of the three branches of the armed forces, just like its 1799 model, with an added but not really significant member coming from the Carabineros force.

Moreover, the model may have been suggested to Pinochet by Allende himself. That is, by the latter's decision to effectively lead a government that from late 1972 and until 11 September 1973 included 'a head' (the president, Allende in this case) and 'a sword' (a general to back him, first Prats and then Pinochet) in the midst of and in order to confront a deepening political crisis. This would have suggested to Pinochet, who knew about and studied the events leading to Napoleon's rise to power, the choices made by the leader of the French Directory government, Emmanuel-Joseph Sieyès, after 18 June 1799. Like Allende in 1972 and 1973, Sieyès decided that the protection and if necessary the revision of the Constitution through a plebiscite would require a head, his own, and a sword.

Famously, Sieyès favoured Barthélemy Catherine Joubert as his sword, but when Joubert died in battle he turned to General Napoleon Bonaparte. The parallels with the situation in 1972 and 1973, when Allende favoured Carlos Prats to protect and revise the Constitution through a plebiscite, and when he stood down turned to Pinochet, must have seemed striking to an officer obsessed with Napoleon. The inclusion of Napoleon as the military sword in the French Directory government is widely seen as paving the way for the 18 Brumaire coup and his rise to power.

This also means that Pinochet knew he was the second-best choice after Prats was forced to resign. If it is true, as Cristóbal Peña and others have argued, that well before the coup Pinochet was jealous of Prats's prestige and intellectual clout inside and outside the armed forces, among hardliners as well as in the Executive office, then to have been selected as second-best choice for the position of Allende's sword must have deepened his animosity against the revered general as well as against the president. At that point Pinochet's jealousy would have turned to resentment, the kind of base passion that has led other historical characters in like circumstances to commit the most heinous crimes.

In his study of the Roman emperor Tiberius, the writer Gregorio Marañón observed that lack of understanding about his real capacities creates in the resentful person a disharmony between, on the one hand, his real capacity to achieve and triumph, and on the other, his perceived capacity to do so. 'It is precisely such lack of understanding about his own capacities,' points out an article on the subject of Pinochet's relationship with Prats posted by the respected Chilean journalistic blog CIPER (Centre for Journalistic Research), 'that led Pinochet to write texts on geopolitics and military affairs, as well as to seek a career in teaching. In setting such a goal for himself, the crucial motivation was a desire for recognition that had so far eluded him . . . while Prats's career was brilliant, Pinochet's was marked by dark and light moments.'[5]

Given the different course of their careers until 1973 – one

brilliant, the other mediocre – the fact that Prats and Allende
promoted Pinochet to the position of commander-in-chief in late
1973, believing him capable but most of all loyal, should have been
a motive for gratitude towards those who had finally recognised
something of value in Pinochet, and the source of a firmer commitment to the constitutionalist cause. If it was, it lasted only seventeen
days, the CIPER bloggers maintain.[6] It is more likely, however,
that being chosen second to Prats, and the implication that the
circumstances of his promotion would make him more grateful and
loyal towards those who had chosen him, in fact had just the opposite effect. Some of Pinochet's biographers, for instance Gonzalo
Vial or Heraldo Muñoz, assert that the general was highly aware of
the fact that Allende and the UP politicians looked down on him
intellectually. This would not mean they thought him untrust-
worthy, for it was reasonable to believe that Pinochet would rest
content with the fact that his promotion was not a reward for
outstanding capacities, but rather a tribute to his loyalty. In his essay
on Tiberius, Gregorio Marañón contends that the resentful character, while often giving the impression of being silent and cautious,
in fact nurses his grudge in private. 'But once in a position of power,
he is capable of anything.'[7]

The day before the coup, Pinochet drove to the Mountain
Training School in the Andes together with his younger children
and his wife Lucía, whom Heraldo Muñoz has likened to a sort of
Lady Macbeth who 'fed his ambition for power . . . convinced him
that he had to cultivate relations with powerful people – and that it
might be necessary for him to do evil things to succeed'.[8] There, he
gave them into the care of Colonel Gustavo Cantuarias, who was
both a good friend of Carlos Prats and a constitutionalist. In his
classes on Geopolitics at the War Academy, Prats would invite his
students to consider one of Napoleon's strategies. His point was to
show that there are not always immediate solutions, the past does
not always show the way to the future.

Pinochet, who like Prats also taught Geopolitics and like him

taught Napoleon's life and career, seemed to draw the opposite
conclusion. He used the heroic past as a model for reiterating history
in the future. However, he may have ended up repeating not so
much his historical hero, Napoleon, but the emperor's nephew,
Louis Napoleon, who became Napoleon III. Caught in the balance
between conservatives, liberals and socialists, just like Louis
Napoleon, Pinochet would move from a commitment to the
conservatives early on during the coup, and before it an oath of
loyalty to a socialist leader, to an uneasy alliance with the liberalising
forces in pursuit of economic reform. A wooden public speaker, he
failed to impress fellow politicians and colleagues but gained popular favour when he appealed for the restoration of order, strong
government and national greatness.

The Chilean aristocracy supported Pinochet as the man who had
prevented communist revolution. He won over a good portion of
the industrialist class through more or less vague indications of
economic progress, the restoration of legal order, and, in time, an
electoral resolution to the emergency crisis.

And like Napoleon's nephew, he appealed to the example of
the French emperor whom popular memory credits with raising
the nation to the peak of its international greatness after the turmoil
of revolution. Appointed as the sword of the Executive while the
aristocracy and the industrialists plotted against it, Pinochet saw an
open door and walked through it. He surrounded himself with
lieutenants completely loyal to him, people like the future director
of the Intelligence Services (formally renamed DINA on
12 November 1973),[9] Lieutenant Colonel (later General) Manuel
Contreras, who set to work the day the coup began, or Jaime
Guzmán, introduced to Pinochet by Air Force General Leigh, just
as Louis Napoleon linked himself with Morny and Persigny. In
doing so, Pinochet blurred the boundaries between force and law
once more, securing the support of the army and his own position
through referenda and terror.[10] If needed, he would even give way
to the occasional populist gesture, as when he pressured the

Catholic Church into offering a Te Deum mass to thank God for 'national liberation'.[11]

On 11 September 1973 Pinochet would lead a coup d'état he did not stage, but managed to turn it in his favour. Some might say that his politics in power swung between the authoritarian and the liberal, something that has also been said of Louis Napoleon. And eventually, like Napoleon III, Pinochet would alienate even the reactionary classes who had helped to bring him to power.

At 7:00 a.m. on 11 September 1973, Pinochet was driven to his command post at the Telecommunications Centre in Peñalolén. He took a detour to visit one of his older children. That made him late, and the other plotters thought he might not show up. When his car did finally arrive, General Oscar Bonilla was about to take Pinochet's place. After placing under arrest his own aide-de-camp, who refused to take part in the coup, Pinochet's period of vacillation between his oath to a socialist president, the Constitution, Schneider's doctrine and Prats's instructions was over. His reservations about his ability to match his predecessors, Schneider and Prats, were assuaged and replaced by a resentful determination. He had said that a truly useful soldier must know how to follow and obey orders. Now it was his turn to give them.

Nothing made this new side of his personality as evident as the tactical and strategic move that Joan Garcés has called the true 'achievement' of General Pinochet: 'his major achievement, his work and creation, was to transform the apparatus designed to defend the government into a centre for the direction and support of the insurrection.' This was precisely the role of Command Post Number One in Peñalolén. 'The centralisation of all information and intelligence services effectively took place, as described in Plan Hercules,' writes Garcés. 'But its nature was changed, it became subordinate to Pinochet, thereby giving rise to the DINA (National Intelligence Direction) which would become the instrument of death and torture of dozens of thousands in Chile and elsewhere.'[12] The decisive fact on 11 September 1973, according to Garcés, was the absence of any organisation with military capability to confront the military and intelligence apparatus. Effectively, as both Garcés and Robert Barros contend, the death, torture, sabotage and terror machinery of DINA – complete with army majors and colonels, but also with terrorists in the rightist paramilitary network of Fatherland and Freedom and the ex-Cadet Commandos, some of whom had been linked to the Viaux plot of 1970 – began to operate on the day of the coup.[13]

Thus, on 11 September Plan Hercules would be used against Allende and the elected government. Not only had Pinochet transformed the plan to serve his purposes, but, as we have seen, with or without his knowledge, other modifications had been introduced by Federico Willoughby and those in charge of Operation Silence. Civilian 'generals' like Willoughby, but also Agustín Edwards, Roberto Thieme, Jaime Guzmán and Sergio de Castro, each in his own way, were actively involved in the plot and/or its execution, through such organisations as the Cofradía Náutica, the National Agriculture Society and the other *Gremialistas*, the rightist parties, and their paramilitary groups Fatherland and Freedom and the ex-Cadet Commandos.

The latter had waged a campaign of terrorist violence against the state and the Allende government from the outset. They played a central role in the plot to stop Allende's confirmation, led by General Viaux and supported by the CIA, which culminated in the assassination of the constitutionalist General René Schneider in 1970. Armed counter-revolution showed its hand in the 'Pots and Pans Protests' in December 1971 and during the 1972 October Strike. Since then, the contacts between these groups and the armed forces became ever tighter, especially with the navy. The paramilitary resurfaced in June 1973, assuming responsibility for the failed June 1973 coup – with hindsight a dress rehearsal for the coup of 11 September. In July 1973, after Fatherland and Freedom's military leader Roberto Thieme returned from his self-imposed exile in Argentina to declare all-out war on the Allende administration, the armed counter-revolution intensified its terrorist campaign: bridges, oil pipelines, energy towers and the national power grid were bombed or otherwise sabotaged; the workers' network, the indus- trial belts and the UP brigades were subject to violent attacks; and plans were drawn up to assassinate the general secretary of the Socialist Party, Carlos Altamirano. This was done in collaboration with the Chilean navy.

On 26 July 1973, a squad led by Navy Intelligence and the rebel sector of the Military Police, either Fatherland and Freedom or the ex-Cadet Commandos, or both, carried out the assassination of Captain Arturo Araya Peters. Araya was Allende's navy aide-de- camp, a member of the constitutionalist sector within the navy, and had become Allende's personal friend and his link with that element of the armed forces. According to Robinson Rojas, Araya's assassi- nation prevented him from being promoted to rear admiral. In that case, Araya, an influential officer trusted by Allende, would have become a member of the Navy High Command. Since the conspir- acy originated in the Navy High Command, Araya would have been well placed to find out about the details of the conspiracy to overthrow the constitutional government, and oppose it. Crucially, in July 1973 the plotting officers had not yet set a date for the coup. The attempt to blame the assassination on the Left was made in the hope of inducing wavering officers in the armed forces to side with the conspiracy.[14]

According to Rojas, in August 1973 Thieme confessed to the Chilean civil police that his men in Fatherland and Freedom and the ex-Cadet Commandos were in contact with Federico Willoughby, and that he had collaborated to make possible their training and other contacts with the US embassy.[15]

As all these developments were taking place, the White House was in crisis-containment mode, now that the journalists Carl Bernstein and Bob Woodward had begun to publish the allegations behind what would soon become known as the Watergate scandal. Watergate was a symptom, revealing the malady rooted at the heart of the US government: a White House grown convinced of its authority to break the law in order to curb dissent at home and smash perceived enemies abroad. 'When the President does it,' replied Nixon when confronted on this issue by David Frost, 'that means that it is not illegal.'[16] That argument, very similar to ones made in more recent years by the George W. Bush White House, justified curbing dissent in the US and smashing popular governments abroad – acts that belong to the same continuum. It also helped to shape the mindset that would allow those doing the dirty work in places like Chile – people like Fatherland and Freedom's Roberto Thieme, Federico Willoughby and others, enabling the hand of the US to stay unseen – to feel justified in breaking the law and doing their bit of smashing themselves. 'I am going to smash that son of a bitch Allende,' Richard Nixon had said to US ambassador Korry back in 1970, and pounded his fist against his hand.[17] In July and September 1973, the economic smashing and covert lawbreaking were finally paying off. Earlier that year, the CIA had urged its agents in Chile to 'induce as much of the military as possible, if not all, to take over and displace the Allende govt'.[18]

Chile's mainstream media were all too quick to pin the Araya assassination on the socialist Left and the president's GAP guards, conditioning their audience with the notion that Allende had unleashed forces he could not control and had been superseded by the radical Left.[19] The hope of inducing hesitant members of the armed forces to side with the plotters shows that at least one of the aims of Araya's murder followed directly from the instructions given by the CIA to its Chilean agents earlier that year. The assassination, and the responsibility of the Left alleged by the Edwards-controlled media, also impacted on the conversations between Allende and Aylwin and the possibility of a pact between the UP and the PDC. Those negotiations ended on 7 August 1973. On 8 August, a new industrial and *Gremialista* transport strike began.

The subsequent investigation by the Homicide Squad of the Policia de Investigaciones, the Chilean FBI, revealed a different truth: the man arrested as the assassin had signed a statement that he had not even read, under torture. The text of the confession was known to a National Party legislator, Gustavo Alessandri, who had read it in part over the National Agriculture Society's radio station where Federico Willoughby worked, two hours before the alleged lone gunman was arrested. Two of the actual members of the death squad had connections with a senior naval officer. On the morning of 8 August Allende discussed the Homicide Squad report with the leaders of the armed forces, observing that if the people were to discover the whole truth about Araya's murder they would assault the military and police barracks in order to bring justice to the conspirators. A second report revealed the connection between Araya's assassins, the paramilitary groups, and foreign military or intelligence services.

If the armed forces wished to avoid half a million dead in Chile, Allende pointed out, they must demonstrate their loyalty to the law and the Constitution, join a Cabinet of national unity as the sword loyal to Allende, its head, and contribute to finding a solution to the *Gremialista* strike before it got as serious as the previous one in October 1972. On the morning of 13 August, Allende announced the formation of a National Security Cabinet with members of the three branches of the armed forces – effectively a triumvirate – with him at the helm, as 'the last chance to avoid a confrontation between Chileans'.[20] According to Robinson Rojas, in the ensuing days Vice-Admiral José Toribio Merino voiced the opinion that Allende was getting too close to learning the whole truth about the international and national conspiracy, which he could use to great effect in exile, and thus the coup, which was now a matter of urgency, must end with his death.[21]

Allende's foretold fate was hastening towards him on the morning of 11 September. Merino's men launched the coup in Valparaíso, Willoughby carried out Operation Silence in Santiago, with the help of the Hawker Hunter jets that blew up the antennas of Radio Portales and Corporación early that morning. The leading players in the coup – Pinochet among them – occupied their command positions to coordinate the attack, intent on robbing Allende of any freedom he might still possess by deciding the manner of his final end. Admiral Patricio Carvajal orchestrated the efforts from the Ministry of Defence building, supervising the exchange of orders between the different posts of the armed forces coordinating military operations. Also at the ministry building were generals Nicanor Díaz Estrada, Ernesto Baeza, Sergio Nuño, and the 'civilian general' Federico Willoughby. Their job was to facilitate communications between the different posts and sectors of the armed forces that day, but also to monitor any communications coming out of the presidential palace that might offer a clue to the potential response from the militants loyal to Allende, as well as selling the coup to the majority of Chileans.

Pinochet was at Post Number One in Peñalolén, in charge of the communications network within the army, the key player in the coup, and therefore he effectively controlled it from the outset, though he himself did not stage it. Having turned Plan Hercules into a device to centralise intelligence services and deploy them from that day onwards, he would also control the brain of the armed forces and its most lethal executive arm. This gave him the edge. Crucially, many of the terrorists working with Fatherland and Freedom and the ex-Cadets since the days of the Viaux conspiracy would resurface in Chile and elsewhere as agents of the centralised intelligence services (DINA) emerging that day at Pinochet's beck and call.

The men at the Ministry of Defence were using the communications link established at Post Number Three in the Military School. Air Force General Leigh was at Post Number Two in Las Condes Academy, while Merino and Huerta remained in Valparaíso at Post Number Four. Pinochet oversaw the action and deployed the reconfigured DINA on 11 September from Peñalolén, in the army's Communications Centre.

'Within [La Moneda] the battle raged,' Beatriz Allende wrote:

The president was supported by a group of friends that belonged to his personal security detail, all of whom had occupied their positions and readied themselves for the fight. A couple of RPGs were distributed, together with some lighter weapons left behind by the Carabineros. A group of men belonging to the CSI [Servicio de Investigaciones] had also joined in and coordinated their efforts with the GAP. Besides them, there were the ministers, sub-secretaries, a group of former ministers, technicians, journalists and members of the Information and Communications Office. The physicians belonging to the medical team were present, as were the members of the administrative team of La Moneda palace who did not want to leave the building. They were ready to fight side by side with Allende. Finally, there were his closest collaborators, eleven of whom were women.[22]

According to Beatriz, measures were taken to make ready for a pitched battle. Allende walked around the palace ordering people to seek shelter against an imminent air strike and to ration food and water. The medical team was ordered to set up a sick bay and be ready to tend to the wounded. 'It was then that he and I had a conversation, alone,' says Beatriz.

He said to me once more that he was going to fight to the last. He said he knew what was going to happen, the outcome was already clear to him, and he would take measures to guarantee we gave them a good fight despite our clearly disadvantageous position. It was going to be hard, he said, but there was no other option for him as a revolutionary, as a president defending the authority given to him by the people, or as a father. He said that by denying the generals the satisfaction of his surrender, they would be revealed as fascist traitors. By acting in such a way he would stand witness to their betrayal and that of their civilian masters.[23]

In a way, she says, her father was relieved that this moment had finally arrived, for everything was now in the open. He was finally liberated from the shackles of a situation that had mortified him during the last months of his presidency.

According to Beatriz, Allende was troubled by the fact that on the one hand he was the representative of a popular government that had made a commitment not to use violence against the people, while on the other the armed forces responsible to him were using the Arms Control Law to unleash their own violence against the peasants, the slum-dwellers and the workers, raiding their factories, beating them up, insulting them and generally subjecting them to inhuman treatment. According to Beatriz they had talked about that before:

> His spirit at that moment was extraordinary. He was ready to keep fighting. His words reflected the clarity of those who can see the situation as a whole. From such a viewpoint he understood that the revolutionary struggle would take a very different course. What matters now, he said, is the political direction of the future. 'We must secure a common purpose of the different revolutionary forces,' he observed . . . For that very reason he wanted to avoid unnecessary sacrifices. He said to me we would have to make a huge effort to achieve the unity necessary to lead the resistance that would begin that day. Such a task, he said, would require the right political orientation.[24]

Allende's decision not to call for armed resistance or mass mobilisation on 11 September sprang from his awareness that the various parties and groups that made up Popular Unity and the Left were divided, lacking both the right political orientation and what he and Beatriz called 'a common purpose'.[25] A common vision of the future, a plan for the day after, complete with the actual legal mechanisms and the political organisation capable of gathering and translating differences into a unity of purpose and movement without betraying or sidelining some of them. These were the conditions for effective resistance.

This would entail putting in place the right institutional and normative framework as well as a decision-making process specific to the aims of resistance and transformation, like the 1792–5 French National Convention. If as a result of that process those in the resistance acquire both the authority and the power to contain greed and betrayal tomorrow, while advancing their plans for the proper allocation of existing resources and their logistical programmes today, their huge effort will have been worthwhile.

Implicit in the terms of the conversation between Beatriz and her father is the recognition that the problems confronting such a task – to ensure a future for the struggle and the Chilean Way – lay not so much in the logic of historical development as in the minds of the people. The psychological obstacle that blocks the Promethean task of ensuring a future has been summed up in that same old weary statement that 'It'll all be the same a hundred years from now.' It is tempting to think that whatever we do to change things for the better, our deeds will be a drop in the ocean. And whatever we achieve, doing it will land us in hot water. So the temptation is to shrug off any responsibility and to disavow our capacity – as individuals or a group – to change the present in order to shape a different future. The future seems bound to repeat itself – tragedy and farce – and the transformative capacities of individuals and groups seem limited, if valid at all.

In today's culture, the scepticism expressed in the phrase 'It'll all be the same a hundred years from now' has combined with narratives that tell of past injustice as something done to someone else by someone else, to persuade us that each atrocity is the repetition of an earlier atrocity, that cruelty is a permanent flaw in human nature, and that justice takes time. We have come to accept that what we do to change past injustice is, at best, inconsequential, just a drop in the ocean, and at worst, it will generate further cruelty and injustice. The conclusion seems to be that justice will have to wait; that there is always more time. But we also know that for the vast majority of humanity living in poverty or under the effects of entrenched inequalities there is little time.

The view for the beneficiaries of past injustice – people like Agustín Edwards, Jaime Guzmán or Federico Willoughby in 1970s Chile – is that they have not received an imperative for change, but more time. For instance, in the Christian theological narrative that Guzmán inherited from his teacher Osvaldo Lira, which informed his views on law and politics, as a protector of the faith, a good Christian ruler governs so that humanity will not fall under the deception that 'the day of the Lord' and revolutionary justice 'is already here'.[26] The provisional winners of history past and present, which the novelist John Berger calls 'profiteers', always want more time.[27]

Beatriz's use of the future perfect and the conditional tense in her account of her last exchange with Salvador Allende goes against that view: it aims to show that things can be quite different, for if you and me will be dead in one hundred years 'then those who are alive at the time will be new people'.[28] In her account of Salvador Allende's speeches on 11 September, his words can be interpreted as a prophetic call for justice now. It is exactly the same image that Gabriel García Márquez used in order to describe Allende, without naming him, in his powerful Nobel Prize lecture 'The Solitude of Latin America'.[29]

It is best to deal with her testimony on its own terms, for her account displays a truth of a different order. Not merely a historical or legal truth, its judgements based on fact-checking, and in the case of law, dealing with new cases or challenges in terms of patterns set in the past. In contrast, the kind of truth that emerges from Beatriz's account takes the specific form of a judgement of history: one that acquires a wider significance no matter what the details of an encounter, a challenge or a conflict.

The significance of that final conversation is universal because it concerns death, which comes to all yet takes us by surprise. We know it will take place, but never exactly when or how; no amount of past experience eases the pain or anxiety that may come with it. It divides the past and the present from the future in a decisive way.

Death can be understood in the sense of those inexorable moments that bring our histories to a close and also allow us to keep moving. Examples of such ultimate judgement and closure, the judgement of history that organises Beatriz Allende's account of those last moments with her father, include the notion of *kairós* in the Judeo-Christian tradition, the idea of apocalypse in Muslim thought, the language of prophecy, Milton's poetry, the figure of the Angel of History or divine violence in the writings of Walter Benjamin, or the storm that sweeps away the town of Macondo at the end of Gabriel García Márquez's *One Hundred Years of Solitude*.[30] We should add to this account the nowadays nearly forgotten genre of manifestos, allegories and declarations, from Gerrard Winstanley's 1651 *The Law of Freedom* to Stéphane Hessel's 2011 *Indignez-vous!*[31]

The point of these experiments in writing and practice is to transform reality and tradition, rather than just repeating it. Beatriz's account of 11 September belongs to that genre. From her point of view, shared with Salvador Allende and the men and women present in La Moneda in the hour of their greatest danger, the task of resistance born at that very moment on 11 September was bound up with the creation of non-hierarchical relations in society and the state. Crucially, in the early 1970s new technologies and changes in social behaviour that opened up new spaces of personal freedom and identity were making it possible to explore and experience non-hierarchical relations. Computers, pioneering social networks (as in Project Cybersyn) and new social sensibilities were beginning to cohere with the aspiration of actual freedom ideals and political experiences such as that of the revolution from below and 'popular power' in Chile. To consider the actuality of a new relationship between the state and the people made sense in that context.

The question of the state, which according to Joan Garcés Chilean society had inherited from the nineteenth century, could now be reformulated in new terms.[32] When we ask: 'OK, this is what we want, this is what we have, now how do we get from A to B?' we tend to deal with such questions by embedding regulatory processes and systems of regulation in the Constitution and the law. Constitutions are powerful devices. They can be used to foretell, project and bind the future out of fear of the past, for example by stifling civil liberties and social rights for the sake of security in the wake of communism, terrorism or crisis. But those same processes can also be used to set the future free, for instance by creating models and narratives of well-being and community that are different from those ushered in by the realities of industrialisation, colonisation and global competition in the context of accumulation and legalised plunder.

This was the fork in the road that Chileans and other younger nations reached at that time of decolonisation and the Cold War in the early 1970s. At the time, emerging technologies were opening new spaces of personal freedom with the potential to alter the ways in which the state and its institutions could relate to society, and the members of society could relate to each other. They could develop both the will to shape their future and the practical tools to realise that will, unimpeded by the global institutions created after the Second World War that favoured only the interests of the wealthy and the powerful. Experiments like Cybersyn made sense in such a scenario, as well as experimental notions in the sphere of international law, such as Allende's doctrine of excess profits – the attempt to bring about new international economic relations in the context of Third World views on global and remedial justice.

According to Vergara and Varas, after the last conversation between Beatriz Allende and her father some forty people gathered in Toesca Hall, nervously checking their weapons and whispering about the air raid on its way. Hush filled the hall once Allende began to speak. He had put on a green helmet given to him by Captain José Muñoz. He wore it while speaking to the Chilean people from the presidential office earlier in the morning and he kept it on as he talked to those remaining in the palace. Beatriz says her father repeated pretty much the entire content of their conversation to the men and women gathered in the hall. Once more, he insisted upon his decision to fight to the last, and to defend with his life the authority of the president, which for him meant the rule of the people. 'Those who are armed must take their combat positions and prepare for a long fight,' he said. Then he ordered the rest to abandon the palace.

The women did not want to go: not Beatriz, not Payita, not Isabel Allende, not Nancy Jullien de Barrios, not the journalists Frida Modak, Cecilia Tormo and Verónica Ahumada. None of them wanted to go; they wanted to stay and fight.

Allende begged them to leave. They met in the waiting room of the office of the Intendencia de Palacio. He told them he had spoken to General Baeza on the phone. There would be a temporary cease-fire so that they could reach the street. 'A jeep will be waiting for you at the corner of Morandé, near the Intendencia,' he said.

Verónica Ahumada replied: 'Mister President, I'm not leaving. I'd rather die here than be shot out there.' The sound of machine guns and bullets shattering windows and riddling walls was clearly audible from where they were. Coco Paredes was with Allende, together with the physician Danilo Bertulín and Arsenio Poupin, under-secretary general of government. Paredes had his eyes fixed on Cecilia Tormo, his girlfriend, but would not say a word.

Poupin asked the president: 'What if the jeep's not there?'

'In that case Baeza will go down in history as a killer of women and someone who is not a man of his word,' said Allende.

At that moment, they heard the sound of combat jets passing over the palace. The president's tone of voice changed. Very firmly, he now ordered them to leave the palace at once. According to Beatriz he spoke to each one of them, explaining why they were needed outside and telling them about the revolutionary duty they must fulfil from then onwards. Once again, he told them that the only thing that mattered right now was the organisation, the unity of purpose of the people and the future. That was their duty. He even told Beatriz off for seeking to remain in the palace despite being heavily pregnant, and impressed upon her that she should be with her *compañeros* in the Cuban embassy. Allende explained to her how embarrassed he was because of the provocations and the aggressions against the embassy in the last months, and that he had suffered them as his own. He believed they would be pushed into combat that day, and that was why Beatriz should be with them.

In fact, the Cuban embassy had kept itself in the loop via telephone communication with the presidential palace and with the offices of its Latin American News Agency, Prensa Latina, located opposite La Moneda. Beatriz had called them earlier in the morning to convey to them her father's desire not to involve them in the battle of La Moneda. Both Beatriz and Salvador Allende were keenly aware that the world was watching. For the president, the presence of Cubans in the presidential palace fighting side by side with UP militants against Chilean soldiers would have played into the hands of the generals, Fatherland and Freedom and the Americans; it would confirm their scare stories about a plan hatched by the Cubans or the Soviets to plunge the country into civil war and reap the benefits, premised on their belief that Allende's commitment to democracy was opportunistic and would soon be abandoned.

Nothing could be further from the truth. Allende was neither an opportunist nor a fool, unleashing forces he could not control on the far pro-Cuban left, or playing second fiddle to alleged Cuban or Soviet masters. In the context of Cold War and détente, Moscow did not want to risk a confrontation with the United States by getting its hands dirty in Chile.

As previously mentioned, the fact is that the results of Allende's trip to Moscow after his UN appearance in late 1972 were disappointing. Moscow declined to help the Chileans both because it lacked faith in Allende's project and because it was 'financially unable to commit to a new Cuba', as the historians Olga Ulianova and Tanya Harmer observe. 'I never imagined that they would do this to me,' a bitter Allende complained to the Chilean diplomat Ramón Huidobro and chief physician Óscar Soto after the trip to

Moscow. 'They have stabbed me in the back.' 'Our Soviet *compañeros*' – he was referring to Alexei Kosygin, Leonid Brezhnev and Nikolai Podgorny – 'don't understand us.' Rather than increasing economic aid to Chile, the Soviet Union actually reduced it from $144 million in 1972 to $63 million in 1973.[33]

The Cubans, on the other hand, welcomed Allende as a true friend. When Allende visited Cuba the year after Castro's tour of Chile, the Cubans pledged solidarity, bread and forty tons of the Cuban population's sugar rations to help the Chilean Way. 'We must launch a gigantic wave of solidarity around our brothers the Chilean people,' said Castro, warning that what the Americans had 'tried to accomplish with bombs in Vietnam they are trying to accomplish in Chile by economic asphyxia'. However, neither sugar nor rum were what Chile needed to confront its economic problems. It worried the Cubans that the far Left's attacks on Allende undermined the Chilean Way, and diminished its political capital to achieve some consensus with the Christian Democrats, confront the fascists, and gain some progress on the economic front. In spite of their sympathies with the sector of the Left calling for armed revolution, they wondered how exactly any call to arms could be made to count in defending the Chilean government, while privately urging Allende to prepare more decisively for an armed confrontation.

Allende relied on Cuban advisers for personal security and intelligence and respected the resilience of the Cubans and of Castro personally in the face of overwhelming threats, but the turn to one-party rule in the island had actually reinforced his faith in democracy. Castro warned him that the military would not abide by the Constitution, but 'until at least early 1973 Allende believed otherwise', as Greg Grandin observes. And in any case, he never accepted that the only option was to choose between suspending democracy and letting the revolution die.

By mid-1973, as events began escaping his control because of the renewal of the *gremialistas*, industrialists and transport owners' strike, the political blockade in Congress and the decline of Chile's economic standing due to the fall in the price of copper, dwindling reserves and the US economic blockade, Allende acknowledged that to ease Chile's financial travails some sort of compromise would be required with the US. Between April and June 1973, the Chilean government demanded to know why the US policy of détente and opening towards China and the socialist bloc countries was not available to Chile. At the same time, Santiago did everything it could to rescue talks on its offer of legal arbitration to solve the issue of compensation and 'excess profits' in the wake of nationalisation, along the lines of the 1914 US–Chile bilateral treaty. The suggestion was that an understanding would be possible if only the Americans eased their economic pressure and stopped interfering.

In early April 1973, Ambassador Nathaniel Davis received author-isation from Secretary of State William Rogers to approach Allende's government and state that the United States had not categorically rejected arbitration, and as representatives of both countries sat in Lima for a third round of negotiations, the UP began to consider accepting some of the US demands contained in their counter-proposal to the 1914 treaty. By then, however, events on the ground had acquired a dynamic of their own. Besides, as Tanya Harmer observes, by mid-1973 the Nixon administration 'calculated that regional counter-revolutionary victories, combined with the UP's mounting difficulties in Chile, made it unlikely Allende would open the floodgates of . . . revolution in the continent'.[34] Rather than easing the pressure on Allende, the new attitude meant that, when Rogers and Allende met on 25 May 1973 in Argentina, their encounter was a sideshow and accomplished little. The US was back at its default position of benign neglect towards Latin America, as became abundantly clear to everyone during the July 1973 meet-ing of the Organization of American States, attended by Orlando Letelier as Chile's new foreign minister.

The lesson to be drawn from Chile's travails on the international front is that the main obstacle to turning widespread frustration with

US policy in the region into systemic change was the lack of any substantial Latin American bloc. Although many Latin American nations were wary of the US basic assumption that they knew best and could tell others what was best for them too, talk of Latin American unity rang hollow. Behind the scenes, America continued to work through its Latin American clients, especially Garrastazu Médici's Brazil, to undermine Chile's position. From the US perspective, when whole swathes of Chile's population appeared unlikely 'to recognize the error of their ways' in the wake of the surprisingly good results for Allende of the 1973 mid-term election, 'Washington singled out the coup as the only way it could truly "save" Chile and ensure "the battle of ideas" was decisively won in favour of capitalism and the United States.'[35] For their part, the Cubans became more convinced than ever that the Chilean military intended to intervene and that the only option left for Allende was to suspend democracy, or at least for the revolution from above to put itself at the head of the revolution from below and organise mass resistance. However, faced with little choice or none at all, Allende refused to take the violent road. Instead, he began focusing on a long-term road for the Chilean Revolution, even if it meant one without him, as Beatriz correctly understood after spending the morning of 11 September with her father during the blitz on La Moneda.[36]

When their father urged them to get out of the presidential palace on the eve of the blitz, Beatriz and Isabel insisted they wanted to stay. Allende said that if they did not leave he would be forced to go out in the street with them and risk being shot. Isabel began to cry. One by one, they began to leave the office of the Palace Intendant. Nancy Jullien de Barrios gave up her Walter PPK pistol and kissed her husband Jaime goodbye; she would never see him again. Beatriz gave Óscar Soto her Colt Cobra, together with the last box of bullets left in her handbag. Allende walked his daughters to the gate in Morandé Street. There, Salvador, Beatriz and Isabel came together in one final embrace. Isabel went out into the street. Beatriz lingered for a few seconds, gazing at her father. 'And that's how we left him, just before the bombs started falling. Fighting together with a small group of revolutionaries, among them a *compañera* who hid in a room because she preferred to keep fighting with them. That is the last image I have of my father,' she wrote.[37]

After the women had left, Salvador Allende walked to the Winter Courtyard and told Joan Garcés he needed him to leave as well, but the Spaniard was in no mood to listen. Allende put it to him that there was nobody else who could tell the world what had happened during those three years, and the events they had witnessed that morning. Persuaded by Allende's argument, Garcés left through the gate leading towards La Moneda Street, together with René Largo Farías, a photographer, and a member of the National Youth Council named Francisco Díaz. Now it was the turn of the physicians, who in Allende's mind had done more than their share that morning. They were also invited to leave, but rejected the suggestion in no uncertain terms: 'If there was a time I could demonstrate the kind of man I am, this is it. I stay,' said Doctor Patricio Guijón.[38]

A squadron of Sherman tanks and armoured cars made an attempt to storm the palace through the main gate at Moneda Street, only to be driven all the way back to Agustinas Street by a hail of bullets and RPG fire coming from the windows of the palace. Allende himself led the action, blowing up the turret of one of the tanks with a bazooka.[39] In Morandé, the army's infantry confronted the GAP snipers positioned at the Ministry of Public Works and the garage of the palace, coming under heavy fire. There were now more rifles, left behind by the Carabineros, than experienced people to fire them. But there were fewer gas masks.

According to Óscar Soto, the uncertainty about how to deal with an air raid was beginning to creep in. With the exception of Osvaldo Puccio, who had been through the bombardment of Berlin when he was fourteen and lived with his Chilean diplomat father, nobody had that kind of experience. At first, Allende and others tried to take cover in a basement room near the office of the Palace Intendant, but the room was too small. Allende moved to the second floor, between Toesca and Independence Hall. There, following Puccio's advice, he sat on the floor between two big walls and protected himself with a blanket, together with Jaime Barrios, Óscar Soto, Patricio Arroyo, Arturo Jirón, Eduardo Coco Paredes, Ricardo Pincheira, Juan Seoane, and two members of the GAP named Carlos and Aníbal, while another one, Daniel Vergara, mounted guard standing up in front of the small hole where Puccio and his son were hidden. From there, they could see the helicopters flying over the buildings near the presidential palace, shooting at the rooftops where UP militants were holding out. Barrios began issuing instructions: if they were hit directly by a rocket there wouldn't be much they could do. But if the rocket exploded at some distance they should protect themselves from the smoke and the shockwave, which were equally dangerous. He remained calm. All the others were scared out of their wits.

Barrios was interrupted by the unmistakable sound of fighter aircraft coming from the south, from the direction of Bulnes Avenue, followed by a sharp noise, like a whistle, made by an approaching rocket. The explosion sent huge shards of glass flying into the air while walls crumbled around them and parts of the roof collapsed onto them. The shockwave caught detective David Garrido running downstairs in search of weapons, sending his body upwards and backwards and blowing the shoes off his feet. The earth trembled, doors and windows were blown open, and almost at once the central part and the northern wing of the historic building caught fire. A huge column of smoke spewed into the air, visible from all four corners of Santiago.

The attack went on for over twenty minutes, during which the fighter jets hit the palace with at least eighteen rockets. Ernesto Amador González, aka 'The Bomber', fired the first rocket against La Moneda, blasting the main gate of the palace. The second airplane followed, piloted by Fernando Rojas Vender. The two planes fired their sura P-3 rockets from 3,000 feet, while flying over the Mapocho train station, some ten blocks from the palace. After firing their rockets into La Moneda, the Hawker Hunter jets flew off to the north of Santiago.

From the studios of Radio Balmaceda in New York Street, the journalist Ignacio González Camus described the scene unfolding before him in downtown Santiago. His words were being recorded on tape, but could not be heard by the people of the capital because the generals had bombed the transmitting antenna of his radio station earlier on. He could not see La Moneda, hidden from view behind a line of buildings, but could see the smoke and the jet planes leaving for the air base. He saw a few people were beginning to gather near Club Unión intent on seeing what was happening in Alameda Avenue and the palace, protected by the high concrete walls of the building; others sought refuge under the statue of the nineteenth-century linguist Andrés Bello, near the main building of the Universidad de Chile. When the exchange of fire between the soldiers and the defenders intensified, the people fled or hugged to the walls. There were corpses of civilians in the street.

'There are some onlookers in the street near The Mall,' González Camus said into his microphone, 'and a cameraman is filming the air bombardment from La Moneda Street. This is historical: they're demolishing the building, destroying La Moneda presidential palace . . . The president had said last week to the leadership of the UP coalition that only' – another flyover by the Hawker Hunter jets, another explosion in the presidential palace drowning out the recording – 'only dead would he leave the palace. He said he would go from the presidential palace straight to the cemetery . . . these are dramatic moments in the history of this country.'[40]

Inside La Moneda the fire was taking hold. Some fifteen minutes after the final attack, a black cloud of smoke began to choke the air and blind everyone. It was already hard to breathe, and some people were sharing the few gas masks while others tried to protect themselves with their jackets, when the survivors of the air raid inside the presidential palace heard the helicopters approach the blown-out windows and the huge gashes left in the building by the rockets. From the helicopters, the soldiers began firing canisters of tear gas into the palace. They could hear the cries and the screams of some of their colleagues and *compañeros* burning in the flames, but the sharp pain in their eyes and the terrible headache stopped them from leaving their refuge. The pipes were broken, and the water began flooding the first floor of the palace.

Cabinet members Almeyda, Briones and the brothers Tohá who had sought refuge in the cellar of the Foreign Affairs offices could not remain there any longer. Wrapping wet shirts and handkerchiefs around their faces, they ran to the first floor and locked themselves in an office near the exit to Morandé Street. José Tohá took the phone and gave their position to the soldiers in the Ministry of Defence. A second phone call from La Moneda palace reached the Ministry of Defence. General Baeza picked up. On the other end of the line was Osvaldo Puccio, who informed him that the survivors were ready to negotiate the terms of their surrender. A commission made up of himself, Daniel Vergara and Fernando Flores would leave the palace to parley with the generals. Flores sounded nervous. After hanging up they met with President Allende on the second floor of the palace, under a table. The president had just been informed that the military were attacking the slums in the outskirts of Santiago. The air force jets had bombarded the presidential residence at Tomás Moro, supported by helicopter fire. After a few phone calls made to find out the fate of his wife Hortensia, Allende learned the house had been destroyed. His heart sank. According to Óscar Soto, they could all see it in his face.[41]

Back at Tomás Moro, the savage fight between the GAP guards and the army was still going on. Taking advantage of the situation, Hortensia's chauffeur Carlos Tello and a member of the medical team, Doctor Stein, managed to smuggle her out of the house, walking her through the outbuildings of the nearby Convent of the Sacred Heart. Tello got hold of a car and drove her to the house of the head of the International Development Bank, Felipe Herrera. According to J. M. Vergara and Florencia Varas's account, the Mexican ambassador, Gonzalo Martínez Corbalá, picked her up there and took her to his embassy. The Tomás Moro residence was now deserted, and as the soldiers withdrew, making room for the bombers to return, the GAP seized the opportunity to flee. After the bombers and the soldiers were gone, the flies descended upon the ruins of the mansion. 'They came by the dozens, men, women, and children,' say Vergara and Varas. 'It was not sympathy or solidarity that prompted them to pour into the house of the president. They came only to loot.'[42]

The entire contents of the mansion, the modernist paintings by Latin American artists, the pre-Columbian objects arranged on the shelves in Allende's study, the radios, record players, women's jewellery, clothes, chandeliers and TV sets passed along a human chain and into a van parked outside in spite of the efforts of a handful of neighbours protesting against the behaviour of the looters. Laura Allende arrived at Tomás Moro after the soldiers had returned and the looters were gone. A neighbour who recognised her told her that Mrs Tencha Allende had been able to escape by car through the rear of the house, and that it was better for her to leave.

Allende had told Puccio, Vergara and Flores they should negotiate an end to the bombardments, the formation of a military government without civilian participation, and a guarantee that social and political rights would be respected without introducing any changes to the laws and the Constitution of the country. Only under such conditions would he resign. However, he was sceptical.

On the fifth floor of the Ministry of Defence, Flores, Vergara and Puccio met with the chief of staff, Vice-Admiral Patricio Carvajal, who informed them that he had been instructed by the Junta to demand the unconditional surrender of the president. From there, he spoke on the radio several times with Pinochet and the others.

General Leigh intervened from his post at Las Condes: 'State of exception, I ask for state of exception and curfew at 1800.'

'Right, Patricio I'm okay with declaring the state of exception,' responded Pinochet, 'but we must add that martial law will be applied to any person found in possession of weapons or explosives; they'll be shot at once without trial.'

'Former Minister Flores and Allende's secretary have called from La Moneda. Their intention is to leave through Morandé 80 to parley. They've been told to use a white flag to avoid being shot . . . the idea is not to talk but to capture them immediately.'

'Agreed, Patricio . . . we must consult with General Leigh. My opinion is that these gentlemen should be captured, put on a plane and sent anywhere. Actually, just throw them from the airplanes on the way out.'[43]

The journalist Augusto Olivares had spoken to Colonel Pedro Ewing at the Ministry of Defence, using the intercom from La Moneda palace. Having learned that the three envoys had been placed under arrest, Olivares looked for Allende, who was trying to coordinate with the GAP guards still fighting at the Ministry of Public Works, and told him about their failure. Then Olivares went down to a bathroom under the staircase leading to the kitchen, sat on a wooden stool and shot himself in the head. Alejandro Cuevas and Carlos Jorquera, for whom Olivares was like a brother, found him still alive. Jorquera shouted for help and the physicians Patricio Arroyo, Patricio Guijón and Arturo Jirón came quickly and tried to resuscitate him without success. Jorquera cried bitterly, while Jirón held Olivares's head until he died.

The physicians climbed the stairs to the second floor to inform Allende of what had happened, followed by all the others: Jorquera, who could not stop crying and shouting to the heavens that his lifetime friend was gone, Danilo, Eladio, Óscar Soto, some members of the GAP, Juan Seoane, Coco Paredes, Jaime Barrios and Miriam Contreras. The troops of General Palacios had entered La Moneda through the Morandé gate and would soon be there. Allende asked them, gathered in the corridor between Toesca and Independence Hall, to hold a minute's silence for their friend before surrendering to General Palacios. Allende had removed his helmet.

The physicians tied a white apron to a broomstick and stuck it out of the window for the soldiers to see it. Some twenty soldiers jumped on them, kicking them down to the floor and out onto the pavement of Morandé Street. Bullets whizzed past them as the GAP continued to shoot from the Ministry across the road. A bespectacled commander whose right lens had been shattered ordered everyone face-down on the ground. General Palacios began to check the identity of his prisoners, and seemed surprised when he found Miriam Contreras among them. Payita was shouting and writhing, and the general ordered an ambulance to take her to the military hospital.

The palace was in flames. The beams sustaining the structure had began to collapse, blazing, threatening to engulf them. The bespectacled commander asked Doctor Óscar Soto how many people remained on the second floor. 'I don't know,' he answered. 'Go upstairs and tell them they have ten minutes to surrender their weapons and come downstairs,' said the commander. Soto did as he was told. Having reached the second floor, he shouted at the group around President Allende that the first floor was under the control of the military and they must give themselves up. Allende told them to go downstairs, and said he would be the last.

The military had to destroy the presidential palace with rockets and fighter jet planes, set the building on fire and flood it with tear gas canisters to defeat a handful of amateur opponents, most of them civilians, who fought, as Beatriz Allende put it, until the end. They held out against the combined assault of the artillery, the Carabineros and the air force for eight hours.

Doctor Patricio Guijón went back to the end of the corridor in order to collect his gas mask. It was the first time he had been in a war and he wanted his sons to keep something to remember what had happened there. As he passed in front of the door of Independence Hall, he noticed it was open, and he could see a baroque red sofa at the end of the hall. On it lay the body of Salvador Allende. Part of his skull was missing. Between his legs was the rifle that Fidel Castro had given Allende as a present. Guijón looked at the clock, and the painting of the Chilean declaration of independence. It was two in the afternoon on 11 September 1973. He took the weapon and placed it at Allende's right-hand side. Then he sat down on the floor and mourned the Promethean president who had died in his sombre palace fighting against an entire army.[44]

III

AFTERMATH AND CONSEQUENCES

12

Laws of Darkness

'This guy will not surrender,' said General Pinochet to Admiral Carvajal. The general had contacted Admiral Patricio Carvajal in the Ministry of Defence, concerned that the pace of events on 11 September was too slow. 'At eleven in the morning sharp we have to bomb La Moneda,' the general commanded.[1] Carvajal relayed Pinochet's concern and his orders to Air Force General Leigh. At eleven fifteen, the Hawker Hunter jets had not yet reached their objective. After the long flight from the south of the country and the bombing of the radio transmitters targeted by Operation Silence, they had had to refuel. Leigh was losing face before his army colleague.

The army's commander-in-chief, an admirer of Sun Tzu's *The Art of War* as well as of Napoleon, seized his chance.[2] Pinochet's displeasure at Leigh's failure was explicit, but the general also stressed that his own initiative would save the day. He ordered General Brady to launch a decisive ground offensive on La Moneda presidential palace. According to Heraldo Muñoz, 'artillery shells, mortars, missiles, and high-calibre bullets slammed into the northern side of the palace'.[3] The former interior minister José Tohá contacted Carvajal from the palace to ask General Pinochet for a truce. He would convince Allende to surrender. 'No negotiations. You hear: unconditional surrender!' screamed General Pinochet to Carvajal after hearing the proposal.

'Unconditional surrender,' Carvajal responded, 'and do we keep the offer to take Allende and his family out of the country?' he asked.

'As far as Allende is concerned, we maintain the offer to fly him out of the country, but the plane falls in mid-flight,' was Pinochet's reply.[4]

In the afternoon of 11 September, while Allende fought his last battle to the death at La Moneda, groups of socialist militants led by the party's Political Commission member Arnoldo Camú, and members of the Leftist Revolutionary Movement, MIR, who had access to weapons, attempted to reach the palace and help those inside. However, the armed forces had effectively cordoned off Santiago's downtown. Obliged to retreat to the Indumet metal foundry, where they joined other comrades and the factory workers, the group was surrounded by members of the Carabineros forces, who opened fire. Workers and militants fired back. The standoff was bloody and lasted until three in the afternoon, when news of Allende's death had begun to spread by word of mouth.

Some of the fighters at the Indumet factory surrendered. Others, led by Camú, managed to escape the siege and left for the Sumar textile factory. Together with another group of militants, they engaged a Puma army helicopter and forced its withdrawal. Then they moved on to La Legua, a slum on the outskirts of Santiago where slum-dwellers and militants fought together against members of the Carabineros. The popular forces defeated the policemen, at least temporarily. They hoped this would be the beginning of a longer and more violent campaign of popular resistance. Earlier that day, Allende warned: 'If I die, the people will keep going.' He observed that 'they will continue down the road, with the difference that it will be harder and a lot more violent. For the masses will have learned, clearly and objectively, that these people – foreign capital, imperialism and reactionary forces – would stop at nothing.'[5]

In the town of Concepción, Marcelo Ferrada and other members of the MIR moved to their safe houses awaiting orders from the movement's headquarters in Santiago. The orders were contradictory. Although they launched resistance operations on the night of

11 September, Ferrada and his *compañeros* were obliged to rush from one safe house to another, constantly on the move, waiting for orders that never arrived and losing their organisation contacts. This was the situation everywhere in the country that acts of resistance took place. The leadership of the UP coalition parties and the militant groups failed not only to secure the weapons required for protracted and decisive resistance action, 'but also to communicate any coherent instructions to its armed or unarmed regulars', as Heraldo Muñoz observes.[6]

Shortly after Allende's death, the Chilean air force bombarded La Legua. An army raid followed. The rage of their punitive operations now targeted all the residents of the Santiago shantytown, and others like it elsewhere in the country. Agents of the then emerging DINA services were deployed in La Legua. Over two hundred men and women were captured. Some were tortured to death, others disappeared.

Ferrada was captured when his father, a man of strong right-wing convictions, tried to smuggle him out of Concepción under curfew. Their car was intercepted by an army patrol in Las Higueras Street. He was taken to the football stadium in Concepción. Ferrada was transported there by members of an army artillery unit under his brother's command. Later on, his brother would save his life. It would not be the last time. The head of Ferrada's MIR unit was also captured in Las Higueras and taken to the prison camp of Quiriquina Island. Ferrada would meet him there; he had been horribly tortured. He never talked. His courage saved many lives. Camú was killed a few days later, as he tried to escape an army checkpoint in downtown Santiago.[7]

By late afternoon on 11 September, the coup had succeeded. A light rain fell on the deserted streets of bloodied Santiago. The government officials who had survived the siege at La Moneda were first taken to the Ministry of Defence, and then flown to the Dawson Island prison camp in Chilean Patagonia. The other fighters from La Moneda were taken in two navy buses to the Tacna

Regiment army barracks. 'All of you are going to be executed,' yelled Colonel Joaquín Ramírez at the prisoners as they entered. Two days later, an army officer arrived. He was carrying a list with the names of those present in the presidential palace on 11 September. Those who were professional members of the Investigaciones homicide squad were separated from the rest. Some were released. The Director of Investigaciones, Coco Paredes, was savagely tortured. He died later on. The remaining twenty-four security guards, lawyers and government clerks were loaded onto trucks and taken twenty miles west of Santiago. They were shot that night.[8]

A few hours earlier, General Augusto Pinochet received a phone call from Admiral Patricio Carvajal. The admiral informed Pinochet that a meeting of the three commanders-in-chief of the armed forces was to take place at the Ministry of Defence. 'No,' replied Pinochet. 'You must come here, to Peñalolén.' He told Carvajal that the other two members of the coup triumvirate would have to come to him. The three would meet at Post Number One. This was no accidental move. Pinochet was taking possession. He was defining the propriety of roles, the proper names and the acceptable rules for the emerging situation, not least his title as 'president' of the Junta, and his role as 'Supreme Command of the Nation'.

Certainly, there was no detailed plan and no institutional design for the day after the coup. The men who plotted it were in no position to arrive at detailed agreements regarding 'the institutional contours of military role nor the content of specific policies', according to Robert Barros.[9] Planning, we know, had begun later than Pinochet claimed in his memoirs.[10] But it would be a mistake to conclude from this that Pinochet was clueless about the institutional line he was likely to take after the coup, and particularly as regards his own position among the other members of the Junta triumvirate about to meet up in the late afternoon of 11 September 1973, and the political-legal implications of such a position.

What we have learned about Pinochet's bibliophile tendencies, thanks in great part to the research published recently by the Chilean journalist Juan Cristóbal Peña, shows a different side of the would-be dictator.[11] His awareness that most people around him, General Prats among them, considered him intellectually second-rate had caused him to nurse deep grudges towards his former commander-in-chief. But he also developed an obsession with books from an early age, seeking to compensate for his perceived lack of intellectual ability, especially on the subjects of history, geography, military strategy and also post-revolutionary French political-legal institutions. In particular, he came to treasure an important collection on Napoleon Bonaparte, almost nine hundred volumes and a dozen miniature sculptures of his political and military hero. A considerable number of them, almost a third, deal with the period commencing 18 Brumaire 1799 – when Napoleon rejigged a coup he did not initiate to become First Consul of a triumvirate. Chief among them is Jean Thiry's *Le coup d'état du 18 Brumaire* in the 1947 edition. There, Pinochet would have found a very precise model for how to govern and remain in power, as well as the institutional, legal and political design for the day after the coup and clues to securing his own position among the members of the Junta, which his biographers and examiners of the period seem to have overlooked.[12]

That is precisely the model that would be established in the Junta's Decree Law No. 1 a few days after 11 September, and in previous administrative decrees called *Bandos*. Decree Law No. 1 stated that the three plus one officers had constituted a government Junta and assumed the 'Supreme Command of the Nation', and designated General Pinochet as 'President' of the Junta. Such a designation has no meaning or legal precedent in Chile's constitutional tradition, but it most closely resembles the role of the First Consul (in a triumvirate) assumed by Napoleon after the coup of 18 Brumaire. Crucially, the decree law, together with the *Bandos* (nos 1 and 5) issued by the triumvirate of generals on 11 September, also provided for the formal designation of the situation in Chile in and after 11 September as one of 'emergency' and a 'vacuum of power'.[13]

Thus began the coup after the coup. General Pinochet assumed his position as first among the members of what would become the Junta's triumvirate next day, and the keystone of Chile's counter-revolutionary constitutional and socio-legal structure.[14]

When Chile's armed forces ousted the democratically elected president of the country, took power and loosed the Furies against the democratic structures of the Left and broad sectors of the people as a whole, they broke unambiguously with the Constitution, the doctrine of military non-intervention, democracy and the rule of law.[15] They also undid the Allende doctrine and practice that divorced the force of law from force pure and simple. In doing so, Pinochet and the Junta set in motion the process that would result in the Chile of permanent transition and exception that the Chilean sociologist Alberto Mayol denounces as one of thorough depoliticisation. Mayol observes that: 'Depoliticisation must be understood as the destruction of the polis, the absence of criteria of political orientation based on the coming together and the consensus of citizens, the loss of any possibility to appeal to the common good or any utopian horizon.'[16] The non-political model examined by Mayol corresponds, strictly speaking, to the contention born in early twentieth-century Germany and Franco's Spain according to which the market economy and its leading light – the normalised consumer – produce public law, not the other way around. It was imported into Chile and the Americas in 1973, by way of an imitation of Napoleon's 18 Brumaire coup. From there, it would go global.

As pointed out earlier in this book, an important corollary of that notion is the idea that any collective desire to use the state and the laws to regulate the economy or transform it can be considered a violation by the state of some allegedly basic individual rights, and hence the loss by such a state of its right to represent these individuals. The latter – strictly speaking, their professional guilds and enterprises – can from this viewpoint make rightful use of violence, and overthrow any state that attempts to put law and politics before the presumed sovereignty of economics. This means that not only the market, but also the tacit doctrine of a permanent state of insecurity (with economic agents always at risk of political intervention by states, or politics as such, and ready to react violently against politics), produce public law, not the other way around. This effectively prevents any meaningful law and politics from taking effect – any significant practice of distributive, remedial or transformative justice. The result – a market culture dictating what kind of desires and political visions are henceforward acceptable and normal – has nothing to do with the law, order or politics. In fact, it means provoking great disorder, as Mayol points out in the case of contemporary Chile or, in a different but related manner, in Iraq or Afghanistan.[17] It is about qualifying respect for law and politics, as the Chilean Junta did in 1973.

Although the military Junta pledged to uphold the law and the Constitution, its actions on and after 11 September effectively made such a pledge null and void for at least two reasons. First, the members of the triumvirate (whose fourth member, Carabineros General Cesar Mendoza, was simply tacked on by the others – Army General Pinochet, Navy Admiral Merino and Air Force General Leigh – on the day of the coup, and would play no meaningful decision-making role) made it explicit from the outset that their respect for the Constitution would go only 'insofar as the situation permits'.[18] Second, this qualification, setting a strict proviso on the Junta's alleged respect for the rule of law, acted as the triumvirate's Law of Laws, a universal get-out clause. That is to say that as such, as a Law of Laws, it glossed the whole set of accepted institutions, rules and procedures under the general qualification, classification or determination of what the Junta chose to call 'the situation'.[19] According to the Junta's own legal-administrative decrees, issued between 11 September and 18 September 1973, the situation in question was characterised as 'a vacuum of power', the loss of 'economic and social normalcy, peace, tranquillity and security', and an 'emergency'.[20] This defined the state of the situation in question as one of abnormality, insecurity or an exceptional void, which needed to be filled or reorganised in the sense that things, words and people needed to be restored to their proper places and names, set in tune with a well-ordered, organic, natural classification. Crucially, the one who does the classifying, the ordering – in this case the Supreme Command of the (Chilean) Nation and in particular its president, General Augusto Pinochet – perceives himself as exempted from that order: that is to say, as holding the position of original creator and legislator.

That fantasy position is commonly designated by constitutional lawyers and political philosophers as a 'state of exception' or 'emergency'. The model for its conceptualisation is the role of Consul and Dictator in Roman Law:[21] when the city was in danger of a military attack, nearly unlimited powers would be given to the military chief or consul, or to a magistrate nominated by the consul, to act as if no law bound him, as a matter of exception and only for as long as the threat lasted, although it would be assumed that law did not cease to exist, but was merely 'suspended'. The problem, as the historical examples of Julius Caesar in ancient Rome, Napoleon during the Brumaire coup, the emergency decrees of 1930s Germany, Franco in Spain and most recently the George W. Bush administration demonstrate, is that the supposedly exceptional character of security powers not bound by law may become permanent or normal if not sufficiently restricted by the courts, and therefore the time limit does not really apply.

By then, it makes little sense to speak of the law still existing. And yet, because nothing has been created beyond the existing law to replace it – at least, for instance, in the sense that the Chilean Junta of 1973 declared its purpose as only 'to restore . . . normalcy' and 'to respect the law' – the practical outcome is a sort of limbo or purgatory, a zone of half- or non-being. In such an instance no creative affirmation of the people or humanity as such can take place. What ensues instead, as it would during Chile's 'state of exception' and 'transition', is a sort of antechamber for people awaiting not their affirmation but their destruction. In short, this is how laws write people out of existence while still appealing to the semblance of the rule of law and the Constitution. These may be called laws of darkness, in the sense of being makers of shadows, laws of death provoking disorder, as one end of a spectrum whose other end is the law of life.

According to the philosopher Alain Badiou, the part of the spectrum closer to laws of darkness or death comprises concrete forms of legality, politics and social behaviour that appear in our societies as what he calls 'the dictatorship of normal desires'.[22] This means that the subjects of such forms of law and politics are like those consumers who only search for information on the Internet and the media that will confirm their habits, unexamined beliefs and prejudices. Such a kind of consumerism, never daring to go outside the given choices, or to question what is presented by the media and the powers that be as normal or definitive – what is possible or 'legal' to imagine – reflects in fact the model of behaviour that predominates in our market cultures. There is, therefore, a connection between the semblance of legality constructed under states of exception, insecurity or emergency – such as the one that came into existence in Chile after 11 September 1973, declared in order to contain alleged existential threats and restore socio-economic normalcy – and the establishment of market cultures where once stood more creative and affirmative societies. According to Alberto Mayol, this would be an accurate description of the kind of institutionality and way of life that became characteristic of Chile between 1973 and 2011: a form of permanent exception, a constant state of emergency that also tames or normalises desire and imagination, which Chileans aptly refer to by the name 'transition'.[23]

If General Augusto Pinochet deserves credit, it is for helping to spawn the state of permanent transition as a global model, rather than some economic 'miracle'. As Mayol suggests, the 'miracle' is unthinkable without the permanent state of transition and exception. 'There are those who believe that if we arrived somewhere after transiting through dictatorship, then we arrived in a shopping mall,' he writes. 'But the fact remains we haven't arrived. We fought for democracy from within a dictatorship in order to live in transition, without ever seeing the light at the end of the tunnel, or the end of the road.'[24]

Contrary to what Mayol argues, however, this state of affairs did not come into existence in the 1980s. If the democratic struggle from within Pinochet's dictatorship emphasised the idea of a bridge, evoking the image of a (peaceful) transition between dictatorship and democracy, then we should be reminded that a bridge is never only a one-way street. One can always cross over the other way, from democracy to dictatorship, and likewise from the 1980s to the 1970s. The result is neither merely heaven nor only hell, but rather a kind of purgatory.

This legal, political and social model of permanent transition and purgatory originated in the exceptional situation brought about by 11 September 1973, more specifically with the implications of Pinochet's refusal on the evening of that date to travel to Santiago so as to meet the other members of the emerging triumvirate. Since the rain falling in and around Santiago that afternoon made it impossible for helicopters to ferry the other two commanders to the foothills of the Andes, Pinochet ended up compromising on a meeting nearer to Santiago, but still on his own ground, at the War Academy on the outskirts of the city.

Three decisions emerged from that first meeting. First, the leaders of the coup would communicate to the public the news of Allende's death by means of a written statement read on television. Second, Chile would at once break off relations with the socialist bloc and with Cuba, and would seek an immediate meeting with the Americans. Third, and crucial, was the decision to 'extend' the as yet undeclared state of exception. No less important, a Military Junta ruling over the state of exception had to be formally constituted. It had been assumed by those present at the meeting that the question concerning who would preside over the Junta should be settled on the basis of seniority, as General Leigh argued that afternoon. Based on such a criterion, Leigh put himself forward as the rightful leader of the Junta. General Pinochet disagreed. It was not a question of the seniority of the commanders, but of the respective institutions they led. Since the army had been created first, it should lead the Junta – that is to say, General Pinochet should.

The proposal was accepted on the basis of a 'gentlemen's agreement' that the presidency of the Junta would rotate among the services.[25] It never happened. Instead, the unresolved divisions between the members of the Junta, mainly Leigh, Merino and Pinochet – but particularly Pinochet's constant attempts to secure and further extend his tenure as 'First Consul' in the triumvirate – and of the institutions they represented (and also the ensuing power struggles between members of the Junta's inner circle to succeed Pinochet and the Junta's transitional rule) would from that day onward play a pivotal role in the institutional, constitutional and political shape of Chile's counter-revolutionary Restoration.

Later on the evening of 11 September 1973, the leaders of the uprising appeared on television introducing themselves to Chile and the world. Pinochet, speaking first, announced that the Junta would 'maintain' the courts and respect for the law insofar as the situation permitted, but that Congress would remain in recess until further orders. 'That's all,' he said. It was all that needed to be said that evening, or at least all that really mattered.

Admiral José Toribio Merino, sitting on the far right of Pinochet, almost out of frame, took over and provided the requisite justification that they had been forced into action: 'It may be sad to have broken a democratic tradition,' he said, 'but when the state loses its qualities, there are those who, by mandate, have to enforce them and take on that task. Chile has to understand the sacrifice such an action entails.'

'It isn't a matter of annihilating certain ideological trends,' pointed out General César Mendoza, whom few if any Chileans would have recognised, and whom Admiral Merino had only met earlier that afternoon. 'It's a matter of restoring public order.' Mendoza's message, so clearly out of joint in comparison with the expressed intentions of the other three Junta members, demonstrates the extent to which he was the non-member of the self-proclaimed triumvirate.

As if to make such intentions fully explicit and crystal-clear, while his partners opted for half-truths and apparent legal formalism, General Leigh, cigarette in hand, talked straight:

> After three years of suffering the Marxist cancer that led us to the brink of economic, moral and social disaster, which could no longer be tolerated, and for the sacred interests of the fatherland, we found ourselves forced to take on the sad and painful mission that we have undertaken. We are not afraid . . . We are convinced, with absolute certainty, that the vast majority of the Chilean people are with us, willing to extirpate that cancer, willing to fight against Marxism until the final outcome!

Undefined 'recess' of Congress; an end to oppositional party politics; 'sacrifice'; 'restoring order'; 'extirpate that cancer'; 'absolute certainty'; 'the final outcome' and solution to the perceived problem. The language matched the occasion. What problem? Whose sacrifice? Which law and which order? 'After 11 September,' observed Patricio Guzmán in his documentary *The Battle of Chile*, 'all the resources available to the army were used to repress the popular movement, with the compliance of the US government.'

There is no exaggeration in his statement: on 12 September 1973 General Pinochet held a secret meeting with the US military attaché, Colonel Carlos Urrutia. Pinochet gave a detailed account of the Junta's outline for the sacrifice and final solution to the 'cancer' problem – the destruction of the popular movement, and popular legal politics – while also touching on the thorny issue of diplomatic recognition for the regime. US ambassador Nathaniel Davis sent a cable to Washington advising 'that obviously [the United States] should not be the first to recognize'. A classified cable sent on

13 September 1973 from the White House Situation Room clarified: 'The US government wishes to make clear its desire to coop-
erate with the Military Junta and to assist in any appropriate way . . .
We welcome General Pinochet's expression of the Junta's desire for
strengthening friendly ties between Chile and the US . . . [but it is]
best initially to avoid too much public identification between us.'
On 14 September, US intelligence sources described Pinochet as
'decisive' and 'prudent'. In reference to the Junta's designs, the same
source noted: 'the priority concerns are to restore order and
economic normalcy. Political reform will apparently wait.'
Ambassador Davis found General Augusto Pinochet 'gracious and
eloquent'.[26]

The Brazilian dictatorial regime was the first to formally recognise the Chilean regime. The Nixon administration followed nearly
two weeks later, providing the desired recognition on 24 September.
The US had encouraged the new Chilean dictatorship to learn from
the Brazilian military, but observing the level of repression against
the popular movement, commentators noticed that Chile's Junta
had 'leapfrogged' the early stages of the Brazilian process. The
consequences were far-reaching: a month before the coup took
place, intelligence analysts in the US had already predicted that
Allende's fall would be a 'psychological setback to the cause of
doctrinaire socialism in the hemisphere' and that its successors
would 'be favourably disposed toward the United States and to
foreign investment'.[27]

This confirmed Sartre's contention, expressed during his re-
elaboration of the crime of genocide before Russell Tribunal I in
1967–8, about the true significance of the strategy he took the
Americans to be conducting worldwide, from Vietnam to Cuba.
The Russell International War Crimes Tribunal was a citizens'
body convened by Bertrand Russell and hosted by Jean-Paul Sartre,
along with the Italian jurist and politician Lelio Basso, Tariq Ali,
Gunther Anders, A. J. Ayer, Simone de Beauvoir, Isaac Deutscher,
Gisele Halimi, Amado Hernández, Sara Lidman, Shoichi Sakata,

Ken Coates, Ralph Schoenman, Julio Cortázar and others, to investigate and evaluate the conduct of American policy and military intervention in Vietnam. It was directly inspired by the Nuremberg War Crimes trials of the 1940s, which were conducted following the legal theory of the US Smith Act of 1940. According to that theory, Nazism was to be treated as a criminal conspiracy, which could have been legitimately prosecuted before taking power. 'The Nazi regime, its leaders and its institutions would be seen as plotting from the very beginning all the crimes of which they are now accused.'[28]

At the time of the Nuremberg Trials, US Secretary of War Henry Stimson and Supreme Court Justice Robert Jackson – who would be the chief prosecutor there – saw Hitler as another Napoleon and sought to avoid what they saw as the mistake of the victorious Third Coalition that defeated Napoleon in 1815 but failed to try him, and possibly execute him, for leading France into aggressive warfare and mass crimes. The Second World War Allies were keenly aware of Hitler's popularity among Germans and feared that he might emulate Napoleon's return from exile in the island of Elba, so that, as in Napoleonic France, they would have to wage another war against Germany. They sought to discredit the Nazi regime as a criminal conspiracy to take over Germany and lead it into a ruinous and criminal war. Thus, the architects of Nuremberg took seriously the question as to whether the legitimacy of the tribunal would require even-handed prosecution of the crimes committed not only by the Germans but also by their Allied foes.[29]

Bertrand Russell justified the establishment of the 1967 International War Crimes tribunal (hereafter Russell I) by appealing, precisely, to Justice Robert Jackson's contention in this regard, acting as chief prosecutor at Nuremberg. 'If certain acts and violations of treaties are crimes,' Jackson said, 'they are crimes whether the United States does them or whether Germany does them. We are not prepared to lay down a rule of criminal conduct against others which we would not be willing to have invoked against us.'[30]

With this question in mind, Jean-Paul Sartre, acting as the tribunal's Executive President, set out to consider whether Russell I could become a forum for what he and others called the inseparability of politics and morality. Critics of the tribunal at the time, such as the conservative French academic Thierry Maulnier, pointed out in their arguments against Russell I and Sartre's 'political morality' that the kind of justice it sought, 'justice that chooses a side', was no justice at all, and that in any case a tribunal that was outside of (state) law was a sham. This kind of argument, which has become quite familiar in our time among those who seek moral equivalence between rightist counter-revolutionary violence (say the Nazi regime, or Pinochet's dictatorship) and left revolutionary violence (Stalin's, anticolonial and national liberation struggles, or the violence attributed to Allende), though correct in its broad appeal to even-handedness, avoids the larger question that the Russell tribunal wanted to emphasise and debate: why is it that global justice is, to begin with, uneven? Why was there no standing tribunal to hold to account violators of international law, human rights and humanitarian law, including Euro-American powers, because of their actions in wars of colonialism, decolonisation, neocolonialism or intervention? Why is it, to put it in more contemporary terms, that we are more likely to see an African autocrat appearing before the International Criminal Court, or any international forum of a similar sort, but clearly not former Secretary of State Henry Kissinger for his alleged responsibility in the Chilean events of the 1970s, nor US ex-President George W. Bush or ex-Prime Minister Tony Blair for their part in launching a war of aggression in Iraq?[31]

Sartre argued at the time that this was because European and American powers did not want to be held to account for their own actions and those of their allies in such wars and in overt or covert interventions. Although since the time of the first two Russell tribunals we have witnessed the emergence of universal jurisdiction and the International Criminal Court (ICC), thanks in no small part to citizens' efforts such as those spearheaded by Russell, and to the wider resonance of the events of Vietnam and Chile in the 1960s and 1970s, the question posed by Sartre back in 1967–8 is still relevant. It is also the case that citizens' and people's tribunals, though acting outside of state judicial systems and for that reason not considered serious, still seem to present enough of a threat to the law that fails to face up to its own darker side to require them to be criticised, ridiculed or even banned. Therein lies the importance of the Russell tribunals.

As Sartre put it, the US wanted to show others that an alternative to their way, such as socialism, does not pay. 'They want to show all the oppressed . . . they want to show Latin America first of all, and more generally, all of the Third World. To Che Guevara, who said "we need several Vietnams", the American government answered, "they will be crushed the way we are crushing the first."'[32]

Sartre's argument leads to a justification of action taken in support of the oppressed, the popular movements and the least favoured as a matter of political morality. These were the sacrificial lambs invoked by Merino, Leigh and Pinochet in their inaugural address to the people of Chile as a necessary price to be paid in order to restore economic normalcy, *chilenidad*, and the law and order these require.

Sartre's argument goes like this: people who prosper by a system of domination will stop at nothing, not even genocide, to maintain or restore their status. If so, then it is just that the dominated and the least favoured should act on their desire to remedy their unequal situation, against the beneficiaries of that situation. The dominated will be ready to put their lives at risk, given the situation they find themselves in, one in which the possibility of satisfying basic biological, psychological and social needs is being forcibly restricted. In such a case, their acts of revolt, exodus and resistance – including death – signify a rejection of 'this life', which is really only a half-life or a form of non-being. Such is the basis for the political morality of the least favoured, and the reason why everyone, no matter what their social position or nationality, 'should endeavour to help them'.

It better expresses the maxim and the collective project of aiming towards a fuller, more integral humanity, in a future that begins today, 'than do the imperatives of one's own deeply alienated moralities'.[33]

Basic needs such as education, food, shelter, but also, importantly, the need to consider the future satisfaction of all needs, of continued life — or if you prefer, the capacity to remake ourselves in remaking the world around us — designate a generic, more universalisable, conception of life as 'priceless' life. This runs counter to the idea that all of life, and life itself, has a price, and can be bought and sold, or reduced to a matter of preferences, values and incentives, as liberal economic theory and market triumphalism would have it.[34]

The hold of such market values on social life can grow so strong that we may stop considering whether they can actually produce the kinds of humans we can and would like to be. We stop questioning, as Mayol notices in the case of 'prosperous' contemporary Chile, and as a result behave in an almost pre-programmed manner, unworthy of our full potential as humans. And yet it is precisely at that point, the point of alienation when the whole of life seems governed by market values and destructive systems, that we must ask whether we want to live that way. Or else, whether we need to rethink the role that such market values and destructive systems, which deny to so many the possibility of reproducing their bare life, should play in our society.

Rather than elevate blind givens and choices to the status of high commands, the Law of Laws ruling the whole of life, we can consider needs and the possibility of reproducing life as felt exigencies. They include freedom and bodily requirements to sustain life, but also 'our need for others, in particular for their love and valuation'.[35] Sartre refers in these terms to our need for knowledge, a meaningful life, further equality, a public arena free of corruption and free of war (or at least, to begin with, free of nuclear weapons that may destroy all life on Earth). These things, these generic needs, are priceless. Without them we cannot become human. Conversely, to satisfy such needs and to realise them in a future that begins now is to become full or 'integral' humans.

We may consider priceless life as the first norm, as the law of life that commands us to make light instead of only shadows, and to build rather than destroy. Systems of destruction – these are concrete legal and political systems such as colonisation, military intervention, nuclear deterrents, patriarchal societies oppressive of youth, women or native peoples, or in the case of Chile what Alberto Mayol calls 'permanent transition', a form of market culture that produces consumers who seek only to reaffirm their own private habits and prejudices, the rule of the market over the whole of life – treat some or most people as trivial means and never as an end.[36]

When we live such reduced lives we cannot grow fully human. Crucially, more often than not such systems reduce some or most, though not all, lives to instruments of gain and objects of use. These we can call, as Sartre and his commentators do, the 'least favoured'.[37] And we can find it reasonable to entertain the notion that they would be willing to risk their lives as both evidence of and a refusal of the conditioning (the increasing government of the whole of life by the logic of buying and selling) that restricts their chance of living humanly. That is, their action of refusal and construction, which in this condensed form presents us with the range of all action, aims to live now in such a way that their needs may one day be satisfied.

Notice that since those least favoured tend to revolt and resist in order to remedy their unequal situation, it is likely that from the dominators' viewpoint every one of the people who count among the dominated becomes suspect as a possible abetter of the enemy. This makes the whole population a target. In the eyes of the dominators – those who declared the state of emergency and exception, as Pinochet did on 11 September 1973, as the last defence against communism and so on – it appears that the only way to free a place like Chile is to free it of the Chileans themselves, as Kissinger implied with his remark about the irresponsibility of the Chilean people. In such a situation it is just to revolt, and putting one's life in danger becomes the only true method of revolt. That method includes going into exile, as thousands of Chileans did after 11 September, or 'voting with one's feet', boycott, transnational solidarity, demanding the expression of popular sovereignty in whatever form available, even armed resistance.

Notice also that this argument applies to the Americans intervening in Vietnam or Chile as much as to the Chilean generals or to any leader, whether of left or right, who turns their apparatus of repression against their own people. The implications of that argument resonate from Vietnam and Chile in the 1970s to the Arab Spring and Syria or Guatemala in the present.

The argument has many facets. It includes elements of geopolitics such as the relative positions of the countries involved or attempts to establish global hegemony, and human rights issues such as a political morality centred on the achievement of integral humanity, which requires the denunciation of oppressive regimes and opposition to any notion of a 'One World' – for instance, market triumphalism. It also has political elements such as the project for an integral humanity that entails recognising the claims of the least favoured not as a matter of sympathy or compassion but as part of one's own process of leading an ethical life, and a legal element in which the negative 'do no harm' of the UN Charter and the international law of the use of force may be supplemented by the more robust duty to strive towards integral humanity in all our actions.

'If I die,' Allende said on 11 September, 'the people will follow their own path, perhaps with the difference that things will get a lot harder, more violent, because the fact that these people will stop at nothing will have constituted the clearest and most objective lesson taught to the masses.'[38] Those words add a tragic poignancy to the historical farce enacted by the civilian and military generals after the coup. The farce continued as sympathisers harped on an 'economic miracle' that restored economic order in Chile, and a freer culture, while down in the basement of the houses of ordinary Chileans in Santiago the killing and torture proceeded.[39]

The financial prize awarded to the conspirator generals by their Washington supporters after the 1973 coup, the credit that poured out of Washington and the financial institutions under its influence (for as long as the generals stuck to the rules), the denationalisation of copper and other industries, on the one hand, and on the other the tortures and killings that began the day after the coup and deepened in mid-October 1973, have a common origin. Their aim was to bind the population, corrupt its memory and disregard all past history. Both types of action – denationalisation and torture – originated in the state of internal war and exception ordained by the generals on and after the evening of 11 September as justification for their actions.

To bind the population, the Chilean Military Junta used two types of ordinances. First, so-called *Bandos*, legal edicts authorised by the Law of Internal State Security to allow military heads of emergency zones control over civilians. Second, legal decrees. The first *Bando* was broadcast by the radio stations controlled by the military on 11 September. It informed the population that acts of protest and sabotage would be punished 'in the most drastic manner possible, at the very site of the act, and with no limit beyond the assessment or decision of the authorities there'.[40]

That very first act created the conditions for a state of emergency, permanent war or 'exception', termed as safeguards against people judged by the military themselves, in situ, and with no limit as to the form or content of their decision – a universal menace. In doing so, the Junta effectively split their country's population in two: on the one side people at risk, a vulnerable population in need of protection; on the other, an enemy population of resistant combatants. The meaning of the first *Bando* was further clarified by a remark attributed to General Pinochet, according to which 'for every soldier killed [by the resistance] we execute six Marxist prisoners'. And less informally by Legal Decree Number 4, which established the division of Chile into emergency zones, designated their corresponding military heads and declared an exceptional state of emergency throughout the country.[41]

The Junta itself was formally constituted by Legal Decree Number 1, drafted after the event by the navy's legal counsel and signed by the original members on 12 September.[42] As said before, it declared that the Junta had assumed the 'Supreme Command of the Nation', designated General Augusto Pinochet as president of the Junta and committed the Junta to respect the Constitution, the law and the independence of the judiciary 'insofar as the present situation of the country permits'. Thus it subordinated the function of legal and democratic institutions to the Junta's judgement concerning that situation. The 'present situation' referred to by Decree Number 1 was, precisely, the state of emergency or exception already declared by Decree Number 4 and clarified by Decree Number 5. The latter stated that the state of emergency or exception should be understood as having the status of a 'time of war'.

Most legal experts have observed that such a state of war was no more than a fiction. The generals justified the near-suspension of the Constitution by claiming that the threat posed by armed activity on the part of Allende's sympathisers was a real and present danger. However, there was no such activity in Chile once the coup was consummated.[43] If anything, armed assaults on the state at the time of the coup were staged by the sympathisers of the coup, such as Fatherland and Freedom.

The legal precedent for the Junta's actions was the state of emergency declared under article 48 of the Weimar constitution following the Reichstag fire, which handed to Hitler dictatorial powers that he never relinquished. Previous and further precedents, adapted to circumstances, could be found during the years of the Spanish Civil War. Francoist lawyers and ideologues such as Juan Vázquez de Mella, Sánchez Agesta and Luis Legaz y Lacambra merged the tradition of *Hispanidad*, which conceptualised Spanish culture, legality, the right to property and Christian civilisation as threatened by a Jewish–Mason–Bolshevik conspiracy, with the idea that the Spanish caudillo Francisco Franco acted as original legislator or constituent, and with the controversial views of the Reich's crown jurists, for instance Carl Schmitt.[44] Such precedents were studied by the legal counsellors who would advise the Chilean Junta on its legal and institutional plans, chief among them Jaime Guzmán. He gained access to such sources through his teacher Osvaldo Lira, but also in the works of Chilean jurists such as Enrique Evans and Alejandro Silva.[45] Decree Number 1 expressed the aim of the coup as 'the patriotic commitment to restore *Chilenidad*', economic and juridical normalcy, 'on the understanding that our only aim is to maintain our fidelity to the traditions of the nation, the legacy of the founding fathers of the fatherland, and Chile's history'. These traditions included orthodox Catholicism, patriarchal family values and property, and excluded everything else.

To achieve that objective, the Junta would remain in power 'only for as long as the situation requires it', while appointing itself as the final arbiter of the situation vis-à-vis the threat of communism.[46]

Whatever the perceived scale of the crisis in 1973, its manifestations were non-military: blockades, shortages, inflation, land seizures, political paralysis, increasingly heated debates. None of these could be considered adequate material justification for an internal state of war or the kind of violence that was unleashed by the generals during and after 11 September. Furthermore, every attempt by the military to discover large caches of weapons in the hands of Allende's supporters proved fruitless. To argue that this confirmed in the eyes of the generals that weapons were still in circulation may be plausible but, on the basis of the lack of any evidence verifying that belief, unwarranted.

The military were disingenuous: every shred of evidence confirmed the absence of any real threat, but they chose to ignore it. When reality did not suit their plans, the men in control just abolished reality. Why? Because the way in which Pinochet and the others related to the people and the reality around them was pre-determined to take place in line with a set of particular rules. According to such rules, what the generals called 'normalcy' in their initial legal and institutional designs, the future they desired, was threatened by the possibility of the return or the realisation of the project that Allende embodied and prophesied. Such a prophecy was the project of the revolution from below that Allende's electoral triumph had unleashed: an alternative here and now to the economic and social norms considered absolute and untouchable at the time.

Allende died in La Moneda, but like the characters in the magical realist novels of the time he refused to let go. On the evening of 11 September, Military Doctor José Rodríguez refused to enter the room where his colleagues were performing Allende's autopsy. He feared that Allende's ghost would wander among the ranks of his opponents, cursing them.[47] The good doctor was not alone. It would seem that all those involved in Allende's fall feared the return of his spectre. The generals kept his first burial a secret, took two years to register his death in the Public Records, and seventeen years to return his wallet to his widow Hortensia. Allende had said he had neither the vocation of the martyr nor the fervour of the messiah.[48] Rather, on that day in La Moneda his words were infused with the conviction of the prophet, asking people to distinguish between the lies planted by his enemies and the truth.

The truth, which Allende himself may have fully recognised only on that day, was that the creative force and energy of the masses had gathered momentum as the president uncoupled the force of law from force alone, by promising not to use the security forces to repress the people and committing to the non-violence of the Chilean Way. Having caught a glimpse of their old dream of liberation, they sought to realise it here and now. Those energies were unstoppable. The image of a way out and beyond the dread of eternal life under capitalism, pursued without the havoc of violence, became, as it should, a self-fulfilling promise. Unbound, the people moved towards the new future.

There was no emergency or reason of state justifying the Chilean coup. Many of those involved have later claimed in their memoirs that they believed there was a danger of a coup from the Left and simply acted to stop it. But the Nuremberg precedent, which strictly rejected arguments based on 'good faith' beliefs that the state was threatened by an emergency, precludes such a defence. And given the similarities between the German and the Chilean case, that precedent applies.

This also means that 'following orders' was an inadmissible justification for the actions that occurred in Chile (and other countries) under the pretext of containing the communist threat. Were the civilian and military generals 'following the law' (for instance, the congressional opposition declaration in 1973 that Allende was in breach of the Constitution) when they acted to overthrow Allende and bind the people? The problem here is that the suspension of the law under the state of emergency declared by the Junta decrees 1 and 4 in 1973 rendered moot any distinction between 'following orders' and 'following the law'. Such decrees (Chilean law itself) stripped the civilian and military generals of the Chilean coup of any protection that could be afforded to those acting in good faith under the rule of law. They incriminated themselves.

The legal significance of Nuremberg is relevant to the Chilean case, as those taking part in the Second Russell Tribunal on Latin America concluded. Such legal precedent lets no one off the hook – whether soldiers, civil servants or multinationals. It means the individual liability of human rights violators cannot be easily shed in an emergency, 'and that those who give contrary assurances' – alleging for instance that they were stopping communism, or following orders or the law, and even claiming executive immunity or asserting that they had to act to forestall human rights violations (for instance, terrorism) – are not immune from prosecution under international law for such acts as torture or disappearance among the civilian population.[49] In this respect, invoking an emergency actually intensifies the responsibility of civilian and military officials. This means that telling lies about the exceptional conditions that supposedly led them down the slippery slope of emergency, crimes and human rights violations is subject after the event to judicial review. All the more so because we know that regimes do not rely solely on popular indifference or the fear created by repressing their direct opponents, as Jaime Guzmán seems to have thought at first. They also seek to mobilise popular support by persuading the public in general that there is a clear and present danger of catastrophe.

We also know that the fire in Chile quickly spread from the burning Moneda palace to engulf the entire population, which was viewed by Pinochet and the Junta as the potential enemy. The ghost of Allende and the least favoured among the people became one and the same. The fuel for this nationwide catastrophe was the designation of 'emergency zones' on 12 September 1973.

On the basis of that initial blueprint, Pinochet and the Junta would erect an entire institutional edifice, gothic in its meticulous detail and its potential for infinite and contradictory interpretation, to exorcise the wraith of Allende from within the body of the people.

From 12 September onwards, the point was to bind the people, or to be more precise their collective desire for a different future, out of fear of a past that refused to be consigned to history.

In this respect, the Chilean author Luis Klener Hernández has said that Allende's body, in its refusal to lie quiet in the ground, became a sort of cluster bomb raining upon Chileans with 'covering fire of memory'.[50] The very actions of the generals triggered that effect: from the secrecy of the president's first burial and the mysterious circumstances of Pablo Neruda's death on 23 September 1973, to the secrecy of the machinery of death that began to take shape even before Allende's sacrifice, and its ulterior normalisation on the basis of the legal fiction of the state of emergency.

If so, then this is the story of the doomsayers who in

announcing and invoking the spectre of a cataclysm to come, brought about what they wanted to avert in the first place. The Christian Democrat Radomiro Tomic expressed this realisation when he wrote to General Carlos Prats in a letter dated August 1973: 'As in the classic Greek tragedies, everybody knows what will happen, everybody says they do not wish it to happen, and everybody does exactly what is necessary to bring about the disaster.'[51]

The very act of concealing Allende's burial or announcing Neruda's death before the fact, while proclaiming to all corners of the world that the cowards had committed suicide or were dying of cancer, created a particular situation in which silence ruled and society was divided between those who held acceptable political beliefs and those who did not. The latter were declared cowards, and a plague.[52]

The result was a state of collective silence, abject passivity and divisiveness, with the spectral figure of Allende haunting the line of division. Such a situation continues to exist in Chile to this day. It is alive, for instance, in the reaction to the rise to international renown of the student leader Camila Vallejo in the course of the 2011 protests against the institutions put together by Guzmán and Pinochet after 1980: 'But how can she be so pretty and a communist!' goes the usual line – surely an inconceivable combination. She appears to those who hold political beliefs deemed acceptable in line with the post-coup rules as the return of a spectre from the past supposedly exorcised in an ordeal by fire. Unsurprisingly, the spectre threatens, goes the slogan, economic normalcy. Plainly the norms of the economy, restored capitalism or so-called neoliberalism, likewise require that you cannot be a woman, beautiful and a communist. Consider the fact that there were actually many precursors of such a role – Blanca Luz Brum, La Negra Lazo, Allende's last lover Gloria Gaitán, Beatriz Allende among others – and it turns out that 'normalcy' is a by-word for anti-feminist patriarchalism and racism as well as anti-communism. In short, the system itself is rigged against anything resembling a fuller human rights ethics or a more assertive politics.

The point of such reactions is to make it clear that a certain kind of person – a Brum, a Lazo or a Vallejo – does not measure up to the system because of who she is. We must conclude that restoring capitalism after the massive challenge of the 1960s and 1970s was not simply a matter of getting the right combination of regulations, deregulations, liberties and institutions, so that the arcane forces of the market could do their work unimpeded. It was, first and foremost, about producing the right kind of people.

If people don't behave in the proper manner, if they are not content with their shopping malls and consumer goods, and instead take to the streets to demand something else – like free education, an end to police violence in inner-city areas or to war abroad – then the business of government changes. It becomes, as Bertolt Brecht put it, 'easier . . . to dissolve the people, and elect another'.[53] The procedure is to call it a riot or a public order nuisance, or provoke one, put the security forces in charge of the streets, jail those responsible with exemplary sentences, unleash the Furies once more, evict the protesters from the spaces they occupy. This is the phenomenon that the sociologist and legal scholar Boaventura de Sousa Santos has termed 'social fascism'.[54]

According to Klener Hernández, Allende's last words were also intended as a final balance of accounts before the Chilean people. In saying, 'I tell you with complete certainty, that the seed I put today in your hands and plant in the untainted soul and the worthy memory of thousands upon thousands of Chileans will not be uprooted ever,' Allende was presenting his lifetime's work, and himself as a farmer, a peasant or a grower allowing for the cultivation of a hope that cannot be scythed down as easily as bodies can. The connotations of such language – to store, produce, multiply and sow – contributed to the formation in people's minds of an image of a better future beyond sacrifice and death. Diffusing and deferring his authority to that of the people, his words acted as a

life-affirming instrument helping to awaken collective consciousness to the need to appropriate history. 'When Allende says "history
is ours, people make it" he is merely clarifying the question of the
ownership of something as intangible as the construction of history.
He gives value to voice and to oral history over written accounts.'
So says Klener Hernández, thereby indicating the possibility and the
necessity for people to go on reconstructing their history on the
basis of their own voices.[55] In doing so, Allende set up a set of
conditions concerning who can create history, and established moral
authority as a necessary condition for creating and narrating history.
Crucially, as in the argument concerning the crime of genocide,
that authority is on the side of the least favoured.[56]

According to Klener Hernández, this is what happened in Chile
after 11 September. He explains that historical accounts of the period
in Chilean academia were characterised by their silence on the
subject of Allende's death, 'having fear as the driving force of
silence'.[57] The press, controlled by the Edwards family and those in
power, was left to perform the task of governing memory and
supplanting historical analysis and criticism. Those in power,
whether military or civilian, established their own social referents
and wrote their own histories as if in a vacuum.

And yet from the outset such revisionist histories were haunted
by Allende's ghost. In more popular contexts, historical reconstruction unfolded on the basis of storytelling, song, memoir,
poetry, oral testimony and myth-making. That process began in
the killing fields and the places of torture. The folk singer Víctor
Jara, for instance, wrote a song about the condition of the regime's
prisoners in the National Stadium of Santiago during the days
following the 11 September coup. It was written on a paper pad,
hidden and smuggled out of the stadium in the shoe of a fellow
prisoner, Boris Navia.

Jara, a world-famous folk musician who dedicated his lyrics to
chronicle the popular experience of the Allende years, was arrested
on 12 September 1973 during a student and staff revolt at the

Technical State University (TSU) against the military. He was taken to the National Stadium together with some five thousand others. Leading the operation were Captain Marcelo Moren Brito, later to become one of the most feared agents of Pinochet's DINA intelligence service, and Commander César Manríquez, who had been put in charge of the secret burial of Allende and later ordered to install the first prison camp at the stadium.[58]

That same day, Chilean security agents began to interrogate and torture prisoners, among them Jara. His hands and ribs were broken during the interrogations, but he managed to write the lyrics before being shot and wounded by an officer playing Russian roulette with him. He was finished off by a couple of army conscripts in the presence of Lieutenant Nelson Haase, a henchman of intelligence director Manuel Contreras. When Joan Jara managed, by chance and word of mouth, to find and reclaim the body of her husband, she found it had forty-four bullet wounds.

But his words survived and helped put the finger on the regime's atrocities. In 1974 the American folk singer Phil Ochs organised a benefit concert in New York where the song was performed. Joan Jara was present. The concert featured Bob Dylan, Pete Seeger, Arlo Guthrie and Ochs, among others. It was titled 'An Evening with Salvador Allende'.[59] Latin American writers also played their part, beginning with Pablo Neruda and Gabriel García Márquez.

Few people understood the significance of Allende's last words and gesture better than Pablo Neruda, who three days after the siege wrote a piece entitled 'My People the Most Betrayed of Our Times' before dying on 23 September. In the piece, Neruda called the body of Allende an 'immortal corpse', defended the president's principled stance and highlighted the connection that had existed historically between the exploited miners of the north of Chile, the millions of pounds accumulated by the bankers and investors of the City of London, and the tragic symbolism of the bombardment of the presidential palace and Allende's death, which for Neruda evoked the Nazi Blitzkrieg against the defenceless cities of Europe. He concluded: 'His murder was kept silent; he was buried in secrecy; only his widow was allowed to accompany this immortal corpse.' Neruda's piece both questioned the official story concocted by Pinochet's regime and contributed to the popular myth-making that would immortalise the resistance in La Moneda.[60]

On the morning of 22 September 1973, Neruda received the Mexican ambassador Gonzalo Martínez Corbalá in his room 406 at the Santa María Hospital in Santiago. The poet had arrived in the hospital three days before, from his house at Isla Negra. On the morning of 11 September he had received a phone call from his friend the author José Miguel Varas, who told him there had been a military coup in Valparaíso. In the next hours he watched on television as Chilean pilots in British Hawker Hunter jets dive-bombed the presidential palace while Allende and a few others resisted inside. He planned a retort to the reply published by the *New York Times* to an article of his in that paper condemning the International Telephone and Telegraph Company (ITT) for what he termed its constant interference in the constitutional govern-ment of Chile. Later in the evening he watched on TV the infa-mous, sinister image of the triumvirate generals, together with a representative of the Carabineros, declaring themselves the Supreme Command of the nation, informing the people of Allende's death, and announcing the excision of the communist cancer from Chile. The inquisitors had sentenced the country to ordeal by fire. The poet collapsed.[61]

His health had been frail since at least July 1973. On the occasion of his sixty-ninth birthday, a small group of his closest friends made the journey to Isla Negra for a low-key celebration. The mood was sombre. Neruda knew about the state of his mind and body: 'From time to time I'm happy!' he had written in his book *The Yellow Heart* (*El corazón amarillo*). 'And with my melancholy prostate and the whims of my urethra, they lead me unhurriedly to an analytical end.'[62] He was referring to the cancer that afflicted him, which on the day of his birthday obliged him to receive the small group of his friends lying down. That book and six others were written by hand on a board spread across his lap as he lay in bed. He gave the seven manuscripts – one for each decade of his life – to his publisher Gonzalo Losada on the day of his birthday, asking him not to publish them until 1974. He wanted to be there to celebrate his seventieth birthday.

José Miguel Varas, one of the members of the small birthday party that day, felt that the handwriting in the manuscripts showed that Neruda was ill. He was trying to finish his memoirs before death caught up with him. There were also the dark omens announcing a looming disaster for the people of Chile. Like the others, during his birthday Neruda agonised over the worsening political situation. 'His voice broke when he spoke of his country's being divided into violent extremes,' said Salvador Allende's niece, the future novelist Isabel Allende, who saw him in late 1973. Rightist newspapers like *El Mercurio* 'were publishing six-column headlines "Chile, save your hatred, you'll need it!", inciting the military to power and Allende either to renounce the presidency or commit suicide, as President Balmaceda had done in the past century.'[63]

In spite of the political turmoil, on the day of Neruda's birthday President Allende and his wife Hortensia flew by helicopter from Santiago to the poet's house in Isla Negra. They made it in time to join the other members of the small group – Losada, Varas, the Venezuelan author Miguel Otero and his wife, the communist senator Volodia Teitelboim, the Mapuche indigenous congressman Rosendo Huenuman, and Congresswoman Gladys Marín – for lunch with Neruda and his wife Matilde Urrutia. They spoke for hours about the difficult political situation. After lunch, Allende told Otero he would personally lead the preparations for the celebration of the poet's seventieth birthday. Otero replied that the poet seemed very ill and asked Allende for his medical opinion. 'Not just me, but also the oncologists who are treating him are certain he will go on several years more. We will celebrate his seventy years with the grand splendour he deserves,' said Allende. Neither of them would make it to the next year.[64]

On 22 September, Martínez Corbalá came to tell Neruda that a DC-8 airplane was waiting at Pudahuel airport ready to take the poet and his wife Matilde into exile. Pinochet's dictatorship, eleven days into its role as Chief Inquisitor of Chile, had provided passports for the poet and his wife. Ominously, on 16 September Pinochet himself had declared to Radio Luxemburgo: 'Neruda is not dead. He is alive and goes freely wherever he wants to, just like every person who, like him, is old and very ill. In this country we do not kill anyone, and if Neruda dies, it will be a natural death.'[65]

Neruda had agreed to leave the country and go once more into exile after his wife Matilde told him that the house they had built in Santiago had been destroyed by government soldiers. He had also learned about the full scale of the tragedy. 'They're killing people,' he told his wife, who did her best to hide from him the extent of the horror that had descended upon Chile. 'They're handing over bodies in pieces. Didn't you hear what happened to Víctor Jara? . . . they destroyed his hands . . . Oh my God, that's like killing a nightingale. And they say he kept on singing and singing, and that drove them mad.'[66]

Around 14 September, after Neruda felt better and got back to work with Matilde, soldiers had raided their house at Isla Negra. On that occasion, Neruda faced the commander in charge of the raid unit and told him: 'Look around. There's only one thing of danger for you here: poetry.' The soldier removed his helmet, asked for forgiveness, and withdrew his men without breaking so much as a jar.[67] The Santiago house, La Chascona, did not fare so well. The raiders there destroyed it, and in a highly symbolic act proceeded to rip apart and burn his books and his library. For Neruda, it was Nazi Germany and the Spanish holocaust all over again. On 18 September the ambulance in which the poet and his wife were travelling to the Santa María hospital was stopped by a military patrol. They were made to get out of it and wait some thirty minutes in the street as the soldiers meticulously verified the identity of the most famous Chilean in the world. Suddenly, Matilde saw tears rolling down Neruda's cheek: 'Wipe my face, love,' he told her.[68]

The last two visitors on the afternoon of 22 September were Sweden's ambassador Harald Edelstam and the diplomat Ulf Hjertonsson, also a personal friend of the poet. Edelstam asserts he found the poet 'very ill' that day, though not in a state of agitation but rather in good spirits and still willing to travel to Mexico. Neruda told Edelstam: 'These people are worse than the Nazis, they're killing their own countrymen.' In a three-page memo sent to his superiors, Edelstam observes: 'In his last hours [Neruda] either didn't know or didn't recognise he suffered a terminal illness. He complained that rheumatism made it impossible to move his arms and legs. When we visited him, Neruda was preparing as best he could to travel . . . to Mexico. There, he would make a public declaration against the military regime.'[69]

That made the poet dangerous to the new powers of Chile. Allende had died during the coup, fighting the army in his burning palace. The voice of Víctor Jara was silenced soon after. Neruda remained. He was perhaps the loudest, his face certainly the most recognisable worldwide. He was dangerous.

Members of the Junta are on record expressing the view on the morning of 22 September that if Neruda flew into exile, his plane would fall into the sea. In the afternoon, radio stations under military control announced that the poet was likely to die in the coming hours while he was still awake in the hospital. The next day he was dead. That historical mystery alone explains why his body was exhumed in April 2013.

Contributing further to the myth-making of the resistance at La Moneda palace on 11 September, Gabriel García Márquez wrote an article for the Colombian magazine Alternativa, which he had helped to found partly in response to the events in Chile. It was entitled 'Chile, el Golpe, y los Gringos', this time pointing the finger unequivocally at Washington. Back in 1971, García Márquez had made it clear that much as he wanted the Chilean experiment to succeed, it would not be allowed to. He told a New York journalist: 'Chile is heading toward violent and dramatic events. If the Popular [Unity] Front goes ahead – with intelligence and great tact, with reasonably firm and swift steps – a moment will come when they will encounter a wall of serious opposition. The United States is not interfering at present . . . [but] it won't really accept that Chile is a socialist country.'[70]

At eight o'clock on the evening of 11 September 1973, García Márquez sent a telegram to the members of the newly constituted Chilean Junta:

> Bogotá, September 11, 1973. Generals Augusto Pinochet, Gustavo Leigh, César Méndez Danyau and Admiral José Toribio Merino, Members of the Military Junta. You are the material authors of the death of President Allende and the Chilean people will actually never allow themselves to be governed by a gang of criminals in the pay of North American imperialism. Gabriel García Márquez.[71]

In December that year he accepted an invitation to preside over the prestigious Second Russell Tribunal, which focused its Rome sessions of 1974 on the allegations of human rights violations in Chile and Brazil and the link between these events, the US intervention in Vietnam, and the role of the multinationals, interpreting Chile in the light of Vietnam by way of Nuremberg. This would prove a turning point in the history of twentieth-century politics, law and the human rights movement. García Márquez's piece was published in February 1974. The magazine's issue that included it sold ten thousand copies on the first day and went on to sell forty thousand overall, 'an unheard-of figure for a left-wing publication' in conservative Colombia, as biographer Gerald Martin points out. More important, the article received worldwide distribution and was published in the US and the UK in March, achieving 'immediate classic status'.[72] It was instrumental in cementing the popular myth of Allende's death and resistance at La Moneda.

> His greatest virtue was being consequential, but fate could only grant him that rare and tragic greatness of dying in armed defence of the anachronistic mess that is bourgeois law, defending a Supreme Court of Justice which had repudiated him but would legitimise his murderers, defending a miserable Congress which had declared him illegitimate but which was to bend complacently before the will of the usurpers, defending the freedom of opposition parties which had sold their souls to fascism, defending the whole moth-eaten paraphernalia of a shitty system which he had proposed abolishing, but without a shot being fired.[73]

Like Neruda and Fidel Castro, García Márquez contributed to the myth of Allende fallen in combat, his body riddled with bullets by his enemies. At the same time, they contributed greatly to a literature-based critique of law that would be central to the emergence of a new and politicised language of human rights.

Importantly, in the piece cited above, García Márquez arrived at the following conclusion: 'the drama took place in Chile . . . but it will pass into history as something that has happened to us all, children of this age, and it will remain in our lives for ever.'[74] This was the point that Sartre had emphasised during his examination of the crime of genocide before the 1968 First Russell Tribunal on Vietnam.

The point was twofold: first, invoking the precedent of the Nuremberg Trials, Sartre argued that ordinary war crimes in Vietnam should be treated as genocide because the war's aim was to impose civilian casualties to levels at which support for the revolution would cease. The argument was similar to one made by Telford Taylor, Robert Jackson's successor as Chief Prosecutor in Nuremberg. According to the American jurist, the lessons of Nuremberg will finally have been learned when victorious powers at war subject their own leaders and the military to the jurisdiction of international tribunals with the power to convict them of war crimes and crimes against humanity. Individual bureaucrats and soldiers should be held to account for the crimes of those in power, notwithstanding allegations that they were 'following orders', did not know enough, or reacted to exceptional circumstances to restore law and order. Therefore, US citizens must make the equivalent of an existential choice between resistance and complicity.[75]

Second, Sartre introduced a measure of concreteness into the vague sense of the human in the notion of crimes against humanity and human rights by claiming that the Vietnamese were fighting for survival, to make possible a more human future, and ultimately for us all. This argument recognises the fact that justice has an inter-generational and inter-temporal, and not only an international, dimension. The origin of this argument lies in debates concerning debt, reparations and restitution in cases of decolonisation, including the effects of slavery and conquest or indigenous dispossession in the Americas.

According to Paige Arthur, Sartre's argument rested on two propositions: on the one hand, a geopolitical argument according to which the US was trying to establish a 'One World' model, in the form of globally integrated capitalism, through war in Vietnam. On the other, that in resisting the United States, Vietnam was resisting the inexorable necessity of such a future based on the 'One World' model. In the course of the Russell Tribunal, Sartre went on to establish a direct connection between the US intention to 'impose its hegemony', as he put it, and the occurrence of 'exemplary' wars and interventions designed to break the spirit of any other people seeking to find their own future or an autonomous economic and political path. In that sense, he said, 'the Vietnamese are fighting for all men and the American forces are fighting all of us. Not just in theory or in the abstract . . . the group that the Americans are trying to destroy . . . is the whole of humanity.'[76] The argument developed by Sartre and the Latin Americans would in time serve Joan Garcés, Judge Baltasar Garzón and Carlos Castresana to bring justice to the door of Augusto Pinochet and the conspirators of 11 September 1973.

13

Transition

The Latin American writers who took part in the Second Russell Tribunal, among them Gabriel García Márquez, Julio Cortázar and Juan Bosch, picked up on Sartre's point and interpreted it through the experience of what had happened in Chile. Effectively, they interpreted Chile in the light of Vietnam and Nuremberg, focusing on the effects of Allende's decision to nationalise copper, the banks and other industries. Allende's policy of nationalisation and compensation, formulated under the term 'excess profits', basically targeted above-average profits obtained by beneficiaries whose unjustly acquired gains continue to appreciate in value long after the perpetrators of past evils have been driven out through wars of independence, anti-slavery struggles and so on.[1]

The term 'excess profits' refers also to a crucial legal problem concerning feasible schemes of reparative justice. An important difference between the Chilean perspective and that of American multinationals on the issue of nationalisation was that for the latter this was a straightforward matter of compensating them for predictable future losses after the takeover, while for the former it concerned reparative justice that went to the heart of post-colonial legal and political institutions based on rights of conquest and property claims. At first, law tends to take the position that if and when there are good reasons to recognise historical injustice through reparations, these should be minimal and symbolic. The passage of time, issues of causality, financial viability and compounding of interest suggest that these should never be taken as paving the way for restoring social justice in general. But in property law, students encounter cases of 'adverse possession', in which the occupation of someone else's space – as in the case of colonisation – turns into a legal entitlement. There the question is whether law rules out remedies – for instance, through recourse to a right of conquest – or else allows for them – for instance, by way of takeovers, nationalisations and restitutions. Nationalisation, as practised in Chile in the 1970s in the cases of lands, banks and mining, was but an example of back-dated restitution, well grounded in the canon of property law by the early twentieth century. The specific case of copper nationalisation was an application of legal theories of restitution according to which it is unjust for beneficiaries of a perceived offence, such as colonialism and neocolonialism, to keep the portion of their often very sizeable accumulated gains that exceeds the damages their surviving victims might claim. This would amount to profiting from a crime.

Allende's policy was declared under Decree 92 of 28 September 1971. At the time, copper was quite profitable for the US multinationals Anaconda and Kennecott – among other things because of the war in Vietnam, as Allende himself recognised.[2] In 1969, Anaconda made 16.6 per cent of its global investments in Chile and obtained 79.2 per cent of its profits there, while Kennecott invested 13.2 per cent and made 21.3 per cent of its total profits in Chile alone. The Chilean Decree was based on United Nations General Assembly Resolution 1803/1962 on 'Permanent Sovereignty over Natural Resources', which recognised the right of peoples to recover and use their basic resources, allowed for compensation to be awarded in accordance with the rules of the state that enacts the nationalisation, and established the courts of that country as the proper place for any resulting conflict.[3] Decree 92 required compensations and above-average or 'excess' profits to be calculated on the basis of balance sheets available after 5 May 1955, when law 11.828 created the Copper Department and the latter began to record data

about profits. In the previous four decades, copper-mining companies had operated in Chile without any significant regulation.
Innovatively, the Chilean Decree addressed the circumstances in
which the benefits of past injustice were cumulative, the number of
the original indigenous victims dwindling, and individual victims
would have trouble proving losses on the scale of the cumulative
gains that built up.

Challenging common legal assumptions in the West on the issue
of fair compensation and the constructive value of wealth unfairly
accrued, Allende's policy can be seen as construing historical grievances that persist in a global market economy, and that beneficiaries
ignore or undervalue, as entitling the victims of past economic
injustice to demand payback now rather than later. Mainstream
discussions over these questions in law and economics tend to focus
on the probable loss of profits in an unchanged future (one in which
multinationals Kennecott and Anaconda can continue to profit
unimpeded), the value of gains if the injustice had never happened,
the absence of a historical point of past injustice to return to so as to
calculate how to right the alleged wrongs, or whether the ongoing
damage of colonialism can be properly measured as compound
interest over a debt whose term has not yet come and might never
come. The problem with these views is that they are at best
counter-factual or speculative, and at worst they treat the past as a
series of catastrophes that recur over time, including our time, without end or solution. For many of those who hold such views, 'the
time of rectifying the past is never now'.[4]

This is important insofar as such permanent delay – or permanent
'transition' – is often conceptualised by constitutional lawyers like
Carl Schmitt in the case of Nazi Germany or Jaime Guzmán in
Pinochet's Chile as a time of exception marked by a state of emergency, disorder and chaos. In exceptional times, these jurists and
political theorists argue, appealing to a view in Roman Law and
sixteenth-century justifications of colonialism (seen through the
prism of twentieth-century fascism/Falangism), it is legitimate to

suspend liberties and opt for the lesser evil. Such readings of past history and precedent make a mockery of the Nuremberg Trials and the Holocaust (Jewish, Spanish, and any other) and condemn human rights to a form of 'transitional justice' that ultimately defends the (ethical) position that nothing should come (politically) after doing 'just enough to achieve political stability'.[5] The dubious model for such justice would be, precisely, the Chilean 'transition' after the coup and elsewhere in Latin America. Later on, that model and its economic sidekick, the trickle-down theory of economic justice, would be imported elsewhere in the world. It has become the normal state of affairs since the late twentieth century.

Transitional and trickle-down models of justice insist that arguments of justice must disregard all past history, and that political attempts to eradicate inequality should be avoided for moral reasons: to stave off the recurrence of the genocidal past. The result is an untenable separation between ethics or morality and politics. Crucially, the historicism of current discourses of Human Rights and humanitarianism in respect to the past – which conceived of the historical past as a series of catastrophes with no end or resolution – tends to limit our awareness about specific moments of historical injustice that may inspire us to do something about it right now, including forcing a resolution in order to overcome our habit of keeping what we already have at all costs.

This kind of historical awareness is the basis of remedial equality. 'It simply assumes that most inequality is the result of past history,' explains Robert Meister, 'and that most of history was bad.'[6] But once we start to correct for specific moments of historical injustice and inequality, we can legitimately ask: why are we not doing away with inequality all together? 'Were we to treat material equality as both an approximation and a cap on remedial justice,' says Meister, 'then the most a disadvantaged group can legitimately desire is that its ongoing disadvantage be wiped out.'[7] And once we recognise that the many unfair advantages enjoyed by the beneficiaries of past injustice, such as Kennecott and Anaconda in the case of Chile, could not be justified starting now, then the obvious question becomes the one Allende asked in terms of his nationalisation policy: why not start with the recovery of common sources of wealth, such as copper, use the revenue to help us rethink the role of markets in society, consider the extent to which too big a role for markets may provoke or increase inequality and corruption, and then even decide that not all goods are properly valued as instruments of profit or use, as commodities – as for instance knowledge and education, health, family life, nature, art, and civic or human rights and duties?

The point of such a line of questioning is not to destroy private property *tout court*, but the much simpler one that 'some of the good things in life are corrupted or degraded if turned into commodities'.[8] If that is the case, then it is reasonable to have a discussion about where and how markets should operate and where they should be kept at a distance. This means we must also consider other ways to value these 'priceless' goods – from education to family life, and from art and science to rights and duties. We already consider slavery – the buying and selling of human beings – to be appalling, likewise the contemporary trafficking of women for the purposes of sexual exploitation, also of children, votes, elections, and we have placed strict limits on the sale of such things as tobacco, drugs and alcohol, or the materials and know-how to make atomic weapons. This means we already think that there is a place for market economics, but that place is not everywhere.

If so, then we must continue to consider, case by case, the extent, role and place of markets, but also explore other forms of value and motivations for creativity and for work, and to entertain the idea that it is actually possible to bring about greater justice too.[9] This may include not only considering remedies within capitalism for its past inability to regulate itself, but also alternative, socialist, remedies that can be crafted and reduce inequality rather than bringing out some of the less morally appealing characteristics of capitalism, such as greed, the tendency to keep what we have or want at all costs, or to sacrifice others to save our own position.[10]

The problem is that we have not had those discussions for a very long time, certainly not in the era of market triumphalism that started about the time when the voices of Allende and others, asking for such debates to take place, were silenced. Market triumphalism reached its peak some time in the 1980s or 1990s, but in the 2000s, especially in the wake of the Great Recession that started in 2008 and the global protests of 2011, the chorus of voices calling for the renewal of such debates and a more reasonable approach to the role of market values, so that we do not keep drifting from having markets to being a market culture, is growing stronger.

It is important, for the purposes of conducting reasonable debates in the here and now, to acknowledge that Allende and others at the time observed in theory and practice that these issues and questions were political, rather than merely economic. Moreover, they focused on the role that historical injustice – plunder, an evil origin – plays in a proper understanding of every historical moment. They concluded that historical grievances that have become systemic – that is, part of the system of rules or value, but also, conversely, reasons for those least favoured to claim remedial justice – cannot for that selfsame reason be correctly valued by the market.

Indeed, as was the case with Anaconda and Kennecott, but also with the US Nixon administration, or the Edwards and Matte families in 1970s Chile, those who benefit from past injustice will ignore or play down the option that past history gives to the least favoured to demand restitution – particularly if such demands are posited as taking place in a receding future, under conditions that have yet to occur. From their perspective, it would not be clear whether it is too soon or too late to settle. Thus, as it happened in the Chilean case, they would tend to assume that, in any case, the right time to settle historical demands, or to pay to put an end to a grievous history, is never now. Allende's policy took stock of this bias. A relatively unacknowledged feature of his policy of nationalisation, which resonates with other authors of the time such as Frantz Fanon, is that their notion of justice entailed that the time to strike was now. That is, that sometimes a resolution must be forced in order to take into account and resolve the problem that those who possess want to keep what they already possess (and may even want more).[11]

That is why law, the force of law, matters more than liberal legal theorists and their leftist critics would like us to think. For law is a site that can be occupied, and it is also more decisive than such theorists and critics believe, in the sense that it may be wielded and used in order to force a resolution to historical claims. This explains why without having to jettison their commitment to law and democracy, Allende and the militants of the Chilean Way could dare to ask: why not socialism? The question was not ideological. It aimed to treat the past as something that can be rectified rather than as an irremediable wasteland.[12]

Some proponents of transitional justice, the branch of legal theory dealing with reform and redress in cases of massive human rights violations, starting from the perspective that history is irremediably dreadul, tend to view injustice as compounded rather than eliminated, particularly if seen in retrospect. For them, the day of reckoning cannot be determined, it never comes. Hence, they tend to reject the possibility that politics can produce a transformative connection between two historical moments. Though it is true that we may not be able to determine with certainty the baseline, the day or the right moment, for remediation or restorative justice, this does not mean we have to abandon every attempt to deal with justice in regard to all past history. 'We might as easily conclude,' observes Robert Meister, 'that equality, as such, is a remedy for the cumulative injustices that are the sum of all past history.'[13] It is on that basis and at that point that the question posited by Allende and the Chilean Way in the 1970s appears reasonable and relevant, even today.

In fact, nowadays, taking into account the experience of transition in Eastern Europe and Latin America, it has become common sense even among forceful advocates of free markets to accept that there is no reason to treat transitional justice measures that benefit the poor or the least favoured 'as presumptively suspect on either moral or institutional grounds, unless we are to treat the justice systems of consolidated liberal democracies', which also deal with remedies, redress and past injustices, 'as suspect as well'.[14]

The fact that law and participatory democracy are more responsive to questions concerning equality and remedial justice than traditional and Cold War frameworks allowed us to think (being based on a strict opposition between communism and democracy) may explain why, when faced with the prospect of a sustained and transformative use of law for the purposes of remedial justice and achieving greater equality by the UP government of the 1970s, the wealthy of Chile and their US and multinational partners resorted to utterly illegal kinds of violence. Rather than allowing for the debate and discussion of the question 'Why not socialism?' to proceed more or less peacefully and reasonably, they opted to silence those voices and to crush the very possibility of such a discussion ever happening.

In other words, rather than allow the least advantaged peoples to claim and receive settlements that would legitimately terminate their historical claims, perhaps in perpetuity, Chile's elite and the multinationals denied their rights as peoples to make such claims. They reacted to the 1970s crisis in the same way they had towards the indigenous peoples of Chile in the late nineteenth century, by treating such people as an inessential means and never as an end.[15] This also means there is a link between the political extermination of peoples and the termination of their claims. But since their attempt at a 'final solution' did not work, they merely succeeded in postponing the issue. This means that the question was never answered. It remains open today.

Searching for an answer in the language of today's law and economics, and in the politics of human rights, Robert Meister points out that 'the techniques for creating financial derivatives – new property rights – could be used to describe the redirection of social revenue flows as contingent claims to be triggered by future events' – that is to say, as options whose actual use has already resulted in massive transfers of wealth with no pretence of justice.[16] If so, greater justice can be an option too.

A similar train of thought will have led Allende, the jurist Eduardo Novoa Monreal and others in the UP government to issue their policy on excess profits. At its basis lies the kind of historical and existential awareness of contingency that characterised Allende's political career and attitude. Such awareness also accompanied Sartre's conception of genocide in 1968, and García Márquez and Cortázar's conclusion at the end of the Second Russell Tribunal that to right the wrongs of the past and do justice is an option. The meaning of the notion that 'justice is an option' was clearly expressed by Gabriel García Márquez. He said that the time and place comes 'where the races condemned to one hundred years of solitude will have, at last and forever, a second opportunity on earth'.[17]

According to the Latin Americans in the Second Russell Tribunal, even though the US had not perpetrated the acts in Chile directly, it was privy to a broader counter-revolutionary framework that equated all attempts to right historical wrongs and achieve remedial equality, carried out in the various names of socialism or Third Worldism, with assaults on the US and its economic interests. If so, conversely, the US could be pronounced guilty of all violence carried out in the name of anti-communism as directed by the American government and multinational corporations. The Second Russell Tribunal declared that the American government and the multinationals had created a state of 'permanent intervention and strategic domination with the intention to assure the highest economic benefits' to themselves.[18]

This general state of permanent intervention and domination had its particular exemplar in the state of exception and internal war alleged by the Chilean Junta as justification for Allende's overthrow.

The argument presented by Julio Cortázar in his short novella *Fantomas versus the Multinational Vampires*, set against the backdrop of his participation in the deliberations of Russell II, makes this connection. It links Allende's 1972 speech at the UN General Assembly on nationalisation and excess profits and the Chilean and Latin American experience of the 1970s, with the grim reality of a world in which a minority literally sucks the life out of the majority.

Cortázar had no illusions about the power of the Tribunal or the human rights discourse it helped develop. In the absence of 'even a handful of [United Nations] Blue Helmets to stand between the bucket of shit and the prisoner's head, between Víctor Jara and his torturers', he said, it was difficult to avoid feeling that, though important, to develop a culture of human rights in response to the wrongs of the past might not be enough.[19] In getting to grips with what happened in Chile, the members of the Second Russell Tribunal were faced with a fork in the road. They could choose the path of developing a culture of human rights based on feelings of impotence and guilt about always being too late, anxious about pre-empting the next holocaust, and prosecuting others just to show that ours is not a culture of impunity. Or else they could opt for the path that had started in the Nuremberg Trials: encourage underlings to document and question illegal orders and bad laws; take such documented harmful measures as all the more reason for prosecuting higher authorities; make justice more rather than less urgent. This would entail taking seriously the claims of remedial justice and greater equality put forward by those injured by the harmful measures that higher authorities take in 'emergency' situations. It would also entail providing the legal and political conditions that would make it possible to issue arrest warrants against higher authorities that give illegal orders or pass harmful measures everywhere, especially if they seek to excuse themselves under the pretext that they were obliged to produce such measures to contain 'emergency' situations. This would require a prosecuting counsel ready to act against such authorities, in the global North as well as in the South.

To their credit, the presidents and members of the Second Russell Tribunal opted for the second option. Some two decades after the tribunal reached its decision on Chile, people like Joan Garcés – who had escaped La Moneda after Allende told him he should bear witness to the world about what had happened there – Carlos Castresana and Baltasar Garzón would take a step towards realising the possibility of a more urgent and global justice. The legacy of the Russell Tribunals and those that helped to create it would lie at the heart of the proceedings that finally allowed some justice to emerge in the present time.

The work led by Joan Garcés, Judge Baltasar Garzón and many others, chief among them Chilean exiles, building on the legacy of the Bertrand Russell Tribunals, was central to the endeavour of achieving urgent global justice. Starting from the precedent set at Nuremberg, and a seemingly narrower conception of genocide, their work broadened the horizon of law and politics, allowing issues of political morality, the urgency of human rights, geopolitics, the anxiety of injustice's beneficiaries, and global political economy to take shape and take central stage.

On 16 October 1998, twenty-five years after he left the presidential palace in Santiago to tell the world the story of the Chilean Revolution, Joan Garcés sent to the Spanish judge Baltasar Garzón a petition asking for the urgent questioning of General Augusto Pinochet, who was preparing to leave London after a back operation and afternoon tea with his admirer, ex-Prime Minister Margaret Thatcher.

Over tea and scones, an older Pinochet told the Iron Lady that opinion polls predicted that Chile could have its first socialist president since 1973. He was referring to Ricardo Lagos, an economics scholar who had worked for the UN and in his youth was Salvador Allende's nominee for the USSR embassy and Chile's delegate to UNCTAD III. After the coup, Lagos had gone into exile in Argentina, and taught for a year at the University of Carolina in Chapel Hill before returning to Chile in 1978.

Once there, Lagos played a central role in the reconstruction of the Socialist Party and opposition to the Junta. After 11 September 1973, the tensions within the party and the Chilean Left in general that were already visible during Allende's presidency intensified. Repression drove most leaders into exile, just as it had done at the time of the Damned Law in 1948, when Neruda and others had had to flee their homeland. Those who remained were arrested, and many tortured, killed or disappeared by Pinochet's DINA secret police. A leftist External Secretariat was formed abroad under the leadership of Carlos Altamirano, who by then had abandoned his notion that Allende's overthrow happened because they lacked a military plan, and advocated an understanding with the Christian Democrats. But the leaders of the Internal Secretariat in Chile disagreed, removed Altamirano, and replaced him with Clodomiro Almeyda, another of Allende's close colleagues. The Altamirano group responded by disowning the decisions of the Internal Secretariat. Once again, when unity was needed the Left fell apart.

In the background were broader discussions about the future of the Left and democratic politics that extended beyond Latin America. In Europe, reflections on Allende's experience led the secretary-general of the Italian Communist Party, Enrico Berlinguer, to call for a compromise between the Left and the Christian Democrats to find a way towards socialism on the basis of consensus and a 'democratic alternative' rather than a purely leftist alternative. According to Heraldo Muñoz 'the European debate on Chile would lead to what later would become widely known as Eurocommunism'.[20] This was the option suggested by Lagos and Muñoz, (who became a magnet for Chilean exiles, including Salvador's sister Laura, and international solidarity activists at his new home in Denver). Together with folk singers Ángel and Violeta Parra, the Quakers and Amnesty International, they spearheaded what would become the international human rights movement.[21] Muñoz was also a seasoned community activist involved in the US Civil Rights movement, linked to the Latino farm workers network led by the iconic

César Chávez. Together with other 'renovated socialists', Muñoz saw the possibility for a historic compromise that would confront dictatorship in Chile, and ensure 'a majority coalition for future democratic stability and social change' in a post-Junta era.[22]

This group was active mostly in academic institutions within Chile and anywhere with a space for dissidents to regroup, diagnose what had gone wrong with the Allende government, and develop an effective plan to challenge the dictatorship. Most of the work was led by one of the former founders of the Dependency school of economic thought in Latin America, the Chilean sociologist Enzo Faletto. His 'Thursday Group', as it became known, included Lagos, Muñoz and a few others. The group led the call for self-criticism, urging the party to accept that its lack of unitary direction during Allende's years bore a significant share of responsibility for its downfall. They also had to confront the decline of industrial worker unions due to deindustrialisation, deregulation and repression, paving the way for an explosion in the services and finance economy that pushed the so-called 'economic miracle' founded on the designs of Jaime Guzmán, Federico Willoughby, Sergio de Castro and his Chicago Boys. In the midst of repression and exile, Faletto and the Thursday Group set out to recover the value of human rights and the rule of law.[23]

Faletto recognised that in Chile a mixture of Catholic orthodoxy, authoritarian rule and the defence of unbridled freedom and scope for economic markets – the kind of synthesis embraced by influential advisers to the Junta such as Jaime Guzmán, Willoughby and De Castro – had precluded any debate on the consequences of granting free rein to market values in society. As a result, without quite realising it, and without ever having reached a consensus to do so, Chileans drifted from having a private sector and a market economy to becoming a market culture with a thoroughly depoliticised society. These are the conditions that according to Alberto Mayol configured the situation of 'permanent transition' that has become so characteristic of Chile.[24] Such conditions coincided with and were intricately related to the process of globalisation and financial-isation of the capitalist economy under the aegis of multinational corporations. From the outset, Faletto saw the roots of both phenomena in the past events of 11 September 1973.

Admiral Merino's and De Castro's Chicago Boys had successfully staged what could be called Merino's other coup, pushing Pinochet and other less sympathetic members of the Junta regime such as the minister of finance Admiral Lorenzo Gotuzzo to implement the reforms proposed in the document *El Ladrillo* (*The Brick*, so called because of its thickness).[25] In October 1973 De Castro locked horns with Hugo Araneda, a lawyer specialising in financial law who was Pinochet's military schoolmate, and other 'statist' members of the military such as General Horacio Bonilla and General Sergio Arellano Stark, who were complaining that the negative social impact of the Junta's economic policies was undermining its hold on power. These men abhorred Allende's expropriations but were not denationalisers (especially not copper, linked to their budget and thus to national security).

By the spring of 1975, the Junta acknowledged that unemployment was out of control and inflation had skyrocketed. The Chicago Boys' Roberto Kelly – former navy officer, a member of the Cofradía who had secured Brazilian support for the coup, and a friend of Sergio de Castro and his group – was given forty-eight hours by Pinochet to come up with a strategy to turn things around. A month before, Milton Friedman had been in Chile giving a lecture at the Junta headquarters entitled 'Gradualism or Shock Treatment?' On 21 March 1975, he and his former student Rolf Lüders met with Pinochet in private. Friedman advocated shock treatment, 'otherwise the patient will die'.

What Friedman proposed to Pinochet that day has since become an article of faith for governments around the world: inflation obsession, massive cuts in government spending, labour-market flexibility, deregulation, abandonment of capital controls, free exchange rates and/or austerity. 'If you want to cut off a

dog's tail you don't do it gradually; you do it in one single chop,'
Friedman reportedly said. Kelly's strategy drew heavily on
Friedman's paper, on the report called *The Brick* that he, De
Castro, Guzmán and the navy had prepared before the coup, on
Guzmán's influential merging of Catholic corporatism – the
medieval theory of the liberty of professional guilds – and the
legacy of Francoism with economic individualism, and on
Friedman's sales pitch to Pinochet.

The pitch worked. Pinochet bought into Friedman's notion that
he had to snuff out the 'statist' disease, which sounded to his ears
like the need to snuff out the 'Marxist cancer' disease, as General
Leigh had put it on 11 September. Leigh had introduced Jaime
Guzmán into his circle of advisers on 20 September 1973. There,
the young conservative, former founder of the *Gremialista* movement that had played such a crucial role during and after the 1972
October Strike in undermining Allende's legitimacy, also a constitutional lawyer inspired by the Francoists in Spain, caught Pinochet's
attention. They may have had very little in common, other than a
fervent admiration for Francisco Franco.[26]

Upon meeting with Kelly and consulting Guzmán around 6
April 1975, Pinochet gave Sergio de Castro's 'Chicago Boys'
complete control over the Chilean economy. De Castro and
Guzmán, together with Kelly and Willoughby, the Junta's new
press secretary, knew each other well from the *Gremialista* movement that connected the industrial and professional guilds, the
inner circle of National Party leader Jorge Alessandri and the
Cofradía Náutica. They were now in a position to effectively
shape Chile's legal and economic model. General Leigh and
others were opposed at first to the shock treatment advocated by
De Castro and Kelly, fearing that the strategy would trigger a
deep recession. 'Witnesses recall Pinochet and Leigh leaving the
room together and yelling at each other in the next room.'[27] This
period between March and April 1975 could be deemed the birth
date of the austerity–authoritarian creed that Naomi Klein has

termed 'the shock doctrine', and the starting point of disaster capitalism.[28]

This means that so-called neoliberalism and disaster capitalism should be treated either as relics of the Cold War or at the very least as Cold War formations by another name, rather than belonging to the period after the end of the Cold War. Their temporality, as something new or 'post', comes from elsewhere: the grammar of human rights discourse that insisted on putting moral constraints on politics originated in the Vicariate of Solidarity, an organisation set up by Cardinal Silva Henríquez on the ruins of the Ecumenical Committee of Cooperation for Peace (which had emerged in the aftermath of the coup, mostly led by left-wing Christians and closed by Silva Henríquez at the Junta's behest).

What linked the austerity and authority creed with Christian notions of the authority of morals over politics was the common ground dug by ideologues like Jaime Guzmán in Chile: the notion that the liberty and moral values of individuals and their associations, especially professional guilds, are naturally prior to and autonomous from any state or collective action. From the 1930s onwards, that notion had spawned the idea that any state action encroaching on such basic individual rights signified a violation of the rights of individuals, and therefore disqualified the state from representing them. Thus emerged a conception of human rights as purely individual rights claimed in advance of the state, and in particular rights to property and industry. It is important to notice that the 'prehistory' of such a conception of human rights – roughly speaking between 1948 or 1949 and 1986 – runs parallel and in many ways counter to another conception of human rights as people's rights, closer to the establishment of the right to self-determination and a moral politics of solidarity at the heart of Third World discourses of liberation.[29]

The case of Chile illustrates this opposition: arguably, between 1964 and 1973 the dominant conception of rights was the Christian-social and socialist notion of human rights as people's rights, articulated around the right to self-determination and economic emancipation through state action. Thereafter, between September 1973 and the late 1980s or 1990s, the dominant conception is of rights as (purely moral or legal natural) individual concerns of property and entrepreneurship vis-à-vis any moral–political action through the state. The latter is the credo that Jaime Guzmán introduced into the legality emerging from the dictatorship period, and in time into Chile's 1980 Constitution. The other, more rebellious, language of rights as people's rights is the one invoked by the members of the Second Russell Tribunal in 1974–5, the pro-democracy movement of the 1980s (although much closer to the Christian-social/Liberal/socialist compromise of post-1948 Germany) and, more forcefully, by the Chilean student movement of 2011.

After September 1973, and not only in Chile, the more rebellious language of rights as people's rights was rescued and 'tamed' by the conception, still predominant in the global North and its human rights governmental or non-governmental organisations, of rights as natural individual securities against the state, especially rights to property and enterprise. The latter has provided the basis for the thoroughly conformist fiction of the autonomy of moral and natural rights from politics, as a condition of their moral relevance. As the case of Chile illustrates, this naturalistic conception of rights and the priority of morals over politics is for the most part of Christian origin, and compatible with the more recent defence of individual property and enterprise. But in spite of its apparent roots in Christian medieval orthodoxy, it has in fact rewritten (or at least glossed over) orthodox Christian and other religious injunctions against the extension of market and money values to the whole of society.

A similar dependence on the fantasy of separating morals from politics unites the early attractions of Amnesty International, the Helsinki (later Human Rights) Watch groups, and the turn to human rights in the Americas and Eastern Europe. The latter would lead to disenchantment and feelings of guilt among many former 'fellow travellers' of the Left and Third Worldism in the Americas, such as the Argentinian literary critic Beatriz Sarlo, Guatemalan author Mario Roberto Morales, Óscar del Barco, or the Mexican biographer of Che Guevara and secretary of state under the conservative PAN government, Jorge Castañeda, and would help to forge the self-destructive tools of French 'new philosophy', which by 1977 went as far as indicting politics as such (as the realm of utopias destined to catastrophic failure) in the name of ethics.[30] That slippery slope ends in the justification of military intervention and massive human rights violations in our time, in the name of human rights. Perhaps the creation by Henry Kissinger in 1975 of the State Department human rights bureau should have set alarm bells ringing.

It is significant in this respect that one of Pinochet's staunchest allies, the *El Mercurio* editor Arturo Fontaine, pointed out in his account of Chile's economic 'miracle' that the general came to view De Castro's Chicago Boys and the young conservatives as 'a commando battalion in the political and economic fields' – one could add the moral field – 'with the capacity to . . . destroy old-fashioned routines and norms'.[31] Pinochet's moral–economic commandos perceived themselves as the vanguard of a national counter-revolution, 'a neo-right that resurrected the principles inherent to liberalism, as well as setting off a revival of the authoritarian tradition'.[32] If so, then it is no exaggeration to call the strategy for the consolidation of the restorative model that emerged out of the 6 April meeting in Santiago a blueprint for a moral economy of torture.[33]

By the end of 1976, the almost defunct Chilean economy began to show signs of vitality, moving forward in zombie-like fashion. De Castro became finance minister, ratcheted up the shock treatment to an even higher level of pain, and sided with Pinochet against General Leigh. By 1977, Leigh and Pinochet had locked horns in all-out war. At the underlings level, Guzmán and Willoughby were also locking horns with Pinochet's chief henchman, DINA's Colonel Manuel Contreras. The issue was not so much the notorious cruelty and inhumanity of Chilean intelligence when it came to torturing and disappearing, but rather, succession. Who would inherit?

According to Robert Barros, many of the constitutional and legislative developments that ended up binding the Junta itself grew out of the confrontation between its members, mainly Leigh and Pinochet. He fails to observe the degree to which Jaime Guzmán, the author of many such developments, was also paving the way for a transition towards a protected democracy in which a civilian – perhaps himself – could succeed the military leaders.

Throughout these developments, however, Pinochet maintained and reinforced his hold over the intelligence and repression apparatus, principally DINA, led by his protégé Colonel Manuel Contreras. According to Barros, the National Directorate of Intelligence began operating on 11 September 1973 as an informal group of army majors and colonels with contacts in the far-right paramilitary groups that had terrorised Chile from 1971 onwards.[34] Quickly, it came to supplant the independent intelligence services of the army, the navy and the air force.

In the days after the coup, Pinochet delegated his authority as head of military tribunals under the terms of the state of emergency to General Sergio Arellano Stark. Arellano was commissioned, together with a group of army officers, to review cases pending before such tribunals, accelerate proceedings and pass harsh sentences. During October 1973, the group travelled around the country by helicopter, issuing sentences accompanied in many cases by extrajudicial executions officially explained as the result either of such judicial decisions or of escape attempts. Seventy-two men were executed, forty of them members of the Socialist Party, and the rest either communists or members of the MIR. Later, all of the members of the delegation, which came to be known as the Caravan of Death, bar General Arellano, became DINA agents. They were joined by former members of Fatherland and Freedom and the ex-Cadet Commandos, who were deployed as agents in Chile,

Argentina and elsewhere to carry out covert operations and political assassinations, and become the pivot for the counter-revolutionary network linking the intelligence services of the continent's anti-leftist governments that launched the notorious Operation Cóndor.[35]

DINA was formally constituted by the Junta on 12 November 1973, and given legal form under Decree Law 521 of 14 June 1977. Although in principle it was ascribed to the Junta, a secret article authorised the Junta to have recourse to DINA in order to carry out arrests in exercise of the exceptional powers bestowed by the declaration of the state of emergency and whose exercise became a prerogative of the president of the Junta as Supreme Command of the Nation, General Augusto Pinochet, within days of DINA's creation. Effectively its head, Colonel Contreras, received orders from and was subordinate to Pinochet, not the Junta. As such, Contreras soon became the most powerful and feared man in the country and abroad, after Pinochet.

At the end of 1973, CIA contacts with DINA assumed a more ominous significance when one of its operatives, Michael Townley, arrived in Chile, according to Contreras, with the specific intent of carrying out orders received from 'the highest national authority' – meaning Pinochet – 'in agreement with what had already been planned by the CIA' to kill General Carlos Prats, who had sought refuge in Argentina after the coup.[36] Two months after the coup a man named Enrique Arancibia Clavel turned up at the headquarters of the recently created DINA 'to present my respects to then Col. Contreras, and offer my services to help acquiring any information he might need'.[37] At the time of joining DINA's foreign service, Arancibia resided in Argentina. He had escaped Chilean justice after being indicted for terrorist activities, as part of the Fatherland and Freedom/ex-Cadet groups led by General Viaux, in collaboration with the CIA, which had assassinated General René Schneider in October 1970.

Arancibia was known as 'El Dinamitero' (the Bomber) for his role in the paramilitary campaign against the Allende government, planting charges in the Bolsa de Comercio, the School of Law of Universidad de Chile, television Channel 9, and the airport at Santiago. He confessed to such acts before a Chilean court, where he also accused General Viaux of being the mastermind behind the series of terrorist strikes he had carried out together with other members of the paramilitary far right. Their aim, he said, was to create a climate of chaos and violence that would lay the ground for the kidnapping of Schneider and hinder Allende's confirmation as Chile's president in 1970. After each explosion, the paramilitary would leave behind pamphlets signed by the bogus 'Workers-Peasants Brigades' to make it look as if an ultra-leftist group had carried them out, and thereby smear Allende.

Arancibia's father was a naval officer. So was his brother. Another brother was in the army. In spite of his confession and the explosives found at his home in October 1970, inexplicably the judge let Arancibia out on bail and he escaped into Argentina. There he was helped by the aide-de-camp of General Juan Carlos Onganía, an Argentinian dictator from the 1960s who had proposed at a Conference of Armed Forces of the Americas the creation of an inter-American task force with a continental mandate against the communist menace. General Schneider opposed the initiative.

With the assassination of Schneider and the displacement of Prats, the plotters of the September 1973 coup, especially Pinochet, thought they had for ever exorcised the spirit of constitutionalism in the armed forces and the principles advocated by the two previous commanders of the army. However, the fact that Prats exerted his moral authority and influence from Argentinian exile, by criticising Pinochet's regime, reawakened the attention of the Chilean rulers.

Some time in mid-1974, Colonel Pedro Ewing approached the Junta's press secretary, Federico Willoughby. 'There's a very dangerous atmosphere for Prats,' Ewing told Willoughby. 'For some reason . . . Pinochet has got very irritated with Prats, because of his weight abroad and the fact he did not approve of the military regime.'[38] Ewing, a former student of Prats in the War Academy, admired and respected his former teacher. Ewing told Willoughby that DINA agents were following Prats in Buenos Aires, and said that he 'honestly feared something bad might happen' to General Prats. Willoughby remembers having witnessed Pinochet cursing Prats after a critical article penned by the constitutionalist general appeared in the foreign press. It was an article on geopolitics, the subject that Pinochet had claimed as his own. On 5 June 1974, Prats wrote Pinochet a letter demanding that the president of the Supreme Command put an end to the machinations against him, and emphasising that 'since I left the army's ranks, I had not intervened in the activities of my successor'. Pinochet interpreted this as a challenge to his authority. It marked a point of no return in their relations.

On 1 October 1974 DINA agent Michael Townley detonated the explosive device that killed General Carlos Prats and his wife Sophia Cuthbert in the Pañermo street of Buenos Aires. Prats and his wife were returning to their residence. He was about to park his car in the garage when a bomb placed under the gearshift exploded, blowing the couple to pieces. The order came from Santiago. Enrique Arancibia Clavel followed the general and provided all the information about his habits and daily routine, as well as the schematics of his house, in a report. The report was forwarded by DINA agent Juan Morales directly to Colonel Manuel Contreras. The DINA agents Commander Raúl Iturriaga and Officer Armando Fernández Larios coordinated the mission to assassinate Prats teamed with Argentinian members of the far-right group Triple A.[39]

In April 1975, these same agents and their foreign partners among anti-leftist paramilitary groups and intelligence services abroad would launch 'Operation Colombo', aimed at the execution of over a hundred Chilean detained-disappeared militants whose corpses would appear in Argentina as if they had been killed by their own comrades. One such partner in the foreign intelligence community, Jorge Osvaldo 'Rawson' Riveiro, second in command of the Argentinian inteligence services and a protagonist of the dirty war against leftist militants in that country, was described by a

27 August 1975 intelligence report as 'having an idea to form a central intelligence coordinated network between Chile, Argentina, Uruguay and Paraguay'.[40] This was the origin of the infamous Operation Condor.

From the outset, DINA carried out operations throughout Chile and abroad. Its members were outside the law and could operate under the orders of its director, Colonel Manuel Contreras, who, as we have seen, reported to and received orders only from Pinochet, with total impunity. Its capacity to operate within the armed forces, and especially the army, gave it power irrespective of rank and seniority, while also cementing Pinochet's hold on the armed forces and the other members of the Junta. The resulting power differential between the original members of the Chilean triumvirate would be a persistent source of internal conflict. Strictly speaking, it meant the continuation of the coup within the coup, beyond the events of 11 September.

As early as June 1974, Pinochet would dismiss the complaints of potential adversaries within the armed forces, such as Air Force General Leigh or Army Generals Bonilla and Lutz, who openly denounced Contreras's habit of overruling his superior officers by saying: 'Gentlemen, I am DINA.'[41] Often this power struggle would be expressed in a language that made use of the differential involvement of the various branches of the armed forces in the repression. The commanders-in-chief of the navy and the air force would in time grow critical of the repressive methods and absolute power embodied by DINA, and by extension, Pinochet. Thus, for instance, Air Force General Leigh would claim that he withdrew virtually all his personnel from the DINA once it became apparent that he had no power within the organisation.[42]

This allowed for the power struggle taking place within and around the Chilean Military Junta between 1973 and the late 1980s to be formulated largely in the language of human rights: civilian and military members or advisers to the Junta would enlist the moral authority of the language of human rights in order to exculpate themselves, cement their 'democratic' credentials, or in any case keep themselves at arm's length from the worst aspects of the regime they had helped bring about. This would prove particularly useful to those among them who sought to carve a space for themselves in the politics of the transition period beyond the late 1980s. Internal power struggles erupted not only between the Junta members, leading to what Robert Barros calls 'autocratic institutional self-limitation' – the kind of military regime specific to Chile, which featured self-binding rules and in a way helped to secure a constitution – but also among their underlings. Colonel Contreras, for instance, subsequently clashed with Jaime Guzmán and Federico Willoughby. The latter would in many instances resort to the language of human rights, or in any case distance themselves from the most horrific aspects of Pinochet's dictatorship, thereby cementing their democratic credentials in the new political context of the transition and the 1980 Constitution. Whether this had anything to do with a genuine concern for human rights, law and so on, is an altogether different matter.

Like the restorative liberal economic model that began to take shape during the dictatorship, DINA was going global, always under the pretext of fighting the good fight against godless communism, the normalisation of the state of emergency, sound economics and war.[43] This was also the justification for South American dictatorships to pool their resources and set up in Chile a coordination and operations centre that would serve as a clearing house for intelligence information backed by the latest computer technology. A sort of evil twin of Cybersyn's Operation Room, it enabled the crusaders to engage at least six countries in operational activities and extend their covert actions, in particular political assassinations, beyond South America. What ensued was a veritable worldwide web of murder and torture, which became known as Operation Condor.

The investigation by the journalist John Dinges into Operation Condor convincingly concluded that the CIA knew about Condor long before the 21 September 1976 car-bomb assassination of

Allende's former minister of defence, Orlando Letelier, and an American citizen, Ronni Moffitt, at Sheridan Circle in Washington, by DINA agents – among them Michael Townley – and anti-Castro operatives. As Townley confessed during his 1976 trial in the US, he recruited five anti-Castro Cuban exiles, belonging to the Coordination of United Revolutionary Organisations (CORU) in consultation with its leadership, to carry out the assassination. Among them were Virgilio Paz and the brothers Guillermo and Ignacio Novo. Those contacts had been cemented before, at the time of the assassination of Carlos Prats and thereafter, with people who included Martín Ciga Correa, formerly a member of an armed group of the National Socialist Youth of Argentina, and the Italian fascist Stephano Delle Chiaie. In the papers found at the Buenos Aires flat of Enrique Arancibia there are accounts of meetings between Ciga Correa, Virgilio Paz and the others in the house that Michael Townley occupied in the exclusive Lo Curro quarter in Santiago.[44]

Two weeks after Henry Kissinger's visit to Santiago in June 1976, the DINA team comprising Townley, Paz and the Novo brothers, among others, received the order from Santiago to kill Letelier. All those directly involved in the murder would later point the finger at the president of the Supreme Command, Pinochet. On Tuesday morning 21 September 1976, Letelier was on his way to work at the Institute for Policy Studies in Washington DC. As his Chevrolet Chevette entered Sheridan Circle, a bomb exploded under it. Letelier died instantly. Ronni Moffitt, a young colleague at the institute who was sitting in the front passenger's seat, was also killed. Her husband, sitting in the back seat, miraculously survived with only a few injuries. Townley had placed the explosive device. Virgilio Paz denotated it. The Chilean Captain Armando Fernández Larios and Mónica Lagos, another DINA agent, ran surveillance before and during the assassination.

Washington had been warned several times about the operation. A Paraguayan source inside the Operation Condor network tipped off US ambassador George Landau about operatives entering the US with false passports provided by Paraguay's military intelligence. Landau photocopied the passports and sent them to the CIA and the State Department. After the murder, CIA director George H. W. Bush launched an investigation. As it pointed towards Santiago, people involved paid the price. The Chilean consular serviceman who had issued Chilean passports for the DINA team was found dead with a gunshot wound at his home in Santiago later the following year. He had been approached by FBI agents in Panama, and as soon as he got back to Santiago went to the foreign minister, Admiral Patricio Carvajal, and told him about the incident. Soon after that he was dead, and the notebook in which he kept the numbers of all the passports he had issued to DINA agents had disappeared. There was no autopsy and a summary investigation concluded that he had committed suicide. In his memoirs, Pinochet does not even mention Letelier's assassination while accounting for important events in 1976. But he had complained to Kissinger about Letelier's influence in Washington when they met on 8 June 1976.

Up until then, Pinochet and Contreras were certain that they had America's support. In fact Contreras received at least one payment from the CIA as a regular asset in 1975. In August 1975, some months after DINA assassinated General Prats and his wife in Buenos Aires, Contreras, who liked to be referred to as 'Condor One', travelled to Washington to meet the CIA deputy director, General Vernon Walters, for the third time. He also met members of the US Congress, to explain Chile's human rights policy. On at least one occasion, he was accompanied by Federico Willoughby.

'While Operation Condor was active,' says Heraldo Muñoz, 'Chile became a safe haven for right-wing terrorists.'[45] Cuban extremists opposed to Castro's rule received training and were welcomed in Santiago by Pinochet and the Junta themselves. At least some of those trainees took part in Letelier's bombing. The Italian neofascist Stefano delle Chiaie was a guest of Pinochet in 1974, accompanied by Mussolini's former naval officer Junio Valerio

Borghese. DINA and Condor's first collaboration took place in Rome, where the Chilean Christian Democrat Bernardo Leighton and his wife were shot in the head with a Beretta 9mm by two of Delle Chiaie's henchmen while walking on a street near the Vatican.

After Letelier's murder, the FBI and the US Justice Department had started joining the dots. Chile's foreign minister Admiral Patricio Carvajal soon found himself in hot water. So did Pinochet. The subject of Chile became an electoral issue in the US campaign when the Democrat hopeful Jimmy Carter questioned President Ford on the subject and the latter failed to respond during the 1976 television debates. When Carter won the election, Operation Condor unravelled. From then on until June 1980 Pinochet was at his weakest, under attack at home and abroad. He managed to get rid of General Leigh on 24 July 1978, after sending the army to surround the Ministry of Defence building, the Junta's building, and every air force base in Chile, forcing Leigh's resignation. Another chapter in the drama of the coup after the coup unfolded that day. By 1977 economic growth seemed more robust. Pinochet's new rising star, the economist José Piñera, had managed to pass labour flexibility reforms and replaced the old pension system with a system of private savings. The economic miracle was now in full swing, untroubled by ongoing repression, torture and killings at home and abroad.

However, by now even Milton Friedman had begun to keep his distance from Pinochet. The shock-therapy model had worked, among other things, because it was rewarded internationally. First, under Nixon and Ford, and the ever-watchful eye of Henry Kissinger, the US finally endorsed the renegotiation of Chile's debt at the Paris Club of creditor nations, which it had vehemently denied to Allende, and pumped sizeable funds into the Chilean economy, as opposed to the $19.8 million Allende received. The Import-Export Bank that had refused to lend Allende anything over $4.7 million lent Pinochet $183.6 million. Between 1973 and 1976, the World Bank provided Pinochet's Chile with $66.5 million, and the Inter-American Development Bank chipped in with $237.8 million. In return, Pinochet compensated all the American companies affected by expropriation in full, including Kennecott, Anaconda and even ITT. The prevailing wind started to change direction in Washington as the full picture of rights violations in Chile was recognised internationally, and revelations about the extent of US intervention began to emerge in the Senate; the result of the investigations into Letelier's murder made matters worse.

In Chile, people like the leader of Fatherland and Freedom, Pablo Rodríguez, still active, called for the regime to strengthen its relations with 'natural allies of anti-communist orientation', such as the apartheid regime in South Africa or Saudi Arabia. Pinochet blamed Carter for his travails, and credited the Virgin Mary for his luck when it became apparent that Ronald Reagan was going to defeat Carter in the 1980 presidential election. Soon after, the ban imposed by the Carter administration on subsidised credits was lifted and Pinochet became popular once more among the likes of Senator Jesse Helms, Strom Thurmond and Britain's prime minister Margaret Thatcher.

But in view of Pinochet's continuing disavowal of human rights, international pressure increased. Not even Pinochet's powerful new friends in Washington and London could keep turning a blind eye. To stave off international pressure, but also as a consequence of internal debates and the succession struggles involving Leigh, Merino, Pinochet and their underlings, the Junta began considering a project that included establishing constitutional limits and a timetable for moving towards Guzmán's 'protected' democracy, including its ratification by referendum on 11 September 1980.

The notion of 'protected democracy', and images of the type of civilian such a democracy would consider acceptable, became the cornerstones of current approaches to liberties and rights under conditions of allegedly permanent threats to security, widely used nowadays to contain social protest against economic shock therapy and austerity reforms. On the whole, the aim of the 1980 Constitution was not to restore democracy as it was before, nor to establish formal systems of representation constituting an order apart from civil society and external to it, as a republican arbiter of the tensions within civil society that result from economic inequality. On the contrary, the objective was to institute forms of practical behaviour internal to civil society, socially ordered practices and norms pre-empting social conflict over economic inequality to which people must submit at all times. The time of remedial equality would be postponed permanently.

Such norms and rules were based on the premise of protection against a vaguely defined enemy waging an effectively unending 'internal war'. This became evident in the dual character of the proposed 1980 Constitution, which included permanent and transitory articles. The latter effectively reinstated the organisation of military rule codified during the first years of the dictatorship, based on the fiction of internal war and the moral constraining of politics. It provided for General Pinochet to remain in office during an additional eight-year presidential term, as well as granting him new and broader discretionary powers irrespective of whether or not a state of emergency was declared, and for the Junta to continue exercising legislative powers. In fact, at the moment of its promulgation this dualism made the permanent mass of the Constitution largely declarative and nominal, for it amounted to the normalisation of the state of emergency.

The 1980 Constitution had been presented as heralding a period of interregnum or transition towards democracy. This entailed moving from one stage to another and closing off the previous one. The time of transition is thus, allegedly, the time after the dictatorship, after evil, the time of nevermore. And yet, as opposition observers noticed at the time, the 1980 Chilean Constitution actually entrenched and radicalised the exceptional 'emergency' purportedly being superseded, foreclosing more substantial forms of participation and popular politics. Through its transitory articles and the appeal to the alleged threat by an enemy vaguely defined, 'emergency' and 'war' became the constant element of the suppos-edly new 'protected' democracy.[46] Nevermore is, after all, when the present is delayed and disabled as a time for justice.

In spite of such vagueness, the actual enemy could be defined quite accurately: even with Allende gone, the unreconstructed socialists, the violent subversives, the new terror could come liter-ally out of anywhere, or to be more precise, take the form of anything that could be construed as harming the normal functions of the economy: Mapuche Indians doing what they have been doing for over five hundred years and passively resisting, protesting students, human rights activists, journalists, magic realist writers, everyone. Especially problematic would be the case of internal dissent over the rules of the economic game.

This is exactly the kind of language we have grown used to in the wake of the other 9/11 in New York, Washington, Madrid and London. Rather than waning with the popularity of people like Pinochet or Bush Jr, and in the aftermath of the 2008 financial crisis and the 2011 global protests, we have seen the languages and prac-tices of the War on Terror bleed into and fuse with representations of 'Broken Britain', a 'socialist' president in the White House, permanent crisis, powers engaging in human rights violations and wars of aggression supposedly in order to contain human rights violations, inevitable austerity and uncertainty, unending terror, and permanent asymmetrical war. This is the true legacy of the events of 11 September 1973 in Chile.

Under pressure from abroad, facing an increasingly organised opposition, and confronting an ambiguous relationship with the Reagan administration, the Chilean regime had it hard in the 1980s. To top it all, the one thing that everybody lauded, the economic model, came tumbling down. In 1981 Chile was in the midst of what the standard indicators call an economic boom. A formerly discreet bourgeoisie, says Muñoz, 'now flaunted its prosperity with luxury cars, mansions and shopping sprees abroad'.[47] Chileans borrowed heavily in an international market crammed with 'petrodollars', wooed by increasingly sophisticated financial schemes dreamed up by clever people in the increasingly clever financial services sector of the economy. Against the theory of the Chicago Boys and the optimism of finance minister Sergio de Castro that his austerity measures would make room for the needed corrections of the market, the American recession that began in 1982 started to drain Chile's reserves, money got scarce, and the banks collapsed.

On 2 November 1981 the Chilean state seized and bailed out a number of private banks and finance companies. Divisions within the Chicago Boys became more pronounced, and military men came back to the cabinet economic posts. Facing uncertainty, Pinochet decided to devalue the Chilean peso. Disaster followed: savings disappeared, businesses went bust, and the banks' bad debts soared to 54 per cent of the financial system's capital and reserves. More banks were seized and bailed out, at a cost of some $7 billion to the taxpayer. After years of denationalisation dogma, the Pinochet regime was in control of 80 per cent of Chile's financial sector.

The economic crisis mobilised people once more, the rock band Los Prisioneros sang *Muevan las industrias* (Move the factories), and the renovated socialists felt encouraged to unify and go on the offensive. Enzo Faletto, leader of the Thursday Group and the man many saw as the best intellectually prepared for the job, declined a nomination as new leader of the socialists and the chance to confront Pinochet in the coming elections. Ricardo Lagos went on to join the leadership of the new Socialist Party of Chile headed by Allende's former interior minister Carlos Briones. Next they sought an alliance with the Christian Democrats, the Radical Party and an anti-Pinochet group on the right, constituting in 16 August 1983, ten years after the siege of La Moneda, the Democratic Alliance (AD). Coordinated protests meant the return of the masses to the streets between June and September 1983. Lagos became president of AD in December, and the protests continued unabated until mid-1984. In November that year Pinochet reinstated a full state of emergency and unleashed the Furies once more.

Only in 1985, when the Junta abandoned the Chicago Boys' medicine to cure the communist cancer, did the economy began to show signs of recovery. By then, the Reagan administration had distanced itself considerably from Santiago. By 1988, both the Pope and 'Superman' had told Pinochet the time had come to transfer power to the civilians. The fiercely anti-communist John Paul II did so during a visit to Chile in April 1987. During a visit to the country in November that year, the actor Christopher Reeve, world-famous for his film portrayal of the Man of Steel and Kryptonian defender of American values, expressed his support for Chilean democracy and for Chilean actors active in the opposition against the military regime who were targets of anonymous death threats.

From then onwards, the opposition's plan would be rooted in what Muñoz called 'hard-nosed analyses of the present reality and not preconceived ideological schemes'. The opposition distanced itself from the violent resistance alternative embraced by the likes of FPMR (Frente Patriótico Manuel Rodríguez), a wing of the Communist Party that opted for the military option after Allende's death and was inspired by developments in Nicaragua, El Salvador, Iran and Afghanistan – where the Soviet intervention had been justified by Moscow in April 1980 as a determination 'not to permit another Chile'.[48] This faction, led by Raúl Pellegrin, a former combatant in Nicaragua, almost succeeded in killing Pinochet on 7 September 1986.[49] On 1 April 1991, an FPMR young cadre named Ricardo Palma, whose sisters Marcela and Andrea had been detained and tortured by the CNI (Centro Nacional de Investigaciones, the successor of DINA) shot and killed Jaime Guzmán as the latter stopped at a red light in his car, after finishing his constitutional law lecture in the East Campus of Universidad Católica.

As Allende had predicted, things became a lot harder and more violent.

Things got even worse for the regime before they could get better. Pinochet lost the 1988 presidential plebiscite, as Chileans

went to the polls for the first time in fifteen and a half years to deny
the dictator eight more years in power. The graffiti scrawled on the
walls of Santiago summed up the importance of what had happened:
'we expelled him with a pencil'. The murals of Santiago were speaking once again.

Pinochet asked the Junta to grant him special emergency powers
in an attempt to launch another coup, but this time General
Fernando Matthei, who had replaced Leigh, and Admiral Merino,
the only other remaining original member of the leading plotters,
refused. It was the end of a long story of internecine battles between
the former victors of 11 September. Still, a resounding defeat this
was not: Pinochet won 43 per cent of the vote.

On 6 October, another of Allende's prophecies came to pass:
thousands of people walked down The Mall (La Alameda) singing
'Chile, happiness is coming'. As Muñoz says: 'Pinochet and his
economic team had trusted that Chile's undeniable economic
growth would win them the election. But the new prosperity benefited only a small portion of society.'[50] Pinochet and the Chicago
Boys had created a structurally divided Chile: 'the clearest expression of this socioeconomic apartheid was the fact that Pinochet lost
in boom cities and towns . . . which, because of their recent export-
driven prosperity, had been thought to be government
strongholds.'[51]

According to Enzo Faletto, to make possible the new relation of
dependency that he termed, following economist Paul Singer,
'consented dependency', the new dominant groups had to transform existing social relations.[52] Put simply, they had to allow market
values to play an ever-greater role in shaping social life. Economics
would become 'an imperial domain' in which the logic of buying
and selling goods and services 'no longer applied to material goods
alone but increasingly governs the whole of life'.[53] As a result,
people's identities and subjectivity changed, prevailing values were
modified, determined by the imperial reign of an entrepreneurial
spirit driven solely by profit motives and consumption drives. And

this was called 'liberty'. If so, on the other side of 'liberty' lies the space inhabited by the poor, and the precarious middle classes – those who suffer inequality and the effects of past injustice. The beneficiaries of that 'model', which Alberto Mayol fittingly calls permanent transition, can, and indeed do, dream about ever-greater growth, purchasing power and consumption. The dreams and desires of the rest have been indefinitely postponed.

The numbers do not lie, but they demonstrate this: by 1990 inequality was much deeper in Chile than in 1970, with economic reforms enlarging the previous gap between rich and poor, and poverty affecting 39 per cent of the population in the last year of the dictatorship. Hence the chanting in the streets of Santiago, 'Happiness is coming'.[54] The question continues to be: when?

After Joan Garcés expanded his legal complaint to include the names of two disappeared Chileans who had been arrested in the context of Operation Condor, Judge Baltasar Garzón issued an order for the international pursuit, and arrest with a view to extradition, of now Senator-for-Life General Augusto Pinochet Ugarte. At 5 p.m. on Friday 16 October 1994, Detective Inspector Andrew Hewett and Sergeant David Jones of Scotland Yard detained the man who had declared only a few days before to the journalist Jon Lee Anderson: 'I was only an *aspirante dictator*' – a candidate dictator. 'I've always been a very studious man . . . I read a lot, especially history. And history teaches you that dictators never end up well,' he said to Anderson.[55] Gone were the dark glasses; others in Latin America would take to using them while saying to anyone ready to listen that they were not Pinochet.

'Lamentably,' Pinochet told Anderson, 'almost everyone in the world today is a Marxist – even if they don't know it themselves. They continue to have Marxist ideas.'[56] It seems laughable, but in a sense, he may be right. As the crisis that started in 2008 deepens, many in the world are beginning to wonder if the path opened up by the Chilean Way of Allende and so abruptly interrupted on 11 September 1973 may have to be retaken. Many in Greece are

wondering, and in Spain, and in the occupied and evicted public
spaces of Britain and America. Those still hopeful in the wake of the
Arab Spring and the Occupy movements everywhere in 2011 and
2012 are wondering too. And, of course, in Chile.

In May 2012, the leftist student leader Camila Vallejo responded
in Chile to an article published in the *Wall Street Journal* a few days
before. The article was titled 'Chile's Cautionary Lesson for
Americans'. The columnist argued that it was incomprehensible
how a twenty-three-year-old whose parents were supporters of
Salvador Allende could lead thousands of protesters demanding free
education, nationalisation of the copper industry and an end to the
restorative economic model in Chile. The author could not fathom
how a young woman like Vallejo could put the rightist government
of Sebastián Piñera on the defensive, let alone how something like
that could happen in the country that was 'the poster-child of liberal
economic reform'. The article concluded: 'Chile has been intellectually swamped by leftist ideas.' The columnist was repeating
Pinochet's nonsense. In her response, Camila Vallejo quoted
Cervantes. She replied: 'It pains them to see Chile's consciousness
awakening. It is a sign that we are moving forward.'[57]

Vallejo is running for Congress, as a representative of the
Communist Party, during the 2013 elections. Another student leader
of the 2011 protests, Giorgio Jackson, decided to create a new party
to challenge the compromises of the transitional period. Furthermore,
a campaign is under way to ask Chilean voters to jot down the
letters 'CA' on their ballot forms, meaning that they call for the
gathering of a 'Constitutional Assembly' with extended popular
participation, which could abolish the 1980 Constitution inspired
by Guzmán and those who helped bring about Pinochet's dictatorship, the state of emergency and permanent transition. The
Constitutional Assembly could agree on a new one, and in the
process could hold the debate about where the market belongs,
whether or not it should continue to be the centre of society or
rather be displaced to its periphery, and how to value education,

health, family life, art and science, nature, democracy, law, and people's rights and duties. That would be a revolutionary act, and an example in today's world.

If after all that has been said there is still a need for a conclusion to this story, it would be this: forget all you may have heard or read about the mismanagement of the Chilean economy by the Allende government. Forget what you think you know about leftist hostility towards business, their idiotic anti-Americanism, and the stupidity of nationalising everything. Forget the notion that these were quixotic characters engaged in an act of surreal naiveté, an adolescent fad or utopian madness. Forget the internal divisions, the pressures from abroad, Kissinger's anxieties and the CIA's mastery of the dark arts.

All that was true. Every single one of such objective conditions was there, and they all exerted their causal force to one extent or another. But not a single one of them, nor all of them put together, could explain the bombs that began to fall immediately after Beatriz and her father sealed their pact to defy destiny in one final and tragic embrace a few minutes before noon on 11 September 1973. The fury that would be unleashed from that moment onwards, would lead to the 40,018 victims – the disappeared, the executed and the tortured – and the hundreds of thousands of exiles, the Caravan of Death that spread its poison of politically motivated assassination across at least three continents under the code name Operation Condor, the assassination of General Carlos Prats and his wife in Buenos Aires, the bomb that scattered the entrails of Orlando Letelier and Ronni Moffitt across the sidewalk of Sheridan Circle in Washington, DC on 21 September 1976, the copycat killings during the 'years of lead' in Italy, and in the midst of that circle of Dante's hell, the so-called economic 'miracle' and success of Chile. According to Camila Vallejo, Giorgio Jackson, Alberto Mayol, Alejandro Zambra and many others – the protagonists of the story of the future of Chile, yet to be written – the period of transition between 1988 and 2011 became, in fact, a version of purgatory.

None of it could be explained, if not for the fact that a sector of Chilean society relinquished its duty to ensure a future, denied another sector its capacity to hope and dream reality, and turned its collective gaze away from the present, in the direction of a mythical safe past. It is time for another past – the one that brought about the heroic, loving, honest, human example of Salvador and Beatriz Allende – to inspire a new future, here and now.

Notes

Introduction

1. Quoted in Beckett, *Pinochet in Piccadilly*, 26.
2. D. Cordingly, *Cochrane the Dauntless*, London: Bloomsbury, 2007, 293.
3. Beckett, *Pinochet in Piccadilly*, 39–40. According to Beckett, by 1822 his estate had come 'to look more and more like a rival power centre to Valparaíso and Santiago'.
4. B. Vale, *The Audacious Admiral Cochrane*, London: Conway Maritime, 2004, 123–4; NAS Edinburgh: GD233/39/261, GD233/20/450, quoted in Cordingly, *Cochrane the Dauntless*, 298 n. 6. See also Beckett, *Pinochet in Piccadilly*, 39.
5. Beckett, *Pinochet in Piccadilly*, 45.
6. Ibid.

1 Outlaws and Political Cobblers

1. S. Allende in conversation with Debray, *Conversación con Allende*, 61. On the long tradition of autobiographical memoir and storytelling in African, Latino and indigenous history in the Americas, see Gordon, *Existentia Africana*, 23–4, and Martín-Alcoff, 'Caliban's Ontology', 9–25, at 21.
2. S. Allende in conversation with Debray, *Conversación con Allende*, 61–2.
3. Ibid.
4. For the history of this idea see Wey Gomez, *The Tropics of Empire*; C. Bracken, *Magical Criticism: The Recourse of Savage Philosophy*, University of Chicago Press, 2007.
5. Martín-Alcoff, 'Caliban's Ontology', 24.
6. E. Hobsbawm, 'Political Shoemakers', co-written with Joan W. Scott, in *Uncommon People: Resistance, Rebellion and Jazz*, Abacus, 1999.
7. Winn, *Weavers of Revolution*.
8. In the *Convivio*, Dante calls *accidia* the vice that results because of lack of outrage, action and indignation. It appears also in Cantos VII and XVII of the *Divine Comedy* in connection with the images of the uncommitted and purgatory. It was against this vice that Marx would declare his famous 11th Thesis, calling for the transformation of reality. Others speak of revolutionary love (Guevara), fidelity to a truthful cause and consistency as virtues, in a similar vein.

9. Hobsbawm, *Uncommon People*, ch. 3, I.

10. Winn, *Weavers of Revolution*.

11. Quoted by Hobsbawm, *Uncommon People*, ch. 3, I.

12. See Bolívar, *Letter From Jamaica*.

13. See Guardiola-Rivera, *What if Latin America Ruled the World?*; also 'Absolute Contingency and the Inaugural Event of International Law, Chiapas-Valladolid, ca. 1550'.

14. A. de Ramón, *Historia de Chile*, Santiago, Catalonia, 2004, 72–3.

15. Galeano, *Las venas abiertas de América Latina*, 15.

16. Ramírez Necochea, quoted in Amorós, *Compañero Presidente*, 39.

17. For a history of liberties and commons centred upon transatlantic exchanges, see Linebaugh, *The Magna Carta Manifesto*; and P. Linebaugh and M. Rediker, *The Many-headed Hydra: Sailors, Slaves, Commoners and the Hidden History of the Revolutionary Atlantic,* Boston: Beacon Press, 2001.

18. Dosman, *Life and Times of Raúl Prebisch*, 23; and García Linera, *La potencia plebeya*, 373–4.

19. Dosman, *Life and Times of Raúl Prebisch*, 22–3; and Feinstein, *Pablo Neruda*, 24. For the Chilean poet and Czech author Jan Neruda, see 'Interviews: Pablo Neruda, the Art of Poetry', by R. Guibert in *The Paris Review*, no. 51, Spring 1971.

20. Neruda, 'Infancia y poesía', also cited in Feinstein, *Pablo Neruda, A Passion for Life*, London: Bloomsbury, 2004, 19.

21. For 'long duration', crisis and 'bifurcation' in the sense used here, see Immanuel Wallerstein in conversation with Alfredo Gómez-Muller and Gabriel Rockhill, 'The Present in the Light of the Longue Durée', 98–112, at 106–7.

22. Feinstein, *Pablo Neruda*, 24.

23. F. Fanon quoted by E. Laclau, *On Populist Reason*, London: Verso, 150–1. Fanon writes: 'all who turn in circles between suicide and madness, will recover their balance, once more go forward and march proudly in the great procession of the awakened nation.' This image can be linked, on the one hand, to the question of the transit between the passive series and the militant group in Jean-Paul Sartre's philosophy, and on the other with the image of the procession of free men through the great avenues (*las grandes alamedas*) that appears in Salvador Allende's speeches. See also Arthur, *Unfinished Projects*; and Bosteels, *Marx and Freud in Latin America*, 51–74.

24. *Los Olvidados* (Luis Buñuel, Mexico, 1950); Revueltas, *Ensayo sobre un proletariado sin cabeza*, and *Los Errores*; Gunder Frank, *Capitalism and Underdevelopment in Latin America*, and *Lumpenburguesía: Lumpendesarrollo. Dependencia*.

25. S. Allende, speaking to the students of the University of Guadalajara, 2 December 1972, quoted in Witker, *Salvador Allende*, 4–5.

26. Ibid. Allende speaks of a *consecuencia difícil*.

27. 'Being young and not being a revolutionary may even be a biological contradiction. But to keep going in life and staying a revolutionary in a bourgeois society, that is the real difficulty.' Witker, *Salvador Allende*, 4–5.

28. For the relationship between prose narrative (memoir and the novel), the disavowal of revolutionary anti-slavery and republican constitutionalism in

the Americas, see Fischer, *Modernity Disavowed*. For the sense of Quixotic errancy and adventure used here, see Garcés, *Cervantes in Algiers*; and Pinet, 'On the Subject of Fiction'.

29. Arrate and Rojas, *Memoria de la izquierda chilena*, 151.
30. S. Allende in conversation with Debray, *Conversación con Allende*, 59. Also Amorós, *Compañero Presidente*, 45. For captivity and trauma in the Cervantine tradition of memoir and the novel, see Garcés, *Cervantes in Algiers*, 6–14.
31. Moulian, *Conversación interrumpida con Allende*, 35.
32. Gunder Frank, *Development and Underdevelopment in Latin America*, xi.
33. García Linera, *La potencia plebeya*, 373; Ampuero, *El último tango de Salvador Allende*, 20.
34. S. Allende in conversation with R. Debray, *Conversación con Allende*, 57–8. Contrary to common belief, the Declaration of Principles of the Socialist Party did not dismiss the 'dictatorship of the proletariat' and actually showed scepticism towards the 'democratic road'. See Amorós, *Compañero Presidente*, 44–5.
35. S. Allende, *Informe al IV Congreso del Partido Socialista, 1943*, cited in Garcés, 'Prólogo', in *Salvador Allende. Presente*, 21 n. 11. See Debray, *Conversación con Allende*, 57–8.

2 The Owners of Chile

1. E. Matte, in *El Pueblo*, 19 March 1892, cited in Ramírez Necochea, *Balmaceda y la contrarevolución de 1891*, 221. Also Gunder Frank, *Capitalism and Underdevelopment in Latin America*, 93.
2. Lazo, *Carmen Lazo: Su última entrevista*.
3. J. C. Mariátegui, *Nota autobibliográfica*, 10 January 1927, published in the journal *La Vida Literaria*, May 1930.
4. Christian and Jackson, 'Luis Buñuel: That Obscure Object of Desire'.
5. Ibarz, 'A Serious Experiment: Land Without Bread, 1933'.
6. See, among others, De Andrade, 'Manifesto Antropófago', and García Márquez, 'Possibilidades da Antropofagia'; also Warat, *Manifesto of Legal Surrealism*; I. rua Wall, *An Introduction: Legal Surrealism*; and Barreto, *We Wish To Inform You that Tomorrow We Will Be Killed With Our Families*.
7. Neruda, *Memoirs*, 115–16.
8. Redmond, 'Square Pegs. The Political Function of Ambiguous Gender in Three Novels of the Southern Cone', 127.
9. Moulian, *Conversación interrumpida con Salvador Allende*, 35.
10. Ibid.
11. C. Lazo, 'Carmen Lazo. Su última entrevista', Biblioteca del Congreso Nacional, at www.youtube.com/watch?v=K7PI_HF9cBA, viewed 13 February 2012.
12. S. Allende, *Higiene mental y delincuencia*, 115, quoted by C. Franz, 'La mala memoria de Allende', in *Letras Libres*, January 2006, 40.
13. Farías, *Salvador Allende contra los judíos*, and *Salvador Allende: El fin de un mito*.
14. Franco, *Cruel Modernity*, 63.

15. Cited in Traverso, *Origins of Nazi Violence*, 50.
16. C. Lombroso, *L'uomo delinquente*, 1876, cited in Traverso, *Origins of Nazi Violence*, 115,
17. Preston, *Spanish Holocaust*, 34.
18. Ibid., 36.
19. Jorquera, *El Chicho Allende*, 81.
20. P. Quiroga (ed.), *Salvador Allende Gossens: Obras Escogidas 1933–1948*, vol. I, Santiago: LAR, 1988, 59.
21. Gunder Frank, *Capitalism and Underdevelopment in Latin America*, 92–3.
22. Nolff, 'Industria manufacturera'.
23. See Nolff, 'Industria manufacturera', 162; also Gunder Frank, *Capitalism and Underdevelopment in Latin America*, 91, 98–120.
24. Extracts from London *Times*, 28 April 1891, and *El Mercurio*, 19 July 1964, cited in the journal *Vistazo*, 1964, also in Gunder Frank, *Capitalism and Underdevelopment in Latin America*, 93.
25. See Winn, 'The Furies of the Andes'; and Grandin, 'Don't do what Allende did'. See also Robin, 'Kissinger: Allende More Dangerous Than Castro'.

3 The Age of Anxiety

1. 'It's like the beginning of *Andalusian Dog* . . . Everything in our America is the beginning of that dog. Few times we have been able to see things straight without the knife or the razor emptying our eyes out.' In Cortázar, *Fantomas contra los vampiros multinacionales*, 45–6. Cortázar refers to the 1929 film *Un Chien Andalou*, by Luis Buñuel.
2. H. Kissinger to R. Nixon, 1970, NSA Archive, available at gwu.edu/ nsaarchiv/NSANEEB110/index; also Kornbluh, 'National Security Adviser Advocates a Hard-Line Toward Chile's Salvador Allende, 1970', in *The Pinochet File*, 121–8.
3. Moyn, *Last Utopia*, 1–10.
4. R. Parker, 'Russian War Zeal Lightens Big Task', in *New York Times*, 4 April 1942, also cited in Stone and Kuznick, *Untold History of the United States*, 106.
5. Ibid.
6. F. D. Roosevelt cited in Roosevelt, *As He Saw It*, 37; and Stone and Kuznick, *Untold History of the United States*, 112.
7. Losurdo, *Liberalism: A Counter-History*; also Guardiola-Rivera, *What If Latin America Ruled the World?*, 107–45.
8. Wallace, *The Price of Vision*, 635–40. See also H. Luce, 'The American Century', in *Life*, February 1941, 61–5.
9. G. Grandin, *Fordlandia*, Metropolitan Books, 2009.
10. Preston, *Spanish Holocaust*, 36.
11. H. Kissinger to R. Nixon, 1970, NSA Archive.
12. Ibid.
13. S. Allende, Archivo Salvador Allende, *América Latina: Un pueblo continente*, 1, Santiago, 1990, 15: 'Those who try to imitate the Cuban Revolution, in its tactics and methods, are making a huge mistake.' See also Debray, *Conversación con Allende*, 69–72.

14. Guevara, *Notes critiques d'économie politique*; R. Piglia, 'La lucha ideológica en la construcción socialista', in the journal *Los Libros: Para una crítica política de la cultura*, 25, 1972; and 'Ernesto Guevara: Rastros de lectura', in *El último lector*, Barcelona: Anagrama, 2005, 132; also Taibo II, *Arcángeles*; and J. Revueltas, 'Un fantasma recorre México', in *México 68: Juventud y Revolución*, México: Era, 197. The latter cited in Bosteels, *Marx and Freud in Latin America*.

15. See, for instance, Ribeiro, 'Allende y la izquierda desvariada'. See also García Linera, 'Indianismo y marxismo. El desencuentro de dos razones revolucionarias', in *La potencia plebeya*, 373–91.

16. H. Kissinger to R. Nixon, 1970.

17. Ibid.

18. Garcés, 'Prólogo', 30.

19. Bosteels, *Marx and Freud in Latin America*, 116–17, citing L. Rozitchner, *Ser Judío*, Buenos Aires: Ediciones de la Flor, 1967, 17.

20. Rozitchner, *Ser Judío*, 36.

21. F. Castro, 'La historia me absolverá', 16 October 1953, at www.granma. cubaweb.cu/marti-moncada/jm01, retrieved 12 January 2012.

22. Berger, *Bento's Sketchbook*, 79–80.

23. For the case of this argument in the work of Hegel concerning right, violence and 'necessity' (*Notrecht*), see Losurdo, *Hegel and the Freedom of Moderns*; and in the Americas, Bolívar, *Letter From Jamaica, 1815*. For a more contemporary appraisal, Sandel, *What Money Can't Buy*.

24. See McWhinney, *The International Court of Justice and the Western Tradition of International Law*; Pahuja, *Decolonising International Law*; Moyn, *Last Utopia*, 176–211; and Dosman, *Life and Times of Raúl Prebisch, 1901–1986*.

25. A telegram sent on 26 November 1938 and signed by Allende together with 75 other Chilean parliamentarians read: 'in the name of the principles of civilised life we express our strongest protest against the tragic persecution of the Jewish people in that country, and demand that His Excellency the Chancellor acts to put an end to it and restore the right to life and justice so humanely and eloquently reclaimed by President Roosevelt.' See Pey (ed.), *Salvador Allende*, xi. As a member of the Spanish Refugees Support Committee, Allende collaborated with the solidarity network that helped settle the refugees brought to Chile on board the *Winnipeg*, a trip organised by Neruda acting as Special Consul during the Popular Front government, of which Allende was a minister. Neruda had become radicalised in the wake of the murder of his friend Federico García Lorca by Francoist troops. In September 1945, Allende denounced in the Senate the complacency of the majority of the congressmen of the right with the Axis powers and the fascist side during the Spanish Civil War. See Martner (ed.), *Salvador Allende*, 134.

26. Martner (ed.), *Salvador Allende*, 143–5.

27. H. Braun, 'Populismos latinoamericanos', *Historia General de América Latina, VIII: América Latina desde 1930*, M. Palacios and G. Weinberg (eds), Madrid: Ediciones UNESCO & Editorial Trotta, 371–94.

28. Neruda cited in Feinstein, *Pablo Neruda*, 198.

29. Ibid.

30. Quoted in Feinstein, *Pablo Neruda*, 199–200.
31. Amorós, *Compañero Presidente*, 70; also Beckett, *Pinochet in Piccadilly*, 88; and Feinstein, *Pablo Neruda*, 194.
32. Garcés, 'Prólogo', in *Salvador Allende. Presente*, 30–1.
33. Prebisch, *The Economic Development of Latin America and Its Principal Problems*.
34. S. Allende, cited in Nolff, *Salvador Allende*, 63–4.
35. Dosman, *Life and Times of Raúl Prebisch*, 24–6.
36. Garcés, 'Prólogo', in *Salvador Allende. Presente*, 12–14; and Dosman, *Life and Times of Raúl Prebisch*, 25–6.
37. S. Allende, 'Discurso en la Cámara de Diputados, 7 de Junio de 1939', cited in Garcés, 'Prólogo', in *Salvador Allende. Presente*, 14–15.
38. Ibid.
39. S. Allende, in Martner (ed.), *Salvador Allende*, 188–91.
40. S. Allende cited in Lavretski, *Salvador Allende*, 64–5.
41. S. Allende, 'Discurso en la Cámara de Diputados, 7 de Junio de 1939', cited in Garcés, 'Prólogo', in *Salvador Allende. Presente*, 14–15.
42. Lazo and Cea, *La negra Lazo*. Also Guevara, 'Socialism and Man in Cuba', in *Che Guevara Reader*, 216ff.; T. Gutiérrez Alea and E. Desnoes, *Memories of Underdevelopment/Inconsolable Memories*, New Brunswick and London: Rutgers University Press, 1990; and L. Rozitchner, *Moral burguesa y revolución*, Buenos Aires: Procyon, 1963.
43. S. Allende, Archivo Salvador Allende, 11, 1990, 139–41.
44. Bosteels, *Marx and Freud in Latin America*, 47–8. He is citing L. Althusser, *For Marx*, trans. B. Brewster, Verso, 1969, 212. Also Amin, *Unequal Development*; and *Cambridge Review of International Affairs* 22, 2009. See Prebisch, *Economic Development of Latin America and Its Principal Problems*; Escobar, *Encountering Development*; and Leyva, *Latin American Neostructuralism*.
45. P. Neruda, 'The Crisis of Democracy in Chile is a Dramatic Warning for Our Continent', in *El Nacional*, 27 November 1947; also his collection of poems *Tercera residencia*, Buenos Aires: Losada, 1947.
46. Grandin, 'Introduction: Living in Revolutionary Time', in *A Century of Revolution*, 17.
47. Ibid. Grandin cites Mayer, *Dynamics of Counterrevolution in Europe, 1870–1956*; and *Why Did the Heavens Not Darken?* See also Boron, 'El fascismo como categoría histórica'.
48. Winn, *Weavers of the Revolution*; and 'Furies of the Andes', 239–40.
49. Grandin, 'Introduction: Living in Revolutionary Time', 18; and Winn, 'Furies of the Andes', 239–75, both in *A Century of Revolution*, ed. Grandin and Joseph.

4 Dawn of the New Man

1. Muñoz, 'The Internationalist Policy of the Socialist Party and Foreign Relations of Chile', 153. He concludes: 'Unlike the various nationalist-populist experiments in Latin America, Cuba was to build socialism from below and not as the imposition of foreign troops.'
2. *Brown v. Board of Education*, 347 U.S. 483. In 1951 Oliver L. Brown and twelve other parents had filed a class action against the Board of Education

of Topeka, Kansas, on behalf of their twenty children, calling for the school district to reverse its policy of racial segregation. The decision declared the doctrine of 'separate but equal facilities' unconstitutional.

3. Stone and Kuznick, *Untold History of the United States*, 274–5.

4. Quoted in Stone and Kuznick, *Untold History of the United States*, 275.

5. Fidel Castro invoked Thomas Jefferson, Thomas Paine and the Founding Fathers in his famous 1953 trial speech, *History Will Absolve Me*, 63–4.

6. See Schrecker, *Many Are the Crimes*; and Stone and Kuznick, *Untold History of the United States*, 212 (quoting an Interior Department Loyalty Board chairman: 'Of course the fact that a person believes in racial equality doesn't prove that he's a communist, but it certainly makes you look twice') and 234. See also Hobsbawm, *Fractured Times*, 27.

7. Salvatore, 'The Enterprise of Knowledge', 83. On the erasure of persistent racism and anti-slavery conflict from Chilean history see V. Vidal, 'La esclavitud en Chile', in *Revista Punto Final*, no. 767, 28 September 2012; G. Feliú, *La Abolición de la Esclavitud en Chile*, Santiago: Ed. Cormorán, 2nd edition, 1973.

8. Salvatore, 'The Enterprise of Knowledge', 83–4.

9. Findlay, 'Love in the tropics', 139.

10. Reproduced from J. J. Johnson, *Latin America in Caricature*, 127, in Findlay, 'Love in the tropics', 144.

11. Stone and Kuznick, *Untold History of the United States*, 275. As the authors observe, three days after Sputnik's launch the USSR anounced it had successfully tested a new ballistic missile-compatible thermonuclear warhead. The sequence thereby opened up would be closed by the events of the Cuban Missile Crisis of 1962.

12. S. Allende in Debray, *Conversación con Allende*, 69–72; also quoted in Amorós, *Compañero Presidente*, 91.

13. A. March cited in Buergo Rodríguez, *Salvador Allende y el Che Guevara: iguales y diferentes*, available in www.rebelion-org/noticia.php?id=68161, last retrieved 4 April 2013. Buergo cites Allende's interview with R. Debray.

14. S. Allende in Debray, *Conversación con Allende*, 69–72.

15. Guevara, *The Motorcycle Diaries*, Introduction.

16. Guevara, *Diarios de motocicleta*, 87.

17. Ibid., 113.

18. Ibid., 114.

19. Guevara, 'El socialismo y el hombre en Cuba' and 'Socialism and Man in Cuba'. See also Yaffe, *Che Guevara*, 199–232, and Bosteels, *Marx and Freud in Latin America*, 97–127.

20. Guevara, *Diarios de motocicleta*, 114–15.

21. Ibid., 115.

22. See *Jodorowsky's Dune* at www.youtube.com/#/watch?v=Q-oBEG-F7uwE, last retrieved 1 May 2013. Also Calder Williams, *Combined and Uneven Apocalypse*; and Bolaño, 'The Colonel's Son'. On law and prophecy in current human rights theory, see Meister, *After Evil*, 286–304.

23. Guevara, *Diarios de motocicleta*, 118.

24. Ibid.

25. 'Four Forrestal Suicide Bids, Says Pearson', *Los Angeles Times*, 23 May 1949; also cited in Stone and Kuznick, *Untold History of the United States*, 225, n. 129.

26. Einstein, *Einstein on Politics*, 404.

27. On national security as the 'sacred word' of US politics, see Fidel Castro interviewed by Oliver Stone, *Comandante* (O. Stone, 2002 & Optimum Releasing 2004). On the Red Scare and the 'Lavender Scare' in the US see Stone and Kuznick, *Untold History of the United States*, 225–9; Schrecker, *Many Are the Crimes*; and D. K. Johnson, *The Lavender Scare*.

28. Faulkner, Nobel Prize Banquet Speech, 10 December 1950, at www.nobelprize.org/nobel_prizes/literature/laureates/1949/faulkner-speech, last retrieved 4 April 2013.

29. Guevara, *Diarios de motocicleta*, 129.

30. S. Allende citing Guevara in Debray, *Conversación con Allende*, 69–72.

31. Gadea, *My Life With Che*, cited by T. Gjelten in his review of the book for the *Washington Post*, 12 October 2008.

32. See J. Stauber and S. Rampton's review of L. Tye's *The Father of Spin: Edward L. Bernays and the Birth of Public Relations*, cited in the BBC documentary *The Century of the Self* (Adam Curtis, 2008); also Stone and Kuznick, *Untold History of the United States,* 262.

33. Westad, *The Global Cold War*, Cambridge: Cambridge University Press, 2007, 149.

34. S. Allende, defending Árbenz's reforms before the Chilean Senate on 4 December 1956, against right-wing senators branding them 'communist', in *Archivo Salvador Allende, América Latina: Un Pueblo Continente*, 1, 127–8.

35. See Prats, *Memorias: Testimonio de un soldado*, 597–8.

36. S. Allende in Debray, *Conversaciòn con Allende*, 69–72.

37. Kapuscinski, 'Guevara y Allende'; also *Cristo con un fusil al hombro*.

38. Kapuscinski, 'Guevara y Allende'.

39. See Zolo, *Victor's Justice*, and Arendt, *Eichmann in Jerusalem*.

40. Grandin, 'Don't do what Allende did'.

41. Ibid.

42. Medina, *Cybernetic Revolutionaries*.

5 A Long Cold War

1. Beer, 'Laws of Anarchy', 'Cybernetics of Humankind', 'An Open Letter to Heinz von Foerster (About Social Cybernetics)', and 'The Will of the People'. Also Wellman et al., 'The Social Affordances of the Internet for Networked Individualism'.

2. Castells, 'Communication, Power and Counter-power in the Network Society'; Hogge, *Barefoot into Cyberspace*; Miéville, *London's Overthrow*. Crucially for the orientation of this book, the questions raised herein can be traced back to two classical and controversial texts on the left: Marx, *On the Jewish Question* and *Fragment on Machines*. See Marx, *Grundrisse*, Harmondsworth, 1973, 704–11, together with E. Dussel, *La Producción teórica de Marx: Un comentario a los Grundrisse*, Méjico: Siglo veintiuno editores, 1985; and P. Virno, 'General Intellect', *Lessico Posfordista*, Milan,

2001, available in English at www.generation-online.org/p/fpvirno10 or C. Marazzi, *The Violence of Financial Capitalism*, Los Angeles: Semiotext(e), 2010; and F. Berardi and G. Lovinck, 'A Call to the Army of Love and to the Army of Software', 13 October 2011, at www.lists.thing.net/paper-mail/idc/2011-October/004867, all last retrieved in April 2013.

3. Mason, *Why It's Still Kicking Off Everywhere*, 131.

4. Guevara, 'Reuniones bimestrales', 149.

5. See Yaffe, *Che Guevara*, 200. In Spanish the term *conciencia* means both moral conscience and consciousness as an emerging awareness, related to truthful-ness as opposed to being in possession of truth or knowledge (including technological knowledge) and being able to charge a price for it. This links up Guevara's lifelong interest in psychology (at twenty-five he described himself as a 'psychoanalyst of dogmas') with the enduring and relevant ques-tion of the price of truth on the one hand, and on the other, with the forms of voluntary and communitarian labour present in the cultural legacy and institutions of indigenous peoples across the Americas. See on this 'Derroteros de la colonialidad y descolonización del pensamiento. Diálogo entre S Yampara, M Hardt, P Mamani, G Cocco, JJ Bautista, J Revel & L Tapia', in *Imperio, multitud y sociedad abigarrada*, Buenos Aires: CLACSO & Waldhuter Editores, 2010, 169–202; also Henáff, *The Price of Truth*.

6. See on this, Yaffe's highly original *Che Guevara*, 163–98, at 166.

7. Weiner, *Legacy of Ashes: The History of the CIA*, 162–3.

8. Kennedy, *On the Alliance for Progress, 1961, Modern History Sourcebook*.

9. Stone and Kuznick, *Untold History of the United States*, 292.

10. 'A Policy on Cuba', *New York Times*, 27 April 1961.

11. Stone and Kuznick, *Untold History of the United States*, 303.

12. Talbot, *Brothers: The Hidden History of the Kennedy Years*, 50–1.

13. Ibid., 95.

14. The Joint Chiefs of Staff, Washington D.C., 13 March 1962, 'Memorandum for the Secretary of Defense: Justification for US Military Intervention in Cuba', at www.gwu.edu/≈nsarchiv/news/20010430/northwoods.pdf. Following presentation of Northwoods, Kennedy removed the chairman of the JCS, who began to perceive the US president as soft on Cuba. The increasing unpopularity of Kennedy within the military came to a head during the Missile crisis of 1962. See also Bamford, *Body of Secrets*, 82.

15. F. Castro in conversation with O. Stone, in *Comandante* (O. Stone, 2005).

16. Stone and Kuznick, *Untold History of the United States*, 309–13.

17. S. Allende in F. Casanueva and M. Fernández, *El partido socialista y la lucha de clases en Chile*, Santiago: Quimantu, 1973, 201.

18. S. Allende, Intervención frente al Senado Chileno, 27 July 1960, in *Archivo Salvador Allende*, 1, 1990, 59–83.

19. S. Allende, 'A dónde va América Latina?', *Arauco*, August 1964, in *Archivo Salvador Allende*, 1, 1990, 17–23.

20. S. Allende, Intervención frente al Senado Chileno, 27 July 1960, in *Archivo Salvador Allende*, 1, 1990, 59–83.

21. S. Allende, 'A dónde va América Latina?' *Arauco*, August 1964, in *Archivo Salvador Allende*, 1, 1990, 17–23.

22. Martner (ed.), *Salvador Allende*, 200–1.

23. Ibid.
24. FRAP, *Programa del Gobierno Popular*, 12–13.
25. *The Times*, 28 April 1891; and *El Mercurio*, 19 July 1964, both cited in Gunder Frank, *Capitalism and Underdevelopment in Latin America*, 93.
26. Richard, *Crítica de la memoria (1990–2010)*, 54–68, at 57.
27. Fernández Fernández, 'La Teología de la Liberación en Chile'.
28. Richard, *Crítica de la memoria (1990–2010)*, 58–9.
29. Ibid.
30. Ibid.
31. Beer, 'The Chilean Experience', in *Think Before You Think*, 362–75; and Medina, *Cybernetic Revolutionaries*, 1–2.
32. S. Allende, 'A dónde va América Latina?', *Arauco*, August 1964, in *Archivo Salvador Allende*, 1, 1990, 17–23.
33. Arrate and Rojas, Memoria, 428.
34. Dorfman, *The Empire's Old Clothes*, Introduction.
35. Cortázar, *Fantomas contra los vampiros multinacionales*.
36. See Castells, 'Communication, Power and Counter-Power in the Network Society'.
37. Kinzer, *Overthrow: America's Century of Regime Change from Hawaii to Iraq*, 175–6; Grayson, *El partido Demócrata Cristiano chileno*, 358–64; Amorós, *Compañero Presidente*, 111, n. 9, citing the *Washington Star* and *Noticias Aliadas*, no. 416, Lima, 25 September 1975, 3; also Stone and Kuznick, *Untold History of the United States*, 372.
38. Beckett, *Pinochet in Piccadilly*, 89.
39. Ibid.
40. S. Allende, *Archivo Salvador Allende, Rumbo de Liberación*, 5, México, 1990, 227–42.

6 The Chilean Way Versus the Multinational Vampires

1. Guevara, *Notes critiques d'économie politique*. As the book's editor, Maria del Carmen Ariet, observes, Guevara's criticism was not directed just to the theoretical shortcomings of Russia's official *Manual of Political Economy* but 'to a number of problems emanating from USSR's reality itself . . . Practice demonstrated the risk involved in the adoption of the Soviet conception of Marxism transformed into a general rule,' that could be imported and applied everywhere. Guevara's conviction at the time is parallel to Allende's conclusion that those who thought to transplant revolutionary experiences – Soviet or Cuban – elsewhere, 'make a huge mistake'. See S. Allende, *Archivo Salvador Allende*, 1, 1990, 15.
2. Goodwin, *Lyndon Johnson and the American Dream*, 95, 230, 251.
3. Ibid.; Young, *The Vietnam Wars, 1945–1990*, 106; McNamara, *In Retrospect: The Tragedy and Lessons of Vietnam*, 337–43; and Mitchell, 'Okinawa's First Nuclear Missile Men Break Silence'; Stone and Kuznick, *Untold History of the United States*, 311–18. For JFK's 1963 American University adress, cited below, see J. F. Kennedy, *Public Papers of the Presidents of the United States John F. Kennedy 1963*, Washington: US Government Printing Office, 1964, 459–64.
4. Daniel, 'When Castro Heard the News'.

5. Guevara, 'Man and Socialism in Cuba', in B. Silverman (ed.), *Man and Socialism in Cuba: The Great Debate*, New York: Atheneum, 1971, 343.

6. For Rawls's 'reasonable pluralism' see among others *The Law of Peoples*. For a critical view on Rawls's pluralism, which I endorse here, Pogee, *World Poverty*, and 'Priorities of Global Justice'. See also Baxi, 'The Death and Rebirth of Distributive Justice' and 'The Failure of Deliberative Democracy and Global Justice'; and De Sousa Santos, *Toward a New Common Sense*.

7. Baxi, *Human Rights in a Posthuman World*, 97.

8. Guevara, *Global Justice*, 6–7 and 18–21.

9. Ibid., 19.

10. Ibid., 21–2.

11. Baxi, *Human Rights in a Posthuman World*, 101–2.

12. Allende in Martner (ed.), *Salvador Allende*, 200–1.

13. S. Allende, Senate Speech, 27 July 1960, in *Archivo Salvador Allende*, 1, 1990, 59–83.

14. Guevara, 'Tareas industriales de la revolución (Marzo 1962)', in *Ernesto Che Guevara: Escritos y discursos*, La Habana: Ciencias Sociales, 1977, vol. 6, 103.

15. Guevara, 'Quelques réflexions sur la transition socialiste. Ernesto Guevara à Fidel Castro, Avril 1965', in *Notes critiques d'économie politique*, 25. See M. del Carmen Ariet García, 'Note éditoriale en préambule à l'édition cubaine', in Guevara, *Notes critiques d'économie politique*, 16, n. 1.

16. Kennedy cited in Daniel, 'An Historic Report from Two Capitals'.

17. Ibid.

18. Ibid.

19. Ibid.

20. See Guardiola-Rivera, *Being Against the World*, 242–57; Malabou, *Ontology of the Accident*, and 'From the Overman to the Posthuman', delivered 22 March 2013 at the Institute of Education, London; J.-P. Dupuy, 'Faire comme si le pire était inévitable', in Yves Cochet, J.-P. Dupuy, Susan George and Serge Latouche, *Où va le monde? 2012–2022: une décennie au devant des catastrophes*, Paris: Mille et Une Nuits, 2012, 21–44; and Mason, *Why It's Still Kicking Off Everywhere*, 127–52.

21. Castro's response to Kennedy, cited in Daniel, 'An Historic Report from Two Capitals'.

22. Ibid.

23. Ibid.

24. Schmitz, *Thank God They're On Our Side*, 265.

25. Smith, *Brazil and the United States*, 161.

26. US Senate, *Covert Action in Chile: 1963–1973*, US Government Printing Office, Washington, 1975; Garcés, *Soberanos e intervenidos*, 138; Amorós, *Compañero Presidente*, 104.

27. 'Text of Johnson's Address on US Moves in the Conflict in the Dominican Republic', in *New York Times*, 3 May 1965; a CIA memo stating that up to eight Castroite agents might be in the Dominican Republic also clarified 'there is no evidence that the Castro regime is directly involved in the current insurrection'. For Bosch's declarations, see H. Bigart, 'Bosch Gives His Version of Revolt', *New York Times*, 8 May 1965, both cited in Stone and Kuznick, *Untold History of the United States*, 346.

28. S. Allende, cited in Amorós, *Compañero Presidente*, 114–15.
29. See J. F. Sombra Saravia, 'Las nuevas relaciones internacionales', in *Historia General de América Latina, VIII: América Latina desde 1930*, M. Palacios and G. Weinberg (eds), Madrid: Ediciones UNESCO/Editorial Trotta, 2008, 339–52. For a critical assessment of contributions to the development of International Law see Pahuja, *Decolonising International Law*, and Salomon, 'Winners and Others: Accounting for International Law's Favourites'.
30. S. Allende, in Modak (ed.), *Salvador Allende en el umbral del siglo XXI*, 299–301.
31. Guevara cited by Tirso Sáenz in an interview with Helen Yaffe, 7 January 2005, in Yaffe, *Che Guevara*, 71, n. 6.
32. Quezada Lagos, *La elección presidencial de 1970*, 41; Pujades and Alsina, *Xile al cor*, 426–8, also cited in Amorós, *Compañero Presidente*, 125.
33. Winn, *Weavers of Revolution*; Fernández Fernández, *La teología de la liberación en Chile*, 249–65; Amorós, *Compañero Presidente*, 126–9; Beckett, *Pinochet in Piccadilly*, 94–5.
34. Winn, *Weavers of Revolution*. The Yarur textile mill was founded by Palestinian-born Juan Yarur, grew during the Second World War on the back of decreasing Japanese cheaper imports, and became an empire that extended into finance with the help of US technical and financial assistance during the 1940s and 1950s. It contributed significantly to the political campaigns of Ibáñez (1952–8), Alessandri (1958–64) and Frei (1964–70). Yarur's sons Amador and Jorge introduced the Taylor system of management that provoked the 1962 strike, broken violently by the Alessandri government.
35. See LaRosa, 'Review of Peter Winn's Weavers of Revolution'; and Gordon, *Existentia Africana*, 26.
36. See on this Simón Yampara's contribution in *Imperio, multitud y sociedad abigarrada*, T. Negri, M. Hardt, G. Cocco, J. Revel, Á. García Linera, L. Tapia et al., Buenos Aires: CLACSO & Waldhuter Editores, 2010, 169–75; also García Linera, 'Indianismo y Marxismo: El desencuentro de dos razones revolucionarias', in *La potencia plebeya*, 373–92. For a critical analysis of the Chilean case by one of Allende's close advisers, Ribeiro, 'Allende y la izquierda desvariada'; Winn, 'Furies of the Andes', 247; and Foerster and Montecino, *Organizaciones, líderes y contiendas mapuches*, 285–7.
37. See Klubock, 'Ránquil: Violence and Peasant Politics on Chile's Southern Frontier'.
38. R. Morales Urra, 'Cultura mapuche en la dictadura', in *Revista Austral de Ciencias Sociales*, Universidad Austral de Chile, no. 3, 1999, 81–108; Carter, 'Chile's Other History'; and Cayuqueo, 'Tiempo de esperanzas'.
39. According to the statistics of the Valech Report on human rights violations during the dictatorship, 47 per cent of those tortured were between twenty and thirty years old. See Ramis, 'Genealogía de una generación maldita'.
40. J. Straw, 'Can Frei Reform Chile?', in *Tribune*, cited in Beckett, *Pinochet in Piccadilly*, 94–5.
41. 'Some people were scandalised by the fact that a Communist poet had such expensive tastes,' writes Jorge Edwards, 'but the . . . justification was pretty simple . . . Socialism was built precisely, among other things, so that poets

and creators could consume a magnum of Dom Pérignon every now and then.' See Neruda, *Memoirs*, 318–19; J. Edwards, *Adiós, Poeta*, Barcelona: Tusquets, 1974, 86 and 206; also cited in Feinstein, *Pablo Neruda*, 305–6.

42. Varas, *Nerudario*, 245–6.
43. Feinstein, *Pablo Neruda*, 367, 374.
44. García Márquez, 'Why Allende Had to Die'.
45. Harmer, *Allende's Chile and the Inter-American Cold War*, 9.
46. García Márquez, 'Why Allende Had to Die'.
47. Hersh, *Price of Power*, 263. Ramón Huidobro, who was present at the meeting between Kissinger and Valdés, confirmed its accuracy to Tanya Harmer during an interview on 28 October 2004. See Harmer, *Allende and the Inter-American Cold War*, 39, n. 100.
48. For the idea of *terra nullius* in the evolution of international legal rules concerning the acquisition of title to territory, see *Western Sahara: Advisory Opinion, International Court of Justice Reports* 1975, 12, 83–7; also Bedjaoui, *Terra Nullius, 'droits' historiques et autodétermination*, 1975, and 'Non-alignement et Droit International', cited in McWhinney, *The International Court of Justice and the Western Tradition of International Law*, 5. On the nineteenth-century version and its impact on current scholarship and policy, see Davis, 'A Compendium of the Obvious. A Review of Jared Diamond's "The World Until Yesterday"'.
49. See Guardiola-Rivera, *What If Latin America Ruled the World?*, 54–66; also Wey Gómez, *Tropics of Empire*.
50. Cited in Hitchens, *Trial of Henry Kissinger*, 55.
51. Grandin, 'Don't do what Allende did'. He cites the work of Seymour Hersh, based on conversations with an NSC staffer.
52. Ibid. See also Harmer, *Allende's Chile and the Inter-American Cold War*, 8.
53. Grandin, 'Don't do what Allende did'.

7 *The Revolution Will Be Televised*

1. Amorós, *Compañero Presidente*, 136.
2. Trumper, 'Ephemeral Histories', 144–5, citing Pierre Nora and David Harvey.
3. R. Matta quoted in Trumper, 'Ephemeral Histories', 145.
4. P. Nora cited in Trumper, 'Ephemeral Histories', 143–4.
5. A. González quoted in Trumper, 'Ephemeral Histories', 145.
6. Ibid.
7. Francis, *La victoria de Allende*, 130–2, also cited in Amorós, *Compañero Presidente*, 135.
8. Collier and Sater, *History of Chile, 1808–2002*, 280.
9. S. Allende, cited in Grandin, 'Don't do what Allende did'.
10. For a more recent version of this conception of law, which has its proximate origins in Sartre–Guevara's political ethics of global responsibility, and further back in the classical tradition of Platonic equality, see Badiou, 'Politics: a Non-Expressive Dialectics'. For remedial equality in terms of human rights, Meister, *After Evil*, 232–316. For the connection with Sartre, Guevara and decolonising strategies, building on the Nuremberg

principles, Arthur, *Unfinished Projects*, 139–76. Also Baxi, *Human Rights in a Posthuman World*, 76–155.

11. Deleuze and Guattari, *A Thousand Plateaus: Capitalism and Schizophrenia*, 448. Like Foucault, Guattari also spent time in Latin America and got involved in the politics of the 1970s. See Rolnik and Guattari, *Molecular Revolution in Brazil*.

12. Grandin, 'Don't do what Allende did'.

13. UK Election Statistics 1945–2003, Research paper 03/59, 1 July 2003; General Elections Results: 1979–2010, Paper SN/SG/2632 at www.parliament.uk/Templates/BriefingPapers/Pages/BPPdfDownload.aspx?bp-id=SN02632, last retrieved 16 May 2013.

14. Grandin, 'Don't do what Allende did'.

15. Cited in Amorós, *Compañero Presidente*, 152.

16. Colby and Forbath, *Honourable Men: My Life in the CIA*, 303.

17. US Congress, Senate, *Alleged Assassination Plots Involving Foreign Leaders, Interim Report of the Select Committee to Study Government Operations with Respect to Intelligence Activities, 94th Congress, 2nd Session*, Washington, DC: US Government Printing Office, 20 November 1975, p. 227. Also Hitchens, *Trial of Henry Kissinger*, 55–6; Amorós, *Compañero Presidente*, 149; N. Guzmán (ed.), *Chile desclasificado*, 17.

18. See Harmer, *Allende's Chile and the Inter-American Cold War*, 51, 61, 69, 72, 126–32; Kornbluh, *Pinochet File*.

19. Cited in Grandin, 'Don't do what Allende did'. Nixon said to Kissinger: 'Our hand doesn't show in this one' – also cited in Grandin.

20. Memorandum of Conversation, the US President et al., The Cabinet Room, 9:40 a.m., 6 November 1970, in Kornbluh, *Pinochet File*, 116–20; and Memorandum, 'Covert Action Program for Chile', 17 November 1970. Also Harmer, *Allende's Chile & the Inter-American Cold War*, 70.

21. Cited in Harmer, *Allende's Chile & the Inter-American Cold War*, 58.

22. Pinochet, interview with Finis Terrae University researchers, cited in Muñoz, *Dictator's Shadow*, 31.

23. Cable, CIA Headquarters to Santiago Station, 'As you will be advised', 27 September 1970. So-called 'false-flag officers' or 'false-flaggers' operate under a false third-party passport. The aim is to increase the 'plausible deniability' of an operation, if compromised.

24. Cable, CIA Headquarters to Santiago Station, 'Highest Levels Here Continue', 7 October 1970.

25. Memorandum, Edward Korry to Crimmins, 11 August, 1970. State Department cables accessed at www.foia.state.gov/SearchColls/CollsSearch.asp>. All cables/memoranda retrieved 14 March 2012. Korry was in fact trying to dissuade Washington from contacting Viaux and Fatherland and Freedom.

26. Memorandum for the Record, CIA, 23 September 1970; Memorandum, Chile Station to CIA Headquarters, 'Intelligence', 26 September 1970; Cable, Santiago Station to CIA Headquarters, 'There is a possibility that coup attempt', 23 September 1970.

27. Memorandum, 'Track II', 12 October 1970.

28. Cable, Santiago Station to CIA Headquarters, 'Station has arrived at Viaux Solution', 10 October 1970.

29. Memorandum, 'Situation Report for Military Move', 13 October 1970.

30. Cable, Santiago Station to CIA HQ, 'Meeting Requested', 16 October 1970.

31. Cable, Santiago Station to CIA HQ, 'Chronology of Events 18 October', 19 October 1970.

32. Hitchens, *Trial of Henry Kissinger*, 63.

33. Ruiz-Esquide Figueroa, *Las Fuerzas Armadas Durante Los Gobiernos de Eduardo Frei y Salvador Allende*, 51.

34. Agüero, 'A Political Army in Chile'.

35. Cable transmissions from US Ambassador Edward Korry, 1 October 1970.

36. Cable, CIA HQ to Santiago, 'Depending How Conversation Goes', 18 October 1970. Also Hitchens, *Trial of Henry Kissinger*, 63–4, citing the cable.

37. Cable, CIA HQ to Santiago, 'Depending How Conversation Goes'.

38. Ibid. Also, Cable, CIA HQ to Santiago Station, 'Realize this Message', 19 October 1970.

39. Hitchens, *Trial of Henry Kissinger*, 63–4.

40. Cable, Santiago Station to CIA HQ, 'Headquarters Will Have Noted', 22 October 1970.

41. Cable, Santiago Station to CIA HQ, 'Although Security Still Tight', 29 October 1970.

42. Memorandum of Conversation, 'Dr. Kissinger, Mr. Karamessines, Gen. Haig at the White House', 15 October 1970.

43. Hitchens, *Trial of Henry Kissinger*, 63–4.

44. Dorfman, *Empire's Old Clothes*, Introduction.

45. Dorfman, *Other Septembers, Many Americas*, 56.

46. Foucault, *Society Must Be Defended*, 15; also Deleuze and Guattari, *A Thousand Plateaus*, 466–9. The result is not anomie but an explosion of top-down regulations that can be added or subtracted at will: anarcho-capitalism or 'neoliberalism', but also the abandonment of the axiom of full employment.

47. Dorfman, *Other Septembers, Many Americas*, 56.

8 The Flies, Act I

1. Collier and Sater, *A History of Chile, 1808–2002*, 343. Also Amorós, *Compañero Presidente*, 225.

2. Winn, 'Furies of the Andes', 241.

3. Collier and Sater, *A History of Chile, 1808–2002*, 333.

4. Guevara, *Notes critiques d'économie politique*, 19–34, 247 ff. Also M. Desai, 'Foreword', in Yaffe, *Che Guevara*, viii–x.

5. S. Allende, 4 March 1971, in Martner (ed.), *Salvador Allende*, 32–6.

6. Ibid.

7. S. Allende, 28 January 1971, in Farías, *La izquierda chilena (1969–1973)*, 623–35.

8. Novoa Monreal et al., *La vía chilena al socialismo*, 44.

9. Moyn, *Last Utopia*, 96.

10. Ibid., 97.

11. Cited in Foucault, *The Birth of Biopolitics*, 80. He quotes F. Bilger, *La Pensée économique libérale de l'Allemagne contemporaine*, Paris: Librairie Générale de Droit, 1964, 211.

12. Foucault, *The Birth of Biopolitics*, 81.

13. Ibid., 84–5.

14. Preston, *Spanish Holocaust*, 34–51.

15. Pinilla de las Heras, *En menos de libertad*, 67–8; I. Jara Hinojosa, *De Franco a Pinochet: El proyecto cultural Franquista en Chile, 1936–1980*, citing G. Fernández de la Mora, *Contradicciones de la partitocracia*, Madrid: Embos-cadura, [1976] 2008.

16. C. Montesinos, M. J. Pavlovic and G. Piergentili, *A diez años de su muerte: El legado político de Jaime Guzmán en la UDI hoy*, A. Santibáñez (thesis super-visor), 13, available at www.archivochile.com/tesis/04_tp0012.pdf, last viewed 23 April 2013.

17. Cited in Preston, *Spanish Holocaust*, 47.

18. See Sombart, *Deutscher Sozialismus*. Together with Max Weber, he repre-sented the last vanguard of the German historical school. Although first reputed a socialist, he adhered to the Führer principle and the programme of the conservative revolution. He taught economics at Berlin and joined the Academy for German Law in 1933. See Foucault, *Birth of Biopolitics*, 112–14.

19. Preston, *Spanish Holocaust*, 47–8.

20. J. Guzmán, *Escritos Personales*, 33.

21. UNGA Resolution 1803 (XVII), 14 December 1962; also A. Kilangi, 'Introductory Note', at www.untreaty.un.org/cod/avl/ha/ga_1803, retrieved 13 January 2013.

22. Collier and Sater, *A History of Chile, 1808–2002*, 276–85.

23. *El Diario Ilustrado*, 21 May 1966, Santiago.

24. For links between Fatherland and Freedom and the CIA, which funded its activities, and their collusion in acts of terror and human rights violations, see Stohl and Lopez, *The State as Terrorist*, 51.

25. F. Willoughby speaking to E. Bucat, see Bucat, *Preparativos golpistas*.

26. Martorell, 'Lo que la DINA escribió sobre Jaime Guzmán'. He cites secret memos from Chile's National Intelligence Directorate (DINA) dated 3 November 1976.

27. See *La Segunda*, 27 September 2000, at ar.groups.yahoo.com/group/chile-l/message/43973. Also Winn, 'Furies of the Andes', 266; Rojas, *Murder of Allende*, ch. 3; López, 'Dos periodistas CIA: Asesinato de Kennedy y Chile'; and Willson, Wiss and Wood Mac Ewan, 'Nosotros acusamos', at inverecun-dos.blogia.com/2009/050306--nosotros-acusamos-federico-willoughby-mac-donald-a-gerad-wood-mc-ewan-.php, last viewed 25 April 2013.

28. Ibid.

29. Memorandum, DINA, 17 November 1976, cited in Martorell, 'Lo que la DINA escribió sobre Jaime Guzmán'. See also www.emol.com/noticias/nacional/2007/08/13/265759/fundador-de-patria-y-libertad-jaime-guzman, retrieved 4 April 2013.

30. See www.inverecundos.blogia . . . cited in note 27 above.

31. Montecino, *Madres y huachos*, 101–8; Richard, *Crítica de la memoria (1990–2010)*, 54–68; Winn, 'Furies of the Andes', 255.

32. Rojas, *Murder of Allende*, ch. 3.
33. Ibid.
34. Collier and Sater, *A History of Chile, 1808–2002*, 343.
35. Rojas, *Murder of Allende*, ch. 3.
36. Ibid.
37. F. Willoughby in conversation with E. Bucat, *Preparativos golpistas*, 1–2.
38. Rojas, *Murder of Allende*, ch. 3.
39. Ibid.
40. Medina, *Cybernetic Revolutionaries*, 17.
41. Dupuy, *The Mechanization of the Mind*, 8.
42. Ibid., 9–11, 33–44, and for the impact of these ideas in social thought and practice, from Hayek's anarcho-capitalism to post-Althusserian Marxism, including principles of government as collective problem-solving, 156–61.
43. Dorfman, *The Empire's Old Clothes*, Introduction.
44. F. Flores, Letter to Stafford Beer, 13 July 1971, box 55, Stafford Beer collection, cited in Medina, *Cybernetic Revolutionaries*, 15–16.
45. Medina, *Cybernetic Revolutionaries*, 5.
46. Ibid., 33.
47. Beer, 'The Will of the People', in *Think Before You Think*, 94–112. My gratitude to David Whittaker for his correspondence, and for bringing these materials to my attention. Also Medina, *Cybernetic Revolutionaries*, 33.
48. Martin and Rosenhead, 'Obituary: Stafford Beer'. See also Gibson, 'Burning Chrome'. Beer's obituary is cited in Medina, *Cybernetic Revolutionaries*, 19.
49. Beer, *Brain of the Firm*, 239. Sartre, *Critique of Dialectical Reason*, vol. 1, 45–8. Guevara, *Notes critiques d'économie politique*, 25, 182–3, 287–91.
50. For all quotes, see Medina, *Cybernetic Revolutionaries*, 74–5.
51. Ibid., 74–6.
52. Castells, 'Communication, Power and Counter-Power in the Network Society'.
53. Medina, *Cybernetic Revolutionaries*, 148; she cites both Grandi and Flores as sources.
54. Ibid., 166.
55. Ibid.
56. Rojas, *Murder of Allende*, ch. 3.
57. Ibid.
58. Medina, *Cybernetic Revolutionaries*, 166.
59. Mendieta, 'The Ethics of (Not) Knowing'.
60. The reference here is double: first to D. Whittaker's letter to the *Guardian*, 9 September 2003, regarding Beer's involvement in Chile as aiming to develop 'a new model of participatory democracy where there is no hierarchy', and to Beer, *Designing Freedom* and *Beyond Dispute*. Second, to an eighteenth-century account of the 19 May 1779 mass meeting in New York City in response to the British blockade of Boston Harbour, 'Gouverneur Morris to John Penn, May 20, 1774', in *The Life of Gouverneur Morris: With Selections From His Correspondence and Miscellaneous Papers*, Boston: Grey & Bowen, 1830, 24–5; also cited in Graeber, *The Democracy Project*, 160.

61. Prats, *Memorias: Testimonio de un soldado*, 597–8.
62. See, for concrete evidence, Solnit, *A Paradise Built in Hell*; and Leeson, 'Better Off Stateless: Somalia Before and After Government Collapse', both cited in Graeber, *The Democracy Project*, 207. Also Gordon and Gordon, *Of Divine Warning: Reading Disaster in the Modern Age*; and Dupuy, 'Faire comme si le pire était inevitable', in Dupuy et al., *Où va le monde?*, 21–44, for a perspective on people's responses to disaster that mixes up phenomenology and cybernetics.
63. S. Beer and D. Whittaker, 'The Chilean Experience', in Beer, *Think Before You Think*, 362–75, at 373.
64. García Márquez's novel was greatly influential in framing Beer's attitudes towards Latin America. See Medina, *Cybernetic Revolutionaries*, 98.
65. Beer, *Think Before You Think*, 372; also correspondence between Stafford Beer and David Whitaker, 22 March 1981, Christmas Eve, 1982 and 14 January 1982, available in Whittaker, *Stafford Beer: A Personal Memoir*, 9–13. My gratitude to David Whittaker for providing me with access to these materials.

9 The Flies, Act II

1. Prats, *Memorias: Testimonio de un soldado*, 597–8.
2. Cable, COS, Santiago to DCI, 14 March 1973, CDP-CIA.
3. UN General Assembly Resolution 1803 (XVII), 14 December 1962. According to A. Kilangi, the resolution resulted from the UNGA's focus on 'the promotion and financing of economic development in under-developed countries . . . and in connection with the right of peoples to self-determination in the draft international covenants on human rights'. At www.untreaty.un.org/cod/avl/ha/ga_1803/ga_1803.
4. B. Allende, interviewed by L. I. López, 'Imagen de Beatriz Allende'.
5. See Amorós, *Compañero Presidente*, 223.
6. S. Allende, *Archivo Salvador Allende*, 1980, 8: 73–81.
7. Ibid., 1989, 13: 157–9.
8. Memorandum of conversation, Letelier and Davis, Santiago, undated, Telegram, Davis to SecState, 23 November 1972, box 2193/RG59/NARA. Memorandum, Crimmins to the Secretary, 11 November 1972, box 2193/RG59/NARA, cited in Harmer, *Allende's Chile and the Inter-American Cold War*, 194.
9. Harmer, *Allende's Chile and the Inter-American Cold War*, 192.
10. F. Castro, Speech to the UN as Chairman of the Non-Aligned Movement, 12 October 1979.
11. Baxi, *Human Rights in a Post-human World*, 87. Also Harmer, *Allende's Chile and the Inter-American Cold War*, 192–3.
12. Neruda, *Invitación al Nixonicidio*, and S. Allende, *Palabras del Presidente de la República de Chile, Salvador Allende Gossens, pronunciadas en la cena ofrecida en su honor en el Kremlin, Moscú*, 6 December 1972.
13. S. Allende, *Discurso de apertura en el XXVII Período de Sesiones de la Asamblea General de las Naciones Unidas*, 4 December 1972, in Martner (ed.), *Salvador Allende*, 626–52.

14. Ibid.

15. See Byers, *War Law: Understanding International Law and Armed Conflict*; Kennedy, *The Dark Sides of Virtue*; Chandler, 'The Road to Military Humanitarianism'; Power, *A Problem From Hell: America and the Age of Genocide*; and Duffield, *Development, Security, and Unending War*.

16. Baxi, *Human Rights in a Post-Human World*, 110.

17. T. Harmer, *Allende's Chile and the Inter-American Cold War*, 195.

18. Meister, *After Evil*, 265.

19. Sartre, 'On Genocide', 619.

20. Ibid., 615.

21. Ibid., 625. Sartre is also recasting the argument that the anti-Semite has a hatred of humanity.

22. Taylor, *Nuremberg and Vietnam: An American Tragedy*.

23. See Baxi, *Mambrino's Helmet*, 34; and 'The Development of the Right to Development'.

24. Prats, *Memorias: Testimonio de un soldado*, 309–10.

25. Prats, 'Entrevista a Carlos Prats'.

26. Briefing on Chile Elections, CIA 1 March 1973, CDP-CIA; Memorandum for deputy Director of Plans, 18 November 1972, CDP-CIA, both cited in Harmer, *Allende's Chile*, 202.

27. Cable CIA Station, Santiago, to CIA Headquarters, 8 February 1973, CDP-CIA; Information Report, CIA, 28 February 1973, CDP-CIA; Cable, Chief, WHD, to COS, 14 March 1973, Memo, Chief, WHD, to DCI, 29 March 1973, CDP-CIA, also cited in Harmer, *Allende's Chile*.

28. S. Allende, *Archivo Salvador Allende*, 1990, 9: 181–94.

29. Winn, 'Furies of the Andes', 246.

30. Joxe, *Le Chili sous Allende*, 193–5.

31. Fontaine, *Todos querían la revolución*, 158–61.

32. Cited in *Chile Hoy*, no. 32, 19 January 1973, 29.

33. P. Guzmán, *The Battle of Chile*, Part One.

34. Cable, COS, Santiago, to DCI, 26 April 1973, CDP-CIA; Cable, COS, Santiago, to DCI, 14 March 1973, CDP-CIA, also cited in Harmer, *Allende's Chile*, 206.

35. Magasich-Airola, *Los que dijeron no*, 14.

36. Ibid.

37. Vergara and Varas, *Coup*, 46.

38. Vial, 'El ocaso de Prats en el gobierno', 11. Also Cavallo and Serrano. *Las vigilias de Allende*, 4.

39. See P. Guzmán, *The Battle of Chile*, Part One and Part Two.

40. Magasich-Airola, *Los que dijeron no*, 13.

41. On 31 July 1972 Allende sent a letter to the UP parties stating his view that the sort of division taking place in the wake of Concepción's People's Assembly threatened the UP's unity and 'serves the enemies of our revolutionary cause'. See Amorós, *Compañero Presidente*, 255–7; *Chile Hoy*, no. 8, 10 August 1972, 6–7; S. Allende interviewed by *Clarín*, 6 August 1972, in *Archivo Salvador Allende*, 12, 1993, 87–91.

42. Some commentators argue, convincingly, that the heightened rhetoric of the Left undermined Allende's authority, isolated him politically, and

422 STORY OF A DEATH FORETOLD

played into the hands of the rightists. Darcy Ribeiro, one of Allende's advisers, refers to these sectors as 'the Left that lost its way'. See Ribeiro, 'Allende y la izquierda desvariada'. Also Winn, 'Furies of the Andes', 247–8.

43. See Preston, *Spanish Holocaust*, 34.

44. For Archbishop Silva's critical views of the ENU Project, see *Mensaje*, no. 209, June 1972, in *Chile visto por Mensaje: 1971–1981*, Santiago: Aconcagua, 1981, 60–2, also cited in Amorós, *Compañero Presidente*, 307.

45. P. Guzmán, *The Battle of Chile*, Part One.

46. Merino, *Bitácora de un almirante*, 510–15.

47. Ibid.

48. Preston, *Spanish Holocaust*, 4–33, at 21.

49. Q. Taylor, *Money and Politics in the Land of Oz*, available at www.usagold. com/gildedopinion/oz. See also Marx, Letter to Kugelman, April 12, 1871, 262–3, cited in Lenin, *State and Revolution*, ch. III, 1 and 2, 33 ff.

50. P. Guzmán, *The Battle of Chile*, Part Two, ch. 1: 'The threat of the coup d'état'.

51. Ibid.

52. Lenin, *State and Revolution*, ch. III, 2, 'What is to replace the smashed state machine?'

53. Garcés, 'Así cayó Allende', 22. Also Marx and Engels, Preface to the New German Edition, *The Communist Manifesto*, 22.

54. Grandin, 'Don't do what Allende did'. He cites both Hersh and Kissinger.

55. Garcés, 'Así cayó Allende', 22. For Pickering's statement, 'La posición del General Pickering', in *Revista Cause*, no. 17, 24 July 1964. The Prats-Cox incident is linked to Poder Femenino and the CIA in *Documentos Especiales, El tancazo de ese 29 de Junio*, Santiago: Quimantu, 1973. For Cox's version, M. Power, *Right-wing Women in Chile: Feminine Power and the Struggle Against Allende, 1964–1973*, Penn State Press, 2010, 263.

56. Willoughby speaking to Bucat, *Preparativos golpistas*, 1–2. Willoughby says at first he did know the plans' purpose, but realised they could be put to good use by the plotters later on.

57. Cavallo and Serrano, *Las vigilias de Allende*, 3.

58. Muñoz, *Dictator's Shadow*, xi.

59. On the USA's crazed environment at the time, see Stone and Kuznick, *Untold History of the United States*, 355–90; the chapter in question is titled 'Nixon and Kissinger: The "Madman" and the "Psychopath"'. On Pinochet's admiration for Franco, his own declarations cited in the far-right website *Despierta Chile*, in 'La situación de los militares españoles después de Franco', *Despierta Chile*, 1, 4, at www.despiertachile.worldpress. com, last seen 7 February 2011.

60. Nerín, *La guerra que vino de África*, 299, arguing that Franco (and by extension, Pinochet) went on to impose on the state the superiority derived from the colonial situation enjoyed by military officers in the colonial protector-ates; also Pinilla de las Heras, *En menos de libertad*, 62, both cited in Malló, *El cártel español*, 43–4.

61. Cited in Muñoz, *Dictator's Shadow*.

62. Garcés, 'Así cayó Allende', 22.

63. Cavallo and Serrano, *Las vigilias de Allende*, 3–4.
64. Ibid.
65. Ibid., Prelude.
66. Ibid., 3–4.
67. Garcés, 'Así cayó Allende', 22.
68. Ibid.

10 The Flies, Act III

1. Garcés, 'Así cayó Allende', 22–3.
2. On this number, CIA Information Report, 9 July 1973, CDP-CIA, also cited in Harmer, *Allende's Chile*, 221.
3. Memorandum, Acting Director of Central Intelligence (Cushman) to Kissinger, 29 December 1971, doc. 145/FRUS/1969-1976/E-10; for Nixon–Médici exchanges, Memorandum of Conversation, Médici, Nixon, and Walters, 11:30 a.m., the President's Office, 7 December 1971, doc.141/ FRUS/1969-1976/E-10; Memorandum of Conversation, Médici, Nixon, and Walters, 10:00 a.m., the President's Office, 9 December 1971, doc. 143 /FRUS/1969-1976/E-10, all cited in Harmer, *Allende's Chile*.
4. Harmer, *Allende's Chile*, 227–30.
5. González Camus, *El día que murió Allende*, ch. 1.
6. Ibid.
7. Ibid.
8. Ibid.
9. Ibid. Also Cavallo and Serrano, *Las vigilias de Allende*, 5; and Cavallo, *Memorias: Cardenal Raúl Silva Henríquez,* vol. II, 265–8.
10. On the difference between concepts and anticipatory images of the future, see Cornell, *Moral Images of Freedom*, 151–64. See also Garcés, 'Prólogo', in *Salvador Allende. Presente*, 9–39, citing Allende at 14-1; S. Allende, Discurso en el Senado, 18 de Junio de 1948 (Opposing the outlawing of the Communist Party); Bosteels, *The Actuality of Communism*, 1–41; Bensaïd, 'Puissances du communisme', 13; and Marx, 'The Civil War in France'.
11. González Camus, *El día que murió Allende*. Also Cavallo and Serrano, *Las vigilias de Allende*, 5; and Cavallo, *Memorias: Cardenal Raúl Silva Henríquez*, vol. II, 265–8.
12. González Camus, *El día que murió Allende*.
13. Ibid.
14. See P. Guzmán, *The Battle of Chile*, Part Two, *The Coup d'Etat*.
15. For the event of the rule of law becoming illegal, see Mattei and Nader, *Plunder*.
16. Bucat,*Preparativosgolpistas*,1–2,availableatwww.cedec.cl/DownloadDokument/ CEDEC_PREP_MARINA.pdf, retrieved 25 April 2013. On the history of the silent revolution, the young conservatives and the media, see Á. Soto, *El Mercurio*; also Lavín, *Chile, Revolución Silenciosa*.
17. Willoughby speaking to Bucat, see *Preparativos golpistas*, 1–2.
18. Ibid.
19. As previously noted in endnote 27, *The Flies, Act I*.
20. Colorado Garcia, 'Jaime Guzmán: Demiurgo de Pinochet', in *Pensamiento*

Crítico, no. 5, 2010, at www.pensamientocritico.imd.cl/index/php?option=com_
content&view=article&id=107:jaime-guzman-el-demiurgo-de-pinochet&
catid=42:nd-5&ltemid=74#_ftnref78

21. Correa de Oliveira, *Revolución y Contra-revolución*, 83 and 95.
22. Philippi, 'Limitación de la propiedad territorial: notas en torno de una
     polémica', and Fontaine and Sierra (eds), 'Escritos y documentos de Julio
     Philippi', 366.
23. Eyzaguirre, *Fisionomía histórica de Chile*, 9, 152–3, 168; A. Edwards, *La
     fronda aristocrática en Chile*, 34 ff.
24. Willoughby to Bucat, *Preparativos golpistas*, 1–2.
25. Báez, *A Universal History*, 244–6.
26. Ibid.
27. Merino, *Bitácora de un almirante*, 510–15.
28. Bucat, *Preparativos golpistas*, 22.
29. According to W. Benjamin 'allegory was the mode of perception pecu-
     liar to a time of social disruption and protracted war, when human
     suffering and material ruin were the stuff and substance of historical
     experience'. See on this, Buck-Morss, *The Dialectics of Seeing*, 178;
     Miéville, *London's Overthrow*; Calder Williams, *Combined and Uneven
     Apocalypse*.
30. Cornell, *Moral Images of Freedom*, especially 137–49; Stern, *Reckoning with
     Pinochet*, Book Three, xxvi–xxix; Rediker and Linebaugh, *The Many-
     Headed Hydra*.
31. Buck-Morss, *Hegel, Haiti, and Universal History*, 133.
32. Hofstadter, *The Paranoid Style*.
33. S. Allende, cited in Winn, 'Furies of the Andes', 240.
34. G. García Márquez, 'La soledad de América Latina', in *Yo no vengo a decir
     un discurso*, Barcelona: Mondadori, 2010, 21–9, at 23; 'Chile, el Golpe, y los
     Gringos', 1–15. For the notion of emulation and reciprocal or mimetic
     violence, see Girard, *Mensonge romantique*, and *Des choses cachées depuis la
     fondation du monde*. See also Winn, 'Furies of the Andes', 240–1.
35. Winn, Furies of the Andes', 240–1.
36. Meister, *After Evil*, 250–9. According to him, in market economies histori-
     cal grievances can be construed as options held in a constructive trust.
     Claims in relation to such grievances cannot be politically terminated. Also
     Baxi, *Human Rights in a Posthuman World*, 149–55, for the related notion
     that remedial justice leads to considering the possibility of crimes against
     the right to development as genocide.
37. B. Allende, 'Combatir hasta el final', 38.
38. Dorfman, *The Empire's Old Clothes*, 4–5.
39. Garcés, 'Así cayó Allende', 28; Ó. Soto, *El último día de Salvador Allende*, 65,
     83; M. Contreras, Letter to B. Allende, Noviembre de 1973, 4–5; Ribeiro,
     'Allende y la izquierda desvariada'.
40. Winn, 'Furies of the Andes', 244; Dorfman, *Empire's Old Clothes*, 3–9. For
     the contemporary relevance of this question, see B. Bosteels, 'In Search of
     the Act', in *The Actuality of Communism*, 170–224. See also Arthur,
     Unfinished Projects, 170–1, and Kirwan, *Discovering Girard*, 61–2.
41. 'Winn, 'Furies of the Andes', 246. He cites, as evidence of the impact of

this sort of intervention, US Senate, *Covert Action in Chile, 1963–1973*, 7–8, 16–17, 21–3.

42. J. Guzmán, 'La iglesia chilena y el debate político', and Fontaine, 'El miedo y otros escritos', 274.

43. Ribeiro, 'Allende y la izquierda desvariada'.

44. Winn, 'Furies of The Andes', 244–5.

45. 'If I refuse to use force and violence against our class enemies, I could not even imagine using violence against the revolutionaries. Never!' See S. Allende 'Discurso de despedida a Fidel Castro. Estadio Nacional, 4 de diciembre 1971', in Garcés (ed.), *Salvador Allende. Presente*, 101.

46. Ibid., 97.

47. Oña interviewed by Harmer, *Allende's Chile*, 232.

48. López, 'Imagen de Beatriz Allende'.

49. Muñoz, *Dictator's Shadow*, 7.

50. 'Detienen a General de la FACh Alberto Bachelet', *La Tercera*, Tuesday, 11 September 1973.

51. 'Carta del General Bachelet a su hijo Alberto y sus nietos en Australia, 16 de octubre de 1973', in *Las Cartas del General Bachelet*; also available at www.lashistoriasquepodemoscontar.cl/bachelet2. On the case, see *Resolución de procesamiento en la investigación por el delito de torturas en el caso de la muerte del General Alberto Bachelet, Ministro en visita [judge] Mario Carroza, 12/07/2012, SML, Fuente: Poder Judicial, Chile.* Also *La Fach y las torturas al General Bachelet*, available at radio.uchile.cl/cartas-al-director/162407.

52. Ibid.

53. 'Servicio Médico Legal establece que General Alberto Bachelet murió a causa de torturas', at www.radio.uchile.cl, 20 June 2012; also 'Exsubsecretario de Aviación identifica a torturadores del General Alberto Bachelet', at www.radio.uchile.cl/noticias/120401, retrieved 26 April 2013.

54. Telegram, Davis to SecState, 30 July 1973, DOS/CFP. Also Rojas, *Murder of Allende*, ch. 1, The Background of the Conspiracy.

55. Muñoz, *Dictator's Shadow*, 8.

56. Garcés, 'Así cayó Allende', 27.

57. Ibid., 27–8.

58. Ibid.

59. Ibid.

60. Ibid.

61. Garcés, *Allende y la experiencia chilena*, 385. Also Cavallo and Serrano, *Las vigilias de Allende*, 35.

62. Garcés, 'Así cayó Allende', 27–8.

63. S Allende, 'Últimas palabras. La Moneda, Santiago de Chile, 11 de Septiembre de 1973', in *Salvador Allende. Presente*, 105–6.

64. González Camus, *El día en que murió Allende*, 66 ff. Also Ravest Santis, *Testimonio*, and Cáceres, *Testimonio*, available at ciperchile.cl/2008/06/26/la-verdadera-historia-del-rescate-del-ultimo-discurso-de-salvador-allende, last consulted 7 September 2012.

65. González Camus, *El día en que murió Allende*, 66.

66. Pinochet Ugarte, *El día decisivo*, 127. Also Rojas et al., *Páginas en blanco*, 1 Parte.

67. For the sources of these paraphrases, see Ralston Saul, *Voltaire's Bastards*, 460;

Yeats, 'Meditations in Time of Civil War, VI: The Stare's Nest By My
Window', 173; and Hedges, *Empire of Illusion*, 1.

68. Ravest Santis, *Testimonio*, and Cáceres, *Testimonio*.

69. Ravest Santis, *Testimonio*.

70. S. Allende, 'Últimas palabras', in *Salvador Allende. Presente*, 108–10. Also
Vergara and Varas, *Coup*, 51–3; and Goldsmith, *The Deserted Village*, available   at   www.poetryfoundation.org/poem/173557,   last   consulted
3 September 2012.

11 A Death Foretold

1. Amorós, *Compañero Presidente*, 335–6.

2. Garcés, *Orlando Letelier*, 25; Dorfman, *Mas allá del miedo*, 156, relating an
anecdote according to which Letelier observed that Pinochet's obsequious-
ness reminded him of the attitude of a barber in an old-fashioned
barbershop.

3. J. C. Peña, *La secreta vida literaria de Augusto Pinochet*, Santiago: Random,
2013; CIPER, 'Los resentimientos intelectuales de Pinochet contra el
General Carlos Prats', 10 May 2013, available at www.ciperchile.
cl/2013/05/10/los-resentimientos-intelectuales-de-pinochet-contra-el-
general-carlos-prats, last retrieved 20 May 2013. Thanks to Alejandro
Zambra for bringing this material to my attention.

4. Barros, *Constitutionalism and Dictatorship*, 45. He cites Captain Sergio Rillón,
naval justice officer and president of the Juridical Advisory and Coordinating
Committee of the Government Junta, set up by *Decree 668 of 12 September
1973*.

5. CIPER, 'Los resentimientos intelectuales de Pinochet contra el General
carlos Prats', 10 May 2013, available at www.ciperchile.cl/2013/05/10/los-
resentimientos-intelectuales-de-pinochet-contra-el-general-carlos-prats,
last retrieved 20 May 2013.

6. Ibid.

7. Ibid., citing Marañón on Tiberius, and Vial on Pinochet's biographical
detail. See also Muñoz, *Dictator's Shadow*, xi, 25–7, 38 (for Pinochet confess-
ing his jealousy towards leftist Senator Volodia Teitelboim) and 40.

8. Muñoz, *Dictator's Shadow*, 27.

9. See *Annals of the Honourable Junta of Government (AHJG) 33, 12 November
1973*; for legal framework, see *Decree Order no. 52, 14 June 1977*, especially its
secret article 10; and *Decree Order no. 527, article 10, no. 14, 26 June 1974*.
Within days of DINA's formal creation, the exercise of powers conferred
by the declaration of the state of exception or emergency, carried out by
DINA, became the sole prerogative of the President of the Supreme
Command, Augusto Pinochet, not the Junta. DINA's director, Lt. Col.
Manuel Contreras, was accountable only and directly to him.

10. See *Decree Order No. 5, 22 September 1973*; and Barros, *Constitutionalism and
Dictatorship*, 117–66, especially 125, n. 9. DINA emerged out of a group of
army majors and colonels with contacts in right-wing paramilitary groups.

11. On 18 September 1973. See Muñoz, *Dictator's Shadow*, 45–6.

12. Garcés, 'Así cayó Allende', 24.

13. Ibid. Also Barros, *Constitutionalism and Dictatorship*, 129.

14. Rojas, *Murder of Allende*, ch. 1: The Artful Staging of a Suicide, 8.

15. Ibid., 8–9.

16. S. E. Ambrose, *Nixon: Ruin and Recovery, 1973–1990*, New York: Simon & Schuster, 1991, 508.

17. Kornbluh, *Pinochet File,* 25, 26, 28–9, 72.

18. Kinzer, *Overthrow*, 190.

19. Corvalán Márquez, *Los partidos políticos y el golpe del 11 de septiembre*, 340–2; Amorós, *Compañero Presidente*, 322.

20. Rojas, *Murder of Allende*, ch. 1: The Artful Staging of a Suicide, 14.

21. Ibid. Rojas argues that this led to Allende's 'staged suicide'. The mystery over Allende's death was solved after a scientific autopsy conducted in 2011 confirmed the witness testimony of Allende's doctor Patricio Guijón. See 'Autopsy Confirms', *Guardian & Associated Press*, 20 July 2011.

22. B. Allende, 'Combatir hasta el final', 34–40, at 37–9.

23. Ibid.

24. Ibid.

25. Jurists, political philosophers and political scientists call this 'General Will'. See Gordon, 'Of Legitimation and the General Will'.

26. *2 Paul's Epistle to the Thessalonians*, 3-10. The claim that God's rule is already here reinterprets world history in a way that refuses any transcendental justification of imperial or oppressive rule. From that perspective, justice takes the shape of a chiliastic judgment, the decision that time has run out and justice must be done now. This corresponds to the moment of kairós in Judeo-Christian theology or apocalypse in Islam. See E. Dussel, *Kairós: El acontecimiento liberador en Pablo de Tarso*, manuscript on file with the author, also available at www.enriquedussel.com/txt/II-CAP-4-31.pdf, for a critique of legal fetishism that can be extended to humanitarianism and human rights. Also, T. Ramadan, 'Prometheus and Abraham', in *Islam, the West and the Challenges of Modernity*, Leicester: Islamic Foundation, 2001, 203-212; *Islamic Ethics and Liberation*, Oxford: Oxford University Press, 2008; and *The Quest for Meaning: Developing a Philosophy of Pluralism*, Penguin, 2012. See also R. Meister, *After Evil*, 304-16.

27. Berger, *Bento's Sketchbook*, 146.

28. Ibid.

29. On the use and meaning of prophetic language in politics, including secular politics, see E. Pagels, *Revelations: Visions, Prophecy & Politics in the Book of Revelation,* New York: Viking, 2012; also Isasi-Díaz and Mendieta, *Decolonizing Epistemologies*, especially 247-64; and C. West, 'A Prisoner of Hope in the Night of American Empire', in *Politics of Culture and the Spirit of Critique: Dialogues*, G. Rockhill and A. Gómez-Muller (eds), New York: Columbia University Press, 2011, 113-27. See also B. Allende, 'Combatir hasta el final' and García Márquez, 'La soledad de América Latina', 23.

30. For current instances of such judgement in literature and philosophy see also Miéville, *London's Overthrow*, and Calder Williams, *Combined and Uneven Apocalypse*. On the currency and political or jurisprudential import of prophetic language, especially on such issues as American imperialism, Jim Crow laws, socialism and democracy see West, 'A Prisoner of Hope', 124-7.

31. See, among others: Winstanley, *The Law of Freedom*; F. Picabia, *Manifesto Canibal Dadá*, 1920 and Andrade, *Manifesto Antropófago*, both included in *Anthropofagia Hoje? Oswald de Andrade em cena*, J. Ruffinelli and J. C. de Castro Rocha (eds), São Paulo: É Realizações, 2011; A. Césaire, *Discours sur le colonialisme, suivi de Discours sur la Négritude*, Paris: Éditions Présence Africaine, [1955] 2004; García Márquez, 'Posibilidades de la antropofagia'; S. Hessel, *Indignez Vous!*, Montpellier: Indigènes Éditions, 2011; R. M. Artal (ed.), *Reacciona!*, Madrid: Aguilar, 2011. On the latter, see Guardiola-Rivera, 'A Jurisprudence of Indignation', in *Law & Critique*, vol. 23, issue 3, November 2012, 253–70.

32. Garcés, 'Prólogo', in *Salvador Allende: Presente*, 9.

33. O. Ulianova, 'La Unidad Popular y el Golpe Militar en Chile. Percepciones y análisis soviéticos', in *Estudios Públicos*, 79, Winter 2000, 83–171, at 102. Also Harmer, *Allende's Chile*, 197–202, citing Ulianova.

34. Harmer, *Allende's Chile*, 213.

35. Ibid., 218.

36. Harmer, *Allende's Chile*, 201–19. Grandin, 'Don't do what Allende did', 6–7; and Winn, 'Furies of the Andes', 256.

37. B. Allende, 'Combatir hasta el final', 38–9. Also González Camus, *El día en que murió Allende*, 82–3; and Vergara and Varas, *Coup*, 60–4.

38. Soto, *El último día de Salvador Allende*, 83.

39. Letter from Miriam Contreras to Beatriz Allende, November 1973, Archivo Chile, Centro de Estudios Miguel Enríquez.

40. González Camus, *El día en que murió Allende*, 87.

41. Soto, *El último día de Salvador Allende*, 88.

42. Vergara and Vargas, *Coup*, 74.

43. The entire conversation between the generals during the morning and early afternoon of 11 September 1973 was recorded. A transcript of the recording was rescued and made public by the magazine *Cauce* in its issue of 24–30 December 1985. See Soto, *El último día de Salvador Allende*, 100–12.

44. García Márquez, 'La soledad de América Latina', 23.

12 Laws of Darkness

1. Muñoz, *Dictator's Shadow*, 14.

2. On Pinochet's unrecognised bibliophile tendencies, see J. C. Peña, *La secreta vida literaria de Augusto Pinochet*, Santiago: Random, 2013; also 'Viaje al fondo de la biblioteca de Pinochet', in CIPER, at ciperchile. cl/2007/12/06/exclusivo-viaje-al-fondo-de-la-biblioteca-de-pinochet, last retrieved 28 May 2013.

3. Muñoz, Dictator's Shadow, 14.

4. Ibid.

5. S. Allende, 'Últimas palabras', in *Salvador Allende. Presente*, 106 and 109.

6. Muñoz, *Dictator's Shadow*, 18.

7. M. Ferrada, 'Ferrada-Noli versus Pinochet', at antifascist.worldpress.com/ category/uncategorized, retrieved 10 October 2012. Also Muñoz, *Dictator's Shadow*, 18–19.

8. Muñoz, *Dictator's Shadow*, 20.

9. Barros, *Constitutionalism and Dictatorship*, 42.

10. Pinochet, *El día decisivo*, 75–6.

11. Peña, *La secreta vida literaria de Augusto Pinochet*; also 'Viaje al fondo de la biblioteca de Pinochet', in CIPER, at ciperchile.cl/2007/12/06/exclusivo-viaje-al-fondo-de-la-biblioteca-de-pinochet, last retrieved 28 May 2013. With thanks to A. Zambra.

12. *Ejército de Chile, División Escuela, Escuela Militar: Relación de la colección de libros de Napoleón*, available at ciperchile.cl/wp-content/uploads/libros-napoleon.pdf, last retrieved 30 May 2013. See also P. J. McDonnell, 'Chile's Pinochet: Napoleon Wannabe?', in *Los Angeles Times*, 10 October 2007, at www.latimesblogs.latimes.com/laplaza/2007/10/chiles-pinochet, last seen 26 May 2013; Barros, *Constitutionalism and Dictatorship*, 43.

13. *Decree Law No. 1, 18 September 1973*, was the *Act of Constitution of the Government Junta*, proclaiming that the Triumvirate Junta assumed the supreme command of the nation, and designating Pinochet as president of the Junta. The administrative–penal military decrees or *Bandos* were used from 11 September to turn the entire population into an enemy if found to be involved in acts of resistance (*Bando No. 1, 11 September 1973*), impose curfews, summon opposition figures to turn themselves in at the Ministry of Defence, institute press censorship, dissolve Congress (*Bando No. 29, 18 September 1973*) and provide ideological justification for the coup (*Bando No. 5, 11 September 1973*). Their authority derived from articles 77 and 78 of the *Chilean Code of Military Justice* and article 34 of the *Law of Internal Security*.

14. *Decree Law No. 1, 18 September 1973*, dated retroactively to 11 September 1973, published in the first edition of the *Official Gazette* published after the coup.

15. Barros, *Constitutionalism and Dictatorship*, 36.

16. Mayol, *No al lucro*, 20–1.

17. Ibid., 17–49. Mayol speaks of a 'crisis of legitimacy' and 'the making of shadows', as opposed to the making of light, in the case of Chile. For 'provoking disorder', see Badiou, 'Politics: a Non-Expressive Dialectics', in *Philosophy for Militants*, 75.

18. *Decree Law no. 1, 18 September 1973*, dated retrospectively 11 September 1973.

19. Article 3, *Decree Law No. 1, 18 September 1973*, dated retrospectively 11 September 1973. On the constructive role of a Law of Laws, see Badiou, 'Politics: a Non-Expressive Dialectics', 68 ff.

20. *Bando No. 5, 11 September 1973*; *Decree Law No. 8, 19 September 1973*; and Actas de la Honorable Junta de Gobierno (AHJG) 1, 13 September 1973, declaring emergency situations.

21. Consuls were elected positions in ancient Rome, comprising both civilian and military functions. The Roman Senate authorised consuls to nominate a dictator, an exception to the legal principles of collegiality and responsibility, chosen as highest magistrate and not legally liable for official actions. They were more often than not chosen *rei gerundae causa* ('for the [exceptional] matter at hand'), *seditionis sedandae et rei erundae causa* ('for the putting down of rebellion and the matter at hand'), and *legibus faciendis et rei publicae*

constituendae causa – 'for the making of laws and for the setting of the consti-
tution'. See A. Lintott, *The Constitution of the Roman Republic*, Oxford:
Oxford University Press, 1990; C. Schmitt, *Dictatorship*, Cambridge: Polity
Press, 2013, for the modern notion of 'state of emergency' and commissarial
dictatorship originating in the power of the Reichspräsident to declare it.
Also D. Dyzenhaus, 'Are States of Emergency Inside or Outside the Legal
Order?', at www.creum.umontreal.ca/IMG/doc/Schmitt_v_Dicey_1_.
doc, last retrieved 25 May 2013, for a recent account, and *A versus Secretary
of State for the Home Department*, [2004] UKHL 56.

22. Badiou, 'Politics as a Non-Expressive Dialectics', 74.

23. Mayol, *No al lucro*, 15.

24. Ibid.

25. S. Huidobro, *Decisión Naval*, Valparaíso: Imprenta de la Armada, 1989,
264–6.

26. Telegram, Sec State to Amembassy, Santiago, 'USG Attitude toward
Junta', 12 September 1973, DOS/CFP. Telegram, Davis to SecState, 'Gen.
Pinochet's Request for Meeting with MILGP Officer', 12 September 1973.
Telegram, Davis to SecState, 'Relations with the New Chilean
Government', 13 September 1973, DOS/CFP. DCI Briefing, Washington
Special Actions Group Meeting, 14 September 1973, CDP-NSC. Citations
from Muñoz, *Dictators' Shadow*, 87–8, and Harmer, *Allende's Chile*, 247.

27. Intelligence Memorandum, 'Consequences of a Military Coup in Chile', 1
August 1973, CDP/CIA, cited in Harmer, *Allende's Chile*, 247.

28. A. Tusa and J. Tusa, *The Nuremberg Trial*, New York: Atheneum, 1984, 54–5.

29. G. J. Bass, *Stay the Hand of Vengeance: The Politics of War Crimes Tribunals*,
Princeton: Princeton University Press, 2000, chs 1 and 5.

30. See J. Waiting, *Bertrand Russell*, Edinburgh: Oliver & Boyd, 1970.

31. See Sartre, 'On Genocide'. For his notion of 'political morality', see 'Notes
for Gramsci Lecture, Rome 1964 (typed manuscript corrected by Sartre)',
John Gerassi Collection of J.-P Sartre. General Collection of Rare Books
and Manuscripts, Beinecke Rare Book and Manuscript Library, Yale
University, GEN MSS 411, Series II: "Other Papers". Box 4, Folder 57, 70.
[Hereafter, 'Rome Lecture, 1964'], f. 63. For an enlightening commentary,
T. C. Anderson, *Sartre's Two Ethics: From Authenticity to Integral Humanity*,
Chicago: Open Court, 1993, and Arthur, *Unfinished Projects*, especially chs
8–9. For the link between Russell I and Russell II on 'political morality'
and Chile, see J. Cortázar, 'Violación de derechos culturales' (1975) and
'Chile: otra versión del infierno' (1975), in *Papeles Inesperados*, Buenos
Aires: Alfaguara, 2009.

32. Sartre, 'On Genocide', 619.

33. Arthur, *Unfinished Projects*, 161.

34. Sartre, Rome Lecture, 1964, 79; also E. A. Bowman and R. V. Stone,
'"Socialist Morality" in Sartre's Unpublished 1964 Rome Lecture: A
Summary and Commentary', in *Existentialist Ethics*, W. L. McBride (ed.),
New York: Routledge, 1996, 170. See also Sandel, *What Money Can't Buy*,
6–11.

35. Anderson, *Sartre's Two Ethics*, 148–9.

36. Sartre, Rome Lecture, 1964, 63.

37. Arthur, *Unfinished Projects*, 143, n. 17. Sartre speaks of '*classes défavorisées, exploitées, opprimées*'. Cortázar uses the Spanish term '*los pobres*' in relation to what Pablo Neruda called 'an incitement to Nixonicide', to be carried out not by agents or assassins but by the American people themselves, 'who take charge of erasing from history he who was covering them with abject shame'. See Cortázar, *Papeles Inesperados*, 278–9.

38. S. Allende, 'Últimas Palabras. La Moneda, Santiago de Chile, 11 de Septiembre de 1973', in *Salvador Allende. Presente*, 106.

39. See Bolaño, *Nocturno de Chile*, 141. Bolaño's narrative is based on actual facts.

40. *Bando No. 1*, 11 September 1973.

41. Law of Internal Security, art. 34. *Bando* No. 1 established control over the population; *Bando* No. 5 declared the need for military intervention in the face of the perceived risk embodied by the Allende government, 'to prevent greater evils' and 'restore the economic and social normalcy'; *Bando* No. 29 dissolved Congress – all of these from 11 September 1973. See Barros, *Constitutionalism and Dictatorship*, 44–5.

42. It was backdated to 11 September and published in the first edition of the *Official Gazette* on 18 September 1973.

43. Barros, *Constitutionalism and Dictatorship*, 120–3; *Informe de la Comisión Nacional de Verdad y Reconciliación*, Santiago: Nacion, 1991, 309–11, 396–8, 437–8.

44. See Colorado García, 'Jaime Guzmán: El demiurgo de Pinochet', at www.pensamientocritico.imd.cl/index.php?option=com_content&view=article&id=107:jaime-guzman-el-demiurgo-de-pinochet&catid=42:nd-5&Itemid=74#_ftnref2 .

45. Cristi, *El pensamiento político de Jaime Guzmán*, 77. See also O. Lira, *Nostalgia de Vázquez de Mella*, Santiago: Editorial Difusión Chilena, 1942, especially 111, and Philippi, 'Limitación de la propiedad territorial'.

46. Decreto-Ley no. 1, 11 September 1973; also J. Guzmán, *Escritos personales*, 100.

47. A. Cavallo and M. Serrano, 'Las 24 horas que estremecieron a Chile', in *Salvador Allende: Cien años, todos los sueños*, A. Ortizpozo (ed.), Caracas: Ministerio del Poder Popular para la Información y la Comunicación, 2008, 246.

48. 'I don't have the make-up of the apostle or the messiah. I lack the conditions of the martyr,' S. Allende, 'Últimas Palabras', in *Salvador Allende. Presente*, 105.

49. Meister, *After Evil*, 282; Colorado García, *Jaime Guzmán*.

50. Meister, *After Evil*, 282–3.

51. Tomic to General Prats, August 1973, cited in Collier and Sater, *History of Chile*, 330.

52. See O. Guardiola-Rivera, 'Pablo Neruda's Importance Was as Much Political as Poetic', in the *Guardian*, 10 April 2013.

53. B. Brecht, 'The Solution', in *Poems 1913–1956*, J. Willett and R. Manheim (eds), Methuen, 1976, 440.

54. 'Manifiesto de historiadores. Revolución anti-neoliberal social/estudiantil en Chile', in *Otro Chile es Posible*, 53–8; for a European case of protest and eviction, see City of London v. Tammy Samede and Others [2012] EWHC

34 (QB), 18 January 2012. For social fascism, De Sousa Santos and Rodríguez (eds), *Law and Globalisation From Below*, 60.

55. L. Klener Hernández, 'Allende y el encendido fogoso de la memoria', in *Salvador Allende: Cien años, todos los sueños*, A. Ortizpozo (ed.), Caracas: Ministerio del Poder Popular para la Información y la Comunicación, 2008, 265–6.

56. S. Allende, 'Últimas Palabras', in *Salvador Allende. Presente*, 108. Klener Hernández, 'Salvador Allende y el encendido fogoso de la memoria', 265–6. Sartre, 'On Genocide', 615, asking: 'Is it possible for us, in objectively studying the facts, to unveil their hidden intention?' On hidden truths and intentions in the case of the exemplary war in Vietnam before the 1967 Russell Tribunal, see Sallah, Weiss and Mahr, 'Buried Secrets, Brutal Truths', cited in Arthur, *Unfinished Projects*, 161.

57. Klener Hernández, 'Salvador Allende y el encendido fogoso de la memoria', 266.

58. See V. Jara, 'Estadio Chile', in *Chile: El otro 11 de septiembre*, 31–3. Also J. Jara, 'El dia del golpe' and 'Un canto inconcluso', in the same collection, 12–30.

59. Délano, 'La muerte lenta de Víctor Jara', available at www.cultura.elpais.com, last retrieved 26 September 2012.

60. P. Neruda, '*Mi pueblo ha sido el más traicionado de este mundo*', available at www.cubadebate.com, last retrieved 25 September 2012.

61. L. A. Mansilla, 'Los últimos días', in *Anales de la Universidad de Chile*, Sexta Serie, No. 10, Santiago, December 1999, and 'Vivir con Neruda: Conversación con Aída Figueroa y Sergio Isunza', in *Araucaria*, Santiago, no. 26, 1984.

62. P. Neruda, 'Sin embargo me muevo', in *El corazón amarillo*, Buenos Aires: Losada, 1974.

63. I. Allende, *Paula*, London: Flamingo, 1996, 180–3.

64. Amorós, *Sombras sobre Isla Negra*, 'Luto en Isla Negra. Último encuentro con Salvador Allende'.

65. Ibid.

66. M. Urrutia, *Mi vida junto a Pablo Neruda*, Barcelona: Seix Barral, 1986, 15–17.

67. Feinstein, *Pablo Neruda*, 413.

68. Ibid., 415.

69. The memo was located in Sweden's National Archive by the Spanish historian Fernando Camacho Padilla, together with a telegram sent by Edelstam to his Ministry of Foreign Affairs. Both documents are cited by Amorós in *Sombras sobre Isla Negra*. See also 'El misterio de la muerte de Pablo Neruda', in *La Tribuna*, 31 March 2013.

70. G. Martin, *Gabriel García Márquez: A Life*, London: Bloomsbury, 376.

71. The interview and the cable are cited in G. Martin, *Gabriel García Márquez*, 376–7.

72. Martin, *Gabriel García Márquez*, 379.

73. García Márquez, 'El Golpe en Chile (I) y (II)' (also cited as 'Chile, el golpe, y los gringos'), in *Alternativa*, No. 1, 15–28 February 1974, and No. 2, 1–15 March 1974, also available at www.cubadebate.com, last retrieved 28 September 2012. An English version titled 'Why Allende Had to Die' was

published in *New Statesman*, London, 15 March 1974 at 358, cited in Martin, *Gabriel García Márquez*, 379 (here modified slightly). It has since been republished on 3 April 2013, available at www.newstatesman.com/world-affairs/2013/04/why-allende-had-to-die.

74. García Márquez, 'Why Allende Had to Die', cited in Martin, *Gabriel García Márquez*, 379, n. 12.

75. Sartre, 'On Genocide'; Taylor, *Nuremberg and Vietnam: An American Tragedy*, and *The Anatomy of the Nuremberg Trials*, New York: Knopf, 1992, suggesting that Allied generals should have been tried for the terror bombing of Dresden and Hiroshima or Nagasaki. See also Meister, *After Evil*, 265.

76. Sartre, 'On Genocide', 626.

13 Transition

1. See, for some of the intellectual sources of this policy, Fanon, *Wretched of the Earth*, 75–84. Also P. Baran and E. Hobsbawm, 'Un manifeste non-communiste', in *Les Temps Modernes* 193, June 1962, 1226–61. For a contemporary take on the legal argument, Meister, *After Evil*, 232–59.

2. S. Allende cited in Farías, *La izquierda chilena (1969–1973)*, 983–97, and Amorós, *Compañero Presidente*, 214.

3. UN General Assembly Resolution 1803 (XVII), 14 December 1962.

4. Meister, *After Evil*, 255–8.

5. Teitel, 'Transitional Justice Genealogy', 69–94, and *Transitional Justice*, also cited in Meister, *After Evil*, 259, n. 76.

6. Meister, *After Evil*, 258.

7. Ibid.

8. Sandel, *What Money Can't Buy*, 10. See S. Allende, 'Nacionalización del cobre. Discurso en la Plaza de la Constitución. Santiago, 21 de diciembre de 1970', in *Salvador Allende. Presente*, 49–57. Also J. Cortázar, *Papeles Inesperados*, on the popular editions of Editorial Quimantú in Allende's Chile as a concrete example of priceless goods and remedial justice, 268–9; against the liberal rejection of remedial justice on the basis that all history is irremediably horrible, 276 and 282–3.

9. See Sandel, *What Money Can't Buy*, 11 ff.; Guevara, *Notes critiques d'économie politique*, 19–34, 247–80; Yaffe, *Che Guevara*, 1–11, 199–275.

10. Meister, *After Evil*, 246.

11. S. Allende, 'Últimas palabras', in *Salvador Allende. Presente*, 106. Also Fanon, *Wretched of the Earth*, I, Concerning Violence, 27–84, especially 80, and Meister, *After Evil*, 256.

12. For the concept of law used here, see E. P. Thompson, *Whigs and Hunters*, New York: Pantheon, 1975, 263, 266; E. Hobsbawm, *Echoes of the Marseillaise*, New Brunswick: Rutgers University Press, 1990; D. Kennedy, 'The Rise and Fall of Classical Legal Thought', AFAR, 1975, 1998, at http://duncankennedy.net/legal_history/essays.html#Rand&F, retrieved January 2013, and 'The Stakes of Law, or Hale and Foucault!', in *Sexy Dressing, Etc.: Essays on the Power and Politics of Cultural Identity*, Cambridge: Harvard University Press, 1993; B. Fried, *The Progressive Assault on Laissez*

Faire: Robert Hale and the First Law and Economics Movement, Cambridge: Harvard University Press, 1998; A. Chase, *Law and History: The Evolution of the American Legal System*, New York: New Press, 1997, 51–219; S. Amin, G. Arrighi, A. Gunder Frank and I. Wallerstein, *Transforming the Revolution: Social Movements and the World System*, New York: New Press, 1990; E. Guevara, *Global Justice,* Melbourne: Ocean Press, 2002; J. Sen, A. Anand, A. Escobar and P. Waterman, *World Social Forum: Challenging Empires*, The Viveka Foundation, 2004; B. De Sousa Santos and C. Rodríguez, *Law and Globalisation From Below*, Cambridge: Cambridge University Press, 2004; Losurdo, *Hegel and the Freedom of Moderns*; R. Mangabeira Unger, *Free Trade Reimagined*, Princeton & Oxford: Princeton University Press, 2007; Arthur, *Unfinished Projects*, 254–74; and Meister, *After Evil*, 237.

13. Meister, *After Evil*, 258, referencing the critical work of Walter Benjamin. Also I. Ayres, *Optional Law: The Structure of Legal Entitlements*, Chicago: University of Chicago Press, 2005.

14. E. Posner and A. Vermeule, 'Transitional Justice as Ordinary Justice', in *Harvard Law Review*, 117, 2003, 764, also quoted in Meister, *After Evil*, 257, n.70.

15. Sartre, Rome Lecture, 1964, 63, cited in Arthur, *Unfinished Projects*, 143.

16. Meister, *After Evil*, 258–9.

17. García Márquez, 'La soledad de América Latina', in *Yo no vengo a decir un discurso*, 29. In that closing paragraph of his Nobel lecture, as at the outset, he refers to Allende's death. See also Cortázar, *Fantomas contra los vampiros multinacionales*, 58, and *Apéndice: Sentencia del Tribunal Russell II, 1974–1975*, 69–77, at 76.

18. *Tribunal Russell II Sobre la situación de los países de América Latina*, appendix to Cortázar, *Fantomas contra los vampiros multinacionales*, available at www. literaberinto.com/cortazar, last retrieved 28 September 2012. Available also, together with other highly relevant documents, in the archives of the Lelio Basso Foundation in Rome. See also Kelly, *When the People Awake*.

19. Cortázar, *Fantomas contra los vampiros multinacionales*.

20. Muñoz, *Dictator's Shadow*, 125.

21. Moyn, *Last Utopia*, 142–8.

22. Muñoz, *Dictator's Shadow*, 125–6.

23. Muñoz, *Dictator's Shadow*, 125–7. See also Faletto, *Dimensiones del desarrollo*, 51; also Basso, *Il principe senza scettro*.

24. Mayol, *No al lucro*, 15, 143; and *El derrumbe del modelo*, 15.

25. US Senate, *Covert Action in Chile: 1963–1973*, cited in Muñoz, *Dictator's Shadow*, 67.

26. Montecinos, Pavlovic and Piergentili, *El legado político de Jaime Guzmán*, 45.

27. Muñoz, *Dictator's Shadow*, 71.

28. Klein, *The Shock Doctrine: The Rise of Disaster Capitalism*.

29. See Foucault, *The Birth of Biopolitics*, 80–1; Baxi, *Human Rights in a Posthuman World*, 93–123, 124–55; Escobar, *Encountering Development*, 4; De Sousa Santos, *Toward a New Common Sense*. Also Moyn, *Last Utopia*, 84–119.

30. Moyn, *Last Utopia*, 120–75; Arthur, *Unfinished Projects*, 199–224; Beverley, *Latinamericanism After 9/11*; and Bosteels, *Marx and Freud in Latin America*, 1–27, 299–310.

31. Muñoz, *Dictator's Shadow*, 71, citing Fontaine's *Historia no contada de los economistas y el presidente Pinochet*.

32. Ibid.

33. Klein, *The Shock Doctrine*, Part 1, highlighting the link between CIA-funded experiments on shock therapy, torture techniques, and the implementation of free market reforms; and Part 2, discussing the transformation of South American economies in the 1970s. Also Fontaine, *Historia no contada de los economistas y el presidente Pinochet*, cited in Muñoz, *Dictator's Shadow*, 71–2.

34. Barros, *Constitutionalism and Dictatorship*, 129.

35. P. Verdugo, *Los zarpazos del puma*, Santiago: Ediciones Chile-América CESOC, 1989. On 15 October 2008, General Arellano was indicted and sentenced to six years in prison by the Chilean Supreme Court for the Caravan of Death case.

36. National Security Archive, Summary of Information, 6–8, at www.gwu. edu/nsarchiv/NSAEBB/NSAEBB8/cho208, last retrieved 24 April 2013. Also M. González, 'La historia que no se cuenta de Arancibia Clavel', in *CIPER Chile*, 1 May 2011, at www.ciperchile.cl/2011/05/01/la-historia-que-no-se-cuenta-de-arancibia-clavel, last retrieved 30 May 2013.

37. M. González, 'La historia que no se cuenta de Arancibia Clavel'. She cites Arancibia Clavel's testimony before Argentinian courts on 28 November 1978.

38. CIPER Chile, 'Los resentimientos intelectuales de Pinochet contra el general Carlos Prats', in CIPER Chile, 10 May 2013, citing Willoughby's declaration before Argentinian courts.

39. A copy of Arancibia's report to Contreras was found during a raid on his apartment in Buenos Aires. Townley had confessed to his part and that of his contacts and superiors in the DINA on 2 September 1992 in the US: González, 'La historia que no se cuenta de Arancibia Clavel'. In July 2003, the Chilean judge Alejandro Solís condemned Manuel Contreras and other DINA members for the murder of Carlos Prats, as members of a criminal organisation, in application of the Nuremberg doctrine.

40. González, 'La historia que no se cuenta de Arancibia Clavel'.

41. Muñoz, *Dictator's Shadow*, 62.

42. F. Varas, *Gustavo Leigh. El general disidente*, Santiago: Ediciones Aconcagua, 1979, 78.

43. See Barros, *Constitutionalism and Dictatorship*, 165.

44. González, 'La historia que no se cuenta de Arancibia Clavel'.

45. Muñoz, *Dictator's Shadow*, 95–6.

46. Barros, *Constitutionalism and Dictatorship*, 168–74; also Muñoz, *Dictator's Shadow*, 127.

47. Muñoz, *Dictator's Shadow*, 130.

48. The Soviet ambassador to France, Stephan Chernovenko, cited by Muñoz in *Dictator's Shadow*, 165.

49. Muñoz, *Dictator's Shadow*, 169. The rocket launched by an FPMR fighter directly at Pinochet's armoured Mercedes Benz slammed into the frame of one of its doors 'but skidded off without exploding'. Pinochet attributed his luck to an image of the Virgin Mary who he said had appeared to him during the attack.

50. Muñoz, *Dictator's Shadow*, 211.
51. Ibid., 211, 234. Faletto, *Dimensiones del desarrollo*, 64–5.
52. Faletto, *Dimensiones del desarrollo*, 64–5.
53. Sandel, *What Money Can't Buy*, 6.
54. Ibid.
55. J. L. Anderson, 'The Dictator', in *New Yorker*, 19 October 1988.
56. Ibid.
57. 'Chile: polémica de Camila Vallejo con diario estadounidense', in *La Jornada*, 2 May 2012, 13, available at www.jornada.unam.mx, retrieved 29 September 2012. Also, M. A. O'Grady, 'Chile's Cautionary Lesson for Americans: A free market is at risk when a demand for equality is not answered by a defense of liberty', in *Wall Street Journal*, 29 April 2012.

References

Selected Archive Sources

Archivo Chile, CEME. 'Ni rendición ni avión, respondió Allende a los generales golpistas', by M González, at www.archivochile.com/S_Allende_UP/doc_sobre_sallende/SAsobre0047.pdf

Archivo Salvador Allende, América Latina: Un pueblo continente, 1, Santiago, 1990

– Las tareas de la juventud, 2, México, 1990

– El gobierno popular, 9, Tlaxcala, 1990

– El partido socialista de Chile, México, 1990

– Los trabajadores y el gobierno popular, 8, Morelia, 1990

– Rumbo de liberación, 5, México, 1990

Beer, S., *One Year of (Relative) Solitude: The Second Level of Recursion, December 1972*, box 60, Stafford Beer collection

Conteras, M., Letter to B. Allende, Archivo Chile, Centro de Estudios CEME, Noviembre de 1973

Ejército de Chile, División Escuela, Escuela Militar. Relación de la colección de libros de Napoleón, available at www.ciperchile.cl/wp-content/uploads/libros-napoleon.pdf , last retrieved 30 May 2013

Flores, F., Letter to Stafford Beer, 13 July 1971, box 55, Stafford Beer collection

Intelligence Memorandum, 'Consequences of a Military Coup in Chile', 1 August 1973, CDP/CIA

H. Kissinger to R. Nixon, 1970, NSA Archive, available at gwu.edu/nsaarchiv/NSANEEB110/index.htm

Letter from Miriam Contreras to Beatriz Allende, November 1973, Archivo Chile, Centro de Estudios Miguel Enríquez

National Security Archive, Summary of Information (Michael Townley), 6-8, at www.gwu.edu/nsarchiv/NSAEBB/NSAEBB8/ch0208.htm, last retrieved 24 April 2013

Schwember, H., Letter to Stafford Beer, November 12, 1972, box 64, Stafford Beer collection

Telegram, Sec State to Amembassy, Santiago, 'USG Attitude toward Junta', 12 September 1973, DOS/CFP

Telegram, Davis to SecState, 'Gen. Pinochet's Request for Meeting with MILGP Officer', 12 September 1973

Telegram, Davis to SecState, 'Relations with the New Chilean Government', 13 September 1973, DOS/CFP. DCI Briefing, Washington Special Actions Group Meeting, 14 September 1973, CDP-NSC

The Joint Chiefs of Staff, Washington, DC, 13 March 1962, 'Memorandum for the Secretary of Defense: Justification for US Military Intervention in Cuba', at www.gwu.edu/~nsarchiv/news/20010430/northwoods.pdf

US Congress, Senate, *Alleged Assassination Plots Involving Foreign Leaders, Interim Report of the Select Committee to Study Government Operations with Respect to Intelligence Activities, 94th Congress, 2nd Session*, Washington, DC: US Government Printing Office, 20 November 1975

US Senate, *Covert Action in Chile: 1963-1973*, US Government Printing Office, Washington, 1975

Published Sources

Agüero, F., 'A Political Army in Chile', in *Political Armies: The Military and Nationbuilding in the Age of Democracy*, ed. K. Koonings and D. Kruijt, London: Zed Books, 2002

Allende, B., 'Combatir hasta el final. Plaza de la Revolución José Martí, La Habana, 28 de Septiembre de 1973', in A. Dorfman et al., *Chile: El otro 11 de septiembre*, ed. P. Aguilera and R. Fredes, Melbourne: Ocean Press, 2003

Allende, S., *La vía chilena al socialismo*, Madrid: Fundamentos, 1971

—, *América Latina: Voz de un pueblo continente. Discursos del Presidente Allende en sus giras por Argentina, Ecuador, Colombia, y Perú*, Santiago: Consejería de Difusión de la Presidencia de la República, 1971

—, *Higiene mental y delincuencia*, Santiago: Ediciones CESOC, 2005

—, *Salvador Allende. Presente*, ed. J. Garcés, Madrid: Sequitur, 2008, 101

Althusser, L., *For Marx*, trans. B. Brewster, London: Verso, 2005, 212

Ambrose, S. E., *Nixon: Ruin and Recovery, 1973–1990*, New York: Simon & Schuster, 1991

Amin, S., *Unequal Development: An Essay on the Social Formations of Peripheral Capitalism*, New York: Monthly Review Press, 1976

Amin, S., Arrighi, G., Gunder Frank, A. and Wallerstein, I., *Transforming the Revolution: Social Movements and the World System*, New York: New Press, 1990

Amorós, M., *Compañero Presidente: Salvador Allende, una vida por la democracia y el socialismo*, Valencia: Universitat de Valencia, 2008

—, *Sombras sobre Isla Negra: La dolorosa muerte de Neruda*, Barcelona: Editorial B, 2012

Ampuero, R., *El último tango de Salvador Allende*, Santiago: Plaza & Janés, 2012

Anderson, T. C., *Sartre's Two Ethics: From Authenticity to Integral Humanity*, Chicago: Open Court, 1993

Arancibia Clavel, P., M. A. Alwyn and S. Reyes del Villar, *Los hechos de la violencia en Chile: del discurso a la acción*, Santiago, CIDOC/Universidad Finis Terrae, 2003

Arendt, H., *Eichmann in Jerusalem: A Report on the Banality of Evil*, London: Penguin Classics, 2006

Arrate, J. and E. Rojas, *Memoria de la izquierda chilena, 1850–1970*, Santiago: Javuer Vergara Editor, 2003

Arthur, P., *Unfinished Projects, Decolonization and the Philosophy of Jean-Paul Sartre*, London & New York: Verso, 2010

Auden, W. H., *The Age of Anxiety*, Princeton University Press, [1947] 2011

Bachelet, A., *Las Cartas del General Bachelet*, Santiago de Chile: Editorial Norma, 2006

Badiou, A., 'Politics: a Non-Expressive Dialectics', paper delivered at Birkbeck Law School, University of London, 26 November 2005, later published in *Philosophy for Militants*, London & New York: Verso, 2012

—, 'The Saturated Generic Identity of the Working Class', an interview with D. George and N. Veroli, in *Carcelaglio*, 16 October 2006, 176–216

Báez, F., *A Universal History of the Destruction of Books*, New York: Atlas & Co., 2008

Ballard, J. G., 'The Assassination of JF Kennedy Considered as a Downhill Race', in *The Atrocity Exhibition*, London: Flamingo, Annotated edition, 1993

Bamford, J., *Body of Secrets*, New York: Doubleday, 2001

Barros, R., *Constitutionalism and Dictatorship: Pinochet, the Junta, and the 1980 Constitution*, Cambridge: University of Cambridge Press, 2002

Bass, G. J., *Stay the Hand of Vengeance: The Politics of War Crimes Tribunals*, Princeton: Princeton University Press, 2000

Basso, L., *Il principe senza scettro*, Milan: Feltrinelli Editore, [1958] 1998

Baxi, U., *Human Rights in a Posthuman World*, Oxford: Oxford University Press, 2007

—, 'The Failure of Deliberative Democracy and Global Justice', in *Democracy Unrealized: Documenta 11_Platform 1 113.132*, ed. O. Enwezor et al., Ostfildren-Ruit: Hatje Cantz Publ., 2001

—, *Mambrino's Helmet: Human Rights for a Changing World*, New Delhi: Har-Anand, 1994

—, 'The Development of the Right to Development', in *Human Rights: New Dimensions and Challenges*, ed. J. Symonides, Aldershot: Ashgate & UNESCO, 1994

—, 'The Death and Rebirth of Distributive Justice', in *Marx, Law, and Justice: Indian Perspectives*, Bombay: N. M. Tripathi, 1993, 51–84

Beck Matuštík, M., *Radical Evil and the Scarcity of Hope*, Bloomington and Indianapolis: Indiana University Press, 2008

Beckett, A., *Pinochet in Piccadilly: Britain and Chile's Hidden History*, London: Faber and Faber, 2003

Bedjaoui, M., *Terra Nullius, 'droits' historiques et autodétermination*, 1975

—, 'Non-alignement et Droit International', *151 Recueil des Cours*, vol. 151, 1976, 408 ff.

Beer, S., 'Laws of Anarchy' (1975), 'Cybernetics of Humankind' (1976), 'An Open Letter to Heinz von Foerster (About Social Cybernetics)' (1976), and 'The Will of the People' (1982), in *Think Before You Think: Social Complexity and Knowledge of Knowing*, ed. D. Whittaker, foreword by Brian Eno, Charlbury: Wavestone Press, 2009

—, *Designing Freedom*, London: John Wiley, 1974

—, *Beyond Dispute*, Chichester: John Wiley, 1994

—, *Brain of the Firm: The Managerial Cybernetics of Organization*, New York: J. Wiley [1972] 1991

Bensaïd, D., 'Puissances du communisme', in *ContreTemps. Revue du Critique Communiste*, no. 4, 2009

Benton, L., *Law and Colonial Cultures: Legal Regimes in World History, 1400–1900*, Cambridge: Cambridge University Press, 2002

Berger, J., *Bento's Sketchbook*, London: Verso, 2011

Beverley, J., *Latinamericanism After 9/11*, Durham, NC: Duke University Press, 2011

Bisama, Á., *Estrellas muertas*, Santiago: Alfaguara, 2010

Bolaño, R., *Nocturno de Chile*, Barcelona: Anagrama, 2000

Bolívar, S., *Letter From Jamaica, 1815*, in *The Bolivarian Revolution*, foreword by H. Chávez, London: Verso, 2009

Bosteels, B., *The Actuality of Communism*, London: Verso, 2011

—, *Marx and Freud in Latin America: Politics, Psychoanalysis and Religion in Times of Terror*, London & New York: Verso, 2012

Bowman, A. E. and R. V. Stone, '"Socialist Morality" in Sartre's Unpublished 1964 Rome lecture: A Summary and Commentary', in *Existentialist Ethics*, W. L. McBride (ed.), New York: Routledge, 1996

Brecht, B., *The Solution*, in *Poems 1913–1956*, J. Willett and R. Manheim (eds), Methuen, 1976

Buck-Morss, S., *The Dialectics of Seeing: Walter Benjamin and the Arcades Project*, Cambridge: The MIT Press, 1989

—, *Hegel, Haiti, and Universal History*, Pittsburgh: Pittsburgh University Press, 2009

Byers, M., *War Law: Understanding International Law and Armed Conflict*, New York: Grove Press & Atlantic Monthly Press, 2007

Calder Williams, E., *Combined and Uneven Apocalypse*, Ropley: Zero Books, 2011

Castells, M., *La lucha de clases en Chile*, Buenos Aires: Siglo XXI, 1974

Castro, F., *History Will Absolve Me*, New York: Center for Cuban Studies, 1953

Cavallo, A., *Memorias: Cardenal Raúl Silva Henríquez*, Santiago: Copygraph, 1991

—, and M. Serrano, *Las vigilias de Allende, Pinochet, Merino y Leigh: La Sangre de los Generales*, 5: www.Salvador-allende.d/Golpe/el 11/24%20HORAS.pdf

Césaire, A., *Discours sur le colonialisme, suivi de Discours sur la Négritude*, Paris: Éditions Présence Africaine, [1955] 2004

Chase, A., *Law & History: The Evolution of the American Legal System*, New York: The New Press, 1997

Christian, D. and B. Jackson, 'Luis Buñuel: That Obscure Object of Desire', in *Buffalo Film Seminars*, Buffalo: Market Arcade Film & Arts Center and State University of New York at Buffalo, 2007

Cockcroft, J. D. (ed.), *Chile's Voice of Democracy: Salvador Allende Reader*, Melbourne: Ocean Press, 2000

Colby, W. and P. Forbath, *Honourable Men: My Life in the CIA*, London: Hutchinson, 1978

Collier, S. and W. F. Sater, *A History of Chile, 1808–2002*, Cambridge: Cambridge University Press, 2004

Colorado, J. I., 'Jaime Guzmán: Demiurgo de Pinochet', in *Pensamiento Crítico*, no. 5, 2010

Comité Creativo, *Memorandum: La Junta y su opción como destino histórico. Implicaciones próximas*, Guzmán Papers, Fundación Jaime Guzmán, Santiago, 1973

Cornell, D., *Moral Images of Freedom: A Future for Critical Theory*, Lanham, MD: Rowan & Littlefield, 2008

—, *The Philosophy of the Limit*, New York: Routledge, 1992

Correa de Oliveira, P., *Revolución y Contra-revolución*, Barcelona: Cristiandad, 1959

Cortázar, J., *Fantomas contra los vampiros multinacionales*, México: Excelsior, 1975

—, *Papeles inesperados*, Barcelona: Alfaguara, 2009

Corvalán Márquez, L., *Los partidos políticos y el golpe del 11 de septiembre*, Santiago: CESOC, 2000

Cristi, R., *El pensamiento político de Jaime Guzmán: Autoridad y Libertad*, Santiago: LOM, 2000

Davis, N., *Los dos últimos años de Salvador Allende*, Barcelona: Plaza & Janés, 1986

De Andrade, O., 'Manifesto Antropófago', *Antropofagia Hoje? Oswald de Andrade em cena*, ed. J. Ruffinelli and J. C. de Castro Rocha, São Paulo: Realizações Editora, 2011

De Ramón, A., *Historia de Chile*, Santiago, Catalonia, 2004

De Sousa Santos, B., 'Toward a Counter-Hegemonic Globalization', Parts I and II, in *Challenging Empires*, ed. J. Sen, A. Escobar and P. Waterman, New Delhi: The Viveka Foundation, 2004

—, *Toward a New Common Sense: Law, Science and Politics in the Paradigmatic Transition*, London: Routledge, 1995

— and Rodríguez, C. (ed.), *Law and Globalisation From Below: Towards a Cosmopolitan Legality*, Cambridge: Cambridge University Press, 2005

Debray, R., *Conversación con Allende*, México: Siglo XXI, 1971

Deleuze, G. and F. Guattari, *A Thousand Plateaus: Capitalism & Schizophrenia*, London: Athlone Press, 1998

Dorfman, A., *Mas allá del miedo: el largo adiós a Pinochet*, Madrid: Siglo XXI, 2002

—, *Other Septembers, Many Americas: Selected Provocations, 1980–2004*, London: Pluto Books, 2004

—, Introduction, *The Empire's Old Clothes: What the Lone Ranger, Babar, and Other Innocent Heroes Do to Our Minds*, Durham, NC: Duke University Press, 2010

Dosman, E. J., *The Life and Times of Raúl Prebisch, 1901–1986*, Montreal & London: McGill-Queen's University Press, 2008

Duffield, M., *Development, Security, and Unending War*, Cambridge: Polity Press, 2007

Dupuy, J.-P., *The Mechanization of the Mind: On the Origins of Cognitive Science*, Princeton & Oxford: Princeton University Press, 2000

— et al., *Où va le monde? 2012–2022: Une décennie au devant des catastrophes*, Paris: Mille et Une Nuits, 2012

Dussel, E., *Kairós: El acontecimiento liberador en Pablo de Tarso*, manuscript on file with the author, 2009. Also available at www.enriquedussel.com/txt/II-CAP-4-31.pdf

Edwards, A., *La fronda aristocrática en Chile*, Santiago: Editorial Universitaria, 1989

Edwards, J., *Persona Non Grata*, Santiago: Tiempo de Memoria, 2000

Einstein, A., *Einstein on Politics: His Private Thoughts and Public Stands on Nationalism, Zionism, War, Peace, and the Bomb*, ed. D. Rowe and R. Schulmann, Princeton: Princeton University Press, 2007

Escobar, A., *Encountering Development: The Making and Unmaking of the Third World*, Princeton University Press, 1985

Eyzaguirre, J., *Fisionomía histórica de Chile*, Santiago: Editorial Universitaria, 1988

Faletto, E., *Dimensiones del desarrollo*, Buenos Aires: CLACSO/Siglo del Hombre, 2009

Fals Borda, O., *La subversión en Colombia*, Bogotá: Universidad Nacional/Tercer Mundo Editores/Fica-CEPA, [1967] 2008

Fanon, F., *The Wretched of the Earth*, London: Penguin Modern Classics [1961], 2009

Farías, V., *La izquierda chilena (1969–1973): Documentos para el studio de su línea estratégica*, Santiago: Centro de Estudios Públicos, 2000

—, *Salvador Allende contra los judíos, los homosexuales y otros 'degenerados'*, Santiago: Áltera, 2005

—, *Salvador Allende: El fin de un mito*, Santiago: Editorial Maye, 2007

Feinstein, A., *Pablo Neruda: A Passion for Life*, London: Bloomsbury, 2004

Findlay, E. J., 'Love in the tropics', in *Close Encounters of Empire: Writing the Cultural History of U.S.–Latin American Relations*, ed. G. M. Joseph, C. C. LeGrand and R. D. Salvatore, foreword by Fernando Coronil, Durham, NC: Duke University Press, 1998

Fischer, S., *Modernity Disavowed: Haiti and the Cultures of Slavery in the Age of Revolution*, Durham, NC: Duke University Press, 2004

Foerster, R. and S. Montecino, *Organizaciones, líderes y contiendas mapuches, 1900–1970*, Santiago: CEM, 1998

Fontaine, A., *Todos querían la revolución: Chile, 1964–1973*, Santiago: Zig-Zag, 1999

—, *Historia no contada de los economistas y el presidente Pinochet*, Santiago: Zig-Zag, 1988

Foucault, M., *The Birth of Biopolitics: Lectures at the Collège de France, 1978–1979*, London: Palgrave Macmillan, 2008

—, *Society Must Be Defended: Lectures at the Collège de France, 1975–1976*, New York: Picador, 2003

Fowke, E. and J. Glazer, *Songs of Work and Protest*, New York: Dover Publications, 1960

Francis, M. J., *La victoria de Allende*, Buenos Aires: Francisco de Aguirre, 1972

Franco, J., *Cruel Modernity*, Durham, NC: Duke University Press, 2013

FRAP, *Programa del Gobierno Popular*, Santiago de Chile, s.f., January 1963

Fried, B., *The Progressive Assault on Laissez Faire: Robert Hale and the First Law and Economics Movement*, Cambridge, Mass.: Harvard University Press, 1998

Gadea, H., *My Life With Che: The Making of a Revolutionary*, New York: Palgrave Macmillan, 2008

Galeano, E., *Las venas abiertas de América Latina*, Madrid, Siglo XXI, 2010

Garcés, J., 'Prólogo', in *Salvador Allende. Presente*, Madrid: Sequitur, 2008

—, *Soberanos e intervenidos: Estrategias globales, americanos y españoles*, Madrid: Siglo XXI, 1996

—, *Allende y la experiencia chilena: Las armas de la política*, Barcelona: Ariel, 1976, reproducido en Santiago: Bat, 1990

—, *Orlando Letelier: Testimonio y vindicación*, México: Siglo XXI, 1995

Garcés, M. A., *Cervantes in Algiers: A Captive's Tale*, Nashville: Vanderbilt University Press, 2002

García Linera, Á., *La potencia plebeya*, Buenos Aires: CLACSO & Prometeo Libros, 2008

—, et al., *Imperio, multitud y sociedad abigarrada*, AA.VV., Buenos Aires: CLACSO & Waldhuter Editores, 2010

García Márquez, G., 'Posibilidades da Antropofagia', in *Antropofagia Hoje? Oswald de Andrade em cena*, J. Ruffinelli and J. C. de Castro Rocha (eds), São Paulo: Realizações Editora, 2011

—, 'La soledad de América Latina', Stockholm, 8 December 1982, in *Yo no vengo a decir un discurso*, Barcelona: Mondadori, 2010

Girard, R., *Mensonge romantique et vérité romanesque*, Paris: Grasset, 1961

—, *Des choses cachées depuis la fondation du monde*, Paris: Grasset, 1978

González Camus, I., *El día que murió Allende*, Santiago: Ediciones ChileAmérica, 1988

Goodwin, D. Kearns, *Lyndon Johnson and the American Dream*, New York: Harper & Row/Saint Martin's Press, 1991

Gordon, J. A. and L. R. Gordon, *Of Divine Warning: Reading Disaster in the Modern Age*, Boulder: Paradigm, 2009

Gordon, L. R., *Existentia Africana: Understanding Africana Existential Thought*, New York: Routledge, 2000

Graeber, D., *The Democracy Project: A History. A Crisis. A Movement*, London: Allen Lane, 2013

Grandin, G., 'Living in Revolutionary Time', in *A Century of Revolution: Insurgent and Counterinsurgent Violence During Latin America's Long Cold War*, ed. G. Grandin and G. M. Joseph, Durham, NC: Duke University Press, 2010

Grayson, G., *El partido Demócrata Cristiano chileno*, Buenos Aires: Francisco de Aguirre, 1968

Guardiola-Rivera, O., 'Absolute Contingency and the Inaugural Event of International Law, Chiapas-Valladolid, ca. 1550', in *Event: The Force of International Law*, ed. F. Johns, R. Joyce and S. Pahuja, London: Routledge, 2011

—, *What If Latin America Ruled the World?*, London & New York: Bloomsbury, 2010

—, *Being Against the World: Rebellion and Constitution*, London: Routledge & Birkbeck Law Press, 2009

Guevara, E., *Notes critiques d'économie politique*, Paris: Mille et Une Nuits, 2012

—, *The Motorcycle Diaries: Notes on a Latin American Journey*, London & New York, Verso, 2005, translated from *Diarios de motocicleta: Notas de un viaje por América Latina*, Buenos Aires: Editorial Planeta, 2005

—, *Global Justice*, Melbourne: Ocean Press, 2002

—, 'El socialismo y el hombre en Cuba', in *Obra Revolucionaria*, and 'Socialism and Man in Cuba', in *Che Guevara Reader: Writings on Politics and Revolution*, ed. D. Deutschmann, New York & Melbourne: Ocean Press, 1997

—, 'Reuniones bimestrales', in *El Che en la Revolución Cubana: Ministerio de Industrias*, vol. 6, La Habana: Ministerio de Azúcar, 1966

Gunder Frank, A., *Capitalism and Underdevelopment in Latin America: Historical Studies of Chile and Brazil*, New York & London: Monthly Review Press Classics, [1967] 2009

—, *Lumpenburguesía: Lumpendesarrollo: Dependencia, clase y política en Latinoamérica*, Barcelona: Laia, 1972

Guzmán, J., 'La iglesia chilena y el debate político', in T. MacHale (ed.), *Visión crítica de Chile*, Santiago: Ediciones Portada, 1972

—, *Escritos Personales*, Santiago: Fundación Jaime Guzmán & Editorial Zig-Zag, 1992

Guzmán, N. (ed.), *Chile desclasificado: Documentos secretos del FBI, Pentágono & CIA*, vol. 1, Santiago: Ernesto Carmona Editor, 1999

Harmer, T., *Allende's Chile and the Inter-American Cold War*, Chapel Hill: University of Carolina at Chapel Hill Press, 2011

Hedges, C., *Empire of Illusion*, New York: Nation Books, 2009

Henáff, M., *The Price of Truth*, Stanford, CA: Stanford University Press, 2010

Hersh, S. M., *The Price of Power: Kissinger in the Nixon White House*, London: Faber and Faber, 1983

Hessel, S., *Indignez Vous!*, Montpellier: Indigènes Éditions, 2011

Hitchens, C., *The Trial of Henry Kissinger*, London & New York: Verso, 2001

Hobsbawm, E., *Gente poco corriente*, Barcelona: Crítica, 1999

—, *Fractured Times: Culture and Society in the Twentieth Century*, London: Little, Brown, 2013

—, *Echoes of the Marseillaise*, New Brunswick: Rutgers University Press, 1990

Hofstadter, R. J., *The Paranoid Style in American Politics and Other Essays*, London: Jonathan Cape, 1996

Hogge, B., *Barefoot into Cyberspace: Adventures in search of techno-Utopia*, London, Barefoot Publishing, 2011

Huntington, S., *Who Are We? The Challenges to America's National Identity*, London: Simon & Schuster, 2004

Ibarz, M., 'A Serious Experiment: Land Without Bread, 1933', in *Luis Buñuel: New Readings*, ed. I. Santaolalla and P. Williams Evans, London: British Film Institute, 2004

Isasi-Díaz, A. M. and E. Mendieta, *Decolonizing Epistemologies: Latina/o Theology and Philosophy*, New York: Fordham University Press, 2012

Jara, J., *Víctor: Un canto inconcluso*, Santiago: Fundación Víctor Jara, 1993

—, 'El dia del golpe' and 'Un canto inconcluso', in *Chile: El otro 11 de septiembre*, with A. Dorfman, S. Allende, P. Neruda, B. Allende, F. Castro et al., Melbourne: Ocean Press, 2003

Jara, V., 'Estadio Chile', in *Chile: El otro 11 de septiembre*, with A. Dorfman, S. Allende, P. Neruda, B. Allende, F. Castro et al., Melbourne: Ocean Press, 2003

Jara Hinojosa, I., *De Franco a Pinochet: El proyecto cultural Franquista en Chile, 1936–1980*, Santiago: Programa de Magíster en TEHA, Departamento de Teoría de las Artes, Universidad de Chile, 2006

Johnson, D. K., *The Lavender Scare: The Cold War Persecution of Gays and Lesbians in the Federal Government*, Chicago: The University of Chicago Press, 2004

Johnson, J. J., *Latin America in Caricature*, Austin: University of Texas Press, 1980

Jorquera, C., *El Chicho Allende*, Santiago: BAT, 1990

Joxe, A., *Le Chili sous Allende*, Paris: Gallimard, 1974

Kahneman, D., *Thinking, Fast and Slow*, London: Allen Lane, 2011

Kapuscinski, R., *Cristo con un fusil al hombro*, Madrid: Crónicas Anagrama, 2010

Kearns Goodwin, D., *Lyndon Johnson and the American Dream*, New York: Harper & Row/Saint Martin's Press, 1991

—, 'The Stakes of Law, or Hale and Foucault!' in *Sexy Dressing, Etc.*, Cambridge: Harvard University Press, 1993

Kennedy, D., *The Dark Sides of Virtue: Reassessing International Humanitarianism*, Princeton: Princeton University Press, 2005

Kinzer, S., *Overthrow: America's Century of Regime Change from Hawaii to Iraq*, New York: Times Books, 2006

Kirwan, M., *Discovering Girard*, London: Darton, Longman and Todd, 2004

Klein, N., *The Shock Doctrine: The Rise of Disaster Capitalism*, London: Penguin, 2008

Klener Hernández, L., 'Salvador Allende y el encendido fogoso de la memoria', in *Salvador Allende: Cien años, todos los sueños*, ed. A. Ortizpozo, Caracas: Ministerio del Poder Popular para la Información y la Comunicación, 2008

Klubock, T. M., 'Ránquil: Violence and Peasant Politics on Chile's Southern Frontier', in *A Century of Revolution*, ed. G. Grandin and G. M. Joseph, Durham, NC: Duke University Press, 121–59

Kornbluh, P., *Pinochet: Los archivos secretos*, Barcelona: Crítica, 2004

—, *The Pinochet File: A Declassified Dossier on Atrocity and Accountability*, New York: New Press, 2003

Kristeva, J., *The Sense and Non-Sense of Revolt*, New York: Columbia University Press, 2000

Lavín, J., *Chile, Revolución Silenciosa*, Santiago: Zig-Zag, 1987

Lavretski, J., *Salvador Allende*, Moscow: Progreso, 1978

Lazo, C. and C. Cea, *La negra Lazo: Memorias de una pasión política*, Santiago: Planeta, 2005

Lenin, V. I., *The State and Revolution*, Whitefish: Kessinger Publishing, 2004

Leyva, F. I., *Latin American Neostructuralism: The Contradictions of Post-Neoliberal Development*, Minneapolis: Minnesota University Press, 2008

Linebaugh, P., *The Magna Carta Manifesto: Liberties and Commons for All*, Berkeley: University of California Press, 2009

López, L. I., 'Imagen de Beatriz Allende', in *Primera Plana*, Madrid, 20–26 October 1976

Losurdo, D., *Liberalism: A Counter-History*, London & New York: Verso, 2011

—, *Hegel and the Freedom of Moderns*, Durham, NC: Duke University Press, 2004

Magasich-Airola, J., *Los que dijeron no: Historia del movimiento de marinos anti-golpistas*, vol. 1, Santiago: LOM, 2008

Malabou, C., *The Ontology of the Accident: An Essay on Destructive Plasticity*, London: Polity, 2012

Malló, O., *El cártel español: Historia de la reconquista española de Méjico y América Latina (1898–2008)*, Madrid: Akal, 2011

Marion, J. L., 'Saturated Phenomenon', in *Phenomenology and the 'Theological Turn': The French Debate*, ed. D. Janicaud, New York: Fordham University Press, 2000

Martner, G. (ed.), *Salvador Allende, 1908–1973: Obras Escogidas (1939–1973)*, Santiago: Ediciones del Centro de Estudios Políticos Latinoamericanos Simón Bolívar & Fundación Presidente Allende, 1992

Marx, K., *The 18th Brumaire of Napoleon Bonaparte*, Preface to the Second Edition (1869), New York: International Publishers/Wildside Press, 2008

—, 'The Civil War in France', in *Political Writings*, vol. 3, *The First International and After*, ed. D. Fernbach, London: Penguin, 1974

—, *On the Jewish Question* (1843) and *Fragment on Machines* (1858), in *Grundrisse*, Harmondsworth: Penguin, 1973

—, Letter to Kugelman, April 12, 1871, in K. Marx and F. Engels, *Selected Correspondence*, Moscow, 1965

—, and F. Engels, Preface to the New German Edition, *The Communist Manifesto*, June 24, 1872, in *Selected Works*, vol. 1, Moscow, 1962

Mason, P., *Why It's Still Kicking Off Everywhere: The New Global Revolutions*, London: Verso, revised edition 2013

Mattei, U. and L. Nader, *Plunder: When the Rule of Law Is Illegal*, Oxford: Wiley-Blackwell, 2008

Mayer, A., *Dynamics of Counterrevolution in Europe, 1870–1956: An Analytic Framework*, New York: Harper and Row, 1977

—, *Why Did the Heavens Not Darken? The Final Solution in History*, New York: Pantheon Books, 1988

Mayol, A., *El derrumbe del modelo, La crisis de la economía de mercado en el Chile contemporáneo*, Santiago: LOM, 2012

—, *No al lucro: De la crisis del modelo a la nueva era política*, Santiago: Debate, 2012

McNamara, R. S., *In Retrospect: The Tragedy and Lessons of Vietnam*, New York: Vintage, 1996

McWhinney, E., *The International Court of Justice and the Western Tradition of International Law*, The Hague: M. Nijhof, 1987

Medina, E., *Cybernetic Revolutionaries: Technology and Politics in Allende's Chile*, Cambridge, Mass.: MIT Press, 2011

Meillassoux, Q., *After Finitude*, London: Continuum, 2008

Meister, R., *After Evil: A Politics of Human Rights*, New York: Columbia University Press, 2012

Mendieta, E., 'The Ethics of (Not) Knowing', in *Decolonizing Epistemologies: Latina/o Theology and Philosophy*, ed. A. M. Isasi-Díaz and E. Mendieta, Bronx: Fordham University Press, 2012, 247–64

— (ed.), *The Frankfurt School on Religion: Key Writings by the Major Thinkers*, New York: Routledge, 2005

Merino, J. T., *Bitácora de un almirante: Memorias*, Santiago: Andrés Bello, 1999

Miéville, C., *Between Equal Rights: A Marxist Theory of International Law*, London: Haymarket Books, 2006

—, *London's Overthrow*, London: The Westbourne Press, 2012

Modak, F. (ed.), *Salvador Allende en el umbral del siglo XXI*, México: Plaza & Janés, 1998

Montecino, S., *Madres y huachos: Alegorías del mestizaje chileno*, Santiago: Cuarto Propio, 1991

Moulian, T., *Conversación interrumpida con Allende*, Santiago: LOM, 1998

Moyn, S., *The Last Utopia: Human Rights in History*, Cambridge, Mass.: The Belknap Press at Harvard, 2010

Muñoz, H., 'The Internationalist Policy of the Socialist Party and Foreign Relations of Chile', in *Latin American Nations in World Politics*, ed. H. Muñoz and J. S. Tulchin, Boulder, CO: Westview, 1984

—, *The Dictator's Shadow: A Political Memoir*, New York: Basic Books, 2008

Nerín, G., *La guerra que vino de África*, Barcelona: Crítica, 2005

Neruda, P., *Memoirs*, New York: Farrar, Straus & Giroux, 1977

—, *Confieso que he vivido: Memorias*, Barcelona: Seix Barral, 1979

—, *Invitación al Nixonicidio y Alabanza de la Revolución Chilena*, Santiago: Quimantú, 1973

Nolff, M., *Salvador Allende: El político, El estadista*, Santiago: Documentas, 1993

—, 'Industria manufacturera', in *Geografía económica de Chile*, vol. 3, Santiago: Corporación de Fomento de la Producción, 1962

Novoa Monreal, E. et al., *La vía chilena al socialismo*, México: Siglo XXI, 1973

—, *Vía lega hacia el socialismo? El caso de Chile, 1970–1973*, Caracas: Editorial Jurídica Venezolana, 1978

Pagels, E., *Revelations: Visions, Prophecy and Politics in the Book of Revelation*, London: Viking, 2012

Pahuja, S., *Decolonising International Law: Development, Economic Growth and the Politics of Universality*, Cambridge: Cambridge University Press, 2011

Palacios, M. (ed.), *Historia general de América latina, VIII. América Latina desde 1930*, Madrid: Ediciones UNESCO & Editorial Trotta, 2008

Peña, J. C., *La secreta vida literaria de Augusto Pinochet*, Santiago: Random, 2013

Pey, V. (ed.), *Salvador Allende: Higiene Mental y delincuencia. Respuesta al libro defamatorio de Víctor Farías*, Santiago: Fundación Presidente Allende & CESOC, 2005

Pinilla de las Heras, E., *En menos de libertad: Dimensiones políticas del Grupo Laye en Barcelona y en España*, Barcelona: Anthropos, 1989

Pinochet Ugarte, A., *El día decisivo: 11 de septiembre de 1973*, Santiago: Editorial Andrés Bello, 1979

Pogee, T. W., *World Poverty: Cosmopolitan Responsibilities and Reform*, Oxford: Blackwell, 2002

—, 'Priorities of Global Justice', in *Global Justice*, ed. T. W. Pogee, Oxford: Blackwell, 2001, 6–23

Power, S., *A Problem From Hell: America and the Age of Genocide*, New York: Basic Books, 2002

Prats, C., *Memorias: Testimonio de un soldado*, Santiago: Pehuén, 1985

Prebisch, R., *The Economic Development of Latin America and Its Principal Problems*, New York: United Nations, 1950

Preston, P., *The Spanish Holocaust: Inquisition and Extermination in Twentieth-Century Spain*, London: Harper Press, 2012

Pujades, I. and J. Alsina, *Xile al cor* (Chile en el corazón), Santiago: Aedos, 1976

Quezada Lagos, F., *La elección presidencial de 1970*, Santiago de Chile, 1985

Ralston Saul, J., *Voltaire's Bastards*, New York: Vintage, 1992

Ramírez Necochea, H., *Historia del movimiento obrero chileno*, Santiago de Chile, 1956

—, *Balmaceda y la contrarevolución de 1891*, Santiago: Editorial Universitaria, 1958

Ramis, Á., 'Genealogía de una generación maldita', in *Otro Chile es Posible*, with Camila Vallejo, Giorgio Jackson, Francisco Figueroa et al., ed. V. H. de la Fuente, Santiago: Editorial Aún Creemos en los Sueños & Le Monde Diplomatique, 2011, 41–5

Rawls, J., *The Law of Peoples*, Cambridge: Cambridge University Press, 1999

Rediker, M. and P. Linebaugh, *The Many-Headed Hydra*, Boston: Beacon Press, 2000

Redmond, E. Hilda, 'Square Pegs: The Political Function of Ambiguous Gender in Three Novels of the Southern Cone', Ph.D. dissertation, Austin: The University of Texas at Austin, 2008

Reinholdt, M., *Flora Tristan*, Copenhagen: Narayana Press, 2004

Revueltas, J., *Ensayo sobre un proletariado sin cabeza*, ed. A. Revueltas, R. Martínez and P. Cheron, México: Era, [1962] 1980

—, *Los Errores*, México: Era, [1964] 1979

Richard, N., *Crítica de la memoria (1990–2010)*, Santiago: Ediciones de la Universidad Diego Portales, 2010

Rojas, P., V. Uribe, M. E. Rojas, I. Largo, I. Ropert and V. Espinoza, *Páginas en blanco: El 11 de Septiembre en La Moneda*, Santiago: Ediciones B, 2001, part 1

Rojas, R., *The Murder of Allende and the End of the Chilean Way to Socialism*, New York: Harper & Row, 1975

Rolnik, S. and F. Guattari, *Molecular Revolution in Brazil*, London: Semiotext(e) & MIT Press, 2008

Roosevelt, E., *As He Saw It*, New York: Duell, Sloan & Pearce, 1946

Rozitchner, L., 'La cuestión judía', in *Volver a 'La cuestión judía'*, ed. E. Vernik, Barcelona: Gedisa, 2011

Ruiz-Esquide Figueroa, A., *Las Fuerzas Armadas Durante Los Gobiernos de Eduardo Frei y Salvador Allende*, Santiago: Centro de Estudios del Desarrollo, 1993

Salomon, M. E., 'Winners and Others: Accounting for International Law's Favourites', in *The Cambridge Companion to Human Rights Law*, ed. C. Douzinas and C. Gearty, Cambridge: CUP, 2012

Salvatore, R. D., 'The Enterprise of Knowledge: Representational Machines of Informal Empire', in *Close Encounters of Empire: Writing the Cultural History of U.S.– Latin American Relations*, ed. G. M. Joseph, C. C. LeGrand and R. D. Salvatore, foreword by Fernando Coronil, Durham, NC: Duke University Press, 1998

Sandel, M., *What Money Can't Buy: The Moral Limits of Markets*, London: Allen Lane, 2012

Sartre, J.-P., *Critique of Dialectical Reason*, vol. 1, trans. A. Sheridan-Smith, London: Verso, [1960] 2004

—, 'On Genocide', in *Against the Crime of Silence: Proceedings of the International War Crimes Tribunal*, ed. J. Duffett, New York: Bertrand Russell Peace Foundation, 1968

Schmitt, C., *Dictatorship*, Oxford: Polity Press, 2013

Schmitz, D. F., *Thank God They're On Our Side: The United States and Right-Wing Dictators, 1921–1965*, Chapel Hill: University of Carolina Press, 1999

Schrecker, E., *Many Are the Crimes: McCarthyism in America*, Princeton: Princeton University Press, 1998

Seeger, P. and B. Reiser, *Carry It On!: a History in Song and Picture of the Working Men and Women of America*, New York: Simon & Schuster, 1985

Sen, J. Anand, A. Escobar and P. Waterman, *World Social Forum: Challenging Empires*, The Viveka Foundation, 2004

Silva Henríquez, R., in *Mensaje*, no. 209, June 1972, in *Chile visto por Mensaje: 1971–1981*, Santiago: Aconcagua, 1981

Smith, J., *Brazil and the United States: Convergence and Divergence*, Athens: University of Georgia Press, 2010

Solnit, R., *A Paradise Built in Hell: The Extraordinary Communities That Arise in Disaster*, New York: Viking Books, 2009

Sombart, W., *Deutscher Sozialismus*, Berlin: Buchhholz und Weisswange, 1934

Soto, Á., *El Mercurio y la difusión del pensamiento político económico liberal, 1955–1970*, Santiago: Centro de Estudios Bicentenario, 2003

Soto, H., and S. Villegas, *Archivos secretos: Documentos desclasificados de la CIA*, Santiago: LOM, 1999

Soto, Ó., *El último día de Salvador Allende*, Madrid: El País & Aguilar, 1998

Soto Kloss, E., *Ordenamiento Constitucional*, Santiago: Editorial Jurídica de Chile, 1980

Stern, S. J., *Reckoning with Pinochet: The Memory Question in Democratic Chile, 1989–2006*, Book Three, Durham, NC: Duke University Press, 2010

Stohl, M. and G. A. Lopez, *The State as Terrorist: The Dynamics of Governmental Violence and Repression*, Westport: Greenwood Press, 1984

Stone, O. and P. Kuznick, *The Untold History of the United States*, New York & London: Ebury Press/Simon & Schuster, 2012

Taibo II, P. Ignacio, *Arcángeles: Doce historias de revolucionarios herejes del siglo XX*, México: Planeta, 1998

Talbot, D., *Brothers: The Hidden History of the Kennedy Years*, New York: Free Press, 2007

Taylor, T., *Nuremberg and Vietnam: An American Tragedy*, Chicago: Quadrangle, 1970

Teitel, R., *Transitional Justice*, Oxford: Oxford University Press, 2000

Thompson, E. P., *Whigs and Hunters*, New York: Pantheon, 1975

Traverso, E., *The Origins of Nazi Violence*, New York: The New Press, 2003

Trumper, C., 'Ephemeral Histories', in S. Zeikmi-Nagy and F. I. Leiva (eds), *Democracy in Chile: The Legacy of September 11, 1973*, Brighton: Sussex Academic Press, 2005

Ulianova, O., 'La Unidad Popular y el Golpe Militar en Chile. Percepciones y análisis soviéticos', in *Estudios Públicos*, 79, Winter 2000, 83–171

Urrutia, M.. *Mi vida junto a Pablo Neruda*, Barcelona: Seix Barral, 1986.

Varas, J. M., *Nerudario*, Santiago: Planeta, 1999

Vargas Llosa, M., *The Way to Paradise*, London: Faber & Faber, 2004

Vergara, J. M. and F. Varas, *Coup! Allende's Last Day*, New York: Stein and Day, 1975

Wallace, H. A., *The Price of Vision: The Diary of Henry A. Wallace, 1942–1946*, ed. J. Morton Blum, New York: Houghton Mifflin, 1973

Wallerstein, I., 'The Present in the Light of the Longue Durée', in *Politics of Culture and the Spirit of Critique: Dialogues*, ed. G. Rockhill/A. Gómez-Muller, New York, Columbia University Press, 2011, 98–112

Walzer, M., *Just and Unjust Wars: A Moral Argument with Historical Ilustrations*, New York: Basic Books, 2006

Weiner, T., *Legacy of Ashes: The History of the CIA*, New York: Doubleday, 2007

West, C., 'A Prisoner of Hope in the Night of American Empire', in *Politics of Culture and the Spirit of Critique: Dialogues*, ed. G. Rockhill and A. Gómez-Muller, New York: Columbia University Press, 2011, 113–27

Westad, O. A., *The Global Cold War: Third World Interventions and The Making of Our Times*, Cambridge: Cambridge University Press, 2005

Western Sahara: Advisory Opinion, International Court of Justice Reports 1975, The Hague: International Court of Justice, 12, 83–7

Wey Gómez, N., *Tropics of Empire*, Cambridge, Mass.: MIT Press, 2008

Whittaker, D., *Stafford Beer: A Personal Memoir*, Wavestone Press, 2003

Williams, B., *Moral Luck*, Cambridge: Cambridge University Press, 1982

Winn, P., *Weavers of Revolution: The Yarur Workers and Chile's Road to Socialism*, New York & Oxford: Oxford University Press, 1986

—, 'The Furies of the Andes', in *A Century of Revolution: Insurgent and Counterinsurgent Violence During Latin America's Long Cold War*, ed. G. Grandin and G. M. Joseph, Durham, NC: Duke University Press, 2010

Winstanley, G., *The Law of Freedom and Other Writings*, ed. C. Hill, Harmondsworth: Penguin Books/Pelican Classics, 1973

Witker, A., *Salvador Allende, 1908–1973: Prócer de la liberación nacional*, México: UNAM, 1980

Yaffe, H., *Che Guevara: The Economics of Revolution*, Basingstoke: Palgrave Macmillan, 2009

Yeats, W.B., 'Meditations in Time of Civil War, VI: The Stare's Nest by My Window', in *The Collected Poems of W. B. Yeats*, Ware: Wordsworth Editions, 1994

Young, M. B., *The Vietnam Wars, 1945–1990*, New York: Harper Perennial, 1991

Zambra, A., *Formas de volver a casa*, Barcelona: Anagrama, 2011

Zolo, D., *Victor's Justice: From Nuremberg to Baghdad*, London: Verso, 2009

Newspapers and Periodicals

Allende, S., 'A dónde va América Latina?', *Arauco*, August 1964

Anderson, J. L., 'The Dictator', in *New Yorker*, 19 October 1988

Bensaïd, D., 'Puissances du communisme', in *Contre Temps: Revue du Critique Communiste*, no. 4, 2009

Bolaño, R., 'The Colonel's Son', in *Granta*, 117, Autumn 2011

Boron, A., 'El fascismo como categoría histórica: en torno al problema de las dictaduras en América Latina', in *Revista mejicana de sociología*, 39, no. 2, April–June 1977, 481–528

Carter, D., 'Chile's Other History: Allende, Pinochet, and Redemocratisation in Mapuche Perspective', in *Studies in Ethnicity and Nationalism*, vol. 10, no. 1, 2010, 59–75

Cauce, 24–30 December 1985

Chandler, D., 'The Road to Military Humanitarianism: How the Human Rights NGOs Shaped a New Humanitarian Agenda', in *Human Rights Quarterly* 23, 2001, 678–700

Colorado Garcia, J. I., 'Jaime Guzmán: Demiurgo de Pinochet', in *Pensamiento Crítico*, no. 5, 2010

Cornell, D., 'Facing Our Humanity', in *Hypatia: a Journal of Feminist Philosophy*, 18/1: 170–4

Daniel, J., 'When Castro Heard the News', in *New Republic*, 7 December 1963

—, 'An Historic Report from Two Capitals', in *New Republic*, 14 December 1963, 15–20

Davis, W., 'A Compendium of the Obvious: A Review of Jared Diamond's "The World Until Yesterday"', in the *Guardian*, 12 January 2013, Review, 6

Délano, M., 'La muerte lenta de Víctor Jara', in *El País*, 5 December 2009, available at www.cultura.elpais.com

El Diario Ilustrado, 21 May 1966, Santiago

Fontaine, A., 'El miedo y otros escritos: El pensamiento político de Jaime Guzmán E.', in *Estudios Públicos*, no. 42, 1991

— and L. Sierra (eds), 'Escritos y documentos de Julio Philippi', in *Estudios Públicos*, no. 74, 1999, 366

Garcés, J., 'Así cayó Allende', in *Revista Triunfo*, 5ª. Época, Año XXX, no. 675, 6 September 1975, Madrid & Barcelona

García Márquez, G., 'Why Allende Had to Die', in *New Statesman*, 3 April 2013, originally published in March 1974

—, 'Chile, el Golpe, y los Gringos' ('Chile, the coup, and the gringos'), *in Revista Alternativa*, no. 1, February 1974, 15–28, and no. 2, March 1974

Gibson, W., 'Burning Chrome', in *Omni Magazine*, July 1982

Gordon, J. A., 'Of Legitimation and the General Will: Creolizing Rousseau through Frantz Fanon', in *The CLR James Journal*, vol. 15, Number 1, Spring 2009

Grandin, G., 'Don't do what Allende did', in *London Review of Books*, 9 July 2012

Guardian, 'Pablo Neruda's Importance Was as Much Political as Poetic', 10 April 2013

—, 'Autopsy Confirms', 20 July 2011

—, 'Obituary: Stafford Beer', 4 September 2002

Hobsbawm, E. and P. Baran, 'Un manifeste non-communiste', in *Les Temps Modernes* 193, June 1962, 1226–61

Kapuscinski, R., 'Guevara y Allende', in *La Jornada*, 17 February 2010

LaRosa, M., 'Review of Peter Winn's Weavers of Revolution', in *Journal of Interamerican Studies and World Affairs*, vol. 32, no. 1, Spring 1990, 182–7

La Tribuna, 'El misterio de la muerte de Pablo Neruda', 31 March 2013

Leeson, P., 'Better Off Stateless: Somalia Before and After Government Collapse', in *Journal of Comparative Economics*, vol. 35, no. 4, 2007

Los Angeles Times, 'Four Forrestal Suicide Bids, Says Pearson', 23 May 1949

Mariátegui, J. C., *Nota autobibliográfica*, 10 January 1927, *La Vida Literaria*, May 1930

Martin, D. and J. Rosenhead, 'Obituary: Stafford Beer', in the *Guardian*, 4 September 2002, 20

Martín-Alcoff, L., 'Caliban's Ontology', in *The CLR James Journal*, vol. 14, no. 1, Spring 2008

Mitchell, J., 'Okinawa's First Nuclear Missile Men Break Silence', *Japan Times*, 8 July 2012

Neruda, P., 'Infancia y poesía', in *El Tiempo*, Bogotá, 31 October 1971

—, 'Sin embargo me muevo', in *El corazón amarillo*, Buenos Aires: Losada, 1974

New York Times, 'A Policy on Cuba', 27 April 1961

—, 'Text of Johnson's Address on U.S. Moves in the Conflict in the Dominican Republic', 3 May 1965

—, 'Bosch Gives His Version of Revolt', 8 May 1965

Noticias Aliadas, no. 416, Lima, 25 September 1975

Philippi, J., 'Limitación de la propiedad territorial: notas en torno de una polémica', in *Estudios*, no. 74, January 1939

Pinet, S., 'On the Subject of Fiction: Islands and the Emergence of the Novel', in *Diacritics* 33, 2003, 173–87

Posner, E. A. and A. Vermeule, 'Transitional Justice as Ordinary Justice', in *Harvard Law Review*, 117, 2003

Prats, C., 'Entrevista a Carlos Prats', in *Ercilla*, no. 1,950, 29 November 1972

Ribeiro, D., 'La izquierda desvariada', in *La Opinión Nacional*, Buenos Aires, 20 January 1974

Sallah, M. D., M. Weiss and J. Mahr, 'Buried Secrets, Brutal Truths', in *Toledo Blade*, 20 October 2003

Teitel, R., 'Transitional Justice Genealogy', in *Harvard Human Rights Journal* 19, 2003, 69–94

Vial, G., 'El ocaso de Prats en el gobierno', in *La Segunda*, no. 6, 5 September 2006

Wall Street Journal, 'Chile's Cautionary Lesson for Americans: A free market is at risk when a demand for equality is not answered by a defense of liberty', 29 April 2012

Wellman, B. et al., 'The Social Affordances of the Internet for Networked Individualism', in *Journal of Computer-Mediated Communication 8*, April 2003

Legal Sources, Decrees, Statutes and Cases

A v. *Secretary of State for the Home Department*, [2004] UKHL 56, and No. 2 [2005] UKHL 71

Annals of the Honourable Junta of Government (AHJG) 33, 12 November 1973

Brown v. *Board of Education*, 347 U.S. 483

City of London v. *Tammy Samede and Others [2012] EWHC 34 (QB)*, 18 January 2012

Comisión Nacional de Verdad y Reconciliación, 1991

Decree-Law [Decreto Ley] 1, D.O. 18 de Septiembre de 1973, dated retroactively 11 September, 1973

Decree Law No. 8, 19 September 1973

Decree Law no. 52, 14 June 1977

Decree Law no. 527, article 10, no. 14, 26 June 1974

Decree Law No. 640, 1974

Decree Law No. 5, 22 September 1973
Edict [Bando] 1, Junta Militar, 11 de Septiembre de 1973
Edict [Bando] 5, Junta Militar, 11 de Septiembre de 1973
Edict [Bando] 29, 18 September 1973
Law of Internal Security [Ley de Seguridad Interna], article 34
Resolución de procesamiento en la investigación por el delito de torturas en el caso de la muerte del General Alberto Bachelet, Ministro en visita [judge] Mario Carroza, 12 September 2012, SML, Fuente: Poder Judicial, Chile
Supreme Decree 668 of 12 September 1973
Tribunal Russell II sobre la situación de los países de América Latina, 1974–1975
UN General Assembly Resolution 1803 (XVII), 14 December 1962; also A. Kilangi, 'Introductory Note', at www.untreaty.un.org/cod/avl/ha/ga_1803.html
UN General Assembly Resolution 41/128 (Annex.), 4 December 1986

Websites

100 Years of Chicano/Latino Music, available at www.latinopia.com, last consulted 16 September 2012
Barreto, J. M., *We Wish To Inform You that Tomorrow We Will Be Killed With Our Families: A Cannibal, Surreal & Subaltern Approach to Human Rights*, at www.criticallegalthinking.com/2010/11/25/manifesto-of-lega-surrealism
Buergo Rodríguez, J. A., *Salvador Allende y el Che Guevara: iguales y diferentes*, available at www.rebelion-org/noticia.php?id=68161
Buscat, E., *Preparativos golpistas*, CEDEC: Centro de Estudios por la Democracia, 2006, also available at www.cedec.cl/DownloadDokument/CEDEC_PREP_MARINA.pdf
Castells, M., 'Communication, Power and Counter-power in the Network Society', in *International Journal of Communication*, at www.ijoc.org, 8 February 2007
Castro, F., Speech to the UN as Chairman of the Non-Aligned Movement, 12 October 1979, available at lanic.utexas.edu/project/castro/db/19701012.html
Cayuqueo, P., 'Tiempo de esperanzas: Salvador Allende y el pueblo Mapuche', in *Azkintuwe*, available at www.rebelion.org/noticia.php?id=69679
CIPER Chile, 'Los resentimientos intelectuales de Pinochet contra el General Carlos Prats', 10 May 2013, available at ciperchile.cl/2013/05/10/los-resentimientos-intelectuales-de-pinochet-contra-el-general-carlos-prats/, last retrieved 20 May 2013
—, 'El control bajó el volumen de la música y yo anuncié al presidente', 26 June 2008, by L. Cáceres, available at ciperchile.cl/2008/06/26/la-verdadera-historia-del-rescate-del-ultimo-discurso-de-salvador-allende, last consulted 7 September 2012
El Mercurio, 'Qué tienen en común Google, Fernando Flores y …?', Revista Sábado, available at www.fernandoflores.cl/node/2288, last accessed 25 May 2012
El Mostrador, 'Jaime Guzmán: Una ausencia tan presente', 31 March 2001, at www.elmostrador.cl
—, 'Fundador de Patria y Libertad acusa a Jaime Guzmán', 13 August 2007, at www.emol.com/noticias/nacional/2007/08/13/265759_fundador-de-patria-y-libertad-jaime-guzman

El Mundo, 'Antonio Banderas se mete en la piel del poeta torturado', by B. Sartori, avialable at www.elmundo.es

El País, 'La muerte lenta de Víctor Jara', December 2009, available at www. cultura.elpais.com, last retrieved 26 September 2012

Entrevista con Carmen Lazo, Biblioteca del Congreso Nacional, available at www.bcn.cl/entrevistas/carmen-lazo-entrevista

Faulkner, W., Nobel Prize Banquet Speech, 10 December 1950, at www. nobelprize.org/nobel_prizes/literature/laureates/1949/faulkner-speech

Fernández Fernández, D., *La Teología de la Liberación en Chile*, at www.revistas. uca.es/index.php/tracadero/article/viewFile/881/745

Ferrada, M., 'Ferrada-Noli versus Pinochet', at antifascist.worldpress.com/category/uncategorized, retrieved, 10 October 2012

Goldsmith, O., *The Deserted Village*, available at www.poetryfoundation.org/poem/173557

Huffington Post, 'Wikileaks: Vatican Dismissed Pinochet massacre reports as "Communist Propaganda"', 8 April 2013, in www.huffingtonpost.com/mobileweb/2013/04/08/wikileaks-vatican-pinochet_n_3038072, last viewed 30 April 2013

Kelly, P. W., *When the People Awake: The Transnational Solidarity Movement, the Pinochet Junta, and the Human Rights Moment of the 1970s*, University of Chicago: Latin American History Seminar, March 2009, 35, available at www.humanrights.uchicago.edu/Baro/PatrickWilliamKelly

Kennedy, Duncan, 'The Rise and Fall of Classical Legal Thought', AFAR, 1975, 1998, at duncankennedy.net/legal_history/essays.html#Rand&F, retrieved January 2013

Kennedy, J. F., *On the Alliance for Progress, 1961, Modern History Sourcebook*, at www.fordham.edu/hall/mod/1961kennedy-afp1

La Jornada, 'Chile: polémica de Camila Vallejo con diario estadounidense', 2 May 2012, 13, available at www.jornada.unam.mx, retrieved 29 September 2012

La Segunda, 27 September 2000, at ar.groups.yahoo.com/group/chile-l/message/43973

Lazo, C., *Entrevista con Carmen Lazo*, Biblioteca del Congreso Nacional, available at www.bcn.cl/entrevistas/carmen-lazo-entrevista

López, M., 'Dos periodistas CIA: Asesinato de Kennedy y Chile', at chiwulltun. blogspot.co.uk/2009/05/dos-periodistas-cia-asesinato-de.html#. UXq1dI6hCoc

Los Angeles Times, 'Chile's Pinochet: Napoleon Wannabe?', 10 October 2007, at www.latimesblogs.latimes.com/laplaza/2007/10/chiles-pinochet, last seen 26 May 2013

McDonnell, P. J., 'Chile's Pinochet: Napoleon Wannabe?' in *Los Angeles Times*, 10 October 2007, at www.latimesblogs.latimes.com/laplaza/2007/10/chiles-pinochet.html, last seen 26 May 2013

Martínez Reinoso, R., *La influencia de Carl Schmitt sobre la praxis política de Jaime Guzmán*, at www.insomne.info/contenido/contenido

Martorell, F., 'Lo que la DINA escribió sobre Jaime Guzmán', in *El Periodista*, at www.elperiodista.cl/newtemberg/1396/article-32991

Neruda, P., *Mi pueblo ha sido el más traicionado de este mundo*, available at www. cubadebate.com

—, 'Exsubsecretario de Aviación identifica a torturadores del General Alberto Bachelet', at www.radio.uchile.cl/noticias/120401, retrieved 26 April 2013

On the Issues Magazine, 'Emma Thompson: The World's Her Stage', by M. Stasio, in www.ontheissuesmagazine.com

Pavlovic, M. J. and G. Piergentili, *A diez años de su muerte: El legado político de Jaime Guzmán en la UDI hoy*, 13, available at www.archivochile.com/tesis/04_tp0012.pdf

Peña, J. C., 'Viaje al fondo de la biblioteca de Pinochet', in CIPER, at ciperchile.cl/2007/12/06/exclusivo-viaje-al-fondo-de-la-biblioteca-de-pinochet/, last retrieved 28 May 2013

Pilger, J., *Dance on Thatcher's Grave, But Remember, There Has Been a Coup in Britain*, available at www.informationclearinghouse.info/article3473, retrieved 26 April 2013

Radio Chile, 'Servicio Médico Legal establece que General Alberto Bachelet murió a causa de torturas', at www.radio.uchile.cl, 20 June 2012

Ravest Santis, G., *Testimonio: 'Necesito que me saquen inmediatamente al aire, compañero'*, available at ciperchile.cl/2008/06/26/la-verdadera-historia-del-rescate-del-ultimo-discurso-de-salvador-allende

Robin, C., 'Kissinger: Allende More Dangerous Than Castro', available at www.coreyrobin.com/2012/07/11kissinger-allende-more-dangerous-than-castro

The Austrian Economics Newsletter, 'An Interview with Jesús Huerta de Soto', in vol. 17, no. 2, Summer 1997, at www.mises.org/journals/aen/aen17_2_1.asp

UNGA Resolution 1803 (XVII), 14 December 1962; also A. Kilangi, 'Introductory Note', at www.untreaty.un.org/cod/avl/ha/ga_1803

Warat, L. A., *Manifesto of Legal Surrealism* (1988); I. rua Wall, *An Introduction: Legal Surrealism* at www.criticallegalthinking.com/2010/11/25/manifesto-of-legal-surrealism

Willson, V., J. Wiss and G. Wood MacEwan, 'Nosotros acusamos', at inverecundos.blogia.com/2009/050306--nosotros-acusamos-federico-willoughby-mac-donald-a-gerad-wood-mc-ewan-.php

Film and TV

Guzmán, P., *The Battle of Chile*, Part One, *The Insurrection of the Bourgeoisie* (1975); Part Two, *The Coup d'Etat* (1976); Part Three, *Popular Power* (1979), Icarus Films

Stauber, J. and S. Rampton, Review of L. Tye's *The Father of Spin: Edward L. Bernays and the Birth of Public Relations*, cited in the BBC TV documentary *The Century of the Self* (Adam Curtis, 2008)

Stone, O., *Comandante* (2002), Optimum Releasing, 2004

Index

A NOTE ON THE AUTHOR

Oscar Guardiola-Rivera teaches international law and international affairs at Birkbeck College, University of London. He has served as an aide to the Colombian Congress and as a consultant to the United Nations in South America. He has lectured in law, philosophy and politics on three continents, writes a regular column for the Colombian newspaper *El Espectador*, is an occasional contributor to the *Guardian* and is the author of *What if Latin America Ruled the World?: How the South Will Take the North into the 22nd Century*. He lives in London.

A NOTE ON THE TYPE

The text of this book is set in Bembo. This type was first used in 1495 by the Venetian printer Aldus Manutius for Cardinal Bembo's *De Aetna*, and was cut for Manutius by Francesco Griffo. It was one of the types used by Claude Garamond (1480–1561) as a model for his Romain de L'Université, and so it was the forerunner of what became standard European type for the following two centuries. Its modern form follows the original types and was designed for Monotype in 1929.